CRITICAL AND CREATIVE PERSPECTIVES ON FAIRY TALES

CRITICAL AND CREATIVE PERSPECTIVES ON

FAIRY TALES

An Intertextual Dialogue between Fairy-Tale Scholarship and Postmodern Retellings

Vanessa Joosen

WAYNE STATE UNIVERSITY PRESS   DETROIT

15 14 13 12 11   5 4 3 2 1

Library of Congress Cataloging-in-Publication Data

Joosen, Vanessa, 1977–
    Critical and creative perspectives on fairy tales : an intertextual dialogue between fairy-tale
scholarship and postmodern retellings / Vanessa Joosen.
        p. cm.—(Series in fairy-tale studies)
    Includes bibliographical references and index.
    ISBN 978-0-8143-3452-2 (pbk. : alk. paper)   1. Fairy tales—History and criticism.   2. Fairy
tales in literature.   3. Intertextuality.   4. Fairy tales—Adaptations—History and criticism.
I. Title.
    PN3437.J66 2011
    809.3'915—dc22

                                                                            2010034197

Published with the assistance of a fund established by Thelma Gray James of Wayne State University
for the publication of folklore and English studies.

Adapted from a design by Chang Jae Lee
Typeset by Westchester Book Composition
Composed in Fournier Regular and Zurich

Written in the fond memory of
a grandmother, a wolf,
and a little girl

Contents

Acknowledgments

In the course of completing this work I was fortunate, to use Vladimir Propp's terminology, to meet with more helpers than adversaries. My research was funded with an FWO scholarship, and I am grateful for their belief in my research project and for their financial support. I am most indebted to Benjamin Biebuyck, Geert Lernout, and Katrien Vloeberghs for their elaborate comments on my work and for their support over many years. Various people have offered pieces of advice in the course of my research, and their feedback and encouragement have been invaluable. They include, in alphabetical order, Sandra Beckett, Ruth Bottigheimer, Majo De Saedeleer, Toin Duijx, Donald Haase, Ute Heidmann, Gillian Lathey, Vivian Liska, Harlinda Lox, David Rudd, Lisa Sainsbury, Karen Sands O'Connor, Claudia Soeffner, Jan Van Coillie, Dirk Van Hulle, Lies Wesseling, Christine Wilkie-Stibbs, and Jack Zipes. I wish to thank three scholars in particular: Kimberley Reynolds, Maria Nikolajeva, and Helma van Lierop-Debrauwer. I believe that they help to secure the future of children's literature studies, not only through the quality of their work but also through the unrelenting support that they give to young scholars. I feel grateful to have been, on several occasions, the beneficiary of their generous help. Much appreciated practical assistance and moral support were granted to me by Laura Atkins, Anke Brouwers, Eva Devos, Lien Fret, and Katrien Jacobs. Finally, I thank my parents, my in-laws, and my dearest Wouter, Aurelie, and Sebastiaan for granting me the chance to write this book, and for the joy, love, and distraction that they gave me when it was completed.

Introduction

Fairy-tale criticism has drawn elaborately on organic metaphors to describe the state of the fairy tale. After the genre was proclaimed dead in Germany after the Second World War, the fairy tale soon rose to life again, as fit as Red Riding Hood when she stepped out of the stomach of the wolf. Guido König remarked in 1975 that "fairy tales can apparently be neither killed nor eradicated" ("Märchen heute" 136; my translation). The tales were to suffer many more blows in the years that followed König's observation, but for every opponent that stood up, at least as many critics proclaimed their interest in or support for the genre. At the beginning of the twenty-first century, fairy tales are still thriving—not only in their traditional forms but also as the subject of a rich body of fairy-tale retellings and literary criticism. In *Why Fairy Tales Stick* (2006) and *Relentless Progress* (2009), Jack Zipes explains the evolution of fairy tales in terms of content, style, function, and address.[1] Darwinist and epidemiological analogies underlie the line of reasoning: in order to survive, the genre of the fairy tale has adapted itself to the changing environments that it has been confronted with over the centuries. One of the survival strategies that Zipes identifies is the emergence of "hybrid genres" (*Stick* 3). Referring to the research of, among others, Jean-Michel Adam and Ute Heidmann, Zipes explores how the fairy tale mutates and absorbs certain characteristics of other genres. The structure and style of traditional tales have been adapted in countless processes (e.g., novelization, versification, and picture-book adaptation), and the content of the best-known tales has been transformed in the form of parodies, updates, role reversals, sequels, and prequels. The traditional versions now coexist with an ever-growing corpus of fairy-tale retellings, which, like criticism, help to keep the interest in the old tales vibrant.

The hybridity of the fairy-tale retelling exists not only in its obvious connection with the traditional fairy tale but also in its overlaps with fairy-tale criticism. Several critics have briefly drawn attention to this connection between retellings and criticism, most notably Stephen Benson in *Contemporary Fiction and the Fairy Tale* (2008): "It is fascinating [. . .] to note the extraordinary synchronicity, in the final decades of the twentieth century, of fiction and fairy-tale scholarship. [. . .] The concerns of the fiction are variously and fascinatingly close to those of the scholarship" (5). Reconsidering the influence of feminism on the fairy tale in *Relentless Progress*, Zipes argues that "since 1980 there has been an inextricable, dialectical development of mutual influence of *all* writers of fairy tales and fairy-tale criticism that has led to innovative fairy-tale experiments in all cultural fields" (122). With the final decades of the twentieth century and the first years of the twenty-first century as my focus, it is my aim in this book to make a number of such parallels between the two discourses of fiction and scholarship concrete. Rather than taking the fairy tale or the fairy-tale retelling as a starting point, as for instance the contributors to Benson's *Contemporary Fiction and the Fairy Tale* and Susan Bobby's *Fairy Tales Reimagined* (2009) do, I will put three critical texts at the center of my intertextual analyses. The fictional intertexts with which I will link these will not be limited to texts in English, as is the case for many studies of fairy-tale retellings. I will also include a substantial number of Dutch and German retellings. In these languages, fairy-tale retellings for children are more popular than those for adults. That children do not read criticism does not exclude these texts from the intertextual range of fairy-tale scholarship, as

I will show. On the contrary, some tales seem motivated by the wish to spread critical ideas to a wider audience, one that specifically includes children. Moreover, the illustrations in children's books have a critical potential that deserves more attention in relation to fairy-tale criticism and retellings. Finally, I will show that although the synchronicity between the occurrence of some ideas in fiction and scholarship is striking, as Benson convincingly argues, some critical views and assumptions from the 1970s continue to live on in the most recent retellings for children.

Rather than examining the influence of criticism on fairy-tale retellings, I consider the relationship between the two discourses as an intertextual *dialogue* in the truest sense. The implementation, as a metatextual dimension, of ideas that were or would become topical in criticism has made the fairy-tale retelling a relevant source of ideas for subsequent studies. Conversely, some authors of fairy-tale retellings have found inspiration in the scholarship on the traditional tales. A direct influence of criticism on a given retelling can only be proved with conviction in a few rare instances. As Linda Hutcheon argues, "A poetics of postmodernism would not posit any relation of causality or identity either among the arts or between art and theory. It would merely offer, as provisional hypotheses, perceived overlappings of concern" (*Postmodernism* 14). In my research, these overlappings of concern have formed the starting point for exploring the intertextual dialogue between criticism and retellings. The objective was to identify not only similarity but also difference—both in content and in form. Two central sets of questions, then, drive this study. First, it provides a description and analysis of the intertextual links that I have observed. Where do criticism and fiction display similar concerns and ideas, and in what aspects do they diverge? The underlying hypothesis of this book is that retellings and criticism participate in a continuous and dynamic dialogue about the traditional fairy tale, yet they do so on different terms. This is the idea behind the second central question: how does the approach to the traditional fairy tale relate to the conventions, limits, and possibilities of the fictional or critical discourse in which the ideas are expressed? "Just as every rewriting of a tale is an interpretation, so every interpretation is a rewriting," states Maria Tatar in *Off With Their Heads!* (xxvi). Although she makes a valid point in recognizing the critical impulse in the retellings and the constructivist aspect of criticism,[2] the status and impact of fictional (performative) and critical (discursive) interpretations substantially differ. Conversely, the extended and intense interaction between fairy-tale retellings and criticism over a period of more than thirty years provides a unique opportunity to increase our understanding of the workings of fiction and criticism and their potential to respond to each other in different modes.

The questions raised are explored through the analysis of a corpus of fairy-tale retellings and criticism that is limited in time from the early 1970s to 2008. The first years of this period mark the beginning of the so-called fairy-tale renaissance, a boom in the production of fairy-tale retellings and criticism in German and English. An early sign of a renewed interest in the fairy tale after the Second World War was the establishment of the *Europäische Märchengesellschaft*, or European Fairy-Tale Society, in 1956. At first, this new appeal did not find a counterpart in literary production. Between 1946 and 1966, "there were hardly any major revisions of the Grimms' tales" in West Germany (Zipes, *Brothers Grimm* 235). The publication of Lutz Röhrich's "Red Riding Hood" parodies in 1967 (*Gebärden*) coincides with what Zipes calls "a radical break in the reception of the Grimms' fairy tales" in the late 1960s (*Brothers Grimm* 238). It was not until then, Haase argues, that fairy-tale studies could shed their association with National Socialism—in fact, the Grimms' fairy tales "became a magnet for scholars coming to grips with the past" ("American Germanists" 295). By the early 1970s, a remarkable increase in the production of fairy-tale criticism and retellings could indeed be perceived.[3]

Several explanations have been offered for this fairy-tale renaissance. It has been linked to developments in literature and literary criticism as well as in society more generally, such as the 1968 movement and the second wave of feminism—societal factors that were inspired by and in their turn reinforced influential academic and literary publications. As such, the rise of fairy tales and retellings in the 1970s became part of a widespread reaction against what leftist critics considered the individualistic, rationalistic, and capitalist ailments of the twentieth century. In the 1960s, the German literary and pedagogical climate had developed a preference for realistic children's books, and until the end of the decade, fairy tales were mainly associated with fancy and illusion (Weinrebe 236). Yet, as the 1970s drew nearer, imagination was revaluated as a means of rebellion against the establishment. James McGlathery sees in the renewed critical interest in the fairy tale a "longing for the simpler life of earlier times, in reaction to the tides that characterized the 1960s" (*Romance* ix), but not all authors and critics approached the fairy tale with such nostalgic longing. An important aspect of the German and American discussions of the 1970s involved the "outdated" ideology that underlies the traditional tales. For this reason, Günter Lange ("Märchenforschung") and Katalin Horn ("Weiterleben" 26) call the post-1968 era a time of crisis for the fairy tale. However, in periods when the traditional fairy tale was under fire, retellings and parodies flourished. Linda Hutcheon has argued convincingly that critical attention for a given text, whether in the form of criticism or fiction (parody and adaptation), paradoxically contributes to its canonization (*Parody* 26). As such, the fairy tale seems more popular than ever during periods when its importance and desirability are under discussion. In addition, fairy-tale retellings have gained critical attention in their turn, which has required critics to reconsider the traditional versions once again.

In this context, Walter Filz sees the discussion in Germany on the "usefulness or uselessness of the Grimms' tales," with participants such as Otto Gmelin, Christa Bürger, Bernd Wollenweber, Dieter Richter, and Johannes Merkel, as an important stimulant for the production of retellings in the 1970s and 1980s (*Einmal* 23–25). The Brothers Grimm's bicentenaries in 1985 and 1986 certainly helped to keep the scholarly interest raised in the 1970s sustained in the 1980s. Moreover, several specific fairy-tale studies and retellings of the 1970s had a snowball effect and launched the appearance of new texts. Bruno Bettelheim's *The Uses of Enchantment* (1976) is considered to be such a work that fuelled discussion and research, as are Alison Lurie's "Fairy Tale Liberation" (1970), Marcia K. Lieberman's "Some Day My Prince Will Come" (1972), Dieter Richter and Johannes Merkel's *Märchen, Phantasie und soziales Lernen* (1974, Fairy Tales, Fantasy and Social Learning), Heinz Rölleke's *Die älteste Märchensammlung der Brüder Grimm* (1975, The Brothers Grimm's Oldest Fairy-Tale Collection), and Jack Zipes's *Breaking the Magic Spell* (1979).[4] Benson (*Contemporary Fiction* 6–7) parallels some of these critical milestones with equally influential retellings, such as Robert Coover's *Pricksongs and Descants* (1969) and Angela Carter's *The Bloody Chamber* (1979). I would also add to this list retellings for children, such as Janosch's fairy tales (1972, *Janosch erzählt Grimms Märchen*) and Robert Munsch's *The Paper Bag Princess* (1980), as well as illustrated tales, such as Trina Schart Hyman's *Snow White* (1974) and Anthony Browne's *Hansel and Gretel* (1981).

In the 1970s, critics occasionally referred to fairy-tale retellings as part of their research on the traditional tales. Anne Sexton's *Transformations* (1971), for instance, proved to be an influential poetry collection that is mentioned in Bettelheim's *The Uses of Enchantment* and Karen E. Rowe's "Feminism and Fairy Tales" (1979). With the rise in the production of retellings from the 1970s onward, the inclusion of these texts in critical analysis has only increased, and it is now common practice for critics to back up their reflections on the traditional tales with examples from fairy-tale retellings. Ruth Bottigheimer, for example, takes into consideration Anne Sexton's use of irony when she discusses gender in the Grimms' tales in *Grimms' Bad Girls and Bold Boys* (1987). In "Reading 'Snow White'" (1990), Shuli Barzilai refers to Donald Barthelme's retelling to oppose the wish fulfillment of the Grimms' ending (524) as well as to Anne Sexton, who "renders with precision the core of this [generational] conflict" between Snow White and her stepmother (528). Just as some fairy-tale retellings include quotations from fairy-tale criticism as mottos, several critical texts start with an extract from a fairy-tale retelling or with a fairy-tale poem. Jane Yolen's *Briar Rose* and Jack Zipes's *Breaking the Magic Spell* offer examples of these practices.

The primary texts analyzed in this book are retellings and illustrated fairy tales that were published in English, German, and Dutch. From these three, English and German are the languages in which the fairy-tale renaissance has become the most manifest in the production of both fairy-tale retellings and criticism. The Dutch context provides an interesting point of comparison because of its relatively late fairy-tale renaissance, in spite of its geographical, cultural, and linguistic proximity to English and German countries and the shared canon of popular tales. Although some appeared before the 1990s, it is only in the past fifteen years that a substantial increase in the number of Dutch retellings can be perceived. In some of these texts, ideas and approaches from German and English criticism and retellings find a deferred and transformed expression.

The majority of the fairy-tale retellings and illustrations that I will discuss are based on a small canon of traditional tales: "Snow White," "Cinderella," "Sleeping Beauty," "Hansel and Gretel," "Little Red Riding Hood," and "Beauty and the Beast." Not only do these belong to the most popular traditional fairy tales in the Dutch-, English-, and German-speaking countries, but they are also among the ones that are most frequently analyzed and retold. As I will argue in the first chapter, the six tales share, moreover, a set of characteristics that makes them suitable for contrastive purposes. Given the large number of retellings and illustrated versions of these six tales published since 1970, this study does not have the ambition to be exhaustive. From a corpus of four hundred picture books, short stories, novels, and poems, my selection of the primary material under discussion is based on thematic links with texts from fairy-tale criticism. These links will be explained in the discussion of the three case studies and backed up, wherever possible, with references to other retellings that explore similar ideas or techniques.

As I explained above, the starting point of my intertextual comparison will not be the traditional tales or the retellings but fairy-tale criticism, and the book is structured around three key texts and momentous debates in fairy-tale criticism. Not only did scholarly research on fairy tales expand at the beginning of the 1970s, but the fairy-tale renaissance also coincided with innovative theoretical approaches to literature that fit the philosophical and social concerns of the period and that still influence the ways that scholars study fairy tales today. Feminism is widely acknowledged as one of the most important twentieth-century approaches to the fairy tale. Although gender issues were relevant to the discussion of the genre before 1970, "scholarly research explicitly devoted to feminist issues in fairy-tale studies began in earnest in 1970 and was propelled by the feminist movement's second wave" (Haase, *Feminism* vii). Marcia K. Lieberman's "Some Day My Prince Will Come," an ideology-critical reading of gender patterns in Western culture's best-known tales, was one of the catalysts of the new surge of feminist fairy-tale criticism and will be the focus of chapter two. Throughout the years that followed the publication of this first key text, the fairy tale was alternatingly criticized for its stereotypical gender patterns and praised for its emancipatory force and possibly subversive power.[5] Sandra M. Gilbert and Susan Gubar's provocative analysis of "Snow White" in *The Madwoman in the Attic* (1979) marked a new, palimpsestic type of feminist fairy-tale reading: behind the surface layer of the Grimms' tale, they detect a model for feminine rebellion. Because I discuss the key texts in chronological order, Gilbert and Gubar will be the starting point of the discussion in chapter four. At a time when the traditional fairy tale had come under heavy fire, one of the greatest defenders of the Grimms' collection was the Austrian-American psychoanalyst Bruno Bettelheim.

The importance of *The Uses of Enchantment* is generally accepted, and Bettelheim's book found a wide international appeal. The 1970s and 1980s saw a wave of psychoanalytical and popular psychological fairy-tale interpretations that were frequently derived from this success. Yet, in academic circles, Bettelheim's ideas found at least as many opponents as supporters, and I will argue in chapter three that aspects of this critique are expressed in several fairy-tale retellings and illustrations that enter into an intertextual dialogue with Bettelheim's interpretations.

As becomes clear from this short overview, the key texts and debates that are the subject of this book originated in the 1970s. They have functioned as starting points or influential milestones in critical paradigms that have developed further since then. In the discussion of the thematic overlaps with the retellings, therefore, I will supplement the key texts with the critical response that they have generated in more recent fairy-tale studies and analyze the position of retellings in these debates. Before we arrive at this discussion, however, chapter one will introduce the broader theoretical framework in which this study is situated and the main concepts and critical tools on which my research has relied.

1 An Intertextual Approach to Fairy-Tale Criticism and Fairy-Tale Retellings

Traditional Fairy Tales and Retellings

As fairy tales have been rewritten at a high frequency in the past four decades, the scholarship on fairy-tale retellings has also expanded. The discussion of contemporary adaptations of fairy tales has led to a mass, or even a mess, of terms and concepts that often lack clear definitions and distinctions: fairy-tale retelling, reversion, revision, reworking, parody, transformation, anti–fairy tale, postmodern fairy tale, fractured fairy tale, and recycled fairy tale.[1] From this long list of alternatives, I have chosen to use the term "fairy-tale retelling" because it is brief and neutral and because the prefix "re-" gives an indication of this genre's defining relationship to a source text, the so-called pre-text.[2] For this pre-text, I will use the term "traditional fairy tale" because I wish to avoid the association of "high quality" implied in "classic fairy tale" and because "old fairy tale" suggests there was a moment of origin before the occurrence of fairy-tale retellings, which is not necessarily the case. "Traditional fairy tales" continue to be written and published to date in the form of what Jack Zipes calls "du-plicates," tales that "reproduce a set pattern of ideas and images that reinforce a traditional way of seeing, believing and behaving" and that are distinct from revisions (*Myth* 9).³ More importantly, I try to avoid the term "origi-nal fairy tale" whenever traditional tales and retellings are compared. As Donald Haase has shown in "Yours, Mine, or Ours?" (1993), originality is a concept that is difficult to apply to the fairy tale. What is, for instance, the original version of "Little Red Riding Hood?" The best-known or most frequently printed version? The oldest written version? The oral versions on which the written versions were presumably based? For Haase, relation-ships between fairy tales should not be understood as linear developments with a beginning and an end but rather as networks or hypertexts: "Inter-textuality, multivocality, and the constructedness of folktales and folktale collections have thus generated a concept of textuality that views each tale not as a text assigned a permanent place in a linear succession or hierarchy that takes us back to an original or a primary form, but as a component in a larger web of texts that are linked to each other in multiple ways and have equal claim on our attention" ("Gutenberg" 225).

Any intertextual analysis of contemporary fairy-tale retellings has to take into account that the best-known tales have been reproduced in innu-merable variants and that fairy-tale material has generated countless verbal and nonverbal manifestations. It is usually impossible to determine which pre-texts were the basis of a given retelling and which other references to fairy tales come into play in the production and reading processes. Even when authors mention a pre-text explicitly, this does not end the matter. The blurb on the jacket of Anne Provoost's *De Roos en het Zwijn* (1997, The Rose and the Swine), for instance, mentions that she based her version on "The Pig Prince" by Giovan Francesco Straparola. The content of the novel runs, however, more parallel to the now better-known version of "Beauty and the Beast" by Jeanne-Marie Leprince de Beaumont. Moreover, as John Stephens and Robyn McCallum argue, "Even where there is a strong pre-text [. . .], retellers are most likely to use intermediary versions—to pro-duce a retelling of a retelling" (4). And this applies not only to retellers but also to readers: the intertextual knowledge of author and reader is inevita-bly discrepant. In the case of *De Roos en het Zwijn*, it is therefore quite plausible that readers are more familiar with other versions of the same tale than the ones that influenced Provoost.

Authors of traditional fairy tales do not consciously and openly allude to other written fairy tales. If they are aware of an intertextual relationship with another text, as is clearly the case for some of the Grimms' texts, the authors do not draw attention to their transformation within the scope of the story itself. In *Children's Literature Comes of Age*, Maria Nikolajeva distinguishes between "open and hidden dialogues" when it comes to authors' use of intertextual references. She uses "open dialogue" to refer to texts that are "written intentionally so that readers recognize the original setting, the characters and the plot pattern" (155). All the retellings analyzed in this book make use of such an open dialogue when it comes to an intertextual link with an earlier fairy tale. They are "consciously played off against some common notion of the shape and content of an 'original' text, and [the authors] might hence assume that the audience will be in a position to weigh one against the other. In such a case, because of the coexistence within the one discourse space of pre-text and focused text the significance of the story will tend to be situated not in the focused text but in the process of interaction between the texts. That is, the effect is intertextual in its fullest sense" (Stephens 88). In Stephens's description of the intertextual interaction, both readers and authors take part. The author "consciously plays off" his or her text against a pre-text, and the implied reader is expected to compare the focused text (the retelling) and the pre-texts (traditional fairy tales).[4] Retellings can signal their intertextual connection with the traditional tales in several ways. Many have a reference to the fairy tale in the paratext (title, subtitle, cover, preface, or blurb).[5] Occasionally, the retelling is printed next to the traditional tale, as in Sara Maitland's "The Wicked Stepmother's Lament." More frequently, the name of the main character is preserved, translated, or slightly modified. Snow White becomes Bianca in Gregory Maguire's *Mirror Mirror* and Tanith Lee's "Red as Blood," and she is called Blanche in Regina Doman's *Black as Night* and Jacey Bedford's "Mirror, Mirror." In addition, all the titles of these retellings contain a marked intertextual allusion to the traditional tale. It is also common practice in children's literature for fictional characters in the focused text to read a pre-text themselves (Kümmerling-Meibauer 51), as you see for instance in Anthony Browne's *The Tunnel*. In other retellings the inclusion of a magic mirror, a trail of breadcrumbs, or a wolf with a bonnet suffices to highlight the text's intertextual relationship with a traditional tale.

The retellings that I have analyzed for this book all do more than briefly allude to a traditional fairy tale. They practice what Linda Hutcheon calls "repetition with critical distance" (*Parody* 6) and transform large parts of the traditional stories, incorporating several elements from the plot while modifying others.[6] Whether marked intertextual references will actually be recognized depends to a large extent on the recipient, as Ulrich Broich stresses: "The threshold for marked intertextual references will be much lower for the literate reader than for the occasional reader. On the other hand, the threshold increases together with the growing temporal distance to the text or pre-text for many later recipients, when the contemporary context is no longer immediately present" (33; my translation).

The two factors that Broich mentions as influential on intertextual recognition may account for the popularity of fairy tales as pre-texts. Their frequent reprinting and their inclusion in most children's reading or viewing to date guarantee a high probability that the marked references will be picked up. For most children, fairy tales belong to the encyclopedic knowledge that is a precondition for intertextual competence. The poet Peter Rühmkorf has even maintained that now that the classics are no longer widely known, fairy tales are the *only* stories with which authors can still expect familiarity in their readership (Horn, "Lebenshilfe" 160). Moreover, the repeated allusions to the traditional fairy tale, not only in literature but also in cartoons, commercials, films, toys, and theatrical plays, prevent the growing temporal distance between the older tales and the contemporary reader from raising the threshold that Broich describes. In this sense, fairy-tale retellings may avoid to some extent the "curious kind of hegemony in children's books" that Christine Wilkie-Stibbs has identified: "Adults who write for children (who by definition are no longer themselves children) consciously or unconsciously operate in and are influenced by the intertextual space which is the literature they read as children" ("Intertextuality" 180). Although the editions and versions through which contemporary children become acquainted with the traditional tales may differ from those of the authors who retell them, these stories do bridge the gap between various generations of readers and writers of children's books.

The use of an open intertextual dialogue with the traditional fairy tale is not the only distinctive feature of fairy-tale retellings. Traditional tales affirm what Hans Robert Jauss calls the typical "horizon of expectation" of the fairy tale. The chronotope of the fairy tale is indefinite and one-dimensional:

both time and place are beyond our reach (Nikolajeva, *Age* 122), and the supernatural is not felt to intrude in human life (Lüthi, *Europäische Volksmärchen* 9). The figures are "flat characters," who do not learn, change, evolve, or age (13–23). The action of the traditional fairy-tale plot progresses quickly, and its ending is optimistic. The narrative style is characterized by fixed formulas, repetitions, and symbolic numbers (Lüthi, *Volksmärchen und Volkssage* 15–17). Finally, traditional fairy tales are told in a linear manner and by an omniscient, third-person narrator who carries no distinguishing mark (gender, race, class, individuality).[7] Not all the traditional fairy tales that are the subject of this book conform to each and every one of the features of the traditional horizon of expectation, but with some aberrations, the aspects listed above constitute the typical characteristics of many of Western culture's most popular traditional tales.

Fairy-tale retellings, in contrast, disrupt this horizon of expectation in several aspects:

1. Chronotope. The chronotope of the fairy tale shifts when the story is relocated to a more concrete contemporary or historical setting, as is common practice in retellings. The time and location of Anne Provoost's *De Roos en het Zwijn*, for instance, are more specific: the story is set in the Flemish town of Antwerp in the late Middle Ages. Even more details are given in *Wolf*, in which Gillian Cross transfers "Little Red Riding Hood" to specific London neighborhoods at the time of the Irish Republican Army bombings. Etienne Delessert dates his retelling of "Snow White" in the autumn of 1613.

2. Attitude to the supernatural. Several fairy-tale retellings renegotiate the boundary between magic and realism, as I have argued in "Disenchanting the Fairy Tale." *De Roos en het Zwijn* once again provides a good example, as does Gregory Maguire's *Confessions of an Ugly Stepsister*, which is based on "Cinderella." In these retellings, the perspective of an unreliable narrator leaves doubt about whether magic really occurs or only happens in the perception of the protagonist. Realistic alternatives are given for several magical occurrences from the traditional tale. The Cinderella figure in Maguire's story does not receive her ball gown from a fairy godmother, for instance, but from her stepsisters. All magic is absent from updated,

novelized fairy-tale retellings such as Cross's *Wolf* and Melissa Kantor's *If I Have a Wicked Stepmother, Where's My Prince?*

3. Characterization. When the fairy tale is adapted to a novel, as is often the case, the psychological development takes prime place. Not only are the protagonist's motives elaborated, but characters in the margin of the traditional tale come to the foreground as well. In the Grimms' "Briar Rose," the prince only appears at the end, whereas in Toon Tellegen's *Brieven aan Doornroosje* (Letters to Briar Rose) his feelings and doubts are described in great detail in 365 letters. Fairy-tale retellings in the form of poems, such as Anne Sexton's or Olga Broumas', often leave out most of the action to focus on the characters' psychology. The fairy-tale prequel is a subgenre within fairy-tale retellings that provides well-known characters with a prehistory. Often this psychological background is used to put an antagonist's evil deeds in perspective (for example in Maitland's "The Wicked Stepmother's Lament"). When an evil character's motivations are added and explained, as in Emma Donoghue's retelling of Snow White ("The Tale of the Apple"), the black-and-white distinction between good and evil fades, and flat characters are replaced by round ones.

4. Optimism. A happy ending is not the standard in fairy-tale retellings, although many retellings for children and young adults still conform to this characteristic feature of the traditional tale.[8] Writers for adults are often more pessimistic and cynical about the possibility of a happy ending (Zipes, "Changing Function" 25). In the final chapter of *Doornroosjes honden* (Sleeping Beauty's Dogs) by Willy Spillebeen, a little girl commits suicide because she wants to sleep forever. The description of the chill of death that takes over her body in the final lines of the book builds a stark contrast to the careless formula of "happily ever after." Sexton's poems locate themes of rape and incest in "Sleeping Beauty" and "Snow White," the victims of which cannot be cured by the simple kiss of a prince. A subgenre within fairy-tale retellings is the fairy-tale sequel, which often unmasks the happy ending of the traditional tale as an illusion.[9] Examples here include Robert Coover's "The Dead Queen," a satiric sequel to "Snow White" in which the prince tries to kiss awake his bride's dead stepmother, and Philip Pullman's *I Was a Rat!*, in which Cinderella's marriage displays similarities to the unhappy

union between Prince Charles and Princess Diana (Joosen, "Pullman" 207).

5. Action versus character development. As I have argued in the discussion of "characterization," the emphasis in many fairy-tale retellings shifts from action to psychological development. The reader is given access to the inner lives of round and complex characters. Some retellings, particularly those in the form of poems, leave out a substantial part of the action, because it is assumed that the reader is already familiar with the plot. Josef Wittmann's "Dornröschen" (1975, Briar Rose), for instance, deals exclusively with the prince's inner monologue as he stands by Briar Rose's bed and asks her not to wake up. Its title suffices to draw the intertextual link with the Grimms' tale.

6. Style. Repetitions frequently disappear from fairy-tale duplicates and retellings, especially in short stories, poems, and picture books. In Babette Cole's *Prince Cinders,* the protagonist only goes to the ball once, in contrast to the Grimms' and Perrault's Cinderella. Fixed formulas and numeric symbolism are usually retained as markers of the intertextual relationship with the pre-text. The seven dwarves, for instance, are transformed into the most diverse forms, from seven jazz musicians (Fiona French, *Snow White in New York*), seven hippies (Uta Claus, *Total tote Hose*), seven partisans (Iring Fetscher, "Das Ur-Schneewittchen"), seven friars (Regina Doman, *Black as Night*), and seven exploited miners (Mary Maher, "Hi Ho, It's Off to Strike We Go!") to seven aliens (Laurence Anholt, *Snow White and the Seven Aliens*) and seven giraffes (Gregory Maguire, *Leaping Beauty*). Yet their number nearly always remains the same.[10]

7. Narratological features. Several fairy-tale retellings are told by a first-person narrator, frequently the protagonist or the antagonist of the traditional versions and sometimes a marginal character. In both Toon Tellegen's *Brieven aan Doornroosje* and Josef Wittmann's "Dornröschen," the prince speaks directly to Briar Rose; Jacey Bedford's "Mirror, Mirror" narrates part of "Snow White" from the perspective of the stepmother; and the title of Melissa Kantor's *If I Have a Wicked Stepmother, Where's My Prince?* reveals that this novel is told in the first person. Retellings frequently make use of a more complex chronological and narratological organization of

plot elements than do traditional tales. In Delessert's *The Seven Dwarfs*, for instance, the traditional "Snow White" is reconstructed in flashbacks a day before Snow White's wedding with the prince. Tom Naegels's "Spiegelliegeltje" is a double retelling of "Snow White": one is a frame tale in which the other retelling is inserted. Polyperspectival novels such as Gregory Maguire's *Mirror Mirror* combine the views on the traditional tale of different first-person narrators.

De Roos en het Zwijn is a rare example that disrupts the traditional horizon of expectation in all seven aspects mentioned above. Most retellings affirm some of the traditional fairy-tale features, while significantly subverting others. *Snow White in New York*, for example, doubles several plot elements from the best-known versions of "Snow White" (the Grimms' and Disney's) and retains the traditional fairy tale's flat characterization and optimistic ending. The shift in chronotope, however, leads to a large number of alterations in comparison to these traditional versions. French's book makes time and location more specific, as the story is set in New York in the 1920s. Several characters, objects, and events are adapted accordingly. The realistic setting is further reflected in a decline of magical occurrences: French replaces the speaking mirror, for instance, with a newspaper called *The New York Mirror*. Other retellings, such as Wim Hofman's *Zwart als inkt* (Black as Ink), follow the plot of a traditional version more closely (in this case the Grimms' "Snow White") but nevertheless qualify as a retelling because of their increased attention to character psychology and elaborate descriptions, as well as their transformation of crucial moments in the traditional tale.

The intertextual relationship between fairy-tale retellings and traditional fairy tales has a double effect. By critically distancing themselves from the fairy tale, retellings invite readers to reconsider the traditional texts. But this is not the only function. Julia Kristeva has argued that "the writer can use another's work, giving it a new meaning while retaining the meaning it already had. The result is a word with two significations: it becomes *ambivalent*" (73). Indeed Hutcheon has identified a paradox at the heart of parody, and that also applies to the fairy-tale retelling: at the same time it criticizes and reinforces the target text; it is simultaneously negative and affirmative, desacralizing and resacralizing, rebellious and conservative. Although a large number of fairy-tale retellings problematize the traditional fairy tale, they are an important factor in its canonization process. Conversely, the higher the status and popularity of the traditional fairy tale, the more critical the analyses and retellings that are published.

Fairy-Tale Retellings and Criticism: A Different Intertextual Approach

The focus of this book is not so much the intertextual dialogue between fairy-tale retellings and traditional tales as the interaction between the retellings and fairy-tale criticism—a literary and a theoretical genre. This requires a different approach to intertextuality, as the "open dialogue" that is typical of the relationship between retelling and traditional fairy tale seldom applies to the intertextual connection that can be drawn between retelling and criticism. The addresser's intent to incorporate, critique, or parody texts and currents in literary criticism can only occasionally be proved. The intertextual dialogue is thus constructed in the reading process and not necessarily in the writing process. When I read Gillian Cross's *Wolf* in dialogue with Bruno Bettelheim's psychoanalytic interpretation of "Little Red Riding Hood," for instance, I do not argue that Cross consciously draws on these theories, even though she incorporates in her text some of Bettelheim's ideas; they may just as well be her own or stem from another source that she has encountered on the subject. In the intertextual dialogue between fairy-tale retellings and literary criticism, it is usually difficult to trace where an idea appeared first or whether ideas that occur on similar occasions were actually "borrowed" from each other. According to Nikolajeva, "The question of who has borrowed the idea from whom [. . . is] totally uninteresting" (*Age* 183) if we apply M. M. Bakhtin's concept of intertextuality as dialogism. One should focus instead on the different use that authors and critics make of the same idea, which is exactly what this study intends to do.

The term "intertextuality," coined in the late 1960s by Julia Kristeva, has been redefined, applied, and problematized in a variety of ways.[11] The congruency of ideas with regard to the traditional fairy tale in criticism and retellings distinguishes my approach from Roland Barthes's theory of circular and "infinite intertextuality" (Wilkie 131), according to which "the reader is free to associate texts more or less at random" (Hutcheon,

Parody 37). Barthes's understanding of intertextuality comes close to Genette's "transtextuality" (Wilkie-Stibbs, "Intertextuality" 180), but Genette foresees the problematics of such a broad concept in *Palimpsests*. He writes that "to subsume the whole of universal literature under the field of hypertextuality [. . .] would make the study of it somewhat unmanageable" (9).[12] As a consequence, many critics narrow down the broad concept of intertextuality when they apply it in the discussion of concrete literary texts.

The model of intertextuality that Manfred Pfister offers is a compromise between two divergent interpretations of the concept—Barthes's poststructuralist interpretation, "in which every text appears as part of a universal intertext," and the structuralist and hermeneutic interpretation, "in which the concept of intertextuality is limited to conscious, intended, and marked relationships between a text and a given text or group of texts" (Pfister 25; my translation). Pfister's alternative model is concentric. Starting from the broad, poststructuralist notion of intertextuality, he splits up the universal intertext into different degrees of intensity of the intertextual relationship. The center marks the highest intertextual density, and "the more we remove ourselves from the 'hard core' of the center, the more [the intertexual intensity] decreases" (25; my translation). In order to determine where pretexts should be located within a focused text's intertextual range, Pfister suggests six qualitative parameters, which he derives from topical discussions on the concept of intertextuality: referentiality, communicativity, reflexivity, structurality, selectivity, and dialogicity. If we apply this model to the intertextual range of fairy-tale retellings, it is clear that the traditional tale is situated close to the "hard core of the center" of the retelling's intertextual scope, whereas fairy-tale criticism is further removed from the center but can nevertheless be considered a relevant intertext.

Referentiality

The first of Pfister's parameters is referentiality, which he bases on the difference between "to use" or "to mention," on the one hand, and "to refer to," on the other. When a citation is integrated seamlessly, that is, when a citation is "used," the intensity of the intertextual relationship between focused text and pre-text is weaker than when the text foregrounds its citations as citations, referring to their original context (26). Although nearly all fairy-tale retellings make use of an open dialogue with the traditional fairy tale, it is obvious that some foreground their intertextual relationships more clearly than others do. In Jon Scieszka and Lane Smith's postmodern picture book *The Stinky Cheese Man* (1992), for instance, the giant from "Jack and the Beanstalk" is shown cutting out parts from a book (Figure 1). On the page that follows this image, he tells his own story in a collage of various fairy-tale quotations (Figure 2). Each line has a different font and is printed on a different piece of paper, most with ragged edges. This fairy-tale collage visually renounces a "seamless" integration of citations into the new work, and a more explicit way of foregrounding citation hardly seems possible. According to Pfister's model, this stress on its own referentiality raises the density of the intertextual relationship that links *The Stinky Cheese Man* with the traditional fairy tale. The metatextual dimension of this collage entails a humorous comment on the traditional fairy tale's use of formulaic expressions—indeed, Wilkie-Stibbs has noted that the traditional tales "themselves are a collage of quotations" ("Intertextuality" 182)— as well as on its prudery and romantic register, which are here grotesquely mocked by the rearrangement of the order.

Although fairy-tale criticism may be a relevant intertext for fairy-tale retellings, only rarely is the pre-text foregrounded and named explicitly in the fictional text itself. There are some exceptions. The title of Willy Pribil's "Schneewittchen—frei nach Sigmund Freud" (1961) contains an explicit reference to criticism, and Dorothea Runow's "Little Red Riding Hood" stages Bruno Bettelheim as a character. The introductions to Iring Fetscher's fictional fairy-tale interpretations, which function as retellings, make it explicit that he finds inspiration in fairy-tale analyses, including those of Sigmund Freud and Ernst Bloch. In some of his retellings, ideas that are borrowed from Freud are italicized, which highlights their status as citations.

Communicativity

Pfister's second criterion draws on the hermeneutic view of intertextuality, when the allusions to the pre-text are intentional and highlighted. He does not consider the author's conscious use of references a criterion sine qua non for intertextuality but rather a factor that helps to raise intertextual density. Examples of signposting have been mentioned above, but the criterion of "communicativity" is relevant here for a different reason, not just

Figure 1. The Stinky Cheese Man and Other Fairly Stupid Tales *by Jon Scieszka and illustrated by Lane Smith.*

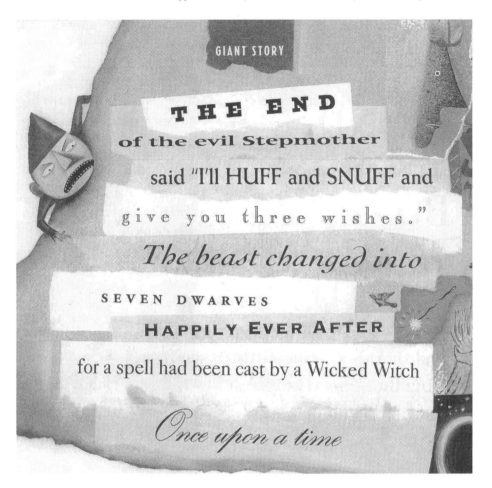

Figure 2. The Stinky Cheese Man and Other Fairly Stupid Tales
by Jon Scieszka and illustrated by Lane Smith.

for pre-texts that are traditional fairy tales but also for pre-texts from fairy-tale criticism. The intensity of the intertextual relationship between pre-text and focused text is higher for canonical texts and for topical, widely received and discussed texts (27). Pfister limits these canonical texts to literary texts, but I will expand this notion to texts from other genres. The key texts that will be discussed in the following chapters are such topical texts of fairy-tale criticism. The canonical status of a critical text is often the only indication that an author of a given fairy-tale retelling may be familiar with it, yet it is no guarantee that a retelling is influenced by it. The theories, ideas, and concepts contained in the key texts have been expressed in various other texts and media; Bettelheim's ideas, for example, have become part of pop psychology through several documentaries and various newspaper articles on him and his theories.[13] Several of Lieberman's and Gilbert and Gubar's ideas were shared, taken up, and elaborated on by other feminist scholars. With just a few exceptions,[14] authors of fiction do not acknowledge explicitly where they encountered certain critical ideas. The pre-text may thus well be a popularized version of a canonical text or another retelling that expresses a similar idea. And of course it is also plausible that an author or illustrator came up with a certain interpretation of a fairy tale without the (conscious) use of any intermediary text.

The communicative situation in children's literature is somewhat different from that in adult literature because of the age difference, and subsequent differences in life and reading experiences, between its authors and readers. It is evident that young readers are not the target audience of fairy-tale criticism, but this does not exclude these texts from the intertextual range of fairy-tale retellings for children. Not only are the authors of these texts adults but many of their readers are adults too. As the communicative situation of children's literature is asymmetrical—there are very few child authors of children's books but many child readers—so is its intertextuality.

Autoreflexivity

Pfister's third parameter is an extension of the first, "referentiality": "The intensity of intertextuality according to the first two criteria can be further increased if the author not only inserts conscious and clearly marked intertextual references but also reflects on the text's intertextual condition and references in the text itself, i.e., that it not only signposts the intertextuality but also justifies or problematizes its presuppositions and effects" (27; my translation).

A retelling that raises the topic of intertextuality and its presuppositions is Barbara Ensor's *Cinderella* (2006), especially in its subtitle: "As If You Didn't Already Know the Story." This phrase can be interpreted in two ways. The subjunctive irrealis can signal that the subtitle is an ironic comment: "You know the story, so why does it still need to be told?" Alternatively, the subtitle can be read without any irony, as an indication of the effect that this retelling wishes to have on the reader. By changing elements of the tale, in this case by adding letters and extra character motivations, fairy-tale retellings disrupt readers' horizon of expectation, giving them a fresh view of the story they thought they knew. The combined meanings of the subtitle of Ensor's book thus function as an autoreflexive comment on its intertextual practice.

Pfister stresses that the parameter of "autoreflexivity" is more specifically intended for texts that blur the boundaries between theoretical and poetic works. Iring Fetscher's mock analyses provide one example, but more explicit reflections on the problems of intertextuality and its effects are rare in fairy-tale retellings. Occasionally, authors do justify their reasons for retelling explicitly within the tale—although the readers still have to take into account irony and author detachment when such fictional motivations occur. Roald Dahl, for instance, explains his dissatisfaction with the traditional "Hansel and Gretel," especially the part in which Gretel pushes the witch into the oven, as follows:

> The Brothers Grimm who wrote this story
> Made it a thousand times more gory.
> I've taken out the foulest scene
> In order that you won't turn green. [. . .]
> It might have been okay, who knows,
> If there'd been humour in the prose.
> Did I say humour? Wilhelm Grimm?
> There's not a scrap of it in him.
>   (*Rhyme Stew* 63)

The first part of Dahl's justification for rewriting "Hansel and Gretel" is contradicted by his corrections; true to his style, he includes *more* cruel details than the Grimms do, describing, for instance, the smell of burning meat when the witch is in the oven. The second part reveals a correction that is more consistent with the poetics that speaks from Dahl's work. His dissatisfaction with the tales stems from their alleged lack of humor, and his strategy of parody is to retell them in a style that severely clashes with the usual solemnity of Grimm. The versification of the tales speeds up the stories, and the many incongruent rhymes intensify the comic effect.

A second example of autoreflexivity in fairy-tale retellings can be found in Sara Maitland's "The Wicked Stepmother's Lament" (1996). Placing her text within a tradition of feminist revisions, the first-person narrator of this transformed "Cinderella" distances herself from other fairy-tale retellings: "There's this thing going on at the moment where women tell all the old stories again and turn them inside-out and back-to-front—so the characters you always thought were the goodies turn out to be the baddies, and vice versa, and a whole lot of guilt is laid to rest: or that at least is the theory" (222). The narrator, Cinderella's stepmother, stresses the complexity of the issues of guilt and innocence, which is ignored in retellings that make use of simple gender or role reversals: "All I want to say is that it's more complicated, more complex, than it's told, and the reasons why it's told the way it is are complex too" (222). With this autoreflexive note, Maitland situates her retelling with respect not only to the Grimms' text but also to the large corpus of feminist revisions and to the reasons for her intertextual dialogue with both these genres. Although the stepmother's words are not to be taken seriously throughout her defense, the introduction of an unreliable narrator like her does add a level of complexity that indeed distinguishes Maitland's short story from those that employ more straightforward role reversals.

Structurality

On the fourth parameter, that of "structurality," most retellings discussed in this book score high: they not only contain isolated allusions to the traditional fairy tale but follow its structure as well. Emma Donoghue's "Tale of the Apple," for instance, is a "Snow White" retelling that parallels the Grimms' chronology: the retelling begins with the biological mother's pregnancy and ends after the protagonist is revived. Yet, prequels and sequels have become a popular subgenre of fairy-tale retellings, and here the retelling does not follow the plot structure of the pre-text(s). Also, several retellings, especially those in the form of poems, zoom into one aspect or scene from the traditional fairy tale. Laurence Snydal's "Grandmother," for instance, is a short lyrical retelling that describes the feelings of Red Riding Hood's grandmother when she is inside the wolf. It relies on the reader's preknowledge to reconstruct the rest of the tale and thus deviates from the principle of structurality.

Several critical texts, including Bettelheim's *The Uses of Enchantment* and Gilbert and Gubar's analysis of "Snow White" in *The Madwoman in the Attic*, in part follow the plot structure of the traditional tale as well. The story is summarized in the typical chronology of the best-known versions, and the critic each time adds an interpretation or evaluation. Some retellings, such as Fetscher's or Pribil's, follow the same pattern. In this way, an intermediary form between fiction and interpretation is created that has structural parallels to both the traditional fairy tale and some texts belonging to fairy-tale criticism.

Selectivity

Pfister's fifth criterion, to measure intertextual proximity, relates to the level of abstraction (28). Literal citations account for a more dense intertextual relationship than do more general allusions to a work as a whole: "As such the citation of a verse from *Hamlet* is a more succinct, pointed reference to Shakespeare's *Hamlet* than the naming or descriptive characterization of its titular hero. By means of analogy the reference to an individual pre-text is more succinct and thus more intensely intertextual than the relationship to the norms and conventions of a genre, to given topoi and myths or to other abstractly defined textually constituted systems" (Pfister 28–29; my translation). The fact that many retellings incorporate literal quotations from traditional fairy tales—the most famous being "Mirror, mirror on the wall" and "Grandma, what big ears you have"—places them quite close to the core of Pfister's circle. Yet, in the retellings discussed in this book, such quotations do not occur in complete isolation. They feature in retellings that follow or rely, at least in part, on the plot structure of the traditional fairy tale. Moreover, fairy-tale retellings, and even the quotations mentioned above, can be related to a group of pre-texts (fairy-tale variants) rather than one specific pre-text. Literal quotations from criticism are rare in fairy-tale retellings. The short stories of Linda Kavanagh and Garrison Keillor will serve as examples of near quotations in the chapters on feminism. Somewhat more frequent is the use of citations from fairy-tale criticism in the retellings' paratext. As mentioned, the motto of Yolen's *Briar Rose*, for instance, is a quotation from Zipes, and Gmelin adds multiple footnotes to each of his retellings in *Märchen für tapfere Mädchen* (Fairy Tales for Brave Girls), in which he cites from fairy-tale theory (Bettelheim's among others).

Dialogicity

Pfister's sixth and final criterion derives from Bakhtin's concept of dialogicity, meaning that "a reference to given texts or discourses has greater intertextual intensity the more the original and the new context share a semantic or ideological tension" (Pfister 29; my translation). Such tensions in fairy-tale retellings are the topic of this book, with regard not only to the traditional fairy tale but also to fairy-tale criticism. What fairy-tale retellings and fairy-tale criticism have in common, that is what makes them relevant intertexts, is in a broad sense that both contain reflections on the fairy tale. Sometimes this broad intertextual concept can be narrowed down to the fact that they contain reflections of one fairy tale in particular. As both are intertextually linked to the traditional fairy tale, it can be argued that they thus become part of the same intertextual network (albeit via a detour).

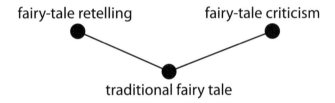

fairy-tale retelling   fairy-tale criticism

traditional fairy tale

The visualization in Chart 1 suggests that every fairy-tale retelling is a relevant intertext to every text from fairy-tale criticism and vice versa. Yet this very broad intertextual network can be further narrowed by shared thematic concerns and ideas. Again, I refer to Nikolajeva's description of intertextuality: "We abandon the idea of one author 'borrowing' from another, but instead are intent on discovering hidden echoes and latent links" (*Age* 154). Such links and echoes will indeed form the starting point for my discussion of specific texts, after which I will proceed to explore how these links carry different meanings within their specific fictional or critical context.

The fact that intertextuality is "dynamic" allows the juxtaposition of retellings with subsequent fairy-tale criticism: Sexton's *Transformations* from 1971 can be intertextually linked with Bettelheim's *The Uses of Enchantment* from 1976, even if we take Sexton's text as the focused text. Likewise, the numerous thematic parallels in Robert Coover's "The Dead Queen" make it a relevant pre-text for Gilbert and Gubar's analysis of

"Snow White" even though the former was published in 1973, six years before the latter. As Nikolajeva argues, "Every line in the dialogue of texts not only looks back at previous texts but forward towards new, yet unwritten texts" (*Age* 155). To some extent, the possibility of reverse chronology in reading versus writing is also relevant to the intertextual link between the traditional fairy tale and the fairy-tale retelling. Although traditional fairy tales may have been *told* and *written* before the retellings, this is not necessarily the order in which they are *read*. Now that fairy-tale retellings are so numerous, not only in the form of children's literature but also in the form of films (the *Shrek* series, *Hoodwinked, Enchanted*) and television programs (*The Simpsons, De Sprookjesboom*), it becomes more and more likely that children will encounter the parody before they read the traditional version. The "aesthetic actualization" (Hutcheon, *Parody* 23) of decoding intertextual references may thus reverse the temporality of the encoding—children may see *Shrek* before they read or see a more traditional version of "Beauty and the Beast." Stephens (with reference to Michael Riffaterre) and Wilkie-Stibbs underline that intertextuality works achronologically, especially for children. When the relationship between criticism and retellings is discussed, it is therefore more adequate to speak about "intertexts" rather than "pre-texts," because the latter term does suggest a chronology.

Moreover, as the textual knowledge of the encoder inevitably differs from that of the decoder, the chance is real that the decoding may not happen at all. If that is the case, that is if the reader (child or adult) "does not notice or cannot identify, an intended allusion or quotation, he or she will merely naturalize it, adapting it to the context of the work as a whole" (Hutcheon, *Parody* 34). Whereas Hutcheon argues that "such naturalization would eliminate a significant part of both the form and content of the text" (34), I would stress that the retelling may still retain other functions, for instance, ideological or political. We will see that this effect is of particular importance to several authors who participate in the intertextual dialogue with feminist discourse.

Fairy-Tale Illustrations as Intertexts

So far, I have mainly stressed the importance of fairy-tale retellings as relevant intertexts for criticism, as this is also the focus of this book. My research has shown, however, that fairy-tale illustrations can also have an interpretative function and that some of them appear as thought-provoking intertexts for fairy-tale studies such as Bettelheim's and Gilbert and Gubar's. In the past two decades, seminal publications on illustration by Maria Nikolajeva and Carole Scott, Perry Nodelman, and David Lewis have drawn attention to the special dynamics that characterize picture books and illustrated texts. Although there are books in which the pictures merely have a decorative function, many exist that provide exciting challenges to readers and researchers. Illustrated texts make use of two different semiotic systems, the verbal (symbolic) and the visual (iconic), and the combination of these two sign systems rarely entails redundancy. Instead, pictures have narrative and interpretative potential (Lewis 25) and can be used to clarify, expand, highlight, and even contradict aspects of the text. Moreover, as Nikolajeva and Scott have noted, "In picturebooks, intertextuality, as everything else, works on two levels, the verbal and the visual" (228), and it is no coincidence that they include illustrated fairy-tale retellings to explore this thought. Fairy-tale illustrations, like fairy-tale retellings and criticism, can thus offer to the reader a variety of interpretations of a given tale, among other means by drawing special attention to aspects or parallels in the story that may have escaped the reader's attention, by contradicting messages in the text, or by situating scenes in a broader context. As Regina Böhm-Korff writes, "Fairy-tale illustrations show certain attitudes toward the tale, and by virtue of this, they comprise an important aspect of fairy-tale reception" (qtd. in Freudenburg 266).

Similar to the retellings, a double intertextual dialogue also applies to the illustrations. Since the pictures are published together with a fairy tale or a retelling, the dialogue with the traditional fairy tale is highlighted (open). Previous fairy-tale illustrations or styles may also come into play here. Sandra Beckett, for instance, has shown how various illustrators of "Little Red Riding Hood" include intervisual references to Gustave Doré (*Recycling* 41) and the collages in *The Stinky Cheese Man* ridicule not only traditional fairy-tale plots but also sugary and stereotypical fairy-tale illustration styles. I will not address such allusions in detail in my analysis, as I will again put fairy-tale criticism at the center of my approach. An intertextual relationship between the illustrations and fairy-tale criticism can be established through analysis, comparison, and interpretation but always remains implicit.

The Uses and Functions of Retellings and Criticism

Even though authors and illustrators of retellings may not openly engage with fairy-tale scholarship, the questions remain of why some do choose to address metacritical ideas about fairy tales in fiction rather than in scholarship and of where the possibilities and limits of the two discourses lie. What then are the features traditionally ascribed to literature and criticism? How fluid are the boundaries between the two genres, and how have they been disrupted? Why do authors feel the need to disrupt them in the first place?

An idea expressed in literature does not have the same significance and impact as the same idea articulated in criticism, and vice versa. It makes a substantial difference whether a literary scholar claims that the mirror in "Snow White" is a patriarchal instrument or Snow White does so herself.[15] Particularly relevant to the status of their content is the difference between fairy-tale retellings as a fictional genre and fairy-tale criticism as nonfiction. Whereas fiction offers imaginary stories, nonfictional texts present content that supposedly corresponds to factual reality.[16] Of course, nonfiction may contain invented elements,[17] and fictional texts never take place in a completely invented universe but always rely to some extent on factual data. In nonfiction, however, the invented parts are by convention clearly distinguished from the rest of the text. In fiction, by contrast, it is left to the readers to assess what they believe is imaginary and what not. In *Snow White in New York*, it is evident, for instance, that the name New York refers to a city in factual reality but that the Snow White character is invented. Readers unfamiliar with New York and its history may be in doubt about whether a newspaper with the title *The New York Mirror* ever existed or whether the Blue Diamond Club, where part of the story takes place, is based on a real venue in New York. Ada Wildekamp, Ineke Van Montfoort, and Willem Van Ruiswijk use the term "indeterminate denotation" for such frequent uncertainties (549).

Linked to the accepted existence of "null denotation" and "indeterminate denotation" in fictional texts is the distinction between fiction and nonfiction based on their specific communicative situations, which require divergent attitudes toward the text from the reader and the author. What comes into play is the so-called fictionality convention, according to which author and reader "play consciously accepted roles, which permits them to step outside their genuine feelings, opinions and the like" (Wildekamp, Van Montfoort, and Van Ruiswijk 555). As a result, authors of fiction have the freedom to use references that do not (accurately) correspond to the world outside the text. In contrast, literary criticism as a nonfictional genre belongs to what Susan S. Lanser calls "attached" or "contingent" texts, which "evoke an 'I' who is conventionally assumed to be the author of the work." The reader expects of such texts that "to the best of her or his knowledge, each author has attempted a factual account, compromised perhaps by errors but not by lies" ("Beholder" 208). It is from the distinction in author attachment between fairy-tale retellings and criticism that the difference in the status of their content arises. When readers encounter an idea in criticism, they can assume it to be the author's truthful and well-researched opinion. When they encounter the same idea in a fairy-tale retelling, they have to form their own judgment about whether they can seriously attribute this idea to the author or not, whether it is perhaps used hyperbolically, as parody, whether the author has deliberately misrepresented or simplified the issue, and so forth.

In practice, assigning fictionality to a given text relies on a judgment by the reader, who tries to ascertain whether the implied author of the text meant the content to correspond to a factual reality and whether the narrative voice in the text is attached to or detached from its real author. Even before the actual reading begins, strong hints are usually given to indicate whether a given text is fiction, and during the reading process readers affirm or adapt their initial judgment on the basis of a combination of bottom-up and top-down processes. In the specific case of fairy-tale retellings and criticism, contextual indices usually provide the reader with clear directions regarding a decision on the text's fictionality. The publication in a scholarly journal or by an academic publishing house, the perigraphic apparatus, and the academic style are strong indices of criticism's nonfictionality. Publishing houses of fiction, the occurrence of peritextual labels such as "a fairy tale retold," and the mention of formulas ("Once upon a time"), places, and characters with zero denotation are clear markers of fictionality in the retellings. The reception of a text and the author's consequent comment or lack of comment on this reception can also be indicative in cases in which there is doubt.

There have been two famous detached texts that were misunderstood to be attached to their authors, and both belong to mock criticism. Iring

Fetscher is a German author as well as a professor of political science and philosophy who has written both fictional texts and criticism.[18] In the preface to the 2000 edition of *Wer hat Dornröschen wachgeküßt?* (Who Kissed Briar Rose Awake?), first published in 1972, he addresses the reception of his fairy-tale parodies: "A few reactions on the fractured fairy tales amused me because of their involuntary humor. An Italian critic praised me for my inventive application of psychoanalytic and Marxist methods of interpretation; a dead serious German Marxist cursed me because I had made a frivolous play of Marxist theories" (9; my translation). That critics have struggled to situate Fetscher's tales in the categories of either fiction or nonfiction is not surprising, as the author combines conventions from both genres.[19] Apart from in the preface and epilogue, it is difficult to discern when Fetscher is addressing his readership seriously versus ironically. Lanser has developed a set of parameters to assess possible author attachment, and on all of these *Wer hat Dornröschen wachgeküßt?* scores high: there is only one, anonymous narrator, and he shares several characteristics with the author—most notably, both are critics with a distinct interest in Marxist theory.

Like *Wer hat Dornröschen wachgeküßt?*, Hans Traxler's *Die Wahrheit über Hänsel und Gretel* (1963, The Truth about Hansel and Gretel) is what Hans Glinz calls a "fictive nonfictional text": a text that carries the features of a nonfictional text but consciously misleads the reader by disregarding relevant information or providing false "facts." In his pseudoscientific report, Traxler claims to describe the findings of the German teacher Georg Ossegg, who, inspired by the discovery of the ancient city of Troy, researches the historical context behind the Brothers Grimm's "Hansel and Gretel." Several experiments lead him to the ruins of the witch's cottage, where he discovers that Hansel and Gretel murdered a solitary-living woman for her gingerbread recipe. Imitating a popular scientific account of folklorist and historical research, Traxler includes detailed descriptions of experiments and complex charts and illustrations.[20] Georg Ossegg uses such schemes to prove, for instance, that Hans was not a small boy but a full-grown man: "The horizon of an adult lies substantially higher than that of an eight-year-old boy. As he thus sees further, he can also spread the marking stones at a substantially greater distance. Therefore the successful experiment could only lead to one, apparently paradoxical conclusion: Hansel and Gretel weren't children! To put it in scientific language: they must have had the height of adults" (Traxler 40; my translation).

In contrast to Fetscher, Traxler was not an academic but worked as a satirist and cartoonist. *Die Wahrheit über Hänsel und Gretel* is a clever parody of popular scientific discourse, and its illusionary effect relies to a great extent on "indeterminate denotation." It turns out that many references in Traxler's text do not correspond to elements in reality, but the abundance of details gives the impression of accuracy, factuality, and reliability. He includes names, places, and numbers, as well as references to other fairy-tale scholars such as Max Lüthi. The book contains an introduction by a (fictional) professor, footnotes, a bibliography, and a detailed index. It is hence not surprising that Traxler's fictional text was interpreted by several readers as nonfiction: "So he was asked for more exact details, teachers wanted to visit the site with their pupils, colleges invited him for lectures, the second edition had to appear with the imprint 'A credible parody'" (Böhm-Korff 136; my translation). Contextual signals of nonfictionality thus needed to be added to clarify the terms of the "contract" with the potential reader.

In addition to their (non)fictionality, fairy-tale retellings and criticism have their own potential and limits in expressing ideas about fairy tales that are linked to their status as literature and/or criticism. The functions and evaluative criteria of these two discourses may also help to explain why someone would choose to express an idea in one or the other. David Lodge distinguishes between three communicative uses for criticism, which usually intertwine: the informative, the evaluative, and the interpretative functions.[21] Linked to these, different objectives can be realized that require different styles: criticism can be "descriptive, prescriptive, polemical, theoretical, and so on" (137). All literary criticism also contains a persuasive and argumentative component. Authors try to convince the reader that their interpretation is valid and that they provide a relevant addition to or correction of previously published material.[22] Like all nonfiction, criticism has an informative function. To truthfully correspond to the factual reality that they describe—mainly fictional texts and other critical texts—literary critics are supposed to obey a number of ethical rules that shape the way research is carried out and results and opinions are communicated to the reader. In *The Craft of Research*, his highly acclaimed manual for students writing research papers and articles, Wayne C. Booth stresses the trust that the public puts in researchers and makes explicit a number of tacit assumptions that underlie the communicative contract between critics and their readers (286):

Ethical researchers do not plagiarize or claim credit for the results of
others.

They do not misreport sources or invent results.

They do not submit data whose accuracy they have reason to question,
unless they raise the questions.

They do not conceal objections that they cannot rebut.

They do not caricature or distort opposing views.

They do not destroy or conceal sources and data important for those
who follow.

Yet, as Lodge has pointed out, criticism carries two important functions
in addition to supplying information. The evaluation and interpretation of
a text vary according to historical, geographical, cultural, and individual
factors, and these factors inevitably have their impact on which information is provided and how. Ideology and personal bias cannot be excluded
from any kind of research, so Marxists have argued against positivist critics
(Kunneman 8). As Ihab Hassan stressed in "Pluralism in Postmodern Perspective" (1986), "The ideological concern declares itself everywhere" and
has affected our idea of what criticism is and what it can and should accomplish (512). This is no reason, however, to put criticism on the same level as
fiction, as some do.[23] Lodge refers, for instance, to T. S. Eliot's suspicion:
"For every success in this type of writing there are thousands of impostures. Instead of insight, you get a fiction" (qtd. in Lodge 139).

Like all theories, critical texts are part of an ongoing discussion, the interests, principles, methods, and arguments of which are subject to change.
The widely divergent interpretations of fairy tales illustrate this practice
perfectly. For Kay Vandergrift this is a second reason to compare criticism
to fiction: "Each theory opens our eyes to new perceptions and new perspectives, but it conceals as well as reveals certain aspects of the literary
work and the literary experience. Each offers a system of useful, but in-
complete, organizing constructs which continually lead to new solutions,
new problems, and new theories. Like all fiction, literary theory requires
a willing suspension of disbelief, that condition of mind philosophers refer
to as the world of 'as if.' "

A third reason is that criticism, like most science, "has its own hidden
agenda," according to Lodge, which is "the demonstration of professional
skill, the refutation of competing peers, the claim to be making an addition

to knowledge" (141). Indeed any type of nonfiction may have a hidden agenda, and all authors may be driven by unconscious ideological and subjective convictions and motivations. What critical texts lack, however, is what Iser considers a constitutive aspect of fiction: the self-disclosure of its fictionality ("Akte" 135). The use of interpretation, the disagreement on methods and principles, and the underlying ideology and hidden agenda do not necessarily turn criticism into nonfiction, nor do they automatically imply author detachment. One can even question the extent to which literary criticism still claims the ability to fix a determinate meaning in the literary text. The relativity of meaning, rather, seems to be one of the catalysts of contemporary writing and criticism,[24] although indeterminate meanings should not be equated with random ones in which any text can be interpreted to mean anything. Paul Feyerabend's famous dictum that "anything goes" has not been taken literally. "The prior existence of the work or works to be criticized, and the prior existence of other critical opinion about them, places limits on the development of the critical discourse," Lodge argues (146), and sets rules to the game. The communicative contract of literary criticism still rests on the reader's presupposition that scholars will use the texts and critical tools that they deem most relevant to supplement an ongoing discussion, even if the ultimate goal is no longer the revelation of truth. The appropriateness of these tools can be evaluated, and Umberto Eco argues, "If it is very difficult to decide whether a given interpretation is a good one, it is, however, always possible to decide whether it is a bad one" (42).

Blurred Boundaries between Literature and Criticism

The attribution of a fictional status to literary criticism can be situated in a broader trend of blurred boundaries between literature and criticism. Literary criticism can indeed assume functions typically ascribed to literature. Robert Dion (1998) speaks of the "aesthetization" of literary criticism (77) and points out that all criticism has a component of narrativity; Lodge argues that good criticism should have some kind of plot and is ideally written with elegance and eloquence (146). More specifically for fairy tales, the impact of traditional tales on the interests and methods of criticism has been explained in a historical context by Stephen Benson, who posits in *Cycles of Influence* that folktale cycles such as *The Arabian Nights* and *The*

Pentamerone not only "provided important access to earlier material for the new discipline" of academic folk narrative studies but also had an influence on the premises and methodology of this new field. "What folk narrative cycles demonstrate is the circulation of motifs and a basic combinatory mechanism," Benson argues (56), and these cycles "*manipulat*[*e*] narrative in a manner which anticipates the basic procedures and conceptions of structuralist narrative poetics" (44). More recent fairy-tale criticism also draws extensively and more directly upon fairy-tale retellings to support critical ideas expressed with regard to the traditional fairy tale. This trend can be noted in the works of renowned critics such as Jack Zipes, Marina Warner, and Maria Tatar and especially, though not exclusively, in monographs that are dedicated to one specific fairy tale, such as Maria Tatar's *Secrets behind the Door* (2004), Jerry Griswold's *The Meanings of "Beauty and the Beast"* (2004), and Sandra L. Beckett's *Red Riding Hood for All Ages* (2008).

The focus of this book lies, however, in the reverse movement: the critical impulse in literature, in the retellings. Several critics have suggested a causal relationship between the simultaneous boom in fairy-tale criticism and fairy-tale retellings since the 1970s, omitting however more concrete explorations of intertextual links. Stephen Benson's comments in *Contemporary Fiction and the Fairy Tale* were mentioned in the introduction. On the situation in West Germany, Walter Filz, Jack Zipes, Hildegard Pischke, and Renate Steinchen have commented as follows:

> The discussion about the value or lack of value of the Grimm tales does not remain without consequence for literary practice. (Filz, *Es war einmal?* 25; my translation)

> Radical fairy-tale opponents and writers from the Weimar period such as Edwin Hoernle, Hermynia zur Mühlen, and Walter Benjamin were rediscovered, and their ideas stimulated contemporary writers to experiment with the traditional fairy tales. (Zipes, *Brothers Grimm* 239)

> Factors that have substantially contributed to their [the transformed fairy tales] genesis are the effects of the fairy-tale debates in relationship to the antiauthoritarian discussion. (Pischke 98; my translation)

There [have] always been critiques and discussions with regard to the fairy tale as children's literature. A result of the critique is the production of anti–fairy tales and the attempt to create a more contemporary fairy-tale literature. (Steinchen 136; see also Born 63; my translation)

All these citations address a critique of the fairy tale, a dissatisfaction with the genre. That such a negative evaluation of the traditional fairy tale should evoke the desire to transform these tales seems logical and will be illustrated with more explicit comments from feminist criticism in chapters two and three. However, more affirmative interpretations of the traditional tales have also inspired retellings, several of which seem written with the intent to transform the fairy tale, not to ridicule it but to demonstrate its relevance for a new age.

The metacritical impulse in literature, whether constructive or destructive, is not new, as Linda Hutcheon has shown in her elaborate discussions of parody and adaptation. Several reasons can be conceived for why authors would consciously opt for fiction rather than criticism to formulate a metafictional comment or interpretation, and they often occur in relation to each other. One reason for using literature as a self-reflexive critical tool is dissatisfaction with literary criticism. This phenomenon has been amplified in the twentieth century, as Hutcheon points out: "Art forms have increasingly appeared to distrust external criticism to the extent that they have sought to incorporate critical commentary within their own structures in a kind of self-legitimizing short-circuit of the normal critical dialogue" (*Parody* 1). In her famous essay "Against Interpretation" (1964), Susan Sontag describes twentieth-century literary criticism as a mostly reactionary activity, an attack on literature. Interpretation that focuses too much on the content of literature rather than its form reduces literature to manageable meanings, Sontag claims, and thus strips it of its potential to unsettle its readers. She prefers to this intellectual approach the "pure, untranslatable, sensuous immediacy" of literature (9), which interpretation takes for granted, yet threatens to destroy. "To avoid interpretation," Sontag suggests, "art may become parody" (10). The psychoanalytic and Marxist approaches that Sontag uses as exemplary cases have exerted a substantial influence on fairy-tale studies. It is no coincidence that Lutz Röhrich (1991) incorporates references to these critical paradigms in his warning against theoretical dogmatism in fairy-tale criticism: "Not only the monocausalists but also the dogmatists, the people who see an astral symbol or an anima or phallus in everything, the dogmatists propounding their Oedipus theories and jargon of mechanisms of suppression and basic drives, are dangerous. But above all we must be aware of those who claim that their interpretation is the only right one. Many truths are sometimes better than one" ("Quest of Meaning" 9–10).

The liberation from fixed concepts of meaning and truth may have enriched criticism on the one hand, yet on the other it is considered one of the causes of a proliferation of criticism at the expense of quality and credibility. In the context of the debates on the death of theory, Perry Nodelman (2005) sees various reasons for a distrust of theory that also affects applied academic criticism: the predictability or sclerosis of "new" readings, the high number of second-rate and derivative analyses, and the absence of any sociopolitical relevance ("What Are We After?" 6–8). Rather than relying on another discourse, literature may thus take over the evaluative and interpretative functions of criticism. As writer and critic Nicole Cooley (2003) states in clear support of the complementarity of literature and criticism, "A great deal is at stake in broadening the array of literary-critical tools we use. If we allow creative writing and literary studies to rejuvenate and replenish one another, both disciplines will gain much" (103).

The dissatisfaction with criticism has found an expression in literature in at least two ways. On the one hand, literature has been used to comment on other literature, and, on the other hand, literature has been used to comment on literary criticism. Such comments can be both (implicitly or explicitly) affirmative and negative, and various examples will be discussed in this book. The anti–theory debates of the 1960s and 1970s did not remain without consequence for the field of fairy-tale studies. Some authors have made it explicit that dissatisfaction with criticism motivated their writing of fairy-tale retellings or parodies of fairy-tale interpretations. The above mentioned German author Iring Fetscher perfectly illustrates Hutcheon's general remark that parody "can call into question the temptation toward the monolithic in modern theory" (*Parody* 116). *Wer hat Dornröschen wachgekübt?* was first published even before fairy-tale criticism had come to its full bloom. In the epilogue to the 2000 edition, Fetscher explains his critique of literary criticism as follows: "The interpreters should not be ridiculed. Only the determined gravity with which some operate has a humorous

effect: they think that only when they can successfully master the reduction of complexity (Niklas Luhmann) have they found the philosopher's
stone" (240; my translation). The various conferences organized for the
Grimms' second centenary in 1985 and 1986 provoked a similar ironic comment from Lothar Borowsky (1984). He claims in his introduction to a collection of fairy-tale cartoons by Heinz Langer that "it would be unwise to
leave the coming festivities only to the scholars" who have wasted almost
two centuries discussing the most trivial details without coming to a conclusion: "Since 1812 [the scholars] haven't even been able to distinguish
clearly between the meaning of Aschenbrödel and Aschenputtel" (7; my
translation).[25]

Nodelman has warned of the conservatism or even reactionary attitude
that may be hidden behind such declarations. Geoffrey Bennington claims
that " 'Post-theory' can easily become an excuse not to think very hard"
(qtd. in Nodelman, "What Are We After?" 12). Yet, such an excuse does
not seem to motivate the retellings. Rather than inviting readers not to
think about the traditional tales, Fetscher, for instance, presents his texts
as an invitation to reflect on the tales in more sophisticated ways and to do
justice to several layers and meanings in these stories. He inserts his critique of fairy-tale criticism in so-called *Umschreibungen*, fictional retellings
of fairy tales with a hyperbolically radical interpretative twist. His parodies
are aimed at three different paradigms: philological textual criticism, psychoanalysis, and Marxist approaches to the fairy tale (see also Joosen, "Back
to Ölenberg"). I will take the first as an example. Fetscher's narrator ridicules the philological paradigm because of its arbitrariness and irrelevant
nitpicking, seeing it mainly as a way for scholars to pave the way for their
own academic career:

> This method is particularly suitable for literary controversies with
> scholarly colleagues, and for many centuries was used by young
> unsalaried university lecturers to gain themselves a lucrative aca-
> demic chair. When the analysis of original texts is too tiresome or
> impossible because the sources are lost or cannot be found, the miss-
> ing pieces can often be successfully and comfortably replaced with
> the help of unbridled fantasy. A few virtuosos in the field of textual
> criticism and exegesis have managed to write hundreds of pages
> on one wrongly placed and therefore meaning-distorting comma.

[. . .] In short, with the help of a good philologist, any arbitrary meaning can be read from any random (and if possible, the most obscure) text. (*Dornröschen* 13; my translation)

The second part of Fetscher's critique is similar to Vandergrift's as well as Eliot's and contrasts with Feyerabend's idea that "anything goes." Fetscher's narrator communicates his views to the reader in two ways: in the metastatement above as well as in the parodies of fairy-tale criticism in which he presents his own analysis. The "unbridled fantasy" that he does not tolerate in (nonfictional) criticism becomes the instrument with which he mocks this discourse in his retellings.

Through his play with the boundaries between fiction and nonfiction, Fetscher invites the reader to reflect on the materiality and conventions of fairy-tale criticism as well as on the characteristics of the traditional fairy tale. *Wer hat Dornröschen wachgeküßt?* requests respect for the multiple layers and meanings in the fairy tale and raises awareness of the illusion of simplicity that is created by any type of criticism that ignores the complexity of this genre.[26] Moreover, in order to comment on and undermine the conventions of criticism, Fetscher makes use of fictional means, which he borrows from the very subject of inquiry of these parodied theories—the fairy tale. Critics such as Anna Altmann and Stephen Benson have stressed the potential for constructive and affirmative meanings that fairy-tale retellings add to their critical component. They can "avoid the appearance of a mere critique" (Benson, *Cycles* 156) and form an active exploration of form and meaning (see also Hutcheon, *Parody* 51). By exaggerating the biased and simplistic approach of some critical paradigms to the fairy tale, Fetscher invests his analyses with an implicit critique, adding extra meaning to the story and reinstalling the polysemantic potential of fiction.

Linked to the debates on the relevance and flaws of literary criticism is a second motivation for bringing fiction into play as a metadiscourse. Those who do value the function and possible impact of literary criticism encounter the problem that it is, in many ways, an elitist practice. Nodelman sees this as a part of its increasing professionalization and institutionalization, so that academic criticism often remains limited to university professors, scholars, and students. In addition to popularized versions of fairy-tale analyses, fiction has helped to spread some ideas from academic contexts outside of the university walls. Several feminist and Marxist critics have formulated the explicit wish for fairy-tale retellings that reflect literary critiques and help achieve their political aspirations. One group in particular is a popular target audience of such retellings with a political agenda: children. The German Marxist Otto Gmelin quotes Maxim Gorky in this respect: "Nowadays a good children's book has a much better effect than a dozen articles. Write a fairy tale!" (*Tapfere Mädchen* 96; my translation). As traditional fairy tales still occupy an important position in the canon of children's literature, and as some critics believe that children are particularly receptive to the ideology that the fairy tale offers, it is not surprising that many retellings try to outbalance this influence by providing other views and values.

Yet the extended readership of fairy-tale retellings does not remain restricted to children. Most adults do not read critical theory either, and in the recent vogue of fairy-tale retellings, many texts are explicitly targeted at them. As Hutcheon argues, "The art forms of our century have been extremely and self-consciously didactic" (*Parody* 3)—the pedagogical aspect does not remain limited to children's literature. Especially for those political groups and movements who see in literary criticism a discourse that can still be effective in changing a larger readership's view on literary texts and even on the world, the academic status of literary criticism is considered an impediment to the widespread dissemination of ideas. Various factors, ranging from the academic jargon and referencing system to its implicit assumptions of basic knowledge and relatively limited availability, exclude large groups of readers. As the radical feminist Andrea Dworkin polemically introduced her analysis of fairy tales in *Woman Hating* (1974), "This book is an action, a political action where revolution is the goal. It has no other purpose. It is not cerebral wisdom, or academic horseshit, or ideas carved in granite or destined for immortality. It is part of a planetary movement to restructure community forms and human consciousness so that people have power over their own lives, participate fully in community, live in dignity and freedom. [. . .] Academics lock books in a tangled web of mindfuck and abstraction. The notion is that there are ideas, then art, then somewhere else, unrelated, life" (17, 24).

Dworkin was a freelance journalist rather than an academic, and her book was written in a rhetorical manifesto style. The simplicity of some of her ideas and her aggressive tone have been criticized by many, but her nonacademic style is now credited for helping her ideas find a wider appeal

(Grant 987; Daly 151). Moreover, in the hope of spreading her feminist ideas as extensively as possible and contributing through this consciousness-raising to an actual change and even revolution in society, Dworkin launches several appeals to writers to assume their responsibility and write feminist works (24–25). As we will see later in this book, several retellings can be linked to her provocative fairy-tale critique, either as a positive reflection of it or as correction and parody.

A third reason for communicating a literary critique or comment through fiction rather than criticism, in addition to the dissatisfaction with criticism and the wider audience of fiction, is to escape the ethics and rules of acceptability that apply to literary criticism. Although various styles of criticism exist, certain conditions and evaluative criteria are attached to all writing within this type of discourse. According to Geert Lernout's manual for academic writing, "There are only two categorical imperatives, two commandments that are [. . .] accepted by all literary critics, no matter their religious, philosophical or ideological stance." These are the following: "Thou Shalt Always Cite Another Author Correctly" and "Thou Shalt Not Commit Plagiarism" (149; my translation). The ethical principles listed by Booth and mentioned above count as further commandments. Other, less imperative guidelines, which may nevertheless function as evaluative criteria for academic writing, include clarity of structure, coherence, and logic of argument (Lernout 185), relevance of the primary and secondary literature under discussion (96), completeness, and adequate use of academic register (104–5). Several aspects of the critical text are affected by these directions, ranging from method and structure to content and style. Helmut Brackert (1980) formulates an even stricter set of ethical rules for the specific interpretation of fairy tales:

> Its very first condition is clearly that no interpretation is allowed—no matter how well one could use it in the course of one's own argument—that is evidently contradictory to the words of the text. The next condition is also that all important and mysterious passages be included in the interpretation; furthermore, that all of this result in a coherence that fits. Finally there is one last condition: fairy tales [. . .] must not be interpreted solely in terms of their surface level, their external course of action; otherwise, one very clearly misses a crucial dimension of their expression, as is confirmed by countless

examples of its reception in practical pedagogy and psychology. Obviously, all these conditions merely mark out an interpretative playground and only in the broadest sense serve judgments about good and bad. ("Märchendeutung" 235; my translation)

The last condition in particular, which stipulates an interpretation beyond the surface layer, has been contested as a principle,[27] and several psychological explanations of fairy tales have been rejected for violating the first principle—the faithfulness to the word of the text. Nevertheless, the practice of fairy-tale interpretation is indeed largely governed by the rules that Brackert describes. This becomes clearest in the implicit and explicit criteria that critics rely on to reject or adapt the works of their predecessors.

Fiction is exempted from several of the ethical presuppositions and evaluative criteria listed by Booth, Lernout, and Brackert. Although plagiarism is not accepted for fiction, the concepts of intertextuality and influence allow the creative use of previously published forms, ideas, and even lines of text in fiction in a way that is less constrained than in criticism. This makes it legally and morally acceptable for authors to use elements from previous texts without quoting sources (in detail). In addition, fiction is characterized by its combination of factual and invented materials. Fiction is not bound to accuracy, and this affects its use of previous textual material. It is free to misrepresent, caricature, and simplify sources and opposing views. Moreover, a metacritical fictional text is by no means limited by a criterion such as "coherence and logic of argument," nor does it make a claim to completeness. The latter is a limit that, although arguably dogmatic in itself, is widely accepted. Eco explains that "any interpretation given of a portion of a text can be accepted if it is confirmed and must be rejected if it is challenged by another portion of the same text" (59). Authors of fiction can step into a story at any given point, without the obligation to finish an argument or to encompass as many aspects as possible of another fictional text or critical discussion. As Christa Kamenetsky confirms, "While satirical writers have always followed their personal impulse, with no obligation to tradition or convention, critics have customarily worked under certain limitations to set logic, evidence, or at least an author's frame of reference" (322). Although the first part of her assertion can be debated, authors of fiction are certainly exempt from the conditions that she consequently lists.

A vast number of critical fairy-tale retellings merely draws attention to a certain passage or oddity, leaving the conclusions and consequent interpretations of other parts of the text to the reader. In chapter three, for instance, I will argue that Dorothea Runow's summary of Bettelheim is a simplification and enigmatic misrepresentation of his theory. Louise Murphy introduces a narrator who claims to tell *The True Story of Hansel and Gretel* (2003): "The story has been told over and over by liars and it must be retold" (1). It is clear that her accusations of the Grimms and her new "truth" are only valid on fictional terms: the story takes place in Poland during the Second World War, more than a century after the Grimms' "Hansel and Gretel" was published. No explanation is given with regard to the relationship between this tale and the "true" version that Murphy's narrator claims to tell, nor is it needed within the fictional context of this book.

Fairy Tales in the Paraliterary Space

The result of the increasingly blurred distinctions between fiction and criticism in postmodernism is what Hutcheon terms the "paraliterary space" (*Postmodernism* 9–10). It encompasses a wide range of practices: the absorption of some literary characteristics in criticism and, conversely, the occurrence in literary works of certain critical functions.[28] It overlaps with what Helen Flavell (1998) calls "fictocriticism"—the "tendency in contemporary criticism to blur the distinction between theory and fiction" (203), which results in a hybrid mixture of fictional and nonfictional genres.[29] Along with mock criticism, practices within fictocriticism also involve the insertion of subjective interpretations and responses as well as autobiographical and ambiguous passages into the text. Occasionally, critics go further in implementing formal features from literary genres.[30] In "Extrapolating from Nalo Hopkinson's *Skin Folk*" (2008), Cristina Bacchilega claims that she wants "to learn more from the cross-fertilization of fiction, folktale and theory" (181). Focusing on intertextuality, hypertextuality, and multivocality in the works of Hopkinson, Bacchilega visualizes a dialogue between various retellings by incorporating quotations and thoughts in text balloons that seem to flow or pop up in the margins of her argument. With this unusual layout, Bacchilega here appears to imitate intertextual echoes that can be heard through literary texts and includes afterthoughts and parallels. It is left to the reader to choose which of these side thoughts to pursue and to make sense of the suggested parallels and remarks. With this approach, Bacchilega brings into practice the "hypertextuality" she ascribes to the fictional texts that are the subject of her article. Such hypertextuality is also introduced in some fairy-tale anthologies, Haase argues, for example in Neil Philip's *The Illustrated Book of Fairy Tales,* in which fairy-tale variants and interpretations are offered to the reader in the margins of the text: "Approximating and anticipating hypertext as they do, these print editions de-center the folktale text, discourage sequential reading, and create the potential for a very different—more cerebral? more scholarly?—experience of the folktale" ("Gutenberg" 227).

A different form of hypertextuality is practiced in Sandra Gilbert and Susan Gubar's "The Further Adventures of Snow White," the closing chapter of their three-volume discussion of twentieth-century woman authors, *No Man's Land* (1994). The bulk of the chapter contains a survey and analysis of seminal feminist scholarship and literature. These parts are preceded by a section in which criticism and fiction are mixed into tales that illustrate some of the evolutions discussed in the survey: "As we now conclude *No Man's Land,*" Gilbert and Gubar write, "we feel we have been reviewing so many new and different plots—all of them explored in various ways by twentieth-century women writers—that it is no longer possible to propose a monolithic 'tale' about the female imagination. What had been a single tradition has become many traditions" (360). Imagining then how a storyteller would write the tale after the gender revolution of feminist criticism, Gilbert and Gubar recast "Snow White" in more than a dozen retellings, which respond, among other things, to the liberation of the female libido (362), the new interest in "lesbianism, bisexuality, transvestism, and transsexuality" (364), and the indeterminacy of deconstruction theories (366). It is clear that they are influenced by authors such as Margaret Atwood and Donald Barthelme, who are also referenced in the nonfictional parts of the text. In offering all these plots, Gilbert and Gubar leave the final course and meaning of the tale to the reader, as they repeatedly stress, "Choose your own adventure" (362), and "Feel free to vote for your own favorite" (363). Intertextual connections can be inferred with both critical and literary texts, some of which are made explicit, many of which are not. More questions than answers can be derived from the hypothetical and often ironic tales. What is nevertheless invoked (and confirmed in the second part of the chapter) is a celebration of the diversity of female voices and stories that feminism has helped to make possible and expressible, both in criticism and in literature.

Not incidentally in a book called *Transcending Boundaries* (1999), Roderick McGillis constructs his article about intertextuality as a dialogue between five historical figures, all of whom have written or illustrated fairy tales: the American nineteenth-century author Harriet Childe-Pemberton, the British turn of the twentieth-century writer Evelyn Sharp, the artist George Cruikshank, the Belgian playwright Maurice Maeterlinck, and the cartoonist Tex Avery. The heading *"Ceci n'est pas un essai"* would evoke, by analogy with René Magritte's painting, the expectation of a traditional essay, but this is not what McGillis delivers. Instead, he explores the boundaries of the fictional and the critical, introducing his characters to an anachronistic talk about contemporary picture books (including *The Stinky Cheese Man*) and recent theories on intertextuality, such as Stephens's and Hutcheon's. The lines with which the article closes seem indicative of how the text should be read:

As they [the authors and illustrators] leave the gazebo, a gaggle of young children race by singing: "Run, Run, / As fast as you may; / You'll not catch us, / Don't care what you say." (124)

This parody of the rhyme from the fairy tale "The Gingerbread Man"[31] is at the same time an intertextual reference to *The Stinky Cheese Man*, a parody of the same tale, in which Jon Scieszka makes similar discrediting statements about the relativism of meaning in the introduction. On the one hand, the speakers of the rhyme remind the adult characters that they have been speculating about a child who remains ultimately beyond their grasp. On the other hand, the rhyme itself seems to escape anyone's attempt to freeze it into a stable meaning: its intertextuality reaches out in various directions. To quote McGillis's fictional Evelyn Sharp: "We speak and in speaking hope to clarify what it means to be a subject by taking up a position in language. But every position is occupied and we can only sit in someone's lap" ("Ages: All" 124). This is true for criticism, as the various references to previous scholars indicate, as well as for literature. Although the attempt to arrive at a final goal or a static meaning seems to have been abandoned, McGillis shows that we still keep running, both because we have to and because we like it. That we can adapt the rules of the game, as

McGillis has done, seems to be motivated not just by necessity but also by the fun of the game.

The overlap between fairy-tale retellings and criticism becomes manifest in a further number of ways. On a macro level, criticism and fairy-tale retellings are published side by side, which suggests that both are important participants in the dialogue on the traditional fairy tale. Examples of this practice include Zipes's *The Trials and Tribulations of Little Red Riding Hood* and *Don't Bet On the Prince*, Jerry Griswold's *The Meanings of "Beauty and the Beast,"* and Maria Tatar's *The Classic Fairy Tales*. More examples have been mentioned in the course of this chapter. Several authors, including Otto Gmelin, Iring Fetscher, Jane Yolen, Neil Philip, Sandra M. Gilbert, Marina Warner, and Jack Zipes, have expressed their views on the fairy tale both in fiction and in criticism. Other authors have attested to reading or studying fairy-tale scholarship.[32] Prefaces to fairy-tale collections, both of traditional tales and retellings, often refer to the best-known critics and theories,[33] and some retellings, such as Yolen's *Briar Rose* and Ellen Datlow and Terri Windling's *Black Heart, Ivory Bones*, have lists with recommended collections of fairy tales as well as nonfictional texts about fairy tales. In German and English, retellings are sometimes published with questionnaires and suggestions for reading group discussions or teaching attached. These questions are frequently influenced by, and occasionally even contain references to, fairy-tale criticism.[34] Other paratextual fairy-tale material may also contain references to fairy-tale criticism. In, for instance, Otto Gmelin's *Märchen für tapfere Mädchen*, critical ideas and references are included in the prefaces and footnotes that accompany each tale. Neil Philip places comments, illustrations, and variants in the margins of his *Illustrated Book of Fairy Tales*.

Several textual strategies for expressing critical ideas *within* the retellings themselves can be discerned. Critical ideas can be introduced in the form of explicit comments. The genre of fictional fairy-tale interpretations, which was introduced above with Fetscher and Traxler, displays author detachment in a text that carries the textual features of a critical text. These interpretations function as parodies of criticism. Linda Kavanagh merges the roles of the subject and object of fairy-tale criticism even further. She lets female fairy-tale characters debate their own portrayal in "The Princesses' Forum" (1985). In this fictional fairy-tale debate, the conventions of critical discourse are exaggerated and exposed and its usual participants mocked. Such examples are rarer than the large number of retellings that contain more isolated comments on the traditional fairy tale expressed by the narrator or the characters. That the displacement of the critic's voice to that of a fictional being gives the content a different status is an issue that will be more elaborately discussed in the following case studies. Whereas in parodies of critical analyses and conference reports the critical ideas are *told* rather than *shown*, in most retellings these comments are demonstrated rather than explicitly mentioned. We will see that the critical evaluation of the traditional fairy tale is "performed" in two ways: first, through exaggeration and exposure and, second, through the correction with a more positively valued ideal.

A simple example can illustrate the three practices. Various feminist critics (including Lieberman, Rowe, and Dworkin) have pointed out the lack of independent and active heroines in the best-known traditional fairy tales. In Kavanagh's princesses' forum, Red Riding Hood remarks this explicitly: "Everyone assumes that in order to live happily ever after, we must each have a prince in tow" (6). Rather than addressing this problem directly, as Kavanagh does, many retellings correct it by providing an alternative, by filling the gap with an active heroine who chooses not to conform to stereotypical gender patterns. Robert Munsch's *The Paper Bag Princess*, in which the heroine saves a prince from a dragon but refuses to marry him, has become a classic example. Others exaggerate the passivity of the traditional fairy-tale heroine to such a degree that it becomes a hyperbolic parody. Anne Sexton's "Snow White" will be seen to exemplify this strategy in chapter four. It is not uncommon that two or even all three strategies—explicit comments, exaggeration, and correction—are combined in one retelling.

Bruno Bettelheim stands apart from the feminist case studies in that he values the traditional fairy tale more positively than do Lieberman and Gilbert and Gubar. His interpretations are written in support of the Grimms' collection especially, as he seeks to recover the latent meanings behind these stories and promotes their therapeutic effect. In fairy-tale retellings and illustrations, the process of psychoanalytic symbolization is often reversed and undone, so that the deeper meaning surfaces again. However, as Bettelheim himself has become the subject of an ample body of criticism, some retellings also incorporate skepticism and even open critique of psychoanalysis. The same is true for retellings that counteract feminist ideals and interpretations. In this sense, the retellings and illustrations truly become part of the intertextual dialogue, talking in different and often more ambivalent voices than the critics but actively and creatively contributing to our understanding and experience of the fairy tale.

2   Marcia K. Lieberman's "Some Day My Prince Will Come"

Marcia Lieberman's "Some Day My Prince Will Come: Female Acculturation through the Fairy Tale" (1972) was one of the first feminist studies in the American fairy-tale renaissance of the 1970s. Published as a reaction to "Fairy Tale Liberation" (1970), Alison Lurie's commendation of the fairy tale as a subversive and potentially feminist genre, Lieberman's polemic reply raised fundamental questions about gender representation in popular fairy tales: "In the catalytic exchange between Lurie and Lieberman during the early 1970s, we witness simultaneously the inchoate discourse of early feminist fairy-tale research and the advent of modern fairy-tale studies, with its emphases on the genre's sociopolitical and sociohistorical contexts. Already anticipated in their terms of debate are nascent questions and critical problems that over the next thirty years would constitute the agenda of much fairy-tale research" (Haase, "Scholarship" 2).

That Lieberman's article is a milestone in American feminist fairy-tale criticism was acknowledged by critics such as Kay Stone ("Feminist Approaches" 230), Donald Haase ("Scholarship" 31), and Jack Zipes, who included it as one of only four critical articles in his anthology *Don't Bet On the Prince* (1983). Lieberman's article is now nearly forty years old, and feminist fairy-tale theory has evolved since then under the influence of various theoretical perspectives, such as semiotics, psychoanalysis, Marxism, deconstruction theory, and queer studies. Both critics and authors of fiction have shown that there are more sophisticated ways of dealing with fairy tales than the social-realistic and political approach that Lieberman represents, for instance by drawing attention to their qualities as fantasies and by taking into account the genre's diversity and developmental history.[1] Problematic as Lieberman's approach may be in comparison to later feminist studies, its influence on fairy-tale research remains undisputed. In his survey of feminist fairy-tale scholarship from 2004, Haase writes that "there was—and still is—widespread agreement with Lieberman's argument" ("Scholarship" 3), and indeed the discourse of critics such as Patricia Duncker (1992), Maria Micaele Coppola (2001), and Gerard Gielen (2006) still echoes several aspects of Lieberman's fairy-tale critique.[2] In addition, aspects of Lieberman's argument can still be discerned in the attitude to the traditional fairy tale expressed in many fairy-tale retellings. They still surface in recent texts—especially, though not exclusively, those intended for children. Examples include Babette Cole's *Long Live Princess Smartypants* (2004), Will and Mary Pope Osbourne's *Sleeping Bobby* (2005), and Marjet Huiberts' *Roodkapje was een toffe meid* (2010, Little Red Riding Hood Was a Cool Girl). Moreover, the older revisions that engage with ideas from the emancipation movement, such as Robert Munsch's *The Paper Bag Princess* (1980), Babette Cole's *Prince Cinders* (1988) and *Princess Smartypants* (1986), and Jane Yolen's *Sleeping Ugly* (1981), are still being reprinted and used in classrooms. According to Manfred Pfister's criterion of "communicativity," the prominence of Lieberman's ideas in the feminist fairy-tale debates makes it a suitable starting point for a thematic comparison on the basis of what he calls "dialogicity."

The Power of the Page

"Some Day My Prince Will Come" is first and foremost a critique of the ideology transmitted through popular fairy tales as they were made available through Andrew Lang's *Blue Fairy Book* (1889) and in Walt Disney's animated films. Lieberman refutes Lurie's defense of the fairy tale's potential for the feminist cause, which is for the most part based on lesser-known tales such as "Clever Gretchen" and "The Sleeping Prince." Lieberman stresses the limited scope that these stories have, arguing instead that "an analysis of those fairy tales that children actually read indicates [. . .] that they serve to acculturate women to traditional social roles" (185). The popular fairy tales of Lang and Disney, she argues, teach children "behavioral and associative patterns, value systems, and how to predict the consequences of specific acts or circumstances" (187). Lieberman's article can be situated in the larger feminist debates on the biological nature or cultural constructedness of gender. Although she acknowledges the unresolvedness of the issue, she emphasizes the second pole. Her approach is characterized by the conviction of the ideological and didactic impact of literature and of children's books in particular: "The best known stories," she writes, "have affected masses of children in our culture" (186). What children read is believed to have a substantial influence on the construction of their own identity, on their beliefs and expectations toward others, and on their conscious and unconscious associations. Popular fairy tales can thus be considered to be what Dieter Richter and Jochen Vogt have called "heimliche Erzieher," surreptitious educators. Lieberman makes this assumption explicit in the following: "A close examination of the treatment of girls and women in fairy tales reveals certain patterns which are keenly interesting not only in themselves, but also as material which has undoubtedly played a major contribution in forming the sexual role concept of children. [. . .] Millions of women must surely have formed their psycho-sexual self-concepts, and their ideas of what they could or could not accomplish, what sort of behavior would be rewarded, and the nature of reward itself, in part from their favorite fairy tales" (186–87). Her confidence in literature's socializing power makes her text illustrative of a strong current in feminist literary theory and children's literature criticism. Like many other representatives of the emancipation movement, she is influenced by the Enlightenment's concept of childhood and children's literature as it is described by Katrien Vloeberghs: "The child is considered the blueprint of a rational subject, a metaphor of a social future that implies an improvement with regard to the present. Crucial is the task of the educator to prepare the unfinished, inarticulate being to a life as an articulate and independent member of the community" (16; my translation).

Indeed Lieberman constructs an image of the child as inexperienced, naïve, and prone to manipulation by what it reads and views. If the child is perceived as a tabula rasa—as Lieberman suggests when she argues with the same imagery of the blank page that the "stories are *imprinted* in children" (200; my emphasis)—adults bear a large responsibility for what they present to the young: "We must pay particular attention to those stories that are so beguiling that children think more as they read them 'of the diversion than of the lesson'" (Lieberman 186). As untrained readers, children are ascribed limited capacity to recognize the explicit and implicit ideology transmitted by the text. Lieberman does not address the possibility that young readers could distance themselves from this ideology: they are assumed to identify with their same-sex characters and imitate the behavior ascribed to them. Moreover, in her article, Lieberman does not denounce the fact that literature is used to transmit ideology—the ideological impact of literature appears rather as something that cannot be avoided. Consequently, her analysis focuses more on the ideological *content* that is communicated through the fairy tale than on its manipulative potential, which is taken for granted.

Lieberman was by no means the only feminist critic in the 1970s who was convinced of the fairy tale's socializing power. The assumptions that lie at the heart of her article were shared by several of her contemporaries—in the United States but also in Europe. "Böses kommt aus Märchen" (Evil Comes from Fairy Tales) was the title of an article by the German pedagogue Otto F. Gmelin (1975), who argued that fairy tales teach children aggression and fear and that they promote sexism and capitalism. In a book by Adri Abbestee et al. that contained several tragic stories of unhappy marriages—ironically titled *En ʒe leefden nog lang en gelukkig . . .* (1974, And They Lived Happily Ever After . . .)—the Dutch feminist publishing house De Bonte Was (The Colored Wash) echoes Lieberman's critique of the fairy-tale ending: "The fairy tale of marriage influences the life of all women, because from childhood onwards all of us have been presented with marriage as the future ideal" (qtd. in Brunt 85). The Dutch critic Eric Hulsens (1979) echoes Lieberman's title when he calls Snow White "a twat who doesn't take her fate into her own hands for a single moment, but only gets saved because of her female charm." Like Lieberman and Gmelin, he believes that such a role model must have a negative effect on children: "Generation after generation this fairy tale teaches girls that what matters in life is to be beautiful and to wait for a prince" (234; my translation).[3] Haase discusses various other examples from British and American scholarship in "Feminist Fairy-Tale Scholarship." The most extreme view is probably taken up by Susan Brownmiller (1975), who blames fairy tales for training women to become rape victims. In *Gyn/Ecology* (1978), Mary Daly states that "patriarchy perpetuates its deception through myth" and makes the following comparison: "The child who is fed tales such as *Snow White* is not told that the tale itself is a poisonous apple" (44). This metaphor ascribes to stories the power to make sick and kill, whereas the young listener is portrayed as an innocent, passive victim. Moreover, Daly compares the child's mother or teacher, the female teller of the tales, to the "wicked queen": she is the ultimate proof that the poison in the apple or the story has been effective, because she passes it on while remaining "unaware of her venomous part in the patriarchal plot" (Daly 44). That Daly thus puts "unawareness" on the same level as "wickedness" underlines the importance that such enlightened thinkers attribute to teaching knowledge and raising a critical attitude toward literature's ideology.

The assumption that children automatically internalize the ideology offered in the fairy tale was countered in the 1970s and more recently by research that focuses on (female) reader response.[4] Critics such as Kay Stone (1975), Madonna Kolbenschlag (1979), and Emma Brunt (1982) stress that not all (generations of) women respond to the fairy tale in the same way. Stone interviewed forty women "of varying ages and backgrounds," and whereas "many admitted that they were certainly influenced by their reading of fairy tales," there were also several others who claimed to be bored by passive fairy-tale heroines ("Disney" 48–49). More recently, Kate Bernheimer (1999) invited various woman authors to reflect on the influence that fairy tales have had on their self-image, and "their wildly different answers suggest some of the multiplicity of ways fairy tales can mirror and form versions of the female self" (Harries 139), thus challenging Lieberman's assumption that the influence of the fairy tale on young readers is homogenous and almost inevitably leads to a confirmation of patriarchal gender stereotypes. More intuitively, Maria Tatar refers back to Jean Jacques Rousseau to remind us of "a child's natural gift for subversion, for moving against every author's intentions" (*Heads* 21). Although this view is in turn a generalization of the child reader's response, influenced by a more Romantic concept of childhood, it addresses the possibility of the child as an active reader rather than a passive recipient of ideology. Finally, several critics who are convinced of the fairy tale's value, such as Bruno Bettelheim and Carolyn G. Heilbrun, have questioned the specific influence of the fairy tale on gender construction, arguing that the reader's sex has little influence on the stories' beneficial impact and that young girls can identify with male as well as female characters.

In spite of these reservations, several fairy-tale retellings testify to the widespread conviction from the 1970s that the fairy tale's ideology had a negative impact on its young reader. This analogy with the sociopolitical feminist approach to literature becomes clearest in the retellings' paratext and in the metacomments on the traditional stories within the retellings themselves. "Consciousness is power," the American feminist Judith Fetterley argued in *The Resisting Reader* (1978): "To create a new understanding of our literature is to make possible a new effect of that literature on us. And to make possible a new effect is in turn to provide the conditions for changing the culture that the literature reflects" (xix–xx). For adult readers, a new understanding of literature can be accomplished through the medium of feminist literary criticism, whose importance Fetterley stresses. Children and adolescents, however, usually do not have access to (feminist) literary theory, and many adults who read literature never come into contact with criticism. Jill P. May (1995) has noted, for instance, that most teachers do not read critical theory (15). This can be and has been a reason for implementing criticism in fiction.

Literature has its own way of opening up other literary texts from without, although metacritical intertextuality and parody inevitably involve taking in aspects of the pre-text. By referring to stories that most children and adults are acquainted with, fairy-tale retellings have the potential to provide a large group of readers with a new—in this case feminist— perspective on a well-known narrative. By exploiting the critical potential of their intertextual links with the traditional story, these "alternative" versions give readers an impression of what literary theory can bring about: fairy-tale retellings try to make readers who draw the connection with the pre-texts aware of issues and possible interpretations in these texts that they may have not noticed before. They show, for instance, that the ideology in the traditional tales is not a natural state but a culturally specific construction. It is the intention of several authors and teachers of fairy-tale retellings that this experience will then lead to a greater alertness and understanding when the children or adults read similar stories in the future. "The first act of the feminist critic must be to become a resisting rather than an assenting reader," Fetterley argues, "While women obviously cannot rewrite literary works so they become ours by virtue of reflecting our reality, we can accurately rename the reality they do reflect and so change literary criticism from a closed conversation to an active dialogue" (xxiii). Yet, feminist authors *have* rewritten fairy tales, entering the dialogue with other literatures and realities not only in criticism but also in fiction, often with the hope of stimulating and training others in becoming resisting readers.

The conviction that fairy-tale retellings can be used to create critical readers characterizes the stories that several feminist authors and movements published during the 1970s and the 1980s. A focus on literature's socializing power and its ideological content is present in several prefaces to collections published in this period. But whereas in the feminist literary criticism of the time (as in Lieberman's article) the influence of (mainstream) children's literature on the young reader's mind was often deplored, in literature itself, this socializing power was a force to be explored and used to the author's own advantage. The primary texts display what Vivian Liska describes as "an optimism derived from the Enlightenment's promises of justice, equality and emancipation" ("Criticism" 96) and a belief that literature can change society for the better when it is written with the "right" ideological stance.

Primary literary texts were used to counteract the gender bias of the best-known tales in at least two ways. First, American and European authors, such as Alison Lurie, Angela Carter, Ethel Johnston Phelps, and Ilse Korn anthologized lesser-known fairy tales with unconventional, empowered heroines in order to break what Lieberman calls "limitations that are imposed by sex" (187) suggested by the more popular tales. Second, many authors have composed new fairy tales and rewritten the most popular tales with a feminist twist. In children's literature, this trend became most apparent in the late 1970s and in the 1980s, with revealing titles such as *Märchen für tapfere Mädchen* (Fairy Tales for Brave Girls, Gmelin, 1978), "The Princess Who Stood On Her Own Two Feet" (Jeanne Desy, 1982), *The Tough Princess* (Martin Waddell and Patrick Benson, 1986), *Princess Smartypants* (Cole, 1986), "Not So Little Red Riding Hood" (Anne Sharpe, 1985), and *Rapunzel's Revenge: Fairy Tales for Feminists* (1985, Anne Claffey et al.).

In the prefaces of feminist collections of retellings, the belief in literature's ideological impact becomes most explicit. If the collection is intended for young readers, the addressee is usually the adult mediator, who is warned about the traditional tales' effect on children. Published in 1972, the same year as Lieberman's article, the Merseyside Fairy Story Collective's retelling of "Little Red Riding Hood" opens with such a warning against the power of the tales: "Fairy tales are political. They help to inform children's values and teach them to accept our society and their roles in it" (qtd. in Zipes, *Subversion* 181). Their retellings are meant to defy this authority and reinforcement of the status quo. Few authors are as fierce in their critique of the traditional tales (and of the society that produced them) as Otto F. Gmelin and Doris Lerche. In the paratext to *Märchen für tapfere Mädchen*, their argument testifies to their belief in the socializing power of literature and the fairy tale in particular: "We are against any one-sidedness, which ONLY wants to change female roles, restyling woman into today's man, forcing the man—economically disempowered—into TODAY'S house. We need to organize both gender patterns ANEW. And such model problems we solve not only with old fairy tales and their criticism, but with new ones" (96; my translation).

Gmelin and Lerche attribute an extraordinary socializing force to literature in claiming that with their new fairy tales they can solve societal problems. This is confirmed in the final sentence of their preface—"fairy-tale education is peace education" (96; my translation)—which implies that a better understanding of literature can make the world a better place. It is not surprising that to the question "Is one allowed to change fairy tales?" Gmelin's answer is clear: "One is not only allowed to change fairy tales, one is obliged!" (*Venus* 4; my translation). Likewise, parents are compelled to think about traditional fairy tales before they present them to their children. Under the title "What One Must Think about Nowadays When One Reads a Grimm Fairy Tale to a Child" and in the form of eight cartoons, Gmelin summarizes some of the basic objections that feminists and Marxists raised against fairy tales—from "all stepmothers are evil" to "everything always stays the same." The rhetorical questions under each cartoon reinforce the dogmatic tone of the title, for example, "Do you believe that such clichés help children of divorced parents get along with their new mothers and fathers?" and "Do you believe that stories that children hear again and again have no influence at all on their thoughts?" (*Venus* 2–3; my translation).

Gmelin's prescriptive style is echoed in the command expressed in the title of Wolfgang Mieder's *Mädchen, pfeif auf den Prinzen* (1983, Girls, Don't Bother with the Prince). In his preface, Mieder reveals himself as a more moderate defender of the fairy-tale retelling: "Fairy tales and fairy-tale poems in the form of anti–fairy tales aim to explain and improve the world, and to that [goal] this little book would like to make a contribution" (10; my translation). Mieder also hopes that literature will have a positive impact on society, albeit a modest one ("this little book"). In a previously published anthology from 1979, he included, to that end, a long list of *"Arbeitsvorschläge,"* or suggestions for discussion, several of which direct the reader to issues of gender.[5]

The fairy tale's power is also thematized in some of the poems included in *Mädchen, pfeif auf den Prinzen*, such as Nelly Wacker's "Veraltete Märchengestalten" (1975, Outdated Fairy-Tale Figures):

> But maybe that is exactly why
> in fairy tales the old must exist,
> so that *all* of today's grandchildren
> understand the environment better,
> in order to, in the battle with the old,
> later shape the world's image anew?
> (16; my translation)[6]

In Wacker's poem, a slight shift in the empowerment of the juvenile reader can be perceived: even the traditional fairy tales help the child *understand* the world and see what is outdated about it. Her poem implies that young readers can distance themselves from the stories' ideology. This is an evolution that can also be noted in feminist literary criticism. Colette Dowling (1983), for instance, thinks of the traditional fairy tale "as a mirror of the forces limiting women" and argues, like Wacker, that a critical interaction with these tales "makes it possible to project alternative ways of constructing lives" (Haase, "Scholarship" 7). The traditional fairy tale is thus brought back into play in order to understand the origin and history of gender stereotypes.

Such a revalorization of fairy-tale material for critical purposes can also be found in the fairy-tale anthology *Neues vom Rumpelstilzchen und andere Hausmärchen* (1981, News from Rumpelstiltskin and Other Household Tales).

Its editor Hans-Joachim Gelberg published several collections with experimental fairy tales and stories for children and is claimed to have "played a major role in bringing about a new more emancipatory children's literature in West Germany" (Zipes, *Brothers Grimm* 241). In the preface to his anthology, Gelberg argues that in light of the fairy-tale debate of the previous decade, "it is no longer possible to give children unmediated and uncritical access to old fairy tales" (10; my translation). The traditional tales have been revitalized, however, in the form of new retellings. Gelberg is aware that the so-called cognitivization of fiction (Dion 77) does not always lead to the best literature. He states explicitly that the literary quality of rediscovered or retold fairy tales is inferior to the supposed effect that these stories may have on the intended (young) reader. Gelberg's aim is to show young readers the variety of fairy tales that can be told. The stories in his book "are partly cheerful or humorous, partly serious and sad, at times also ironic and critical of society. Not everything is successful in a poetic sense; what mattered, however, was the broadest possible range of examples from contemporary fairy-tale telling: An attempt thus to recirculate fairy tales for children. [. . .] These are fairy tales [. . .] to think about and to weave further. [. . .] An appeal also to the reader's fantasy, to a critical awareness of fairy tales and by all means an illustration of the fairy tale beyond the ordinary" (Gelberg 11–12; my translation).

With special reference to the child reader, Gelberg marks with a star the texts "with higher demands on the reader's capacities" (12; my translation). This special status, which applies to the more literary texts in this volume, seems to discourage rather than encourage parents to present them to their children. A similar poetics drives Gmelin's revisions. "Kinder wollen Klarheit" or "children want clarity," he argues ("'Das' Märchen" 143), and in the introduction to *Märchen für tapfere Mädchen* he includes a quotation from Hildegard Pischke, who describes his fairy-tale revisions with formal criteria such as transparency and closure, which should give the young reader a sense of security. This also means that Gmelin consciously abstains from literary techniques to create distance, such as irony: his ideas and values are "transmitted affirmatively and emotionally" (Pischke 110; my translation).[7]

Such a concern with the fairy tale's impact has, in turn, become the subject of critique and parody. Best known is James Finn Garner's *Politically Correct Bedtime Stories* (1994), whose preface begins with a pretended discomfort with the traditional tales' effect on the reader: "When they were first written, the stories on which the following tales are based certainly served their purpose—to entrench the patriarchy, to estrange people from their own natural impulses. [. . .] Today, we have the opportunity—and the obligation—to rethink these 'classic' stories so they reflect more enlightened times. To that effort I submit this humble book" (ix).

The reference to an obligation to rethink the fairy tale is a tongue-in-cheek imitation of the prescriptive tone in the titles and prefaces of critics such as Gmelin. The last sentence mirrors the modesty of Mieder (who was, however, serious about his wish for a better world): "to that [goal] this little book would like to make a contribution." The irony with which Garner regards the "more enlightened times" that he envisages becomes clear from the rest of his book, in which he addresses specific "womyn's issues," including the "inalienable rights of mermaids" (ix). Political correctness, with its effort to promote equality, is shown to inhibit rather than help human understanding.

A similar critique, in a different form, can be derived from Margaret Atwood's "There Was Once" (1994), in which she stages a conversation between a storyteller and a critic who questions every word and idea expressed in the story. Political correctness is what drives many of the issues that are debated, as in the following passage:

> There was once a middle-class girl, as beautiful as she was good—
>
> Stop right there. I think we can cut the *beautiful*, don't you? Women these days have to deal with too many intimidating physical role models as it is, with those bimbos in the ads. Can't you make her, well, more average? [. . .]
>
> There was once a girl, as average-looking as she was well-adjusted, who lived with her stepmother, who was not a very open and loving person because she herself had been abused in childhood.
>
> Better. But I am so *tired* of negative female images! And stepmothers—they always get it in the neck! Change it to *stepfather*, why don't you? (Atwood, "Once" 21, 23)

Feminist and Marxist criticism can kill creativity, the story suggests, as the teller's sentences on the last page get shorter and shorter, and in the end he simply gives up. Although a critique of the traditional fairy tale is voiced, this parody seems to be aimed at sociopolitical fairy-tale criticism rather than at fairy tales.

Twenty years earlier, Iring Fetscher had parodied the fairy-tale discourse of the emancipation movement in a similar vein. His retellings mock the critics' certainty with regard to the fairy tale's transference of sexist and capitalist ideology, as well as their prescriptive tone. In his introduction to "Cinderella's Awakening" ("awakening" being of course another enlightened concept), Fetscher writes that "the motif is unambiguous, the tale is meant to pacify: just wait, you poor and suppressed, exploited and despised being, the day will come when you will walk in gold and silver and triumph over your tormentors by the hand of a handsome and powerful prince. [. . .] The dream is beautiful, but it distracts from the deed and lets the dreamer reside in a bad reality. One should activate the fairy tale, if it is to have an emancipatory effect" (*Dornröschen* 101; my translation). In the tale that follows, Cinderella is portrayed as an independent working-class girl who sets up a union and leads the way for social reform. The radical nature of this revision—which presents a utopian dream in its own right—suggests that Fetscher is poking fun at the belief in the direct impact of ideological literature on the reader, as well as at the simplistic stories with which the emancipation movement has sought to correct the traditional tales.

The negative impact of traditional fairy tales on gender construction that troubles Lieberman is further addressed in metatextual references within the fairy-tale retellings themselves. In particular, the suspicion that children harbor toward stepmothers and stepsisters is frequently blamed on Perrault's, the Grimms', and Disney's exclusively negative representations of stepparents and stepsiblings. These retellings counteract Nicholas Tucker's impression that "common experience dictates that any new parent in the family is going to be at least initially resented by already existing children whether they have come across fairy-tales or not" ("Stepmothers" 49). Most fairy-tale retellings take the same side as Lieberman, who imagines that *all* (Western) children have come across fairy tales and is convinced of their impact on the construction of prejudice.

Róisín Sheerin's "Snow White" (1991) is a monologue by a stepmother who wishes Snow White well. She makes explicit the accusation of the traditional fairy tales' bias and the fear of their socializing force: "She [Snow White] has a lively imagination though and reads a lot. She has read that all

step-mothers are evil, cruel and generally nasty" (48). In Emma Donoghue's "The Tale of the Apple" (1997), the same reasoning is described
from the point of view of the daughter: "I knew from the songs that a stepmother's smile is like a snake's, so I shut my mind to her from that very first
day" (46). Pat Murphy's "The True Story" (1997) presents itself as a truthful correction to the popular versions of "Snow White" and likewise addresses how fairy tales shape prejudices: "The woman let me hold the baby,
but she stayed close by my side. She did not trust me, I thought. [. . .]
I was the child's stepmother, and in the storytellers' tales, stepmothers are
often wicked" (281). In most of these stories, however, the characters that
were at first influenced by the stereotypes of traditional fairy tales eventually develop a more critical distance—an attitude that the implied reader of
the retellings is also invited to take.

A similar shift from influence to critical distance takes place in Evelyn
Conlon's fantastic story "That'll Teach Her" (1986). The title itself gives
an indication of the fairy tale's instrumentalization in teaching gender stereotypes. This story describes the impact of Hans Christian Andersen's
"The Little Red Shoes" on a seven-year-old girl's construction of feminine
identity as even more dramatic. The initial appeal of the tale is enormous:
"The book had stuck to her hands, the words had grabbed on her eyes like
plungers and she could not stop reading" (32). The effects are equally powerful: "She fell asleep chastened, terrified and lonely and she dreamt fright-
eningly all night. [. . .] So it was true. *The Little Red Shoes* was true. She
would stop playing with herself and try to push to the back of her mind the
fact that she wanted to be a dancer when she grew up" (33).

Conlon shows that the traditional fairy tales are "*Grim Words for Children,*" as the girl's storybook is called.[8] The young protagonist in this tale
is, however, more empowered than the child reader that Lieberman envisages, since the girl soon realizes that it is the fairy tale that makes her unhappy. She has a dream of an extremely repressive patriarchy, in which
women are manipulated by men and female bonding is discouraged and
even prohibited. The girl knows "that life wasn't that awful" (33). She is
able to tell the difference between fiction and reality and, unlike Lieberman's implied fairy-tale reader, she takes her contemporary environment
into account when she evaluates the tale. Immediately after the little girl
realizes the fairy tale's impact on her self-image, she decides to put the book
away.

In Conlon's tale it is readers who control stories, not the other way around. Eventually the tale transforms itself because it is no longer read:

> Gradually *Little Red Shoes* itself decided to change a little. First it changed in small ways when no-one was looking, dropped an odd word, changed the occasional sentence around, added bits and pieces here and there. But then it felt patch-worked, some parts just did not fit with other parts so it decided one night, "F——this, I'm going to have to go the whole hog." And it did. In what must be said was an extremely brave swoop it did a complete job on itself, turning inside out upside down to make a completely different story. It was interesting really because when it consulted its individual parts they were all delighted to change. [. . .] *Little Red Shoes* began to feel wonderful. (35–36)

Conlon's retelling illustrates the theory of the "survival of the fittest" that Zipes applies in *Why Fairy Tales Stick*, although with a different conclusion than Zipes, who wonders how the traditional fairy tales can still be popular today. The story of "The Little Red Shoes" has to retell itself and fantastically reshape itself in order to survive the threat of oblivion—and it succeeds, because the girl is willing to give her fairy-tale collection another chance. The title of this story, "That'll Teach Her" is thus used as an ironic comment on the alternative title to Andersen's "The Little Red Shoes" and can function as a metareflection on the impact of fairy tales in general: in today's society, young girls are no longer forced to adapt themselves to patriarchal ideals, Conlon argues, rather it is the stories that have to transform in order to survive.

The doubtfulness of the early feminists' anxiety about the fairy tale's effect is further addressed in a variety of humorous metareflections on the fairy tale's impact in juvenile literature. This stands in contrast to the stories of Sheerin, Donoghue, and Conlon, who seem to take Lieberman's skepticism more seriously. Sophie, the protagonist of Diana Wynne Jones's *Howl's Moving Castle* (1983), believes that nothing extraordinary can happen to her because she is not the youngest of three sisters. This is a reflection of Lieberman's comment on the "special destiny of the youngest child" (188). The story, of course, will prove Sophie wrong, paradoxically affirming another rule of the traditional fairy tale: the righteous and modest are usually rewarded in the end. Melissa Kantor's Cinderella figure, Lucy, tries to draw practical conclusions from the fairy tale as well, as the title of this young adult novel reveals: *If I Have a Wicked Stepmother, Where's My Prince?* (2005). Lucy finds that life after the happy ending is not necessarily a continuation of bliss: "How can you be Cinderella *after* she meets the prince and still feel so incredibly sad?" (73). The fairy tale proves to be a bad manual for real life. Yet, in Kantor's retelling the protagonist is aware of the incompatibility between fairy-tale wisdom and reality, and she is able to detach herself from the traditional "Cinderella." Lucy does find her second and true "prince charming" at the end of the novel but states, "I don't believe in fairy tales anymore" (282). When her new boyfriend asks if she still wants to be a princess, she decides to pass, although they agree that they can "still get to have the happy ending" (283). Whether it will last "ever after" is a question to which the book suggests a positive answer, conforming once again to the conventions of the traditional fairy tale as well as most romantic "chick lit" novels, of which Kantor's is an example. The fairy-tale critique that these two adolescent novels formulate does not place them outside of the fairy-tale tradition, but rather they criticize some aspects and affirm others from within.

As many recent authors distance themselves from the belief in the fairy tale's predictable impact on the young reader, several side with critics who refute the predictability of children's responses to fairy tales and warn against preliminary conclusions. In the short Argentinean book *Caperucita Roja (tal como se lo contaron a Jorge)* (Little Red Riding Hood, as Told to Jorge), Luis María Pescetti (1996) addresses exactly these reservations. The book's frame tale features a father and son in a typical storytelling situation. The father tells Jorge the traditional "Little Red Cap" in a shortened version of the Grimms' story. The text comprises only a small space on the page; most of it is filled with two balloons, each representing, respectively, Jorge's and his father's mental visualizations of the plot. The images that are displayed in the father's balloon are as traditional as the story he is narrating and demonstrate a clear influence from popular "Little Red Riding Hood" illustrations: the girl is pictured in the typical red cloak, the story takes place in a medieval setting, and the German-looking huntsman has half-long blond hair and a feather in his hat. It soon becomes clear that the boy is influenced by visual pre-texts that differ substantially from his father's, and the images that Jorge forms of the same tale create a humorous contrast. His mental representations include a superhero in comic-book style, a flying, pizza-delivering Little Red Riding Hood, and a spectacular spacecraft. Adult and child have dissimilar frames of reference from which they interpret the story. The lack of interaction between the two characters makes it possible for Jorge to construct an entirely different concept of the story in his imagination. Pescetti's tale can thus be read as a comment on adult critics' arrogance when they assume to offer insight into the young reader's mind without ever hearing the child's voice. As such, *Caperucita Roja* opposes itself to critics such as Lieberman, Brownmiller, Gmelin, and Lerche, who predict the effect of fairy tales on readers and society. The fictional rendering of Jorge's mental response to his father's storytelling should not be read as a correction of these critics, in the sense that it does not present a serious claim to the truthful representation of a child's mental images. What is at stake is the humorous contrast between two frames of reference, the interplay of literal and figurative meaning, and the individualistic understandings of a text that result from it. Pescetti's book demonstrates an awareness of how little adults know about the child reader's mind—and how much is assumed about it.

The Passive Ideology of Passive Princesses

The bulk of Lieberman's analysis concerns what Peter Hollindale calls "passive ideology": ideology that is not made explicit in the text but that can be derived from recurrent patterns, associations, and representations. In order to uncover a text's hidden ideology, Hollindale asks the reader (or critic) to reflect on so-called packages, associative patterns "in which separate items appear and interlock," and to question whether "these groups of virtues or vices [are] necessarily or logically connected with each other" (20).[9] In this sociopolitical type of feminist critique, it is mainly the fairy-tale ideology linked to gender that is under scrutiny. The associative packages that Lieberman lists have been radically transformed in the retellings of the late twentieth and early twenty-first centuries; the examples that I will discuss in this chapter either critically reflect the issues that Lieberman addresses or replace the gender models that she rejects with alternative patterns. Her ideas not only occur in self-proclaimed feminist literature but can equally be found in works that do not openly assert a feminist agenda. This is not necessarily the merit of Lieberman herself, but she can be considered a prominent representative for this approach to the fairy tale in criticism.

What follows, then, provides a correction to Natascha Würzbach's model (1985) for the possible modes of interaction between fiction and the social reality of gender conventions. She argues that literature can (a) reproduce sexist norms uncritically, (b) incorporate gender issues both realistically and critically, or (c) present examples of progressive and utopian femininity (207). Würzbach associates the first type of interaction with trivial literature, the second with the Anglo-American novel, and the third with feminist fairy-tale retellings. This classification is not exclusive but nevertheless strikes one as odd, if only because Würzbach compares a genre determined by literary status with one characterized by its geographical origin and one by its ideological stance. Moreover, cross-patterns of the three interaction types now occur in most subgenres that she lists. The novelization of the fairy tale has produced hybrid forms between fairy-tale retellings and the (Anglo-American) novel, for instance in the works of Gregory Maguire, Melissa Kantor, Anne Provoost, and Adèle Geras.[10] These are feminist fairy-tale retellings (Würzbach's type c) with a realistic treatment and critical incorporation of gender issues (type b). Moreover, since the 1970s (when Lieberman's article was published) and the 1980s (when Würzbach's study came out), gender representations in Western society have been further reshaped under the influence of the emancipation movement, so that what may have once been utopian or progressive gender-related behavior has now become standard practice and can also be found in popular literature. Movies such as *Hoodwinked* and DreamWorks' *Shrek* series provide good examples of the fusion between popular culture and (formerly) progressive gender ideals (Würzbach's type c). Moreover, standards of what is progressive are relative, so that some models that appeared as advanced in the 1970s had become stereotypical or conservative by the turn of the twenty-first century.

Who's the Fairest of Them All?

One recurrent pattern that Lieberman interprets as a sign of the traditional fairy tale's patriarchal ideology is the "beauty contest" in the most popular princess tales: "Where there are several daughters in a family, or several unrelated girls in a story, the prettiest is invariably singled out and designated for reward, or first for punishment and later for reward.

Beautiful girls are never ignored" (187). Lieberman here attaches her critique to a wider feminist protest against beauty contests, most spectacularly at the election of Miss America in Atlanta in 1968. Her disapproval has been mirrored in various collections of feminist fairy tales. Even a text as recent as Barbara G. Walker's introduction to *Feminist Fairy Tales* (1996) uncritically echoes a number of arguments from "Some Day My Prince Will Come": "Only to be decorative is the customary female function in these old stories. Girls without any beauty are automatically also without virtue, happiness, luck, or love. [. . .] The message that such stories convey to girls is plain: Your looks are your only asset. Whatever else you might be or do doesn't count" (ix). Walker almost literally mimics Lieberman's assertion that fairy tales "focus on beauty as a girl's most valuable asset, perhaps her only valuable asset" (188). Like Lieberman, Walker, it can be argued, draws this conclusion from a generalization of the fairy tale as a genre.

Jane Yolen incorporates and transforms a critique of the beauty contest in *Sleeping Ugly* (1981), a picture book aimed at young children. It demonstrates an open intertextual dialogue with "Sleeping Beauty" and a few other tales, such as the Grimms' "The Three Wishes" and "Mother Holle" as well as Perrault's "Toads and Diamonds." The plot revolves around three female characters: Princess Miserella, Plain Jane, and an elderly woman with magical powers. At the beginning of the story, Miserella has lost her horse and wants to return home. On her way, she meets the elderly woman and Plain Jane and orders them to help her get back. The elderly woman, who turns out to have magical powers, takes a liking to Jane and grants her three wishes. Jane uses two of these to compensate for damage that Miserella causes with her insulting behavior, at which point the fairy gets so upset that she wishes for all to fall asleep. When after many years a prince arrives, he has to choose who among the three women he will kiss. This is the moment when Yolen explicitly rejects the pattern of the beauty contest. In *Sleeping Ugly,* the prince deliberately discards the most beautiful girl: "The prince looked at Miserella. [. . .] Even frowning she was beautiful. But Jojo knew that kind of princess. He had three cousins just like her. Pretty on the outside. Ugly within" (58–59). Although Miserella would win the beauty contest, she is not singled out and does not get the reward. Prince Jojo chooses Plain Jane as a wife and leaves Miserella asleep forever, thus reversing the traditional pattern identified by Lieberman.

The feminist rejection of the beauty contest is an explicit theme in Linda Kavanagh's "The Ugly Sisters Strike Back" (1991). Whereas in the traditional versions of "Cinderella" the stepsisters would do anything to be the most beautiful, their ugliness is a form of nonconformism to sexist ideals of beauty in Kavanagh's tale: "It was doubtful if either of them would ever have won a beauty contest, since they did not even try to conform to the currently accepted image of female pulchritude. In fact, they were regarded as being somewhat eccentric, because they were both quite content to look like themselves" (20). Kavanagh exposes the relativity of the value that is attributed to beauty in the fairy tale in two ways: by pointing out that these ideals and standards vary in time ("currently accepted") and by replacing the word "beauty" with its Latin-based synonym "pulchritude," which appears as a mismatched artificial and technical term that undermines the romantic connotations of the word "beauty." In a reverse movement, "ugly" is replaced by the more positive "eccentric," which implies that there is an oppressive beauty norm. When the sisters are invited to the royal ball, they criticize it as "a cattle market" (21), once again rephrasing the criticism with which feminists have repeatedly condemned beauty contests.

The beauty contest is also explicitly addressed in Priscilla Galloway's "A Taste for Beauty" (1995). Galloway challenges the reader's expectations by introducing a first-person narrator who seems, at first sight, to be a contemporary version of Snow White. At the beginning of the story, she describes her difficult family situation. Her stepfather is abusive, her mother a passive victim. The competition for beauty that is central to the plot of the Grimms' "Snow White" is here perverted into an unexpected context and meaning. The protagonist finds a job at an abattoir, where she enters a very different type of contest: "To start with, I sharpened the knives and brought them to the assembly-line workers to cut the animals' throats and slit their bellies. Soon I graduated to the line myself. [. . .] It wasn't more than a month before I was getting the biggest bonus for the fastest, cleanest work. A firm hand and total conviction, and you can't stop to think, except about being the best. The best. The quintessential best" (98).

At least two elements in this citation give a twist to the usual beauty competition as it is presented in the fairy tale. First, traditional fairy-tale princesses such as Snow White, Beauty, and Cinderella do not seem aware of the competition, and if they are, they do not display the winner's instinct that characterizes the narrator of Galloway's tale. Traditional fairy-tale princesses are typically modest, and it is usually others (stepmothers, sisters, kings) who make them an unconscious and often involuntary part in the rivalry. In Perrault's "Cinderella," for instance, the stepmother makes the comparison between her daughters and her stepdaughter and thus encourages the competition: "She could not abide the young girl, whose good qualities made her own daughters appear all the more detestable" (450). Second, the type of competition that the protagonist enters in Galloway's story is as unladylike as can be. The quality of having the smallest feet or the most beautiful features as a sign of superiority is transformed into the ability to cut up corpses in the neatest and fastest way.

The corrective function with regard to the traditional "Snow White" is made ambiguous when "A Taste for Beauty" develops. At first, the reader is invited to believe that the narrator is a Snow White figure. In most "Snow White" retellings with a first-person narrator, this is indeed the case. When another character is the narrator, this is usually signaled from the very beginning, for instance in the title (as in Polly Peterson's "The Prince to Snow White") or in the first lines of the tale. In Róisín Sheerin's "Snow White," for instance, the first paragraph takes away all ambiguity about who narrates the tale: "When I married Max, it was like a dream come true. [. . .] I have to try and make Snow White, my sullen, suspicious stepdaughter, happy" (48). Such clear markers are missing from the first pages of Galloway's tale. Several parallels support the initial suggestion that the first-person narrator is a Snow White equivalent: she too is raised by a helpless parent and a violent stepparent (albeit here a stepfather), and after she has fled her home, she ends up in an all-male environment (equivalent to the seven dwarves' home), which she leaves again when she marries the king. Only at the very end of the story does it become clear that "A Taste for Beauty" is a prequel to the Grimms' tale and that the narrator is not Snow White, but her stepmother. The first hints are given after seven pages, when it is predicted that the narrator will kill children "to protect [her] own position" (103). The references to the king's first wife, who died in childbirth, and the appearance of "a plain oval mirror with a black frame" are further indications of the narrator's identity. It is not until the penultimate page that any ambiguity is taken away: "I married the widowed king. His daughter, pale little black-haired thing, was flower girl at our wedding. Snow. What a stupid name" (105).

The fact that the narrator in Galloway's tale is Snow White's stepmother allows an interesting perspective on Lieberman's critique of the beauty contest. Galloway is one of the contemporary authors who make such a critique most explicit: the protagonist of "A Taste for Beauty" actually enters a beauty competition. Her motives are different from the traditional, naïve fairy-tale princess, who, as said, is usually unaware that she is in rivalry with other women. Galloway's narrator wants to escape the predicaments of her social class and satisfy her need to be the best. Through the young woman's insight into the workings of the system, the retelling formulates a critique of the traditional fairy tale. Although the protagonist wins the main prize in the beauty contest and is chosen to marry the king, she realizes that she only has exterior and superficial characteristics to thank: "I have to be the most beautiful, anybody can understand that. [. . .] It doesn't matter what people say about character and intelligence being important and beauty being only skin deep. Nobody ever said much about my character and intelligence. I became queen because I'm the most beautiful of all" (Galloway 106).

It is a statement, critics such as Lieberman and Dworkin argue, that also holds true for Cinderella, Snow White, and Beauty, yet they do not realize it. Although Galloway's story thus provides a feminist critique, there is a conservative twist in this tale. The first part of the short story may play with the reader's expectations about the identity of the first-person narrator, but the final pages bring the story back to the traditional pattern of associations. In "A Taste for Beauty" the opposition is retained between the cruel stepmother, who is aware of the competition and who will do anything to be the best, and the sweet, innocent victim, Snow White. The main difference is that the reader has been given insight into the motivations of the stepmother's deed, which can be considered mitigating circumstances and a break with the traditional black-and-white characterization of the fairy tale that feminists criticize.

Good Pretty Girls

Linked to the beauty contest is the second typical constellation or "package" of female characteristics that sociopolitically oriented feminists see repeated in the traditional tales: "Good-temper and meekness are so regularly associated with beauty, and ill-temper with ugliness, that this itself must influence children's expectations" (Lieberman 188). When one perceives fairy tales as didactic instruments that help instruct children morally and socially, the stories can create prejudices and false expectations: "If a child identifies with the beauty, she may learn to be suspicious of ugly girls, who are portrayed as cruel, sly, and unscrupulous in these stories; if she identifies with the plain girls, she may learn to be suspicious and jealous of pretty girls, beauty being a gift of fate, not something that can be attained. There are no examples of a cross-pattern, that is, of plain but good-tempered girls" (Lieberman 189). In this last sentence, Lieberman points out a gap in the traditional fairy tale, and it is exactly this lack of cross-patterns between beauty and kindness that several (feminist) fairy-tale retellings attempt to fill. The critique coincides, moreover, with a moral inspired by Christian and humanist values that dominates many realistic children's books: a person's inner qualities are more important than one's outward appearance. It is hence not surprising that a great number of fairy-tale retellings apply this correction to the traditional tales.

Before I turn to the discussion of some of these corrective retellings, I want to stress that Lieberman's critique is mainly based on the use of Perrault's and Grimms' fairy tales in popular culture and mass-market collections. She mentions the example of Cinderella, "with the opposition of the ugly, cruel, bad-tempered older sisters to the younger, beautiful, sweet Cinderella" (188). This seems to be based on the portrayal of the stepsisters by Disney rather than Grimm or Perrault. In the *Kinder- und Hausmärchen*, even in the fairy tales that feminists most often criticize, beauty and internal goodness are not necessarily linked. It is explicitly stated, for instance, that Cinderella's stepsisters are beautiful but unkind: "Two daughters [. . .] who had beautiful and fair features but nasty and wicked hearts" (468). In Perrault's version, which is repeated in Andrew Lang's collection, it is said that Cinderella is more beautiful than her stepsisters but not that they are therefore unattractive. The same is true for Snow White's stepmother in the Grimms' collection: "She was a beautiful lady, but proud and arrogant" (83). Although Snow White and Cinderella may win the beauty competition, their stepmothers and stepsisters are not as bad looking as they are portrayed in many mass-market adaptations.

Several fairy-tale retellings are likewise influenced by this trend in popular adaptations. If we take Cinderella's stepsisters as an example, we see that the general assumption in many retellings, too, is that they are bad looking. This is signaled in titles such as *Confessions of an Ugly Stepsister* (Maguire)

and "The Ugly Stepsisters Strike Back" (Kavanagh) and supported especially in illustrated fairy tales for younger children, such as Lynn and David
Roberts's *Cinderella: An Art Deco Love Story*, Scieszka and Smith's *The Stinky
Cheese Man*, and Dahl's *Revolting Rhymes*. In Maguire's and Kavanagh's retellings, the opposition of beautiful and ugly and the related associations of
character are corrected. In *The Stinky Cheese Man* and *Revolting Rhymes*, the
typical patterns of the traditional fairy tale are exposed through ridicule, and
the opportunity that ugly sisters provide for grotesque exaggeration is exploited to the full. These texts are further supplemented or countered by a
very large number of feminist retellings in which the association between inner and outer characteristics is deleted, problematized, or reversed.

The anonymous author of *Anne Sexton's Feminist Re-reading of the
Grimms'* Briar Rose points out that deletion can indeed be one strategy for
responding to Lieberman's critique of the traditional fairy tale: "When
reading a 'classic' fairy tale from a feminist viewpoint (as defined by Marcia
K. Lieberman), a reader will find that women characters are important—
are "chosen"—because of their beauty. Sexton, as a feminist, ignores this
point and goes directly to talk about the issues and problems facing that a
woman character must face [sic]. What the woman is thinking, feeling, and
experiencing is far more important than her appearance, and Sexton makes
this clear by never once describing how the princess looks, but describing
instead what happens to her." Sexton's poem can be considered representative, in this respect, of a large body of fairy-tale retellings that remove
elaborate descriptions of the heroine's beauty found in the traditional versions. Further examples include Donoghue's short stories as well as Shirley
Hughes's picture-book retelling, *Ella's Big Chance* (2003), which features
illustrations of a chubby Cinderella and contains remarkably few textual
references to her exterior appearance.

In his "politically correct" version of "Sleeping Beauty," James Finn
Garner addresses the taboo that the feminist critique of the emphasis on
beauty creates: "Whether she was also physically attractive is of no importance here and also depends entirely on one's standard of beauty. It also
perpetuates the myth that all princesses are beautiful, and that their beauty
gives them liberty over the fates of others. So, please, don't even bring up
the fact that she was quite a looker" (*Enlightened Time* 120). The narrator of this "Sleeping Persun of Better-Than-Average Attractiveness" resorts back to a macho phrase to reveal his position behind an exaggerated

politically correct description. The second sentence bears strong similarities to the sociopolitical analysis of gender patterns in the traditional tales. Garner ridicules the sensitivity raised by politically correct language and points out through his contradiction of self-reflexive passages that a woman's physical appearance still matters in spite of the feminist effort. Indeed, in most picture books, short stories, and novels that are based on the tales that Lieberman discusses ("Snow White," "Cinderella," "Sleeping Beauty," and "Beauty and the Beast"), the element of the heroine's beauty is either retained or turned into the explicit object of discussion and revision, and rarely is it only implicitly corrected.

Jane Yolen's "Fat Is Not a Fairy Tale" (1999) can serve as an example of the second strategy. It is a retelling that explicitly addresses and problematizes the gap that Lieberman has identified:

> I am thinking of a fairy tale
> *that is not yet written,*
> for a teller not yet born,
> for a listener not yet conceived,
> for a world not yet won,
> where everything round is good:
> the sun, the wheels, cookies, and the princess.
>   (158; my emphasis)

Although it is true that there are few fairy tales in which "the princess is not / anorexic, wasp-waisted" (158), quite a few have been produced in which princesses who do not live up to the highest standards of beauty are positively valued. In Yolen's own *Sleeping Ugly*, for instance, the typical dichotomy beautiful/kind and ugly/wicked is openly reversed: "Princess Miserella was a beautiful princess. [. . .] But inside, where it was hard to see, she was the meanest, wickedest, and most worthless princess around" (7–8). External beauty is thus dissociated from inner beauty. Miserella is contrasted with plain, but kind Jane: "In that very same kingdom, in the middle of the woods, lived a poor orphan named Plain Jane. She certainly was. Her hair was short and turned down. Her nose was long and turned up. And even if they had been the other way 'round, she would not have been a great beauty. But she loved animals, and she was always kind to strange old ladies" (10).

A new constellation of external and internal features is established, which disrupts and invites readers to question the traditional association in fairy tales between the quality of inner and outer traits. This is what Hollindale calls the "examination of the negative," and it is used to "show unsuspected blights in the published picture" (19), in this case the traditional tales. After deletion and explicit problematization, it can be considered the third and most popular strategy of response to associative and behavioral patterns related to gender in the traditional fairy tale.

The type of reversal that Yolen employs is most frequently notable in retellings based on "Beauty and the Beast." The fact that the protagonists of both this tale and of "Sleeping Beauty" are called "Beauty" seems to be an open invitation for authors to switch characteristics—hence the titles *Sleeping Ugly* and "Ugly and the Beast." In the introduction to the latter tale, Walker makes explicit why she reversed the exterior features of the main characters: "I thought the heroine might have been more admirable if she had less beauty and more character and I feared that the Beast's transformation into a handsome prince might turn him into a less likable creature, perhaps conceited or selfish, as handsome princes are sometimes known to be" (47). Like Plain Jane, Walker's Ugly fills the gap that Lieberman identifies as "a cross-pattern, that is, of plain but good-tempered girls" in mass-market fairy tales: "The eldest daughter [. . .] was hunchbacked, bowlegged, pigeon-toed, over-weight, coarse-skinned, and lank-haired, with small piglike eyes, a bulbous nose, crooked teeth, and a deformed jaw. The poor girl was so hideous that everyone called her Ugly. Nevertheless, she took it in good spirit, knowing that it was a fair description. Despite her appearance, she had a sweet, warm generous nature" (Walker 49).

Even though Yolen and Walker portray a kindhearted and plain-looking fairy-tale heroine, in both descriptions a trace of irony can be discerned. Walker's Ugly seems to have nearly every physical defect imaginable, and the description of Yolen's Plain Jane is supplemented with exactly the feature that will be useful to her in the course of the story: kindness to strange old women. In this way, these retellings still do not live up to the feminist plea for a realistic female role model with whom young girls can identify (see Lieberman 195–96); instead they affirm the expectation of flat characterization that is conventional in the traditional tale.

Gail Carson Levine offers a more developed heroine in terms of character psychology in her fantasy retelling of "Snow White," *Fairest* (2007). The adjectives with which the protagonist Aza describes herself are reminiscent of Walker's Ugly—yet here they are not the result of a narrator's wit but of a young girl's deeply felt dissatisfaction with herself: "I was an unsightly child. My skin was the weak blue-white of skimmed milk, which wouldn't have been so bad if my hair had been blond and my lips pale pink. But my lips were as red as a dragon's tongue and my hair as black as an old frying pan. [. . .] If anything, I became uglier. I grew large boned and awkward. My chubby cheeks were fine for a babe, but not for an older child" (Levine 4).

Like Kavanagh's "The Ugly Sisters Strike Back," Aza's description of herself draws attention to the relativity of standards of beauty, especially if the intertextual link with the corresponding passage in the traditional "Snow White" is explored. In the Grimms' tale of 1857, the whiteness of the child's skin is compared to snow, the redness of her lips to blood, the blackness of her hair to ebony wood. These are the colors that Snow White's mother wishes for, and so they are presented as desirable and beautiful. Aza has the exact same colors in her skin, lips, and hair, but she lives in a country where they are deemed coarse. Moreover, by comparing herself to such base things as skimmed milk, a dragon's tongue, and a frying pan, she demeans herself further by association. Whereas beauty is quickly discarded as an unimportant or even disagreeable aspect in Kavanagh's, Yolen's, and Walker's tales, Aza's narrative testifies to the impact that exterior features do have on other people's expectations and behavior—and on the self-image that results from this. Nevertheless, her ugliness does not prevent her prince charming from falling in love with her, and in the end she is content with her looks, finding them preferable to a forged beauty. This correction of the fairy-tale pattern is supported by the discussions that Aza has with herself and with other characters, especially when she reminds the adolescent reader that "people don't look as they behave" (Levine 304).

To return to "Beauty and the Beast," this tale is particularly relevant to Lieberman's argument both directly because of the protagonist's name and because the problematic link between interior and exterior features is, in fact, its central theme. The main tension in Leprince de Beaumont's tale focuses on the question of whether Beauty will fall in love with the Beast in spite of his deterring looks. It can thus be read as a warning against putting too much value on exterior rather than interior features: the reader is invited to sympathize with the Beast, and Beauty is praised and rewarded for being able to disregard his appearance. And yet, Leprince de Beaumont's fairy tale seems at the same time to assert and to undermine the message that beauty is only skin-deep. From the very beginning of the tale, great emphasis is put on the exterior qualities of Beauty: "[The merchant's] daughters were very pretty, but everyone admired the youngest one in particular. When she was a small child, they simply called her 'Little Beauty.' As a result, the name stuck and led to a great deal of jealousy on the part of her sisters. Not only was the youngest girl prettier than her sisters, but she was also better" (Leprince de Beaumont 805). Here, the narrator reinforces the association between good nature and appearance that Lieberman rejects. Leprince de Beaumont appears to use different standards for the two sexes: whereas the exterior features of a man may be secondary, in a woman beauty does matter. The end of the tale equally leaves its readership with an ambiguous message. Beauty is rewarded for the fact that she can love a physically unattractive beast, but her reward consists of a man who *is* physically attractive. Just when Beauty has learned that external features are only secondary, this message is undermined by the transformation of Beast into a handsome prince.

In many retellings of "Beauty and the Beast," the ambiguity or even inconsistency of this ending is removed, and the moral that a person's appearance is unimportant is reinforced.[11] In Walker's "Ugly and the Beast," this moral is made explicit. "Beauty is in the eye of the beholder" (53), says the Beast when Ugly apologizes for her appearance. In a metacomment on the traditional horizon of expectation, both characters express their awareness of what would be expected of them in traditional tales such as Leprince de Beaumont's:

> [Ugly] became sufficiently comfortable with him that one day she finally dared to ask him how he came to have such an unattractive exterior.
>
> "I knew that would come up," the Beast sighed, "so we might as well get it over with. You're expecting me to say that I'm under an enchantment, and I'm really a handsome prince, and your love will bring forth my real self. [. . .] The truth is that I'm a Beast. This freakish appearance is the real me."
>
> "Oh, Beast, I'm so glad," Ugly cried, embracing him. [. . .] The Beast was so pleased that she didn't want him to be a handsome prince, and Ugly was so pleased that he didn't want her to be a beautiful princess, that they agreed to marry at once. (Walker 54)

The lesson is reinforced by an equally didactic final line: "They loved each other truly, because they were free of the narcissism that often mars the relationships of beautiful people; and so they lived happily ever after" (54). In this extreme reversal of associations, as well as in Walker's introduction to the tale cited above, the Beast's earlier message that "beauty is in the eye of the beholder" is once again subverted. Appearances do determine both a person's nature and his or her chance of happiness, although not in the way that traditional fairy tales suggest. A new associative pattern is established that is equally limiting: ugly people have a higher chance of true love; beautiful people are narcissistic and cannot engage in meaningful relationships.

The pattern of reversal that Walker opts for has become so popular in late twentieth-century versions that it seems to have established a new standard in retellings of "Beauty and the Beast." Revisions of so-called animal groom tales are now just as likely to end with the nontransformation of the animal groom as with the more traditional closure. The prince in Jon Scieszka and Steve Johnson's *The Frog Prince Continued* (1991) longs for his former days as a pond animal. On the last page of this sequel, both he and his wife are transformed into frogs, and this ending is regarded as more positive than the traditional one. In parodies such as Laurence Anholt and Arthur Robins's *Billy Beast* (1996) and DreamWorks' second *Shrek* movie (2004), the main characters choose to be ogres rather than human beings, thus subverting the expectations established by "Beauty and the Beast" and "The Frog Prince." In literary retellings for young adult readers, such as Anne Provoost's *De Roos en het Zwijn* and Tanith Lee's "Beauty," the transformation of the Beast into a prince is frequently absent, and this closure does not have any influence on Beauty's affection. In his seminal work *Ideology and the Children's Book* (1988), Hollindale invites readers to focus on the endings of (children's) literature to discover its passive ideology, and this is indeed what all these retellings of "Beauty and the Beast" do: they draw attention to the implicit messages of traditional fairy-tale endings in a move similar to ideology-critical fairy-tale theory. "Is the conclusion imaginatively coherent, or does it depend on implicit assumptions which are at odds with the surface ideology?" Hollindale challenges the reader to ask, and, "Are there any loose ends (not so much of plot but of thought and feeling)?" (20). The paradox that lies at the heart of Leprince de Beaumont's "Beauty and the Beast" is such a loose end, and countless modern versions have indeed drawn attention to it. In contrast to Lieberman, however, most of these retellings leave the comparison with the traditional tale, as well as the subsequent interpretation or revaluation of this tale, up to the critical judgment of the reader.

Rich Handsome Princes and Poor Absent Boys

Popular fairy tales use a double standard for the two sexes, Lieberman argues. Whereas fairy-tale heroines stand out in beauty and kindness, fairy-tale heroes are often valued for their wealth: "Good, poor, and pretty girls always win rich and handsome princes, never merely handsome, good, but poor men" (189). Although her critique mainly concerns the representation of women, she briefly recognizes the limited and often equally stereotypical gender roles for male fairy-tale characters. However, this critique immediately turns back to the female figures and readers: "Since girls are chosen for their beauty, it is easy for a child to infer that beauty leads to wealth, that being chosen means getting rich" (189–90). Like most of her contemporaries, Lieberman did not reflect on the effect that fairy tales might have on boy readers—since the male characters are often desired for their status and wealth rather than their personality, it would be equally easy for a child to infer that *money* leads to happiness.

Once again, Yolen fills the gap that Lieberman briefly addresses. *Sleeping Ugly* explicitly corrects the traditional expectations that women are valued for their beauty and that potential husbands are judged according to their power and wealth. Love is dissociated from beauty, status, and money. Prince Jojo "was the youngest son of a youngest son and so had no gold or jewels or property to speak of" (Yolen, *Sleeping Ugly* 46). He is the "handsome, good, but poor" man that Lieberman could not find in the most popular traditional tales, and Jojo remains poor until the end of the book. It is Plain Jane, not Jojo, who provides a place to live—a reversal of the usual gender roles in which the prince brings his own castle or, if not, it is provided by the bride's or groom's father. Through the double reversal, Yolen's tale counteracts the implicit message in the traditional fairy tale "that beauty leads to wealth" (Lieberman 189). The only beautiful character in the story, Princess Miserella, is still asleep at the end of the tale. Happiness, it is stressed, has nothing to do with money or beauty.

Sleeping Ugly can be considered a precursor in this respect, and many of the standards that Yolen sets have been followed in retellings since the late

1980s. At the end of the twentieth century, princes are generally allowed to be scared, disempowered, or poor without losing their charm. In two recent retellings of "Cinderella," Maguire's *Confessions of an Ugly Stepsister* (1999), a historical novel, and Ellen Jackson's *Cinder Edna* (1994), a picture book, Cinderella and her prince are contrasted with another, less glamorous pair. Rupert, Edna's prince charming, is characterized as follows: "He lives in a cottage in the back and runs the recycling plant and a home for orphaned kittens." In *Confessions of an Ugly Stepsister*, the less likable Cinderella figure Clara is contrasted with her good-hearted but ordinary-looking stepsister, Iris. Caspar, the man whom Iris loves, is described as "only a poor boy, an apprentice painter, dingier than dung" (337). And yet, they live more happily ever after than Clara and her wealthy prince: "In time [Caspar] made Iris a good husband" (363), the narrator explains, whereas Clara's prince "did succumb to some pox or consumption" (365) and she "died of a complaint of the heart" (366)—whether the cause of this complaint was physical or emotional is left unexplained.

The strategy that both these retellings use serves a didactic purpose: the contrastive doubling of protagonists is a device that is often employed in cautionary tales and has proven effective in showing which behavior is desirable (and rewarded) and which is not. Think for instance of the Brothers Grimm's "Mother Holle," in which a kindhearted girl is showered with gold and her lazy sister with tar. The multiplication of protagonists and plots in retellings such as *Cinder Edna* and *Confessions of an Ugly Stepsister* facilitates the reader's understanding of the authors' critical positions with regard to the traditional fairy tale. Many elements of this traditional version are still present in the retelling, but they are put in a different and unexpected context so that their limits or disadvantages become apparent. As the readers' sympathy is directed away from the traditional version, which is "repeated with a critical distance" to borrow Hutcheon's description of parody, they are immediately provided with an alternative that suits the feminist ideology better.

In several other retellings of "Cinderella," readers are required to make the intertextual comparison with the traditional versions for themselves, and when they do they are offered similar solutions. The Ella of Shirley Hughes's *Ella's Big Chance*, a version set in the Jazz Age, is offered the hand of a duke but prefers to marry Buttons, the doorkeeper of her father's shop. When he reminds her afterward that she "could have been very rich, you know," she stresses that she wants to make their fortune together: "I don't fancy being a grand lady. [. . .] And anyway, it could get a bit dull doing nothing all day except being dressed up like an expensive doll. We'll go off and start our own little shop and I'll make stunning clothes, more beautiful than anyone has ever seen." The ending of this "Cinderella" revision is strongly reminiscent of *Cinder Edna*. Suggestions are given for how the young couples will spend their future together, and these are more concrete than the traditional "happily ever after." Buttons and Ella, as well as Rupert and Edna, are pictured setting up their own business together, sharing not only work but also, and more importantly, humor. As such they can be read as correcting another aspect of the traditional fairy tale, which Lieberman criticizes for focusing exclusively on courtship and magnifying it "into the most important and exciting part of a girl's life. [. . .] After marriage she ceases to be wooed, her consent is no longer sought, she derives her status from her husband, and her personal identity is thus snuffed out" (199–200). Lieberman's interpretation of the ending that "happily ever after" implies is countered by these "Cinderella" retellings in which the heroines and their husbands are equal partners. Although Jackson and Hughes do not detach their retellings from the traditional happy ending, they do deviate from Perrault's pre-text by giving that ending a more concrete dimension and by showing that marriage is only the beginning of a life full of excitement and laughter if the choice of a partner is based on interior rather than exterior qualities.

Disposing of the Damsel in Distress

Such modifications of the traditional fairy-tale ending can only take place if the heroines are reshaped in a further aspect. Connected with Lieberman's critique that fairy-tale females are only valued for their beauty is her rejection of the genre's generally passive role model for women: "An examination of the best-known stories shows that active resourceful girls are in fact rare; most of the heroines are passive, submissive, and helpless" (190). This is probably the issue that has been most picked up and corrected by authors of contemporary fairy tales for children and adults as well as fantasy stories that draw on fairy-tale narratives and patterns. A few of these have become classics, such as Robert Munsch's *The Paper Bag Princess* and Babette Cole's *Princess Smartypants*. These tales provide young children with alternative role models: the women are active, quick-witted, and independent and no longer perceive marriage to be the only happy ending.

From recent versions of "Cinderella," a tale to which Lieberman also pays great attention, it becomes clear that the role models for women have diversified in the contemporary fairy tale. Lieberman compares Andrew Lang's translation of Perrault with the Norwegian folktales about Espen Cinderlad, a male Cinderella, and comes to the conclusion that "Cinderella plays a very passive role in her story. [. . .] Cinderella's male counterpart, Espen Cinderlad [. . .] plays a very different role. Although he is the youngest of the three brothers, as Cinderella is the youngest sister, he is a Cinderlad by choice. His brothers may ridicule and despise him, but no one forces him to sit by the fire and poke in the ashes all day, he elects to do so. All the while, he knows that he is the cleverest of the three" (192).

With the issue of choice being central to the emancipation movement, it is no surprise that feminist retellings have broadened the example of Espen Cinderlad to include many female Cinderellas as well. Again, the most instantly recognizable example is *Cinder Edna*. Whereas the first protagonist of this double retelling is an exaggerated embodiment of the female aspects from Lieberman's typology, the second carries all the characteristics of Espen Cinderlad. The initial conditions for the two women are the same: both are exploited by an unsympathetic stepfamily. But whereas the hard work is a source of misery for Cinderella—"her loneliness and her suffering are sentimentalized and become an integral part of the glamour," writes Lieberman of Perrault's "Cendrillon" (194)—Cinder Edna knows how to turn it into a source of joy and pride and an opportunity to learn and earn money.

Frances Minters is the author of *Cinder-Elly*, a picture book published in the same year as *Cinder Edna* (1994). Minters declares on the dust jacket that she "wanted to create a Cinderella who wasn't a wimp." Indeed this American Cinderella is not just a helpless victim:

> Elly cleaned up
> 'Cause she like to be neat
> From the hair on her head
> To the toes on her feet

She has a different motivation for cleaning up the mess that is determined by internal rather than external factors. Her deeds are presented as actions, not reactions. The British picture book *Cinderella and the Hot Air Balloon*

(1992), by Ann Jungman and Russell Ayto goes one step further and invests the traditional story with a socialist message. The protagonist Ella resides near the kitchen fire's cinders because she prefers to be with the servants rather than with her haughty family. These retellings correct the observation that in Perrault and Grimm, Cinderella's "victimhood is signified by her enforced affinity with the cinders" (Stott 19).

All of these Cinderellas from the 1990s represent the ideal model of the entrepreneur: eager to learn, tireless, practical, inventive, and optimistic. As such, they offer empowered alternatives to the traditional victim that Lieberman condemns. Although they cannot change the bad conditions from which they start, the way they deal with these circumstances differs substantially from Cinderella's dependent state as described in Perrault's and the Grimms' tales. Lieberman recognizes the importance of choice in the tale of "Espen Cinderlad," and it is exactly this freedom that makes the American Cinderellas of the 1990s different from Lang's: "Elly cleaned up / 'Cause she *liked* to be neat" (Minters and Karas; my emphasis); "What Ella *liked* most of all was to talk to Cook and the other servants" and she explains to them that she "didn't *want* to go to the boring old ball" (Jungman and Ayto; my emphasis).

Escaping the Second Feminist Wave

By the turn of the twenty-first century, feminist ideological critique had gained firm ground in literary studies and in Western culture more generally. Emancipated heroines are now more common in children's fiction than are female characters of the kind that Lieberman rejected. Authors who retell the tale in a more traditional way often resort to a genre that is known for its potential to transmit nonprevailing ideology and role models that are not up to date: the historical tale. As John Stephens argues in *Language and Ideology in Children's Fiction*, "Historical fiction is faced with a problem which threatens to deprive it of a readership, in that the assumptions of its intellectual and ideological bases are no longer dominant within Western society" (203). Stephens sees, however, that not only can this aspect of historical fiction be a disadvantage, but it also can be and has been used as "a very powerful ideological tool, especially for inculcating social conservatism" (205). With regard to the fairy tale, several recent retellings that keep (or even increase) the sentimentality of the traditional pre-texts and that do not alter the gender stereotypes identified and rejected by feminist fairy-tale critics set the events in a twentieth-century time frame before the second feminist wave, that is before the 1960s. The 1920s, for instance, has become a popular period, and several late twentieth-century picture-book retellings are relocated in it.

Lynn and David Roberts's *Cinderella: An Art Deco Love Story* (2001) illustrates this trend perfectly. This picture book shows a helpless and sentimental Cinderella figure, Greta, of the kind that has become rare in retellings that either retain the fairy tale's traditional atemporal chronotope or relocate it to a specific, more recent setting: "Greta was forced to sleep in the kitchen. At night she lay by the fire to keep warm. When she wakened she was always covered in dust and cinders. [. . .] Alone in the kitchen, Cinderella [as Greta has been renamed] sighed and wiped away a tear as she watched the sisters and their mother drive away." The illustration that accompanies this text (Figure 3) affirms Cinderella's state of sadness and helplessness as she watches the others leave through the window of a dirty kitchen, her hands clasped and a tear running down her cheek. Belinda Stott claims that in Perrault's and Disney's versions, Cinderella is "a particularly proficient victim" (15), and indeed at the end of these stories, she displays some agency when she asks if she can try on the glass slipper that does not fit her stepsisters. In Roberts's adaptation of the text, such elements are removed: it is Cinderella's father who invites the prince to let his daughter try. Even more than in the traditional version, her fate is determined by a man.

Combined with Perrault's original French text, Roberto Innocenti sets the illustrations to his *Cendrillon* (1983) in more or less the same time period as Roberts's Art Deco "Cinderella," that is, some sixty years before its publication date. In this picture book too, Cinderella's facial expression is invariably sad before the appearance of her fairy godmother. The focus is on Cinderella's disempowerment and dependence on others, something that has become rare in more up-to-date settings.

Brad Sneed's illustrations to Alan Schroeder's *Smoky Mountain Rose: An Appalachian Cinderella* (1997) indicate that Perrault's story is resituated in the United States in the 1940s. This is supported by the final illustration, which shows Rose, the Cinderella figure, and Seb, her "prince," as an elderly couple in more contemporary clothes. As a young girl, Rose is portrayed as a passive character who hardly ever speaks and lacks even the

Figure 3. Cinderella: An Art Deco Love Story *by Lynn and David Roberts.*

limited initiative of Perrault's and the Grimms' Cinderella figures: "Now Rose, she wanted to go to the party somethin' awful, but she held her tongue for fear of bein' laughed at again." Ruth Bottigheimer has noted that the distribution of speech in literature "offers implicit evidence as well as explicit information about an author's or editor's disposition toward speech use in general and that of specific characters in particular" (*Bad Girls* 52). In "Cinderella" she sees "textual silence and powerlessness unite in the titular protagonist" (53). These two aspects also coincide in Lynn Roberts's *Cinderella* and in Schroeder and Sneed's *Smoky Mountain Rose*. In the narrative comments to the latter book, it is mainly Rose's misery that is stressed: "Rose, meanwhile, sat next to the pigsty and cried. Far off 'cross the creek she could hear the sound of fiddle music. That made her cry even harder"; and "Rose nodded, all teary-eyed." The occasions on which Rose is described as speaking are very rare, and she hardly gets any direct speech in the whole retelling. Whenever she talks, it is in direct response to others, a pattern that Bottigheimer considers indicative of unequal gender relationships in the Grimms' tales (*Bad Girls* 54), which *Smoky Mountain Rose* retains and intensifies rather than corrects. A similar sentimentality and lack of female agency and verbosity are rarely found after 1990, except in parodies that are obviously tongue-in-cheek.[12]

Critical Responses to Marcia Lieberman and Images of Women Studies

Although it cannot be denied that the emancipation movement has helped to accomplish great improvements for women in society and sparked revolutionary insights into literary history, many—both feminists and antifeminists—have deplored the methods used and alternatives suggested in the 1970s and 1980s. The subject, object, and goal of early feminist literary criticism were topics of vehement debate and have substantially evolved and diversified since the late 1960s.[13] In the process, several objections arose to the kind of literary criticism that had been undertaken by the so-called images of women studies, of which Lieberman can be considered a representative. The emancipation movement, which sought to expose and correct patriarchal patterns and stereotypes, faced the problem of turning into a cliché itself. And although it was relatively agreed upon what the problem was, possible solutions provoked more discussions and disagreements. In "Feminist Criticism in the Wilderness" (1981), Elaine Showalter uses the biblical metaphor of the promised land to explain how the goals of feminist criticism became more varied and even partly evaporated as the theory developed: "A few years ago feminist critics thought we were on a pilgrimage to the promised land in which gender would lose its power, in which all texts would be sexless and equal, like angels. [. . .] We may never reach the promised land at all; for when feminist critics see our task as the study of women's writing, we realize that the land promised to us is not the serenely undifferentiated universality of texts but the tumultuous and intriguing wilderness of difference itself" (205). The enlightened ideal of gender equality was partly replaced with a revaluation of difference. In this context, generalizing analyses and statements such as Lieberman's and Dworkin's became problematic. Just as the ideas of the women's liberation movement were expressed both in literary criticism and in primary texts, its opponents also addressed their critiques in theory as well as in fiction. Fairy-tale retellings can thus intensify, transform, counteract, or comment on the negative aspects that have been associated with the early feminist view of literature.

A Dual Model

Although the analysis of the fairy tale in "Some Day My Prince Will Come" is driven by a dissatisfaction with existing gender patterns, sociopolitical images of women studies such as Lieberman's have been reproached with repeating, rather than transforming, the male/female divide. From her perspective as a literary critic, Lieberman draws up a typology of the fairy tale, which she evaluates on the basis of both sociological and pedagogical concerns. In so doing, she addresses gaps and recurrent patterns in the fairy tale and deplores the effect that she believes fairy tales have. Yet, in contrast to such critics as, for instance, Gmelin and Gelberg, Lieberman writes more vaguely about what she values positively and does not offer suggestions for a solution. Her work supports Showalter's thesis that images of women studies lack a theory of female poetics or aesthetics. For that reason, Showalter considers them not so much a contestation of patriarchy as a continuation of it.

An affirmation of the dichotomy between the sexes can be seen in the fact that Lieberman puts her focus so strongly on girls and women, as both characters and readers. In this she does not differ from some of her contemporaries, such as Lurie and Dworkin. The critique of binary thinking applies to some of the feminist retellings to an even higher degree than to the secondary works. As became clear in the examples above, authors have sought to fill the gaps that feminist readings have identified and, in order to do this, they have had to imagine alternatives to the patterns established by the most popular traditional fairy tales. It is exactly in these alternatives that the continuation of the male/female divide becomes most apparently problematic.

One of the earliest, simplest, and most popular strategies to correct the patriarchal model of representation in traditional fairy tales was the reversal of gender roles, a few instances of which have been mentioned. In many so-called upside-down stories or inside-out tales (Beckett, *Recycling* 107), the sex of the characters is inverted. Cinderella, for instance, is transformed into *Prince Cinders* (by Babette Cole), Sleeping Beauty becomes *Sleeping Boy* (by Sonia Craddock) and *Sleeping Bobby* (by Will and Mary Pope Osbourne), and Little Red Riding Hood is turned into *Little Red Riding Wolf* (by Laurence Anholt). It is no coincidence that all these books are marketed for younger age groups. As Kornei Chukovsky affirms, "The mental game involving the 'reversal of the normal relationship of things' is appreciated by very young children and is a cornerstone of children's humour" (qtd. in Beckett, *Recycling* 107). It is mainly in picture books that the reversal of gender roles is still common practice today, but occasionally the strategy is also employed in texts for adults. Donoghue, for instance, ends "The Tale of the Rose" with a thought-provoking gender reversal—in this retelling of "Beauty and the Beast," the Beast is revealed to be a woman. The construction of gender stereotypes is an explicit theme in the story, which reflects on issues of representation in language and the performance of different gender roles. As such, it is more complex than the straightforward replacement of a female with a male protagonist in, for instance, *Prince Cinders* and *Sleeping Bobby*.

The mere reversal of gender is not enough to qualify as a feminist text, Hilary S. Crew argues, nor is the simple "substitution of strong female protagonists for more passive female characters" (205). This is, however, a second popular strategy of reversal, in which it is not the sexes that are reversed but the characteristics ascribed to those sexes. Authors subvert the associative patterns from the traditional fairy tale and provide a literary answer to the observation that the "sexes of the rescuer and the person in danger are almost as constantly predictable" (Lieberman 195).[14] "Hansel and Gretel" is an interesting tale to consider in this respect because it features two siblings of different sexes. Lieberman mentions it to reject Lurie's positive valuation of female role patterns in the Grimms: although it is true that Gretel saves her brother by killing the witch, Lieberman admits, in the rest of the story she is far more vulnerable and dependent. The specific passages in which Hansel and Gretel overhear their parents and are later lost in the forest have often been revised and parodied in fiction. In Grimm (1857), it reads,

> The two children had not been able to fall asleep that night either. Their hunger kept them awake, and when they heard what their stepmother said to their father, Gretel wept bitter tears and said to Hansel, "Now it's all over for us."
>
> "Be quiet, Gretel," Hansel said. "Don't get upset. I'll soon find a way to help us." (711)

And when the children are lost,

> By the time they finally awoke, it was already pitch-black, and Gretel began to cry and said, "How are we going to get out of the forest?"
>
> And when the full moon had risen, Hansel took his little sister by the hand and followed the pebbles. (712)

In "My Stepmother, Myself" (1983), Garrison Keillor's Gretel openly disagrees with these two scenes, humorously attacking the Grimms' tale as if it were the mimetic rendition of facts. After signing a contract with the Brothers Grimm, Keillor's feminist reincarnation of Gretel polemically claims that she was put under a spell. When she awoke, she found that not only had the Grimms cut her part of the financial share, they had also manipulated the story:

> The book was pure fiction. Suddenly he [Hansel] was portrayed as the strong and resourceful one, a regular little knight, and I came off as a weak sister. [. . .] Nothing could be further from the truth. My brother was a basket case from the moment the birds ate his bread crumbs. He lay down in a heap and whimpered, and I had to slap him a couple of times *hard* to make him walk. Now the little wiener makes himself out to be the hero who kept telling me, "Don't cry, Gretel." Ha! The only crying I did was from sheer exhaustion carrying him on my back. (183)

Keillor replaces the passive and vulnerable Gretel with another stereo-type, the macho ladette. The citation functions as what Pfister has termed an "autoreflexive passage," in that it can be read as a motivation for the use of intertextuality. Yet, as was the case with Dahl, such autoreflexive comments need not always be taken seriously. The fear of the manipulative power of fiction that Gretel addresses hyperbolically here is expressed in a text that not only is fictional itself but also ideologically biased. This aspect of Keillor's retelling will be further discussed below.

A similar but less aggressive reversal of the gender roles in "Hansel and Gretel" takes place in Donna Jo Napoli's *The Magic Circle* (1993). As Gretel explains to the witch, who is here of a friendlier kind than the Grimms',

> "The first time, I told Hansel to fill his pockets with white stones. So he did. [. . .] But the next afternoon when they sent us away again," says Gretel, [. . .] "stupid Hansel here—"
>
> "I'm *not* stupid."
>
> "He puts bread crumbs in his pockets instead of stones."
>
> "It takes time to gather that many stones," says Hansel. His eyes water from the onion. I smile. [. . .] Then I move closer to Gretel and put my fingers on her cheek. "You are not just lovely to look at," I say, "you are clever."
>
> "I'm clever too," says Hansel.
>
> "That remains to be seen," says Gretel.
>
> "Don't be hard on your brother," I find myself saying, although I, too, don't know if this boy is clever. (84–88)

The discourses of Keillor's and Napoli's fragments differ from each other and from Lieberman's article, but the function of both fiction and criticism is partly the same: to raise awareness about the stereotypes that the traditional "Hansel and Gretel" puts forward in the description of its main characters. Lieberman notes that the stereotype exists. Keillor and Napoli also recognize the stereotype but then subvert it by rearranging the characteristics of boys and girls. In both retellings, Hansel is portrayed as the weakling who wines and whimpers, and Gretel is the brave, resourceful character. Napoli goes further in her correction than Keillor does. Whereas in his retelling, Gretel is portrayed while explaining her role in the tradi-tional story, Napoli reverses even the discourse of justification. It is now

Hansel who is trying to convince the other characters that he is smart too, something that is contradicted by the behavior that the narrator describes.

By the mere exchange of the characters' genders, Keillor and Napoli remain stuck in a dual model that is also limiting. The narrator's feminist gaze in Napoli's retelling is as ideologically predetermined as feminists argue the Grimms' to be: the witch admires Gretel for her intelligence but glosses over Hansel's attempts to find ad hoc solutions in executing his sister's plans. In the way that images of women studies were reproached for continuing the divide between males and females, Natascha Würzbach remarks that fictional gender reversals display a similar problem: "The main objection, which has also been raised by several feminist critics themselves, is aimed at the maintenance of the dichotomy of the sexes, against a sexism with reversed conditions" (199; my translation). The opposition between males and females is indeed retained in Keillor's and Napoli's "upside-down stories," and the more positive portrayal of female characters is at the expense of their male counterparts. Anna Altmann uses the image of a seesaw to describe this phenomenon: "In order for one end to go up, the other must come down, and both ends are ineluctably separated but connected, whichever one is up" (24). This metaphor is particularly appropriate for various older retellings for young readers, such as *The Paper Bag Princess* and *Princess Smartypants*, in which the positive representation of active females is combined with dominantly negative male characters. The implied reader is expected to read the traditional tales and the reversals dialectically in order to achieve a balance, a form of gender equality at the end of the intertextual process.[15] If you believe, however, as many early feminist fairy-tale scholars did, that children's expectations with regard to gender are more directly influenced by these entertaining stories, then the problematic nature of seesaw gender reversals becomes clear, especially for little boys.[16] The apparent disregard for the possible effects that children's literature may have on men and boys is something that these upside-down stories share with "Some Day My Prince Will Come." Lieberman stresses that "millions of *women*" have formed their (limited) self-concepts on the basis of their favorite fairy tales and that the tales "have been made the repositories of the dreams, hopes, and fantasies of generations of *girls*" (187; my emphasis). The question of whether the tales have also contributed to the development of limited gender constructs for boys is not sufficiently addressed.

It is not only in retellings for young children that gender reversal leads to antimale attitudes, nor is this side effect limited to the retellings of the 1970s and 1980s. When Maria Micaela Coppola (2001) compares Emma Donoghue's tales to the feminist retellings published by Attic Press (including the aforementioned *Rapunzel's Revenge*), she notes the simplistic literary strategies in the latter, calling Donoghue's tales instead "authentically innovative acts of re-writing" (133). Coppola rightly observes that Donoghue's retellings are multilayered as well as highly creative and original; however, she does not recognize that the reversal of gender characteristics is one of the strategies that Donoghue's tales share with many of the stories published by Attic Press. The binary opposition of males and females is largely retained in *Kissing the Witch*, and the rise of women in Donoghue's tales more often than not happens at the expense of men. Their roles are limited and reside mostly in the negative: some have incestuous feelings for their daughters ("The Tale of the Apple" and "The Tale of the Skin") or abuse their wives and children ("The Tale of the Cottage"), others are sick weaklings, coughing blood ("The Tale of the Handkerchief") or kept almost entirely silent ("The Tale of the Shoe").

In Walker's *Feminist Fairy Tales*, the negative representation of men is even more prevalent. Male roles in this book range from rapists and fools ("Little White Riding Hood") and violent creeps who aspire to rise above their class ("Snow Night") to drunks ("Princess Questa") and cruel masters exploiting their harem slaves ("The Weaver"). This exemplifies what Altmann recognizes as a general problem in retellings with simplistic gender reversals: "A woman can be something other than a passive princess only if all men are ineffectual and most of them jerks" (24). In her introduction to "Snow Night," Walker reflects on the double standard that she believes the traditional fairy tale uses when it comes to gender: "One might suspect that female beauty was really a larger issue for men than for women, because male sexual response depends to a considerable degree on visual cues. Placing each 'fair lady' (or anything else) somewhere on an arbitrary hierarchical scale seems to be a male idea" (19). The retelling that follows contradicts this statement. Snow Night's evaluation of men is based on the standards that Walker (like Lieberman) condemns for male fairy-tale characters: exterior features and social ranking. "If my father tries to make me marry a hideous old toad like Hunter, [. . .] I'll run away" (21), Snow Night claims, and, upon his marriage proposal, she replies, "I'm not ready to marry. But when I am, I will certainly marry a handsome prince, not an ugly old huntsman. Lord Hunter, you presume far above your station" (22). Although the power relations have shifted among the sexes in the retelling, the criteria for judgment have remained unaltered. Snow Night dismisses the hunter on the same grounds on which his desire for her is based.

Not all fairy-tale retellings uncritically take over the strategy of gender reversal. The problematic nature of this practice is an insight that is provided not only in literary criticism, such as Altmann's and Würzbach's, but also in some primary texts. Consider, for instance, the following discussion between a group of fairy-tale princesses at Kavanagh's "Princesses' Forum":

> "Well then," said the Sleeping Beauty, "we'll just have to rewrite the stories ourselves. I'd just love to rescue some good-looking fellow who's been imprisoned in a castle or tower by a wicked uncle or stepfather."
>
> "That's a ridiculous plot," said Goldilocks contemptuously.
>
> "I know," said the Sleeping Beauty, "but it's actually the plot of *our* stories in reverse."
>
> "I hope we're not just going to reverse the situation," said Cinderella. "In that event, we'd only be reversing the roles of oppressor and oppressed. I don't want to oppress anyone."
>
> All the women nodded in agreement. (8)

The discussion is reminiscent of a feminist conference, with the issues that were topical in the 1970s and 1980s. In spite of the metacritical reservations that Cinderella expresses toward role reversals, the princesses' agreement not to resort to such problematic techniques is soon undermined, even by Cinderella herself. She talks about "macho idiots" (8) and accuses her prince of a foot fetish. At the end of Kavanagh's forum, the roles of brave prince and helpless princess are exchanged: "Cinderella approached the second prince. 'If you're worried about going home alone—' she whispered, 'I'll go with you and hold your hand'" (11). Kavanagh acknowledges that gender reversal is an unsatisfactory solution to the negative representation of women in the fairy tale, but the challenge of coming up with an acceptable alternative is apparent in her story as well.

From these examples, it becomes clear that the unilateral, prejudiced view on gender with which feminists of the early 1970s reproached the popular fairy tales seems to be repeated in the retellings that rely on gender reversal or a simplistic redistribution of gender traits. Showalter's critique of early feminist literary theory, namely that "the feminist obsession with correcting, modifying, supplementing, revising, humanizing, or even attacking male critical theory keeps us dependent upon it and retards our progress in solving our own theoretical problems" (183), can thus be said to apply to retellings that are thematically linked to that theory as well. As Tina L. Hanlon writes in her discussion of Yolen's *Sleeping Ugly*, satirical retellings are "fun" but do not lead to greater knowledge or insight into "the richer folk traditions that lie behind" fairy tales. Thus, Hanlon argues, a "more productive response to the sexist stereotypes of so many traditional tales involv[es] revising the canon of the classic fairy tales, digging deeply into oral and written folk history" (147). Haase similarly reproaches early feminist criticism for a lack of knowledge about what fairy tales are: "Some feminist fairy-tale analyses remain stuck in a mode of interpretation able to do no more than reconfirm stereotypical generalizations about the fairy tale's stereotypes. Such studies are oblivious to the complexities of fairy-tale production and reception, sociohistorical contexts, cultural traditions, the historical development of the genre, and the challenges of fairy-tale textuality" (*Feminism* ix–x). Later feminist fairy-tale criticism, such as Zipes's *The Trials and Tribulations of Little Red Riding Hood*, Bottigheimer's *Grimms' Bad Girls and Bold Boys*, and Warner's *From the Beast to the Blonde*, does take this folkloric and sociohistorical background into account, as do the retellings that reflect their ideas.

Looking Back in Anger

The use of gender reversal in fairy-tale retellings illustrates the initial lack of satisfying female role models. As equality was put forward as one of the ideals of the emancipation movement (also known as the equal rights movement), it was often understood as promoting sameness.[17] At first participation in masculine behavior appeared as a desirable goal: the right to vote and go to college; the possibility of wearing pants, or even suits and ties, to assume typically "male" jobs (e.g., in the army and the construction industry); and, more recently, the display of so-called ladette behavior. On the level of the fairy tale, this was reflected in female characters defeating dragons and oppressing characters of the other sex (e.g., Gretel in Napoli's tale). This simplistic manifestation of feminism is part of what Showalter has called an "immasculation of women" and seems to confirm the inferiority of femininity, something for which it was heavily criticized from both inside and outside the emancipation movement. The substitution of the passive and the masculine woman with more generally acceptable role models, however, proved to be less straightforward. As Jutta Osinski argues, "A rather significant difficulty for feminism as a 'school' lies in the fact that the shared premises of woman's repression and the common goal of emancipation are too vaguely defined; they allow for a vast number of different positions and interpretations" (125; my translation).

Lieberman limits herself to a typology and ideological critique of the fairy tale, without suggesting a positive femininity as an alternative. "Implicit in such criticism is the assumption that good feminist fiction would present truthful images of strong women with which the reader may identify" (7) writes Toril Moi in a critique of Showalter, and this also applies to Lieberman and several of her contemporaries. Yet, "truthful images of strong women" is a concept that could be filled in various ways. As Würzbach shows, later stages of feminist criticism focused more on revaluing and redefining femininity than on attacking sexism. This shift can be identified not only in criticism but in literature as well. In "Parody and Poesis in Feminist Fairy Tales" (1994), Anna Altmann distinguishes between two kinds of fairy-tale retellings. Tales such as *The Paper Bag Princess* and Walker's "Snow Night" would be ranged under the term "parody"—here used in a more restricted sense than Hutcheon's, as revisions with "a very sharp edge" (Altmann 22). Typical of such parodies, Altmann argues, is that they comment on the ways in which women have been depicted in the past and do not necessarily provide an alternative to the problematics they criticize: "Parody is metafiction, a criticism of established forms. Criticism produces insight, but it does not necessarily make new use of the forms, create new meaning: it is not always poesis" (22).[18] Because parody is a type of metafiction, it always looks back, and feminist parodies, like emancipatory criticism, often look back at the traditional fairy tale in anger. This anger is absent from what Altmann calls "poesis." Poesis "looks forward, creates new meaning" (23) and thus corresponds better than parody to the need in feminist criticism to redefine femininity while looking at the hopeful future rather than the negative past. These poetic texts "use the form of the fairy tale without commenting on it. Or at least, commentary is not the main point. [. . .] They are about what women can be and are" (Altmann 23, 28).[19] They provide positive, realistic role models for women that do not happen at the expense of men and that do not alter "the expected form and tone" of the traditional fairy tale (28).

The exact distinction between parody and poesis is not always easy to make in practice and seems to depend on one's point of view. Altmann remains rather vague in her discussion of concrete examples, and it appears that a retelling can be interpreted as parodic in some aspects and poetic in others. Yet, the distinction that she makes surfaces in other critics' discussion of the fairy tale. Benson's view on the works of Angela Carter, for instance, can be used to illustrate the concept of the "poetic" retelling even though he does not use the term himself: "Carter's idiosyncratic adaptation of the stylistic potential of the folktale tradition means her texts can be both aesthetically constructive and ideologically deconstructive (well aware of the ties between these two), simultaneously located within and reflecting back upon the tradition itself. To varying degrees, what we find in Carter's work is an interest in the fairy tale that goes beyond the purely critical" (*Cycles* 229). Benson acknowledges that Carter is "reflecting back"; however, she does not do so in anger, nor is looking back considered the main quality of her work. Benson locates Carter's potential to overcome the "purely critical" in her own ties with the oral tradition that lies behind the literary fairy tale, an "awareness of the field of wonder tales that lies beyond the rigidly defined boundaries of the standard canon" (*Cycles* 229).

Altmann's description of parody and poesis also helps us understand what several critics have held against explicitly feminist retellings, and her ideas are particularly enlightening in combination with Hollindale's distinction between explicit and implicit ideology. In *Ideology and the Children's Book*, Hollindale posits that there are three different levels on which ideology is transmitted in children's (and other) literature: explicit ideology, implicit or passive ideology, and ideology as inherent to all language. On the first level, the author consciously and explicitly tries to recommend his or her social, political, and moral beliefs to children. Lack of literary talent (11) is not the only explanation that can be given for this foregrounding of ideology—it can also be a matter of choice. The explicit transmission of ideology can suggest, for instance, a lack of confidence in the (child) reader's capacity to understand literary strategies (12): authors may refrain from using more complex forms to convey ideology (such as irony or hyperbole) because they do not believe the implied child reader is capable of recognizing them as such. Furthermore, explicit ideology may also be included in order to evoke resistance in the reader. It is no coincidence that Hollindale mentions "antisexist" and "antiracist" children's books as typical examples of the explicit transmission of ideology. The prefix "anti-" signals that they also belong to Altmann's parody, texts that present themselves as a reaction. Indeed, in self-proclaimed feminist fairy-tale retellings, ideology is often unambiguously expressed in metastatements by the narrator or by fictional characters who try to convince the reader. When in "The Princesses' Forum," Cinderella calls herself a "self-respecting woman," as mentioned above, and Little Red Riding Hood complains that female fairy-tale characters are "all the victims of stereotyping" (5–6), the reader gets a clear view of the story's political agenda, which had already been signaled by the subtitle of the volume in which it appeared, *Fairy Tales for Feminists*. Literary subtleness seems secondary to the conveyance of a clear and powerful message to the reader.

John Stephens argues that the second form of ideology that Hollindale identifies in the literary text, "passive ideology," is, however, more effective: it is implicit or covered and consists of "values taken for granted" (10). These assumptions and values are presented as natural, and the reader needs critical distance to recognize them—otherwise these texts work as what Davies calls "coercive texts" ("Beyond Dualism" 154), stimulating tacit agreement in readers. It is passive ideology that is criticized in "Some Day My Prince Will Come," as Lieberman lays bare implicit assumptions in popular fairy tales. These stories do not explicitly state that beautiful women are singled out for happiness and wealth, but the recurrence of the pattern "beautiful-rich-happy" points to the passive ideology that is conveyed. A countermove against this implicit ideology can be both explicit (e.g., *Rapunzel's Revenge*) or implicit, as shown above, in the form of more silent corrections that rely on an intertextual comparison to be recognized. As Stephens notes, the unambiguous promotion of ideology is typical of "books which openly advocate 'progressive' or 'enlightened' ideas," and such explicitness may evoke resistance in the reader (9); "well-disposed ideological enthusiasm can be counter-productive" (Hollindale 18). However, Hollindale sees the crude didacticism of this type of literature as an inevitable collateral effect of its intention to change the world: "If you present as natural and commonplace the behaviour you would *like* to be natural and commonplace, you risk muting the social effectiveness of your story" (11).

Feminist fairy-tale retellings in the form of Altmann's poesis may form a special case with regard to the dichotomy between explicit and implicit ideology. They may function as an explicitly ideology-inspired narrative without necessarily using a "crudely didactic" narrative voice or resorting to forced utopian models, as do some of the texts that Altmann labels parody. The intertextual link with the traditional fairy tale allows the poetic retellings to present as natural the ideology they want to promote, and to do so without losing their social effectiveness. Readers who make the connection with the pre-text of the traditional tale will be encouraged to understand the corrective function of the retelling, and yet the transformed ideology does not necessarily intrude into the aesthetic aspects of the fictional text. As such, feminist fairy-tale retellings can avoid presenting their antisexist moral code as unnatural while keeping the potential of social effectiveness (although they do not always do so). Instead, they can present this ideology as perfectly normal and natural. The confrontation of the ideology of the pre-text (the traditional fairy tale) and that of the retelling takes place in the reader's mind, without being explicitly positioned in the literary text itself, but is strongly encouraged by the intertextual markers in the retelling.

To illustrate the difference between parody or explicit ideological revision, on the one hand, and poesis or implicit ideological revision, on the other, I will now turn to a selection of retellings that transform the Brothers Grimm's opening scene from "Hansel and Gretel" (1857). This passage has been criticized for its sexism by, among others, Zipes (*Happily Ever After* 50) and Tatar (*Classic* 182), in particular the following lines:

> One night, as he [Hansel and Gretel's father] was lying in bed and thinking about his worries, he began tossing and turning. Then he sighed and said to his wife, "What's to become of us? How can we feed our poor children when we don't even have enough for ourselves?"
>
> "I'll tell you what," answered his wife. "Early tomorrow morning we'll take the children out into the forest where it's most dense. [. . .] They won't find their way back home, and we'll be rid of them."

"No wife," the man said, "I won't do this. I don't have the heart to leave my children in the forest. [...]" She continued to harp on this until he finally agreed to do what she suggested. (Grimm, "Hansel" 711)

In the 1857 edition of *Die Kinder- und Hausmärchen* (and to a lesser extent in earlier editions), Hansel and Gretel's father is by far more sympathetic to the children's fate. The blame for the parents' attempt to rid themselves of their children thus lies predominantly with the stepmother, who is portrayed as heartless, cold, and bossy. Feminists such as Tatar and Zipes have identified this scene as one of the most striking examples of the Grimms' antifemale attitude, and the passage is deleted or modified in several contemporary retellings. In Keillor's "My Stepmother, Myself," the link to the opening scene of the Grimms' tale is made explicit in Gretel's pseudoconfession of "what really happened." After the Brothers Grimm put Gretel under a spell, not only did they rewrite Hansel's part of the story, but they also modified the role of the stepmother:

Dad was shown as a loving father who was talked into abandoning us in the forest by Gladys, our "wicked" stepmother.

Nothing could be further from the truth. [...] As for Dad, he has no bleeding heart. [...] Gladys couldn't send us to our *rooms* without his say-so. The truth is that he was in favor of the forest idea from the word go. (182–83)

Gretel's testimony is an open rectification of the biased portrayal of the parents, as she unmasks the traditional version as a lie with reference to a fictional "truth." With her account she wants to "set the record straight" (180). She is clearly looking back in anger, and the retelling falls under Altmann's description of parody. In a self-reflexive move, it is made explicit what ideology is criticized in the traditional story and why. However, the content of Gretel's plea and her polemic tone underline the fact that the ideology she promotes is not commonplace or natural. This is supported by the material that surrounds this text: two similar testimonies of other fairy-tale characters and a fictional newspaper report about the mistreatment of stepmothers. The explicit way in which Gretel advocates her rights and the fact that she is a fictional character may therefore provoke readers' resistance, as Hollindale and Stephens argue. In this context, it is questionable whether the ideology proclaimed by the first-person narrator is supported by the author of this text. Although Keillor's story may raise awareness about several feminist issues in the Grimms' tales, from his use of hyperbole and fictional characters as feminist critics, the discourse of the emancipation movement does not appear as a particularly interesting or valid one. In this sense, Keillor's tale illustrates that the explicit ideology formulated in a literary text is not always synonymous with the ideology that the text actually tries to convey—the principle of author detachment stipulates that an author's intentions and opinions cannot simply be equated with his or her characters' or narrator's. Note in this respect that it is rather difficult to identify the ideology or view of the fairy tale that Keillor does positively advocate in this tale. According to Altmann, such a negative stance is the precondition of all parody. Its strength lies in attacking what is undesirable and deconstructing what is problematic, rather than in affirmatively promoting a solution or ideology.

The difference between parody and poesis becomes apparent when Keillor's version is compared to Donoghue's retelling of the same passage in "The Tale of the Cottage." Here, too, we find a correction of Grimm, but it is not marked as a correction. The roles of parent and stepparent are reversed. Hansel and Gretel have a stepfather, a huntsman, and he is the one who persuades his wife to leave the children to starve in the forest:

> Then no luck for huntman. Means no meat for us. Brother say mother eat her words. I see only nuts and old bread. She say, Sorry sorry. She put last drops holy water on huntsman gun. Still no luck. One night he came home snowed like pine. Next day lie in smelly furs all day bellyache. Say, How can we feed our children when we can't even feed ourselves?
>
> Moonrise I holding chicken for warm hear him through wall. They talking small not like *whap whap*. She say, It's their home. He say, What's a home with a bare table?
>
> Later after sounds like running I hear him say, Pick one. You can't feed two birds with a single stone. The little one's no earthly use not right in the head.
>
> After mother cry and gone quiet like sleeping I hold my head like apple shake it for see what sick. (134–35)

Donoghue leaves it to the readers to draw the intertextual link with the traditional "Hansel and Gretel." A number of textual markers, from a brother and sister abandoned in the woods to the witch's cottage and Hansel's lockup, stimulate readers to do so. When the opening scenes are compared, it becomes apparent that the roles are reversed. In Donoghue, the mother literally speaks the words of the father in Grimm: "How can we feed our children when we can't even feed ourselves?" Whereas in the Grimms' version, both parents lead the children into the woods, in "The Tale of the Cottage," it is only the huntsman who takes them, while their mother cannot get up.

A further contrast with Keillor's retelling lies in the fact that Donoghue does not include a motivation for her revision, and this is another gap that readers need to fill themselves if they want to make sense of the gender reversal. The transformation of roles implies a shift of guilt from female to male and a correction to the Grimms' vilification of the (step)mother and the exoneration of the father. However, this possible function of the retelling is made explicit nowhere in the literary text itself. To refer back to Pfister's intertextual parameter, Keillor's text is more openly autoreflexive than Donoghue's. In "The Tale of the Cottage," the situation in which a mother defends her children is not promoted as corrective, unnatural, or forced. Instead the mother's love is evoked as a natural relationship that is simply represented as such (as passive rather than explicit ideology). This feminist dissociation from women and evil nature is further reinforced by the fact that Donoghue presents nearly all relationships between female characters in *Kissing the Witch* as kind and supportive, which makes goodness and bonding appear as universal female features within her fictional world. To recognize this new pattern requires the critical distance that Hollindale deems necessary for discovering passive ideology. Whereas Keillor's text forces the reader into such a critical attitude, Donoghue offers it as a possibility but does not oblige. In Altmann's distinction, this difference makes Keillor's retelling parody and Donoghue's poesis.

Lacking Literariness

Feminist literary criticism, Liska argues, "started out with an idea of literature as unmediated representation of social reality" ("Criticism" 95), and this type of analysis was applied to genres that make no claim to realism, such as the fairy tale. Indeed, "Some Day My Prince Will Come" implies a reduction of literature, in the sense that Lieberman treats a type of fantastic fiction as a mimetic rendering of reality. Features such as magic, exaggeration, symbolism, and flat characterization, some of the defining characteristics of the traditional fairy tale, are put on the same level as realistic elements. Thus Lieberman seems to engage in what is called the "realistic fallacy" (Meijer 181) of Anglo-American feminist criticism when she disregards fairies as empowered female characters simply because they are not real: "They are not examples of powerful women with whom children can identify as role models. [. . .] A girl may hope to become a princess, but can she become a fairy?" (196). Because of the predominantly mimetic angle, early feminist criticism "dealt with texts primarily in terms of their content, denotative meaning, and documentary value" (Liska, "Criticism" 96) and thus largely disregarded literariness and other artistic intentions except the wish to render a faithful image of real life (Osinski 44). Not only can such feminist criticism be reproached for not doing justice to the aesthetic pleasure that a literary text can create, but Liska also indicates literary strategies that may jeopardize such a straightforward analysis of images of women, such as narratological undecidability and the difficulty of locating intentionality. Images of women studies have thus been problematized as inaccurate critical tools that can only be applied to a limited number of texts.

Literariness concerns feminist fairy-tale retellings in two further ways. On the one hand, they are a critical treatment of other literary texts, the traditional fairy tales; on the other hand, they are fictional texts that can qualify as literary texts in their own right. Altmann and Benson stress that fairy-tale retellings form an active exploration of form and meaning, and they can thus avoid a reductive view of the pre-text by addressing it in an equally stimulating poetic form. However, like early feminist criticism, many parodic feminist retellings of fairy tales are produced with the same concern with content rather than form. In the reception of fairy-tale retellings, the Aristotelian criterion of the autonomy of a text proves to be a recurrent standard for determining its literariness. As Northrop Frye argues, "Pure literature, like pure mathematics, is disinterested, or useless: it contains its own meaning. Any attempt to determine the category of literature must start with a distinction between the verbal form which is primarily itself and the verbal form which is primarily related to something else" (75). For the specific case of children's literature, with its double address and its history as a pedagogical tool, complete autonomy seems impossible. "By definition, and perhaps also ontologically, this is said to disqualify children's literature from being art," argues Torben Weinreich. Nevertheless, "pedagogy and art are not diametrically opposed to each other," and, he continues, "just as art can be a category of pedagogy, pedagogy can also be a category of art" (107).

The question of whether literature needs to be autonomous to qualify as art has proved relevant not for children's literature alone. As we have seen, feminist authors for adults also found a useful tool in literature for raising awareness about gender inequality and informing and instructing adults. Sara Maitland is the author of several feminist fairy-tale retellings, including the aforementioned "Stepmother's Lament." In her fictionalized autobiographical article "A Feminist Writer's Progress," (1983), she reflects on her evolution and role as a feminist author. About her childhood reading, she writes, "Suddenly the little girl could see that *the stories were just vehicles;* they had been told over and over again for different purposes and could be told one more time at least; they could be told through brand new shining feminist eyes" (18; my emphasis). This view of the fairy tale as a transmitter of ideology meets her ideal that "politics matters" in art too, a premise that is tacitly shared by many authors of feminist retellings. Again, as with Lieberman, the fact that literature is used as a vehicle, as an ideological tool, is not problematized—Maitland seems more concerned about the content than the form. Later, she describes how her alter ego "the feminist writer" did have to negotiate between two groups: on the one hand, "her old education" and "old artistic consciousness," which were "booming out that politics and great writing cannot go together"; on the other hand, "the other feminists," who opposed how the aesthetic form of expression obscures the message and "snapped out that what she was writing was not 'good feminism,' was not 'useful to ordinary women'" (19).

As becomes clear from Maitland's dilemma, the poeticist poetics of the Russian Formalists has influenced many of the criteria by which literature is judged today—literariness is attributed on the basis of meaningful form, of the alienation, estrangement of language through literary procédés and deliberately difficult forms (Fokkema 100). Such aesthetic criteria are now also recurrent in studies of children's literature, and indeed fairy-tale retellings, whether intended for adults or children, are judged on the basis not only of meaning but also of form. A disregard for the generic specificity and complexity of the fairy tale is a recurrent critique that has been aimed at both critics and retellings. Concerns that the didactic impulse in fairy-tale retellings comes at the expense of aesthetic qualities and the reader's enjoyment of the story surface equally in many reviews and critical responses. In particular, artificiality is a criterion frequently raised in reviews of fairy-tale retellings. "Unfortunately, the one-dimensional characterization and overwrought tone will probably put off teenagers looking for books on lesbian themes," writes *The Horn Book Guide* (1997) on Donoghue's *Kissing the Witch* (Rev. of *Kissing the Witch*). Hazel Rochman of *Booklist* (1992) sees a flaw in the explicitness with which fairy-tale themes and symbols are presented in one of Adèle Geras's retellings: "The parallels are somewhat contrived and portentous. You can see the author setting up the literal details to fit the pattern, and then the symbolism is carefully explained." Kathleen Beck reads Tracey Lynn's integration of feminist discourse in *Snow* as equally unsuccessful: "Lynn tries to promote feminism, for example, in Anne's bitterness at society's strictures on women, but succeeds only in sounding artificial and preachy. As for her attempt to rehabilitate the wicked stepmother—please!" She sees this retelling as "a step on the way to more sophisticated revisits to fairy tales" such as those by Robyn McKinley, Napoli, and Geras. In her review of Walker's *Feminist Fairy Tales*, Janet L. Langlois (1997) claims to find anthologies such as Zipes's *Don't Bet On the Prince* "suspect" and prefers "selections drawn from world folktales with implicit feminist themes already in place." She labels Walker's rewritten fairy tales "too obvious" and as having "a broad moralistic sweep" (187).[20] It is striking that these and other factors seem to matter less in Langlois's evaluation of the collection when she starts considering it a text for children: "My comparison here to young-adult fantasy literature suggests a move from 'authentic folk texts' to 'juvenile literary adaptations.' In that space and the shortness of each tale suggest this shift, I rest more comfortably" (188). One explanation for why Langlois finds Walker's tales more acceptable as children's than as adult literature is the tension between literary and didactic features that is inherent to all fiction for the young. However, the adult agenda that drives Walker's retellings gets in the way here too: "Enough textual references hint at a battle being fought on adult ground" (188).

Langlois believes that overly didactic retellings are acceptable in children's literature, but Anna Altmann issues a warning for such reasoning with reference to Bronwyn Davies's reader response research. In *Frogs and Snails and Feminist Tales* (1989), Davies finds that preschoolers' responses to feminist fairy-tale retellings are strikingly conservative, and Altmann attributes this to the type of retellings used in the experiment. Altmann believes that it is logical that the stories lose their appeal if they are stripped of their imaginary power and used as a vehicle to transmit new ideology. She considers the glitter of the traditional princesses and the brown paper bag of Robert Munsch's *The Paper Bag Princess*, the retelling that Davies uses for her interviews with children, metaphors for the appeal of these stories. The children's "refusal to give up satins and jewels for the utilitarian bag may be read as a refusal to exchange the extra-ordinary, the wonder of fairy tales, for a moral in a plain brown wrapper" (Altmann 26). More poetic fairy-tale retellings, Altmann implies, might have led Davies to different results.

In a debate that was highly influential in the German pedagogical context (Born 59), Guido König similarly addressed the absence of literary complexity in Gmelin's retellings.[21] He considers Gmelin's "Hansel and Gretel," for instance, a failed alternative, "in reality a more or less veiled role play" ("Böses" 132; my translation). The absence of literary challenge is, moreover, counterproductive to Gmelin's explicit wish to emancipate children, König argues: "He who instrumentalizes fairy-tale texts to become ideological reservoirs of thoughts (see Gmelin's 15-fold proclamation of propositions about the 'stereotypes'!) automatically lands in the tendentious channelling of absolute contents and this constructed compulsion necessarily has an antiemancipatory effect" ("Böses" 132; my translation; see also "Märchen Heute" 142). König's condemnation of the programmatic fairy-tale retelling relies on John Locke's influential view of children's literature as combining pleasure and instruction. It also addresses the implicitly condescending image of the child that can be discerned in Lieberman's article as well as in Gmelin's work and the paradox in forcing emancipation on a reader who is pictured as naïve and weak. As Monika Born states about the ideology-critical movement of which Gmelin was part, it is contradictory that emancipation and antiauthoritarian attitudes were proclaimed in such an authoritarian discourse (79)—an *"Aufklärungseifer"* or eagerness to enlighten (Osinski 44) that Gmelin shares with other early feminist critics. Instead of straightforward and authoritative messages—what Langlois calls "in-your-face feminist fairy tales" (187)—König combines a psychoanalytic frame of reference with a more romantic image of the wise and innocent child and pleads for an openness to several interpretations (*Vieldeutigkeit*), an inexhaustibility (*Unerschöpflichkeit*) of stories, and fluctuating images rather than fixed concepts ("Märchen heute" 139). Because of their alleged effect on the human psyche, König sees in such symbolic literature neither an affirmation of hegemonic powers and the status quo nor a cheap escapism, but a possibility of personal liberation.

A Literary Playground After All?

Although the clear didactic impulse disqualifies many fairy-tale retellings as literary texts on the basis of an autonomist literariness, several of these texts do correspond to another concept of literariness as elaborated by critics such as Stanley Fish (342) and Wolfgang Iser: the idea of the literary text as a "*Spielraum von Bedeutungsmöglichkeiten*," or a playground of potential meanings (Iser, *Appellstruktur* 8).[22] Iser sees it as characteristic of a literary text that it leaves its intention and most important aspects unsaid (33). Three retellings that can and have been criticized for being overtly didactic do seem to provide such a literary playground: Walker's "Ugly and the Beast," Kavanagh's *Rapunzel's Revenge*, and Yolen's *Sleeping Ugly*.[23]

It is unlikely that anyone would interpret Walker's title *Feminist Fairy Tales* as meaning something other than what it says, and few would label her collection antifeminist. However, some of her tales do not simply formulate one meaning or one truth, as Iser sees happening in nonliterary texts (*Appellstruktur* 33). Certain elements in her retellings do produce fissures in the text, tensions or gaps that open up a space for interpretation, "*einen Auslegungsspielraum*" (15). A detailed analysis of her retellings problematizes the idea that Walker promotes an unambiguous feminist ideology. At various points, she seems to undermine her feminist message with contradictions and even antifeminist passages. Some of her tales can thus be read not so much as feminist fairy tales but as parodies of feminist fairy tales. Parody seems to be used to fight parody or, as Langlois labels the process, Walker is "fighting fire with fire" (189). The fairy tale is used as burning fuel—but, as Altmann has pointed out about parodies, at several instances what it is exactly that Walker wants to gain is open to interpretation. Langlois mentions a well-chosen example with Walker's description of Ugly in "Ugly and the Beast," a fragment that was included in the discussion of Lieberman's text above. Whereas Walker upholds a model of identification in her introduction, her retelling instead offers a character so grotesque that it invites ironic distance.

It is striking that several explicitly feminist retellings at some point lapse into such a moment of self-contradiction or self-parody. *Rapunzel's Revenge* has been mentioned several times as a collection in which feminist debates are explicitly voiced. It was the first in a series of several short story collections by the Irish feminist publishing house Attic Press. The volume explicitly and implicitly places itself along the line of critics such as Andrea Dworkin and Marcia Lieberman—explicitly in the introduction, "The Princesses' Forum," in which some female fairy-tale protagonists discuss their portrayal in the tales, and implicitly by reversing gender roles in the various adapted tales. Little Red Riding Hood complains that they are "all the victims of stereotyping," Sleeping Beauty is "really quite wide awake," and Cinderella calls herself a "self-respecting woman" (Kavanagh 5–6). "Once we're not in competition for men's approval, it won't matter which of us is better-looking" (8), says Snow White, thus aligning herself with Lieberman's critique of the beauty contest.

Despite the overt emancipatory agenda in *Rapunzel's Revenge*, its introductory tale contains several messages that problematize a straightforward feminist reading. Paradoxically, the story is implicitly based on some of the stereotypes it explicitly challenges. The prejudice that most princesses lack intelligence is a good example. When Rapunzel complains she has put on weight and feels sick in the morning since the prince has visited her, all the princesses fear that she is pregnant. She herself says all this in "happy innocence," is "bewildered at the response" of her friends, and even makes "a mental note to keep quiet in future," which she then forgets (5–6). Although it turns out that all the symptoms were caused by the pill, the misunderstanding shows that the other women do not expect Rapunzel to be very bright and the incident confirms the stereotype of bossy, quarrelling women. One of the main goals of feminism is to give women a voice, but Rapunzel is snapped at and so decides to keep quiet. When she does make a remark, Cinderella says, "If I were you [. . .] I'd keep my mouth shut" (6). Another issue the princesses fail to correct is their relationship with men. Although they claim that they have had enough of princes who have foot fetishes (Cinderella) and are too stupid to find a ladder (Rapunzel), as soon as a few princes arrive, the women focus on them. Eventually each princess leaves with her new lover and the female gathering breaks up. Snow White instead goes to her stepmother's laboratory and is thus the only woman who really makes an effort at female bonding. The conclusion of this tale seems to be that although many women advocate a feminist ideology, very few incorporate it in their lives—or is this only true when the feminist critics are fairy-tale characters?

In the discussion of the interaction between Lieberman's article and late twentieth-century fairy tales, I have mentioned *Sleeping Ugly* several times. The previous analysis might suggest that Yolen's tale merely functions as a mouthpiece for feminist ideology. The didactic intent of her tale seems to be marked by the narrator's explicit comments on characters and events in the story and by other suggestions in the tale that direct the reader's sympathies (on the level of both explicit and implicit ideology). The names of the characters, for instance, are an unmistakable indication of their nature: the beautiful but annoying princesses who feature in the tale are called Miserella, Prunella, Bratina, and Nastina. And yet, even in a small book as simple as *Sleeping Ugly*, several elements undermine and make ambiguous this didactic aspect. A number of ambiguities and inconsistencies can be perceived. A resisting reading affirms Hollindale's claim that "sometimes [. . .] the conscious surface ideology and the passive ideology of a novel are at odds with each other, and 'official' ideas contradicted by unconscious assumptions" (14). This is a practice that Barbara Godard often sees at work in feminist rewritings of traditional genres: "Coded ideologies implicit in the genre will overwhelm the feminist message unless they are explicitly addressed and/or deconstructed by the text" (121).

One can question, in fact, to what extent Yolen's story really is a fundamental revision of typical fairy-tale characteristics and to what extent it goes along uncritically with the assumptions of the genre. This ambiguity appears when we consider the evaluation of beauty in the traditional tale and in Yolen's retelling. In *Sleeping Ugly*, beauty and internal characteristics are still linked—people are still defined by their looks. The traditional association of beauty with goodness and ugliness with a bad character may be reversed, but the connection between outer and inner features remains unaltered. It is signaled by the prince's reasoning on "that kind of princess" who looks good but is ugly within. It is not only the prince who judges women according to their beauty; the narrator also constantly stresses Princess Miserella's good looks throughout the story: "She rode and rode and rode, looking beautiful as always, even with her hair in tangles" (13); "So there was the princess, lost in a dark wood. It made her look even prettier" (16); "Princess Miserella looked miserable. That made her look beautiful, too" (39); and "Even frowning she was beautiful" (58). By repeatedly referring to Miserella in terms of her beauty, the narrator may on the one hand contrast this tale explicitly with the traditional fairy tale (in which beauty and good character are associated), but on the other hand, the comments also signal that exterior features are not secondary to a character's (and a person's) description.

The fact that Yolen's prince chooses a plain girl over a beautiful princess appears to be a correction to traditional fairy tales such as "Snow White" and "Cinderella," in which girls are selected for their beauty. However, there is a bias in the choice of the prince. First, his judgment is still based on external rather than internal features: he has not exchanged a single word with Plain Jane when he declares his love to her—he selects her on the basis of her "smell of wild flowers." Critical readers will realize that there may be another reason: if he excludes Miserella and the old fairy, there is simply no one else left. The following conversation is telling: " 'I love *you*,' he said. 'What's your name?' " (60). This prince does not know the object of his love any better than Sleeping Beauty's, Snow White's, or Cinderella's respective admirers.[24] But what does the *reader* know about Plain Jane? Not very much either. Most of the reader's knowledge of her depends on information provided by the narrator, who expresses clear sympathy for this character. When she is introduced, it is explained that Plain Jane is not pretty but that she is kind to animals and old women (10). The first trait underlines the contrast with Miserella (who has just kicked her horse); the second comes in handy when she meets the old fairy. A comparison between Jane and Miserella reveals that the book contains twelve pages of text in which Miserella is the focus point, whereas Jane receives less than half as much attention.

Plain Jane may be endlessly good and kind, but she is also a bit naïve and slightly boring. In the edition of *Sleeping Ugly* illustrated by Diane Stanley, fourteen of the seventeen pictures in which Jane features show her with the same facial expression: a kind, but dumb smile. Miserella, by contrast, is a more varied and dynamic character. Antiauthoritarian readers will certainly feel sympathy for her when she reacts against the old fairy's pedantic lecture:

The princess said, "[. . .] that was a stupid way to waste a wish."

The fairy was angry.

"Do not call someone stupid unless you have been properly introduced," she said, "or a member of the family."

"*Stupid, stupid, stupid,*" said Miserella. She hated to be told what
to do.

"Say stupid again," warned the fairy, holding up her wand, "and
I will make toads come out of your mouth."

"*Stupid!*" shouted Miserella. (34–36)

If we interpret Miserella and Jane as two types of children—and, possibly, the fairy as a parent or teacher—Jane is the good and submissive child,
whereas Miserella is stubborn and has a mind of her own. Although the
narrator obviously tries to direct the reader's sympathy to Jane, Miserella is
definitely more interesting. One can indeed question whether Yolen's own
preference lies entirely with Jane, as the narrator's seems to. In "America's
Cinderella," an essay that she published a few years before *Sleeping Ugly*,
Yolen criticized the reception of "Cinderella" in American popular culture:

Hardy, helpful, inventive, that was the Cinderella of the old tales but
not of the mass market in the nineteenth century. Today's mass-
market books are worse. [. . .] For the sake of Happy Ever After,
the mass market books have brought forward a good, malleable,
forgiving little girl and put her in Cinderella's slippers. However, in
most of the Cinderella tales there is no forgiveness in the heroine's
heart. No mercy. Just justice. (25)

Yolen's description of the pop culture Cinderella is reminiscent of Plain
Jane. She too is extremely humble and forgiving: she wastes two of her
three wishes on a spoiled princess who she does not even know—a princess
who has insulted her and wants to make Jane her maid. Some of the characteristics that Yolen describes as typical of Disney can be applied to Plain
Jane as well: "In the Walt Disney American version, both movie and book
form, Cinderella shares with the little animals a quality of 'lovableness,'
thus changing the intent of the tale and denying the heroine her birthright
of shrewdness, inventiveness, and grace under pressure" ("America's Cinderella" 23). Plain Jane too is typically described and pictured, as Disney's

Cinderella and Snow White are, in the company of animals. If readers are looking for shrewdness and inventiveness, they will find it with Miserella rather than Jane. Only at the end of *Sleeping Ugly* does Jane assume the justness that Yolen valued in the old "Cinderella" variants when she does not forgive Miserella and does not save her from eternal sleep.

"Ugly and the Beast," "The Princesses' Forum," and *Sleeping Ugly* exemplify the tension between the educational purpose of feminist fairy-tale retellings as awareness raisers and their aesthetic function: these "alternative" fairy tales include destabilizing elements within their critical comments on other texts and, according to some poetics, can be argued to function not just as fictional but also as literary texts in their own right. The irony, the exaggerations, the humor, the contradictions, and the ambiguities in these stories do offer the reader a way out of a programmatic feminist-didactic reading of the text.

The tension between these artistic and pedagogical aspects of literature is the central theme to William Brooke's retelling of "Beauty and the Beast." In "A Beauty in the Beast" (1992), he plays a game with the reader's expectations in opposing the main characters of the traditional tale, something that only becomes clear as the story develops. Instead of the usual correlation between names and outward appearance, the names here refer only to inner features:

> Ugliness and physical perfection regarded each other solemnly across the dinner table. [. . .] He was the very semblance of human perfection. If you judged only by looking.
>
> "We have this in common," he said, "that we are both named for our hearts, not our outward appearances."
>
> She smiled at that, her cruelly twisted lips curling like snakes in the midst of the horror that was her face. If you did not know the pure goodness behind that face, you would have called the smile an evil leer. (69–70)

In the metareflective passages on narratives and their allegorical and symbolic meanings that are a recurrent motif in Brooke's retelling,[25] a key is offered to the reader to how this deviation from the traditional version can be interpreted. "As the stories show, appearances are deceptive!" Beast says when Beauty refuses to look at herself in the mirror. "So are stories!" is her reply. "An artful truth is as deceptive as a lie!" (62). Beauty's assertion about the manipulative power of art touches on the difficulty of practicing ideological criticism through a literary text—her statement applies not only to the traditional version of "Beauty and the Beast" but also to Brooke's retelling itself. Each time the two main characters tell each other a story, they ask the other to explain the moral. The respondent's reaction is always similar. In their minds, they formulate the message that the story-within-the-story most straightforwardly suggests, but they always answer with a funny nonsense reply:

> "Tell me, Beauty, what do you think is the moral of this story?" He felt his point was very clear, and was rather smug that he had wrapped it so neatly in a story. [. . .]
> She thought, "There's no riddle to that story: We must love a thing entire if it is to nourish us," but she did not say that out loud. She ran her fingers along the grain of the wood as if deep in thought.
> She finally smiled to herself and suggested, "Opposites detract."
> Beast considered that with a frown. "I suppose the story is not as clear as I had meant it to be." (Brooke 56)

In this fragment, the moral to the story-within-the-story is understood and made explicit for the reader ("We must love a thing entire if it is to nourish us") but not expressed between the characters, so that a discussion that would reveal the heart of the matter can be avoided. The retelling leaves the storyteller's intended moral implicit. Brooke's tale suggests a message that is at least as ambiguous as Leprince de Beaumont's pre-text. On the one hand, "Beauty in the Beast" seems to argue against attributing a clear and explicit moral to a story, and for the appreciation of literature for its own beauty, not for its possible (ideological) use. On the other hand, Brooke uses his tale as a means to convey a very powerful ideological message, which is repeated over and over again in the characters' stories, in their minds, and in their conversations: "We must love a thing entire if it is to nourish us" (56); "We must reckon a thing entire if it is to be of value" (60); "The mathematician cared more for the *appearance* of the thing than for the *substance* of the thing" (61); "Appearances are deceptive" (62); "Beauty and ugliness are the same thing, a chance shaping of the physiognomy" (77–78); "The appearance doesn't matter as long as we find what we seek within" (95); and "I need you for what you are" (96). That the final example matters most is affirmed by Beauty, who states that "the moral is where it belongs, at the end" (77). In essence, these messages are variations on the values that Leprince de Beaumont defended in her tale of "Beauty and the Beast": that outward appearances are secondary to a person's inner value. The retelling thus contradicts Beast's remark on one of his tales: "You will search in vain for the least hint of a moral" (71). Not to be moralistic is paradoxically the moral that this story has to teach.

The Perpetuation of a Heterosexual Model

One of the main hypotheses of this book is that literary criticism and fictional retellings can supplement each other in the debate on the traditional fairy tale. Within feminist fairy-tale studies, there is one area that until very recently displayed a clear gap when compared to other gender studies and to fairy-tale retellings. As the feminist debate evolved after the late 1960s, the assumptions of the earliest critics were scrutinized and their own ideological presuppositions and reductions addressed: "The internal critiques within the women's liberation movement during the 1980s tended to focus on minority group rights and on making visible more dimensions of women's experience of oppression" (Duncker 22). The early feminists were revealed to have been largely white, middle class, and heterosexual, and the scope of the equal rights movement was broadened to include issues of race and class, and of sexual inclination.[26] From the feminist fairy-tale criticism of the 1970s and the 1980s, the issue of homosexuality seems virtually absent. It has come up with regard to the lives of fairy-tale authors and collectors, most notably of Oscar Wilde and Hans Christian Andersen, and some of their tales have been analyzed in that respect.[27] In a few rare instances, critics have attributed Jacob Grimm's lifelong bachelor status to suppressed homosexuality, but this has not been used as a critical tool for the analysis of the Grimms' tales. In Haase's *Fairy Tales and Feminism: New Approaches* (2004), which presents the state of the art of what is topical in international gender studies related to fairy tales, only one article briefly mentions homosexuality, Patricia Anne Odber de Baubeta's "The Fairy-Tale Intertext in Iberian and Latin American Women's Writing," and here it only appears in the margins of a discussion of two late twentieth-century fairy tales. With these exceptions, fairy tales are rarely read as "closet texts," the term used for writing about homosexuality in covert terms, nor have many critics tried to "deconstruct the heterosexual surfaces of seemingly 'straight' forward texts" (Jay and Glasgow 5) with regard to the fairy tale. Fairy tales that would allow such a reading do exist, most notably the tales of so-called reluctant brides, but also tales featuring intense male friendships, such as "Snow White," "The Frog Prince," "The Two Brothers," and "The Queer Minstrel."

In a recent contribution on gay and lesbian fairy tales to *The Greenwood Encyclopedia of Folktales and Fairy Tales* (2009), Lewis C. Seifert notes further avenues that this research may take, for example, considering tales about cross-dressing and tales about same-gender friends or rivals (401). "Queer theory" has now indeed entered the discussion of fairy tales (which is not to be confused here with the study of fairy-tale retellings, in which queer texts and readings have become more frequent) but often in a restricted sense. Queer theory has been applied to literary tales written by one identifiable author (e.g., Oscar Wilde, Hans Christian Andersen, and George MacDonald) rather than to the tales that were collected by the Grimms and Perrault. And when "queer" is employed with regard to the fairy tale, it is often in a sense that excludes homosexuality but retains the aspect of performativity of gender roles, the blurring of female and male gender characteristics.[28] In "Snow White and the Seven 'Dwarfs'—Queercripped" (2007), Santiago Solis does include homosexuality in his use of the word "queer," as he criticizes the heterosexual norm in Western fairy tales: "Queering describes the practices of putting a spin on mainstream representations to reveal latent queer subtexts; of appropriating a representation for one's own purposes, forcing it to signify differently; or of deconstructing a representation's heterosexism" (Carrie Sandhal qtd. in Solis 115). Solis analyzes four picture-book editions of "Snow White" and comes to the conclusion that all four suppress or marginalize homosexual relationships and disabled bodies. That some of these interpretations are indeed *forced* to signify differently, as Carrie Sandhal's definition spells out, can be confirmed with the following example. It is taken from Solis's critique of Elisabeth Wagner-Koch's illustrations to the Grimms' *Snow White and the Seven Dwarfs:*

> As she contemplates the blood, the Queen thinks to herself, "If only I had a child as white as snow and as red as blood, and as black as the wood on the window frame." [. . .] The Queen does not wish for a

lesbian or a disabled child. But why are homosexuality and disability not on the Queen's wish list? Would being a lesbian or having a disability make Snow White less beautiful, less appealing, and less envied? Since homophobia and ableism are often intertwined, what these questions reveal is that we need to examine both heterosexism and ableism as products of cultural values. (Solis 119)

It seems a stretch for Solis to reproach Snow White's mother for not wishing to have a lesbian and disabled child since she does not wish for a heterosexual or able child either. Both the sexual orientation and the child's physical abilities are completely absent from this part of the tale, and it is therefore striking that the opening of "Snow White" leads Solis to the affirmation that "heterosexism and ableism" are intertwined. If there are arguments in favor of such a pairing, they do not arise from this piece of text. The manifest disparity between the overt content of the primary text under discussion and the radical conclusions that Solis draws from it,[29] as well as from the other examples under discussion, violate the common boundaries on interpretation as described in chapter one with reference to Eco and Brackert. The disregard of these limits can be explained by the implication of Solis's work in the "ongoing commitments to activism" that characterize queer theory (Sandahl qtd. in Solis 117). This activism is reminiscent of some of the earliest feminist critics of the fairy tale, such as Andrea Dworkin, who saw her *Woman Hating* more as a "political action" than as part of academic discourse (17). In the meantime, such ideologically driven scholarship has been discredited for its oversimplification for several decades within feminist fairy-tale studies (Haase, "Scholarship" 3). The repeated conclusions to which Solis comes are equally provocative but as unsophisticated as Dworkin's and may mark only the first step in a homosexual, queer critique of the traditional fairy tale.

Much more established and refined is the queer approach in fairy-tale retellings. Solis remarks that "even contemporary variations on the tale continue to produce a public image that supports hetero-corporo-normative desire and identity; none of them depart from or defy heterosexist and ableist norms" (128). Although this case may be argued with regard to duplicates and to most fairy-tale retellings in the domain of children's literature, the main genre in which lesbian and homosexual issues have regularly met with the fairy tale is not fairy-tale criticism but fairy-tale retellings for adults.[30] As in Solis's analysis, "Homosexual relationships are sometimes put forward in revisionist texts not only as a fulfilling option, but also as an efficient way of attacking the establishment" (Fernández Rodríguez, "Deconstruction" 66), of challenging dominant discourses and clarifying which voices have been suppressed in the tales of the past. An example of how queer theory can offer new, exciting readings of older fairy-tale retellings is provided in Bronwyn Davies's "Beyond Dualism" (1993), in which she describes how a discussion at Deakin University gave her the opportunity of seeing the gender relationships in *The Paper Bag Princess* in a different light. Prince Ronald, who has usually been reproached by feminists for refusing Elizabeth as an atypical fairy-tale princess, is here rehabilitated. The formerly progressive feminist reading is shown to be rather conservative and oppressive itself when the story is interpreted as forcing a heterosexual role model on a prince about whom the text gives some indications that he may be homosexual.

Since the 1990s, several homosexual fairy tales and retellings have appeared, such as Priscilla Galloway's "The Prince" (1995), Jan Vander Laenen's "De Schone Slaper" (1998, Sleeping Handsome), Michael Ford's *Happily Ever After: Erotic Fairy Tales for Queer Men* (1996), and Peter Cashorali's *Fairy Tales: Traditional Stories Retold for Gay Men* (1995) and *Gay Fairy and Folk Tales* (1997). Some of the retellings mentioned in this chapter add a lesbian dimension to their feminist parody of the traditional fairy tale. Donoghue's *Kissing the Witch* has now become the best-known homosexual collection of fairy tales and continues to generate critical analyses, but several of the themes that she has addressed were already present in the poetry of Olga Broumas (*Beginning with O*, 1977), Anne Sexton ("Rapunzel" 1971), and Suniti Namjoshi (1981).[31]

As Carolina Fernández Rodríguez (2004) argues, retellings such as Broumas's and Namjoshi's "follow the strategies of recent studies in lesbian literary theory" and help break with the compulsory heterosexuality of the fairy tale ("Cuentos"). Similar intertextual relationships exist between queer criticism and retellings as between Lieberman's critical text and feminist revisions: the primary texts can both draw attention to a gap in the traditional fairy tale and attempt to fill it with an alternative. First, examples can be found of metastatements in which the negative influence of traditional fairy tales on the identity construction of the homosexual protagonist is described. "A Moral Tale" (1981) is a short retelling of "Beauty and the Beast" by Suniti Namjoshi that describes the prehistory of the beast. The title may refer to the retelling itself or to the traditional fairy tales that the lesbian protagonist reads: "She became more and more solitary and turned to books. But the books made it clear that men loved women, and women loved men, and men rode off and had all sorts of adventures and women stayed at home. 'I know what is,' she said one day, 'I know what's wrong: I am not human'" (Namjoshi 21). Lieberman argues that fairy tales have shaped generations of women's self-images based on limitations defined by gender. Namjoshi's tale shares the conviction that children's literature has an enormous impact, broadening the limitations under consideration to those of sexual orientation and focusing the scope of the envisaged female readers on lesbians. Her conclusion is extremely pessimistic: the young girl can find no human protagonist to identify with and resigns herself to becoming a beast, who in this version does not transform but dies. The extent to which Namjoshi sees heterosexual expectations as dominant in Western society is reflected in the last sentence, in which the narrator blames the victim: "No one was at fault: she had been warned but she hadn't listened" (21). The text suggests that fairy tales are complicit in this problematic moral; yet in the rest of the volume, the author shows that the fairy-tale retelling can be employed to counter this effect.

Namjoshi's "Thorn Rose" is as an example of a retelling of "Sleeping Beauty" that overtly addresses a gap. In this poem, the pessimistic fate of a lesbian Briar Rose is described: "She clambered to the attic of her own accord, and when she fell asleep, nobody woke her: no women available" (10). When a female rescuer does show up or when sisterhood and lesbian love relationships can be chosen and lived within, as in Broumas's, Donoghue's, and some of Francesca Lia Block's retellings,[32] the effect is portrayed as liberating, an awakening in the most profound sense. These authors reimagine fairy tales and invest them with new desires and happy endings. Donoghue's *Kissing the Witch* offers the most extended and thought-provoking fictional response to the absence of female love in the traditional tales, since her entire collection is built on a chain of women who establish strong friendships or fall in love with each other and who also share stories. As Jennifer Orme argues, "Because of its recursive structure, the proliferation and staged orality of its voices, and its overt representation of multiple types of female desires, *Kissing the Witch* is a particularly complex text to read from any perspective. These traits, as well as its resistance to easy generalizations, make *Kissing the Witch* a particularly apposite text for queer reading."[33] The roles of teller and listener shift with each chapter as each individual retelling functions as a frame tale for the next; at the end of each story, the protagonist asks another character to tell hers, which then becomes embedded. The chronology of the storytelling in *Kissing the Witch* goes against the fictional course in which the events have supposedly taken place: the last tale in the book is the one that happened first and is consequently retold by all the subsequent storytellers, who each adds her own story to the ever-growing tale. Together they form a line of fictional storytellers from various social classes and backgrounds and build a sense of history and community through their stories. Many of the tales portray society's pressure on women, and lesbians especially, to conform to a patriarchal model. When at the end of "The Tale of the Rose," beauty and her female beast have fallen in love, the villagers' ambivalence is included in the final lines: "Some villagers told travellers of a beast and a beauty who lived in the castle and could be seen walking on the battlements, and others told of two beauties, and others, of two beasts" (40). Before Donoghue's Cinderella figure can open up to the love that her fairy godmother has to offer, she first has to silence the voices in her head, who whisper that she is a "lazy heap of dirt" and try to direct her into the more traditional happy ending with the prince (2–4). When the chapters in *Kissing the Witch* are read one after the other, the book also suggests the difficulty of maintaining a female community, as the transitions between the stories imply that no woman's happy ending has seemed to last, even as the exact cause of each disruption is left to the reader's imagination and the storytellers bond again with other female listeners. Orme connects the gaps between Donoghue's stories not only to the characters' lives but also to the act of storytelling: "The passing of story from teller to teller also leaves significant gaps in the characters' lives, thus suggesting that these tales are 'in process' and never entirely closed" (118). She argues convincingly that *Kissing the Witch* represents a double type of queering, in both the book's representation of female desire and its treatment of the fairy-tale pre-text: "It enables queer readings of its intertexts, and realigns reader expectations and assumptions about what it is possible for the fairy tale to do" (Orme 121). Compared to some of the retellings discussed in this chapter, *Kissing the Witch* does not offer a harsh critique of the traditional fairy tale, but it offers an alternative to the genre's limited possibilities for human relationships—a variety that early feminists have not sufficiently paid attention to.

The Dynamics of the Intertextual Dialogue

As Jutta Osinski writes in her introduction to feminist literary criticism, the main goal of the women's movement was to raise consciousness about gender-related issues (41). Marcia K. Lieberman, like several of her contemporaries in the United States and Europe, reacts against the sexist lessons that she believes the best-known fairy tales teach and makes explicit the passive ideology that these stories implicitly transmit. The didactic potential of literature is not questioned as such, and indeed, many feminists have taken advantage of narrative to teach their own lessons. Countless retellings published from the 1970s to the present display a clear thematic overlap with the issues addressed by the emancipation movement and the fairy-tale criticism that can be associated with it. The scope of this intertextual dialogue was extended in this chapter to critical responses to Lieberman's type of criticism, a dialogue in which retellings and critical texts supplement each other again.

When fiction and theory express similar ideas, the possibilities and limits of the two genres come into play. Fiction has certainly helped to make a larger audience familiar with feminist fairy-tale critiques. Whereas Lieberman's article was intended only for adults, feminist retellings exist for children *and* adults and continue to be published to date. On the one hand, this can be explained by the fact that inclusiveness is one of the aims of the equal rights movement and that politically inspired feminist authors wished to reach as large an audience as possible—children as well as adults, academics as well as others. On the other hand, gender role models in Western culture have evolved substantially since the traditional fairy tales were written, and the correction of ideology can be seen as part of a more general updating.

With Hollindale's theory of ideology in literature in mind, one may wonder, however, to what extent fairy-tale retellings can actually succeed in raising awareness about feminist thought. Those retellings that include explicit feminist metacomments run the risk of provoking resistance and associating the ideology that they want to promote with a state that is unnatural and even forced. Some retellings use explicit ideological corrections with exactly this intent, to parody rather than promote the feminist perspective on the fairy tale. This effect is intensified when a fictional character is the narrator. Moreover, retellings that promote their ideology with too much emphasis and clarity have been reproached with compromising their literariness and have been dismissed by reviewers as uninteresting or unjust responses to the traditional fairy tale.

Retellings that leave their ideological corrections more implicit have to rely on the readers' participation to make the intertextual comparison with the fairy-tale pre-text and give meaning to the differences that they can identify. Reader response critics such as Janet Evans and Lawrence R. Sipe believe that young readers, too, can achieve this goal. On the basis of his experiments with primary school children, Sipe (2008) comes to the following conclusion: "The children used intertextual links to interpret personal experiences that had been brought forward during the readaloud; to make symbolic interpretations of elements of the text; to predict what might happen in the narrative; to create and modify their schemata for stories; to interpret story characters' feelings, actions, or motivations; to position themselves outside and above the dynamics of the narrative; to build up and refine their concept of illustration style; and to make chains of other intertextual connections which raised the discussion to a higher cognitive level" (*Storytime* 147).[34]

Although Sipe noticed some resistance with children in kindergarten who had not yet been exposed to many variants of fairy tales, the young readers "quickly moved beyond this type of intertextual resistance" and "modified their internal schema for a story, becoming more flexible and accepting of differences" (*Storytime* 151). A research project in which Sipe had sixth graders read both traditional and transformed tales led him to believe that retellings can perform a function for children that is similar to that of criticism: "Our reading and discussion of these pairs of stories also evoked literary insights that would have been overlooked if the stories had been read singly" ("Transformations" 21). Children who had read the transformed tales started questioning elements in the traditional pre-texts. Raymond Briggs's *Jim and the Beanstalk*, for instance, "provoked reflection about the Jack of the traditional story, who steals from the giant," and Fiona French's *Snow White in New York* made one student remark, "The Snow White in the old story must have been pretty dumb. After she almost got killed the first time, why wasn't she more careful?" (20). As Sipe has demonstrated with his research, the retellings stimulate children to become creative writers as well as emerging critics. In retrospect and in a broader context, critics such as Shawn Jarvis recognize the effectiveness of the feminist fairy-tale retellings of the 1970s: "The work of the past 30 years has indeed created a generation of 'resisting readers'" (159), and some of these have in turn become resisting writers.[35]

A feminist effect cannot always be accomplished, as the antifeminist reactions of Australian preschoolers to *The Paper Bag Princess* illustrate in Bronwyn Davies's research. Yet, in contrast to Altmann (31), I would argue that the fact that the feminist message of the book irritated the children indicates that these tales do have an impact. Even if the young audience was not yet prepared to have its understanding of gender altered by these tales, their irritation shows the acknowledgment of the existence of a different gender pattern. As Wolfgang Iser argues, "One can imagine the case in which a text so massively contradicts the ideas of its reader that it provokes reactions that can range from shutting the book to a readiness to come to a reflective correction of one's own predisposition" (*Appellstruktur* 13; my translation). Indeed, not all texts for children work with models of identification, and readers' predispositions and subsequent responses to a text can change as they age or gain new literary experiences, as Sipe has shown. Moreover, transformations in society may influence a reader's concepts of text and gender. Children at the turn of the twenty-first century, when some of the goals of the emancipation movement are realized, cannot automatically be expected to react in the same way as readers at the time when this movement was at its height.

Nevertheless, David Rudd has argued that even when readers are open to feminist revisions, the didactic impulse in children's literature always runs the risk of being compromised by other meanings: "Because the word is always half someone else's, as Bakhtin notes, the attempt to avoid hybrid contamination is fated: it refuses to mean just what the author intends, 'neither more or less.' This means that, though [Karin] Lesnik-Oberstein rightly points out that children's literature can never escape 'the didactic impulse' [, . . .] neither can the didactic impulse escape this hybrid relation, the excess and play of the signifier, such that an entertaining surplus is ever present" (38). This is true not only of children's books but also of didactic adult literature, which many feminist retellings can be argued to be. The play of the signifier can lead these stories into both feminist and other, even antifeminist, directions and even the simplest retellings carry the potential for contradictory interpretations.

Marxist Retellings

Before we move on to the next chapter, it should be noted that the approach that I have taken to Lieberman's text can also be applied to Marxist retellings. In fact, the emancipation of female characters often goes hand in hand with anticapitalist and antiroyalist messages. Just as retellings can help to recognize and understand gender stereotypes, they can also draw the reader's attention to class differences and muted lower-class voices in the traditional fairy tales. Most notably the tale of "Cinderella," with its themes of social degradation and rags-to-riches, has been a popular pre-text for anticapitalist rewritings. Many Marxist retellings of this story appeared in the 1970s but also beyond. In Fetscher's "Aschenputtels Erwachen," Cinderella goes on strike; in Wim Povel's "De koetsier van Assepoester" (1980, Cinderella's Coachman), the coachman feels exploited for his services; in Kavanagh's "The Ugly Sisters Strike Back" (1991), the stepsisters overthrow the monarchy; and Ellen Jackson (*Cinder Edna*, 1994) vividly pictures the alienation in a marriage that is mainly based on wealth. "Snow White" retellings often focus on similar themes, turning the seven dwarves into a symbol of the working class. Examples include Maher's "Hi Ho, It's Off to Strike We Go!" (1985), Fetscher's "Ur-Schneewittchen," and "Snow White" by the Merseyside Fairy Story Collective (1972). These retellings criticize the idealization of royalty, beauty, and wealth in the traditional fairy tale and invest it with antiauthoritarian messages. The moral of feminist retellings that beauty is only skin-deep finds its equivalent in the idea that riches do not make people happy, as in *Cinder Edna* and Pullman's *I Was a Rat!* The alternative feminist endings equally have a Marxist counterpart: various retellings depict couples who lead a happy life without financial wealth,[36] and in other stories, marriage as the traditional happy ending is replaced by large-scale political changes[37]: democracies replace monarchies; socialism replaces capitalism. These retellings respond to the Marxist critique that traditional tales can never be truly antiauthoritarian because at best they picture the rise of one lucky or cunning individual, never a profound change of the status quo. Yet, as in feminist fairy-tale retellings that strongly promote the correction of gender stereotypes through the method of simple role reversals, the clarity and explicit assertion of ideological visions sometimes come at the expense of literary complexity or intellectual challenge. The emphatic style in which some Marxist retellings are written invites distance from rather than sympathy for the socialist ideology that drives the revisions, and hints of irony make some of the messages of these tales highly ambivalent. Marxist and feminist retellings thus enter the intertextual dialogue with the criticism of the emancipation movement on terms that are determined by their fictionality and multivocality, raising awareness of issues of gender and class but leaving the ultimate interpretation and validation of this knowledge to the reader.

The subversive potential and aesthetic functions of the fairy tale are aspects that early feminists, such as Marcia Lieberman, with their focus on gender representation, insufficiently addressed. The focus text of chapter four, Gilbert and Gubar's palimpsestic reading of "Snow White," takes these functions more into account. Before their *Madwoman in the Attic* appeared, however, another important key text was published that provoked critics, authors, and readers to consider the psychoanalytic perspective on the fairy tale: Bruno Bettelheim's *The Uses of Enchantment*.

3 Bruno Bettelheim's
The Uses of Enchantment

Bruno Bettelheim's international bestseller *The Uses of Enchant-ment: The Meaning and Importance of Fairy Tales* (1976) was without a doubt the most prominent psychoanalytic study of fairy tales of the 1970s. Not only did it dominate the academic discussion of the fairy tale's role in children's development and education (Haase, "Psychology" 407),[1] but it also found a broad appeal outside the university. In 1995, the New York Public Library listed *The Uses of Enchantment* as "one of the 159 most influential and frequently requested 'Books of the Century'" (Pollak 351). Translations of and articles and documentaries on his work helped spread Bettelheim's theories in various European countries.[2] Wilhelm Solms holds Bettelheim responsible for stimulating the German fairy-tale revival (1), and Monika Born highlights his enormous impact on the didactic approach to fairy tales, especially when *The Uses of Enchantment* was issued in a German paperback edition in 1980 (65).

Many critics have tried to explain this lasting success. Horst Künnemann (1978) attributes it to several factors: Bettelheim's rich experience as a psychoanalyst (which was still undisputed in the 1970s),[3] his invitation to adults to reinterpret their previous responses to fairy tales, and his lucid style, which is comprehensible to readers who are not specialists in psychoanalytic theory. All these aspects have helped make the book's content appealing and accessible to a wide audience (147–48). On a more skeptical note, Maria Tatar claims that Bettelheim's theories are so attractive in spite of their flaws because they "capture more accurately than any other volume what our own culture has wanted to find in fairy tales" (*Heads* xvii). *The Uses of Enchantment,* then, is "deeply symptomatic of our own culture's thinking about children" (xxv) in a way that fits the adult's agenda rather than the child's best interest. Nicholas Tucker ("Dr. Bettelheim," 1984) observes that it is quite rare for someone from outside the field to occupy themselves with "the self-referring world of children's literature" (33). As a result, Tucker argues, these critics often bring new perspectives that have a large impact (33), which is certainly true for Bettelheim.

Not only did Bettelheim have an influence on the study of fairy tales, but his ideas also surface in fairy-tale retellings—although the possessive pronoun should be taken with some reservation, since many of Bettelheim's views were shared by contemporaneous psychoanalyst critics and he has been accused of plagiarizing the work of his predecessors. However, none of these critics has gained the international appeal that Bettelheim had, and according to Pfister's criterion of "communicativity," this canonical status raises the possibility of intertextual density and makes his text a more suitable starting point for comparison.

Fairy Tales as Therapy and Access to the Unconscious

In the introductory chapter to *The Uses of Enchantment,* Bettelheim explains the fairy tale's therapeutic function and more general importance in children's education, an argument that he then applies in a dozen more elaborate neo-Freudian analyses of individual fairy tales.[4] By addressing the unconscious of children in a symbolical language that is similar to dreams, fairy tales help the young deal with unspoken fears and desires, such as sibling rivalry and oedipal conflicts ("Beauty and the Beast"), ambivalent feelings toward their parents ("Snow White" and "Cinderella"), and oral regression ("Hansel and Gretel").[5] The reason fairy tales have such a unique healing and liberating power—according to Bettelheim, in contrast with more contemporary children's literature—has to do with their long oral tradition: "Through the centuries (if not millennia) during which, in their retelling, fairy tales became ever more refined, they came to convey at the same time overt and covert meanings—to speak simultaneously to all levels of the human personality, communicating in a manner which reaches the uneducated mind of the child as well as that of the sophisticated adult" (5–6). The tales crystallize, as it were, the knowledge and wisdom of the many generations of tellers who have passed them on. Essential for its therapeutic effect is the fairy tale's optimism. The good, often children and underdogs, are rewarded; the bad cruelly punished.[6] According to Bettelheim, children identify with the protagonist of the tale and feel relieved and reassured that their problems can be overcome likewise. At the end of their oedipal conflicts lies the promise of self-realization (39). Bettelheim projects this model of identification onto both the child's conscious and unconscious and argues that the fairy tale "offers meaning on so many different levels" (12).

That Bettelheim's popularity has led to an increase in the production of traditional fairy-tale collections, especially the Grimms', seems logical: he strongly argues for their inclusion in every child's education. Many parents felt their love of fairy tales to be affirmed and reinforced by Bettelheim, who reassured them that these often gruesome stories were indeed "good for their children" (Pollak 351). It is, however, paradoxical that Bettelheim's theories have also influenced revisions of the Grimms' tales. On the one hand, the fact that late twentieth-century authors and illustrators incorporate his explanations of the underlying meanings and symbols of individual tales attests to the great influence of *The Uses of Enchantment*. However, authors who revise, explain, or update the tales, as well as illustrators who visualize them, violate two of Bettelheim's central premises: first, that the therapeutic effect of the fairy tale only works if the story is presented in its original form, which Bettelheim usually equates with the Grimms' version of 1857; and second, that the child is capable of spontaneously grasping the deeper meaning of the tales on an unconscious level. As Hamida Bosmajian has noted, "While psychoanalyst critics of adult literature amplify the reader's appreciation of the text, those same critics will, in the case of children's literature, conceal their interpretation from the child" (129).

Indeed Bettelheim stresses that any additions (verbal or visual), alterations, or explanations can only hamper the child's unmediated understanding (18–19). His "noninterventionist policy" (Tatar, *Heads* 77), which affects not only illustrators but also parents, teachers, and contemporary authors, contrasts with the feminist approach that Marcia K. Lieberman represented in the previous chapter. Intervention in the form of revision or explicit contextualization was deemed desirable and was often explicitly encouraged by feminist critics.

Since 1976 and in spite of Bettelheim's advice to leave the Grimms' tales intact, his ideas and interpretations have penetrated into the imagination of several authors and illustrators, who have adapted the stories accordingly.[7] Not all the intertextual connections can be attributed to a direct influence. As explained above, psychoanalytic views on the fairy tale were circulating long before *The Uses of Enchantment* was published, and when some of Bettelheim's ideas entered pop psychology, they often did so in isolation from the whole theoretical framework that he had developed. Moreover, as I argued that fairy-tale retellings that can be intertextually linked to Lieberman not only display but also transform feminist critiques, there is a similar dialogicity in the relationship between retellings, illustrations, and psychoanalytic theory. In the revised tales, convergences with *The Uses of Enchantment* are supplemented with divergences and critiques.

The parallel that Tatar draws between *The Uses of Enchantment* and the work of the American illustrator Maurice Sendak can be expanded to include many contemporary children's books: both Bettelheim and Sendak consider stories "a therapeutic form of play" and deplore "the fallacy of innocence that informs children's literature" (Tatar, "Sendak" 209). Both Bettelheim and Sendak "argue for the instrumentalization of fantasy (whether in adventure books or in fairy tales) even as they deplore children's literature that takes an explicitly didactic turn. [. . . Stories] must never put those lessons into words" (211). The same implicit assumptions also inform many contemporary fairy-tale retellings (for children as well as for adults). In addition, Bettelheim's views and interpretations surface in contemporary literature on more concrete levels: in the prefaces of fairy-tale collections,[8] in stories about children who respond to fairy tales, and in the illustrations that accompany traditional fairy tales. Three aspects of Bettelheim's theories will form the starting point of my comparison. First, I will focus on the belief in the therapeutic function of the fairy tale and the access to the unconscious that it provides. I will then move on to discuss two concrete dream mechanisms that Bettelheim sees at work in the fairy tale—the first is the condensation of characters and places, the second is the resexualization of the fairy tale, which undoes the former repression of sexual elements.

The main hypothesis that lies at the base of *The Uses of Enchantment* is that fairy tales have a therapeutic effect on children—an idea that the German and Dutch translations, *Kinder brauchen Märchen* (Children Need Fairy Tales) and *Het nut van sprookjes* (The Usefulness of Fairy Tales), make explicit in their titles. This assertion has been both reinforced and contradicted in late twentieth-century fairy-tale retellings. The possibilities for a retelling that in no way conflicts with Bettelheim's theory are rather limited. Bettelheim's imperative that only the "original" form of the fairy tale has a therapeutic effect means that all other children's literature cannot aspire to the same impact. Retellings and illustrated fairy tales for children violate the noninterventionist policy. Alan Dundes finds that "Bettelheim's insistence that fairy tales can serve children's emotional growth only if their unconscious, latent content is not revealed [is] somewhat strange" and argues therefore that psychoanalytic interpretations should also be made accessible for children: "One could just as well argue, I should think, that fairy tales ought to be explained to children so that the underlying emotional traumas with which they deal may be less threatening" ("Folklore" 24). Whereas Bettelheim argues that the therapeutic effect of the fairy tale can only work on an unconscious level, Dundes claims that children, like adult patients, should gain conscious insight into the latent content of the tales. In order for such explanations to conform to the codes and conventions of contemporary children's literature, this would require a substantial adaptation of Bettelheim's ideas—an adaptation, it should be noted, that has also taken place in popular psychology. The fairy-tale retellings and illustrations that are discussed in this chapter can be said to solve the dilemma: they offer suggestions for a Bettelheimian interpretation without making them as explicit to the (young) reader as a psychoanalytic study would.

An exception is Paul Biegel's introduction to *Wie je droomt ben je zelf* (You Are What You Dream), the gift book for the Dutch children's book week of 1977. It is one of the most explicit reformulations of psychoanalytic fairy-tale theory intended for children that I have come across. Biegel explains the importance of dreams to his young audience with a clear influence from Freudian ideas, adapting the register and technical terms:

> Dreams happen in your innermost self. That is the place where you feel something without being able to say where it is: happiness, sadness, anxiety, fear. [. . .] Your innermost self is full. There is much more there than what comes out: memories and fantasy images and longings that somehow remain hidden and that you don't know yourself. But every once in a while something comes up; then you know all of sudden what you didn't know before. If you dream, something from inside of you also comes up. Sometimes exactly those things that are hidden. But they don't come openly; they dress up and perform a story like a play. (5–6; my translation)

At the end of the fragment Biegel makes the link between dreams and stories: both contain elements from the unconscious that take the form of characters that act out a plot. Later in his introduction, Biegel makes this thought explicit in an explanation that can be described as "Bettelheim for kids": "Fantasy stories and fairy tales, just like dreams, come from your innermost self. In those stories too, things are dressed up" (7; my translation). Further, Biegel encourages children to play psychoanalyst for themselves: "There is another meaning behind the story. You can try to understand fairy tales the way you can also try to understand a dream, to find out what really lives inside of people, and thus yourself" (8; my translation). Although Biegel is still rather vague about what those "things" could be, he does make the therapeutic function of fairy tales explicit. Moreover, in a self-reflexive passage, he explains to readers how his retelling in particular can help them explore the unconscious messages in the text:

> The story in this book is not new. When you start reading it or look at the pictures, you will think: I already know that. But that is intentional, because if you didn't know the story well, you wouldn't recognize that the narrator has taken something from its deepest inside and brought it up: the wolf. The wolf that you are so afraid of, that you run away from, that is not a wolf in the forest. It is something inside of you, dressed up like a wolf. That's what this story is about: what you dream is what you are. (8–9; my translation)

Biegel is an exception when it comes to making explicit this function of the fairy-tale retelling with regard to psychoanalytic theory, and he openly rephrases assumptions that may also lie at the heart of such retellings as Anthony Browne's *The Tunnel* and Gillian Cross's *Wolf*. He sees the fairy-tale retelling as a means for children to explore their unconscious ("inner-most self") as well as the unconscious elements in the fairy tales they like to read. Note that Biegel equates the two: he shifts from the unconscious of the story (what is "deep inside" the story) to the unconscious of the child. "What you dream is what you are" is his motto and the title of the book, but it could just as well be "What you read is what you are."

Biegel considers the fairy-tale retelling particularly suitable as a tool for beginning psychoanalytic analysis of the self and the literary text. As children already know fairy tales, they are able to compare and discover what is hidden in the unconscious of the text—or rather what the writer of the retelling believes lies hidden there and brings back up. Does Biegel then, as Dundes has suggested that adults should, provide children with insight into the unconscious meanings of the fairy tale? His explanations in the introduction are still rather vague. Although he suggests that fairy-tale elements represent something from the unconscious, that there is a latent content ("dressed up") behind the manifest content, Biegel, in contrast to Bettelheim, does not give precise explanations of what that latent content may be. The wolf, for instance, is not just an element that springs up from the unconscious; it is also clearly present in the overt content of the tale. Moreover, Biegel only interprets the wolf as a symbol of fear and horror, and this hardly needs to be explained—that the wolf causes fear is also present in the overt content of the traditional "Little Red Riding Hood." No further details on the possible unconscious cause for this anxiety are mentioned in Biegel's introduction, as they are in Bettelheim's interpretation. Moreover, the new meanings that are given to the characters in the retelling itself are complex and allow several interpretations, as we will see below.

Reader Response in Realistic Fiction

Both in children's books and in adult literature, examples can be found of children who respond positively to fairy tales, who use fairy tales to explore their unconscious, or who find healing with the help of fairy tales. One of the topics Bettelheim most frequently addresses in *The Uses of Enchantment* is sibling rivalry, which he claims is central to many fairy tales and children's lives. Anthony Browne's *The Tunnel* describes the difficult relationship between a brother and sister who are complete opposites. Although the book begins like a fairy tale ("Once upon a time there lived a sister and a brother"), the illustrations set the story in a late twentieth-century urban environment. The focalization of the narration shifts between the children in the beginning but then resides with the sister. She likes books and appears to enjoy fairy tales in particular: the pictures show her reading illustrated versions of "Hansel and Gretel," "Little Red Riding Hood," "Jack and the Beanstalk," and "Cinderella." Her bedside lamp has the shape of a gingerbread cottage, and her bedroom wall is decorated with a reproduction of Walter Crane's "Little Red Riding Hood" (Figure 4). Her red cloak is reminiscent of Red Riding Hood's, and when her brother wants to scare her at night, he chooses a fairy-tale character for his mask: a wolf.

Forced by their mother to go outside and play together, the brother and sister come across a tunnel—like the rabbit hole in *Alice in Wonderland*, one of the typical psychoanalytic symbols of an entrance into the human unconscious. The difference is of course, that Lewis Carroll wrote *Alice in Wonderland* before Freud's *Traumdeutung* (*The Interpretation of Dreams*) had appeared, whereas *The Tunnel* appears at a time when psychoanalytic theory is long known. This opens up the possibility that Browne uses psychoanalytic theory deliberately. After the appearance of the tunnel, the reader's knowledge is limited to the sister's point of view: she is afraid and stays behind as her brother enters the tunnel. When she does eventually follow him, she finds a space that looks like a surreal fairy-tale forest. Hidden behind or between the trees are wolves, Little Red Riding Hood's basket, Sleeping Beauty's staircase, Hansel and Gretel's bonfire, and a small cottage. The fairy-tale forest is a well-known psychoanalytic symbol for "the dark, hidden, near-impenetrable world of our unconscious" (Bettelheim 94). That one of the wolves strongly resembles the Walter Crane illustration in the sister's bedroom suggests that the forest represents her unconscious, in which fairy-tale and real-life elements appear as a "*Tagesrest*" (day's residue) with which the girl still needs to come to terms (Figures 4 and 5). The same is true for the witch's cottage in "Hansel and Gretel" that appears both in the sister's fairy-tale collection and in the forest.

Browne's story and illustrations affirm Bettelheim's claims that fairy tales provide the child with a place to explore the unconscious, that the stories themselves enter the child's unconscious, and that they help the child to

Figure 4. The Tunnel *by Anthony Browne.*

overcome irrational fears and other problems, such as sibling rivalry. Bettelheim argues that fairy tales offer children reassuring images of how they can overcome their own fears and conflicts (39). *The Tunnel* supports this claim when the sister finds inspiration in a fairy tale to save her brother. The scenes in which he has become a stone statue and she hugs him back to life are reminiscent of "The Snow Queen," according to Bettelheim one of the few stories by Hans Christian Andersen that "comes quite close to being a true fairy tale" (37). Browne's text echoes the passage in Andersen that describes little Gerda bringing Kay back to life after he has been turned to ice:

> She threw her arms around the cold hard form, and wept.
> Very slowly, the figure began to change colour, becoming softer and warmer.

Figure 5. The Tunnel *by Anthony Browne.*

Then, little by little, it began to move. Her brother was there. (Browne)

She knew him directly; she flew to him and threw her arms round his neck, and held him fast, while she exclaimed, "Kay, dear little Kay, I have found you at last."
But he sat quite still, stiff and cold.
Then little Gerda wept hot tears, which fell on his breast, and penetrated into his heart, and thawed the lump of ice, and washed away the little piece of glass which had stuck there. (Andersen)

Browne's use of intertextuality corroborates Bettelheim's claim that the fairy tale offers solutions for overcoming fears and conflicts. By imitating Gerda's gesture, the sister manages to bring her brother back to life with her love and tears. The therapeutic effect can also be felt in real life: when brother and sister leave the forest, they have become friends. Interestingly, it is unclear how they leave the forest. Do they return through the tunnel?

Do they simply walk out of it? Or do they just need to wake up? As in Browne's *Hansel and Gretel*, the various images of sleeping children in *The Tunnel* leave the possibility that the forest scenes take place in a dream. Whether something has changed in reality at the end of the book or whether that closure too needs to be situated in the surreal dream world, is unclear.

Browne makes use of fairy tale allusions in quite a different way in the more recent *Into the Forest* (2004). This picture book contains several inter-visual references to Browne's previous fairy-tale illustrations as well as to some of his other work. The young male protagonist of *Into the Forest*, like the sister from *The Tunnel*, experiences great fear on his path through the woods, and once again the forest contains many hidden objects from fairy tales. In this book, however, the fairy tale seems to instill horror without bringing a model for resolution—at best it leads to comic relief. When the fearful boy enters his grandmother's house in a passage that echoes the parallel scene in "Little Red Riding Hood," he does not find the wolf, but only his grandmother. This surprising twist implies a parody of fairy-tale conventions, as well as of Bettelheim's positive evaluation of those conventions: the fairy tale is blamed for unnecessarily raising anxiety in children, and the knowledge that it offers is not applicable in a real-life context. For Browne, as for many critics of the twenty-first century, the positive impact of psychoanalysis as a model for interpreting fairy tales seems to have passed and made way for a playful parody of its premises.

Such a complex dialogue with psychoanalytic fairy-tale theory also takes place in Gillian Cross's *Wolf* (1990), one of the most acclaimed fairy-tale retellings in British young adult fiction. That Cross's rewriting of "Little Red Riding Hood" displays a high awareness of psychoanalysis becomes clear in the opening phrase: "Of course Cassy never dreams, Nan always said. She has more sense, to be sure. Her head touches the pillow and she's off, just like any other sensible person. There's been no trouble with dreams, not since she was a baby." Although this quotation seems to argue against the importance that psychoanalysis attaches to dreams, the novel will soon prove Nan wrong.[9] Cassy, the protagonist, has dreams every night in which she deals with her anxieties and repressed memories. Christine Wilkie-Stibbs argues that Cassy as a dreaming subject thus "occup[ies] a position analogous to the analysand in analysis," and in her dreams effects "a transition in the transference of latent unconscious contents that is [her] moment of cure." Moreover, "through their acts of dreaming, the narratives themselves subscribe to the structures of the dream as described by Freud and inscribe Cassy [. . . as . . .] the decentered subject of conscious and unconscious contents." Wilkie-Stibbs therefore reads *Wolf*, together with two other young adult novels, as "paradigmatic narratives that lay bare in their textuality Freud's and Lacan's theories of dreaming and the closely related phenomena of memory" (*Feminine Subject* 145). When we take into consideration that *Wolf* makes ample use of fairy-tale references, Bettelheim's views appear as a relevant theoretical framework as well.

As Bettelheim argues that fairy tales can provide the child with a means to access the unconscious without being overwhelmed by it, the dreams in which Cassy incorporates fairy-tale material disturb her at first but are suggested to have an ultimately therapeutic effect: her dreams give her access to her preconscious, latent memories, and repressed fears.[10] They do so in the form of fairy tales and thus affirm Freud's assertion that, for some people, the memory of their favorite fairy tale has replaced their own childhood memories ("Märchenstoffe" 49).[11] Although "Little Red Riding Hood" does not appear in the text as Cassy's favorite fairy tale, it is through this story that she deals with the fear of her father. Her dreams contain elements and quotations from the tale that mingle with what Cassy remembers about her father, an Irish Republican Army terrorist whom she has not been allowed to see or talk about since she was two years old. The intertextual connection with "Little Red Riding Hood" is further maintained in the level of the story that takes place in the fictional reality (London in the 1980s). Cassy makes the opposite journey that Little Red Riding Hood undertakes: she leaves her grandmother, Nan, to stay with her mother, Goldie. This move also implies that she trades a structured and balanced life for one of chaos and, at first sight, danger. Goldie, her new boyfriend, and his son are squatters in an old abandoned house. Their behavior is unpredictable and in Cassy's perception often irresponsible.[12] She has difficulty adapting to her mother's household and is constantly disturbed by inexplicable anxieties. It is only when Cassy is able to draw the link between her own life experiences and her dreams, loaded with references to "Little Red Riding Hood," that she gains insight into her past and present and realizes where the real danger lies. The fairy tale offers Cassy a framework in which to deal with her suppressed fears and provides an added layer of symbolism that prevents the confrontation from becoming too direct.

Although Cassy's fears are not mainly sexual in nature, as in most psychoanalytic analyses of "Little Red Riding Hood," they are closely linked to family ties and the relationship with her father. Wilkie-Stibbs draws persuasive intertextual parallels between *Wolf* and Freud's case of the Wolf-Man (1914) and suggests an "intentional association" by Cross as well as by the dust jacket illustrator of the Puffin edition. In Freud's analysis, the nightmares that his patient had about a group of white wolves were caused by an oedipal fear of the father (*Kinderneurosen* 159). It may seem that Wilkie-Stibbs ignores Cassy's gender when she consequently situates Cassy's fear of the father in an Oedipus complex, but she argues convincingly that Cross similarly conflates people of different gender (as do the Wolf-Man and Bettelheim). For instance, Cassy's father and her grandmother both function as representations of the Law of the Father in Wilkie-Stibbs's Lacanian analysis of the novel. At least in one passage, Wilkie-Stibbs points out that this Oedipus complex is expressed in terms of sexual desire: Cassy's third dream contains several phallic symbols, references to pubic hair, and an invitation to play a game that can be read as a seduction (*Feminine Subject* 157–61). That Cassy's longing for her father is triggered when she is a teenager corresponds to Bettelheim's view of "Little Red Riding Hood" as the reactivation of oedipal feelings in puberty (175). In the final meeting with the wolf in the grandmother's house, in many versions the most sexually loaded scene of the story, another phallic symbol turns up when Cassy's father is described as playing with his gun (*Feminine Subject* 161): "His [hands] were fidgeting with the gun on his knees, stroking the trigger and moving up and down the dark barrel. Cassy looked down at the thin metal tube at the end, pointing at her chest" (Cross 176). In a novel so loaded with psychoanalytic references, this scene carries strong sexual connotations. The symbolic inclusion of dangerous, oedipal sexuality that Bettelheim and Freud have identified in "Little Red Riding Hood" and the figure of the wolf is thus highlighted by the added allusions in Cross's retelling of the tale.

Like Freud and Bettelheim, Cross addresses the possibly dramatic consequences of repressing disturbing memories and desires. Comparable to the function of the ego in Freudian theory, Cassy needs to find a balance between her superego and her id. Her superego seems to speak through Nan, who tries to bring structure and neatness into her life. The main elements that disturb the order that Cassy and Nan try to create are Cassy's dreams, the memories of her father, and the inhabitants of Goldie's squat. Her grandmother sees Goldie as the most important threat: *"Goldie's all right as long as she doesn't get excited,* Nan said. *As long as she's calm, she's quite good at doing what you tell her"* (41). Cassy (the ego) has internalized Nan's voice, as if it is her own conscience speaking. Some of the sentences that are marked in italics, representing Nan, surface unmarked in Cassy's mind at some other point, indicating that she considers them to be her own. When she thinks that "the best remedy for peculiar feelings was to be up and doing," a few paragraphs later, the reader can deduce that this is a piece of advice from Nan that Cassy has internalized: "Nan's voice seemed to be ringing in her ears. *Up and doing. You don't want to waste time mooning about"* (45).

As the narrative proceeds, Cassy learns that she cannot avoid the memories and fears of her past and that it is necessary and liberating to let them disturb Nan's artificial order from time to time. Her fear of the wolf, which is linked to her fear of her father, is brought to a climax during a performance about wolves. This show is organized by Lyall, her mother's boyfriend, and he pressures Cassy to take part. The limit of her repression is reached when the performance addresses the topic of the werewolf, the figure that unites wolf and man. Cassy ventilates her fear and panic with a primal scream: "She couldn't shut it out any longer. Couldn't fight off her terror by pretending to be practical and calm and realistic. The darkness inside her head was real, swelling larger and larger, choking her as it blotted out her small, comfortable world. It was her own voice screaming" (Cross 167). Cross modifies the expectations that she had first raised about the unconscious, showing that what has the external appearance of chaos can actually be safer than the pretence of order and structure. Nan's "neat, white false teeth" (180) can be read as a symbol of her deceptive order, as is Cassy's father's neurotic habit of arranging everything in symmetric piles and rows. Nan's strategy of repression and denial is revealed as the most dangerous, her ideals of tidiness and structure turn out to be illusions. Whereas for Bettelheim the fairy tale can appease the child's unconscious, in *Wolf* the tale of "Little Red Riding Hood" at first causes anxiety but then helps bring Cassy to the confrontation with her id that is inevitable and, at the end of the story, appeasing in its own right. How the ending of Cross's novel can be read to affirm and contradict Bettelheim's reassurance will be further discussed in the final section of this chapter.

The Tunnel and *Wolf* are both aimed at young readers. The therapeutic function of fairy tales is also thematized in several short stories, poems, and novels for adults that address a child's reaction to fairy tales. In Jill McCorkle's "Sleeping Beauty, Revised" (1992), the first-person narrator is a recently divorced mother who has a first date. References to the fairy tale here occur on several levels. They apply to the mother's own situation, where they are used ironically. Her practical problems and cynical tone defy the happy ending and sweet romance that the fairy tale has to offer. Her son Jeffrey, by contrast, uses the fairy tale in play to deal with his parents' divorce and his own ensuing anxieties. As the mother explains, "I always get the sinister roles: witches and ogres and evil stepmothers. I give Snow White the poisoned apple and I make Sleeping Beauty touch the spindle and I talk Pinocchio out of going to school. I indulge my child's fantasy life despite the recent comments I've received about how this might not be healthy. My aunt Leonora has suggested that this is how he's (she leans close to whisper) *dealing with divorce*, these *violent* games" (199).

Although the mother at first seems to accept her part in her son's games out of passivity rather than from a true belief in their therapeutic effect, the fairy tale does function as a frame of reference through which she and her son can communicate. If she plays the role of the ogre, the wicked witch, and the sly cat and fox, it is suggested that Jeffrey enacts the roles of Jack, Snow White, Sleeping Beauty, and Pinocchio. The fairy tale gives the child an excuse to channel his feelings of hurt and blame in an innocent way: "'You be the giant,' Jeffrey says, a rolled-up newspaper in his hand. 'I'm gonna knock you out and steal the golden chicken'" (McCorkle 198). Bettelheim argues that it is liberating for a child when the villain in the fairy tale is punished as cruelly as possible. The child strongly identifies with the protagonist of the tale, not with the villains: "Adults often think that the cruel punishment of an evil person in fairy tales upsets and scares children unnecessarily. Quite the opposite is true: such retribution reassures the child that the punishment fits the crime. The child often feels unjustly treated by adults and the world in general, and it seems that nothing is done about it. On the basis of such experiences alone, he wants those who cheat and degrade him [. . .] most severely punished" (Bettelheim 141).

Bettelheim praises the Brothers Grimm for including harsh punishments, and Jeffrey too shows his delight in the enactment of the gruesome endings. In his game, Captain Hook, here played by his mother, is devoured by the crocodile. He also likes to act out the grim finale of "Hansel and Gretel": "Phil [the mother's date] is talking about Hansel and Gretel and the way Jeffrey has delivered it, the mean ugly witch pushed into the oven and gassed, charred to a crisp. I don't tell how many times in the past week I've sat in the pantry, cackling and then screaming at the victorious Hansel" (McCorkle 202). In order for the fairy tale to fit his personal needs, Jeffrey adapts its content to enhance identification. In the traditional "Hansel and Gretel," it is not Hansel but Gretel who pushes the witch in the oven.

That the fairy tale gives Jeffrey a harmless excuse to deal with his repressed anger is supported by the mother's apologetic comment: "It's the same old story" (202). No realistic story could give the child such a therapeutic cover for safely acting out his anger, Bettelheim argues,

> Revenge fantasies are something every child entertains at this time in life [when the child moves out of the oedipal stage], but in his more lucid moments he recognizes them as extremely unfair, since he knows that the parent provides him with all he needs to survive, and works hard to do so. [. . .] There is no need for the child to repress such fantasies; on the contrary, he can enjoy them to the fullest, if he is subtly guided to direct them to a target which is close enough to the true parent but clearly not his parent. (133–34)

Bettelheim suggests that the fairy tale provides the child with a stepparent as the perfect figure on whom to act out these revenge fantasies without creating feelings of guilt. In Jeffrey's games, the parental substitute approaches once again the real parent, as it is his mother who performs the role of the wicked witch. It is mainly the pretence of the play that creates distance from their situation in real life. Phil, the mother's date, is disturbed by the tales and prefers versions in which the villains are redeemed. As examples, Phil and the narrator mention the evil witch from "Hansel and Gretel," who joins a support group, and the queen in "Snow White," who becomes "a nice grandmotherly type" (McCorkle 206). In contrast, the mother, like a true follower of Bettelheim, recognizes the function of the cruelty in the tales and argues against such retellings: "I begin telling him about taking Jeffrey to see a little production of 'Jack and the Beanstalk,' where the story was not even recognizable. The giant, instead of falling to his death, climbs from the beanstalk and upon reaching the bottom is struck with amnesia and becomes a big-time land developer whereas poor Jack the hero fights the infiltration of shopping malls. I had taken Jeffrey straight home and read him the *real* version. Then we spent the rest of the evening with me falling to my earth-shattering death from the cedar chest" (McCorkle 203).

Whether Jeffrey assigns his mother the role of villain or whether she assumes it actively is not spelled out. Yet, at this point in the story, the enactment of fairy tales seems to have become more than just a habit to which the mother passively resigns herself. Whereas at the beginning she still claimed that "it's the same old story," the title "Sleeping Beauty, Revised" suggests the opposite: it is *not* the same old story. As the mother seems to realize that the fairy-tale play holds the key to restoring the relationship with her son, her role as a Sleeping Beauty is also transformed to become more conscious and active. The comments on her support to the *real* version seem ironic in this sense, since they are presented in a text that is itself a retelling in which the pre-text of "Sleeping Beauty" is barely recognizable.

Although Bettelheim stresses the importance of fairy tales for the child, McCorkle's short story shows that they can equally have a therapeutic effect for adults. The games that Jeffrey and his mother play are also her way of dealing with her own guilt and "fears about having done (or doing) *irreparable damage to a young psyche*" (212). The boy's scenarios are a demonstration not only of anger but also of love: "His trust in me is complete. If it weren't, he'd never give me the *bad* parts to act out. And what's wrong with acting out the bad parts? What's wrong with Jack getting rid of the giant? And why shouldn't Hansel and Gretel kill the witch in self-defense. Hooray for Dorothy, the wicked witch is dead. Then you just turn the page and start all over" (213). As Simon A. Grolnick argues, Bettelheim should be praised for his recognition of the fairy tale's function in the interaction between parent and child: "It is when empathy is missing and parental inconsistency and trauma are too prevalent that the fairy tale can become an instrument of fear" (210). In McCorkle's story, in contrast, the fairy tale and its enactment in play provide a safe place in which the mother and her son can deal with their suppressed feelings of blame and guilt, love and anger. Bettelheim does warn against this: "A parent not attuned to his child, or too beholden to what goes on in his own unconscious, may choose to tell fairy tales on the basis of *his* needs—rather than those of the child" (151). But he also sees the benefit: it will help the child to understand his parent better. That the fairy-tale therapy works for Jeffrey and his mother is affirmed in the last paragraphs of the story. When they have returned home after the failed date—Phil ends up flirting with a waitress—Jeffrey tells his mother another story. He chooses a scary tale, which gives him an excuse to seek physical contact and comfort with his mother, who closes her eyes and hugs him tight (McCorkle 214). The fairy tale in "Sleeping Beauty, Revised" thus provides a way for mother and son to not just communicate their anger and disappointment but also express their need for affection.

Dream Mechanisms in Fairy-Tale Illustration

Not only have several retellings addressed the therapeutic function of the fairy tale, but contemporary authors and illustrators also enter into an inter-textual dialogue with another aspect of psychoanalytic theory: its consideration of literary strategies that function as dream mechanisms in the traditional fairy tale and transform the perturbing latent content into acceptable manifest content. In several of his interpretations, Bettelheim analyzes two or more different characters as the child's projections of one and the same person. This fits in with the neo-Freudian approach that Bettelheim uses to analyze the Grimms' tales: the split of characters and spaces is a reversal of Freud's dream mechanism of condensation.[13] The best-known example is provided by Snow White's mother and stepmother, whom Bettelheim sees not as different characters in essence but as the two projected images that the child has of its mother: "Although Mother is most often the all-giving protector, she can change into the cruel stepmother if she is so evil as to deny the youngster something he wants. Far from being a device used only by fairy tales, such a splitting up of one person into two to keep the good image uncontaminated occurs to many children as a solution to a relationship too difficult to manage or comprehend. With this device all contradictions are suddenly solved" (67). The stepmother is thus a construction of the young child that functions as a scapegoat: it takes on all the bad traits of the biological mother so that the latter can remain an entirely positive image. Other examples of such split projections abound in Bettelheim's interpretations—most siblings in fairy tales are interpreted as the different aspects of one and the same child (in tales such as "The Two Brothers," "Brother and Sister," and "Hansel and Gretel"). In his analyses, Bettelheim undoes this split and refocuses the two projected images onto one single underlying meaning.

Fairy-tale illustrations and retellings for children and adults can similarly draw connections between characters or objects that Bettelheim considers split surface images of one aspect in the latent content. Rachel Freudenburg, for example, found that Bettelheim's theory is incorporated in several picture books of the post-1970s (307). This is paradoxical, because Bettelheim notoriously opposed fairy-tale illustrations, which he thought would interfere with the child's unconscious understanding of the story: "Illustrated storybooks, so much preferred by both modern adults and children, do not serve the child's best needs" (59). He argues that "the illustrations direct the child's imagination away from how he, on his own, would experience the story. The illustrated story is robbed of much content of personal meaning which it could bring to the child who applied only his own visual associations to the story, instead of those of the illustrator" (60). Some illustrators have avoided this paradox by resorting to abstract imagery rather than detailed or realistic pictures. As examples of such visualizations Sandra Beckett mentions Warja Lavater's *Le Petit Chaperon rouge* (1965, Little Red Riding Hood) and Jean Ache's *Le Monde des ronds et des carrés* (1975, The World of Circles and Squares). Although the former was published more than ten years before *The Uses of Enchantment*, Beckett links the two in her study. Lavater's visual coding, in which the characters are represented by colored dots and lines, "address[es], at least in part, Bruno Bettelheim's concern that the illustration of fairy tales robs the story of much of the personal significance" (Beckett, *Recycling* 57).

In children's literature studies, the enriching power of illustrations has been stressed on countless occasions. Pictures, including those in fairy-tale collections, are deemed to stimulate rather than limit the child's imagination. David Lewis writes, "The presence of pictures appears to loosen generic constraints and open up the text to alternative ways of looking and thinking" (66). Psychoanalysis, as one of the most popular theoretical approaches to the fairy tale, has occasionally inspired these new ways of looking, and examples can be found of illustrations that display intertextual connections with Bettelheim's interpretations. The equating of several characters, for instance, is a principle of Bettelheim's that can be found in several illustrated versions of fairy tales. Anthony Browne's *Hansel and Gretel* (Grimm, *Hansel and Gretel*) is the best-known example.

Bettelheim's view of the mother and stepmother as two appearances of one and the same person who alternates for the child between good and bad also applies to the stepmother and the witch in "Hansel and Gretel." This tale, according to Bettelheim, describes the frustrations of the very young:

> This is how the child feels when devastated by the ambivalent feelings, frustrations, and anxieties at the oedipal stage of development, as well as his previous disappointment and rage at failures on his mother's part to gratify his needs and desires as fully as he expected. Severely upset that Mother no longer serves him unquestioningly but makes demands on him and devotes herself ever more to her own interests—something which the child had not permitted to come to his awareness before—he imagines that Mother, as she nursed him and created a world of bliss, did only so to fool him—like the witch of the story. (163)

Similarly, Bettelheim equates the children's home with the gingerbread house as two manifestations of the same latent content: "After they have become familiar with 'Hansel and Gretel,' most children comprehend, at least unconsciously, that what happens in the parental home and at the witch's house are but separate aspects of what in reality is one total experience. [. . .] Thus, the parental home 'hard by a great forest' and the fateful house in the depths of the same woods are on an unconscious level but the two aspects of the parental home: the gratifying one and the frustrating one" (163).

In his illustrations, Browne draws a similar, this time visual, parallel between Hansel and Gretel's home and the witch's house (Figures 6 and 7). The shape of the two roofs is similar, and the two houses have a chimney on the left and a bird in the middle of the roof. That one of these birds is black and the other white, as if one is the shadow of the other, testifies to a Jungian influence that is also present in Bettelheim's view of split projections. Both the parental home and the gingerbread cottage stand in front of a group of trees. To the left of each house is a smaller building: in the case of the parental home this is a small shed, and in the case of the gingerbread house it is an unspecified building that looks like a loaf of bread. It seems to have no other function than to support the parallel with the parental home. Not only are the external characteristics of the houses similar, but parallels can also be drawn between objects within the parental home and the

Figure 6. Hansel and Gretel *by Anthony Browne*.

gingerbread cottage. The wardrobe in Hansel and Gretel's home has the same multiple frames as the oven in the witch's, and the two large objects are pictured from an analogous perspective. That the same black hat can be seen standing above the wardrobe and the oven strengthens the link. The broomstick that is pictured next to the oven can be discerned in the children's living room, slightly obscured from view by a chair that Hansel sits on.

The differences between the two houses in the traditional tale can be explained, according to Bettelheim, by the children's changed perception: the parents' house as the dreary reality, the gingerbread cottage as the (treacherous) fulfillment of the children's fantasy. This is supported by the subtle difference in artistic styles that Browne uses to visualize the two houses: whereas the parental home is drawn in a realistic and detailed style, the gingerbread house looks fuzzier and is reminiscent of a child's drawing, as if it stems from Hansel and Gretel's imagination. This impression is supported by the fact that when the gingerbread house first appears in the

Figure 7. Hansel and Gretel *by Anthony Browne.*

story, the reader follows the children's gaze. If this hypothesis is taken further, several of the elements from the children's home appear in transformed form in their further adventure. The wallpaper in their home has the same shape as the tops of the trees in the forest—something that becomes particularly clear in the illustration in which Gretel crosses the river on the white swan at the end of the story. And is not the swan possibly a transformed *Tagesrest*, a day's residue of a decorative element in the children's home? In the living room of the parental house, a small white swan was pictured as well.

At their return home, the children's perception evolves once again. As Bettelheim argues, "Nothing has changed at the end of 'Hansel and Gretel' but inner attitudes; or more correctly, all has changed because inner attitudes have changed" (165). Browne illustrates this mental shift with another transformation of the house. The twilight of dawn has made way for the colors of bright daylight, the curtains and the windows are open, and the mud on the doors of the shed and the house has been cleaned away. Two elements have disappeared. The bird, which functioned as a connection with the gingerbread house, has flown away; the trees behind the house are gone. The chopped wood that lies next to the garbage can suggests that they have been cut down. Earlier in the book, a strong visual association was created between the trees and the bars of Hansel's cage. This was enforced by the strong bars in the front door, which too have faded to become substantially less prominent in the final picture of the house. The softening, even more than the removal of threatening and depressing aspects of the house, supports the hypothesis that the children's perception is influential in the overt content that the story depicts. Hansel and Gretel's home is no longer threatening, nor is it a fantasy. It appears as a realistically drawn, welcoming place.

Paul O. Zelinsky's illustrations to Rika Lesser's adaptation of "Hansel and Gretel" (1984) likewise draw parallels between the two locations. The cover (Figure 8), in which Hansel and Gretel are pictured on their way to the gingerbread house, shows remarkable analogies to the composition of an illustration further in the book. Here the children are shown as they return home after their parents' first attempt to abandon them in the forest (Figure 9). Both images are constructed along a diagonal line in which Hansel and Gretel are situated at the bottom left and the house is placed on a hill at the top right. The gingerbread house (Figure 10) as well as the parental home stand in a small clearing in the forest surrounded by a low fence. A path with a small bend follows the diagonal line that dominates the two pictures, leading the children to the front door of the houses. The elements in the landscape also follow this line. Both illustrations are framed by a large tree on the left-hand side whose branches extend to the top of the page. Finally, in all three of Zelinsky's illustrations, the house is constructed as a rectangle, with the door facing right. These elements support the hypothesis that the children's home and the witch's cottage are two appearances of one and the same house, and this parallel links Zelinsky's illustrations to Bettelheim's theory.

More striking still is the visual analogy that Anthony Browne draws between the stepmother and the witch in the tale of "Hansel and Gretel."[14] In Browne's illustrations, both stepmother and witch look at the children (and the reader) from a window, and although the frame and the view of

Figure 8. Hansel and Gretel *retold by Rika Lesser and illustrated by Paul O. Zelinsky.*

Figure 9. Hansel and Gretel *retold by Rika Lesser and illustrated by Paul O. Zelinsky.*

Figure 10. Hansel and Gretel *retold by Rika Lesser and illustrated by Paul O. Zelinsky.*

the house differ slightly, the frontal perspective is exactly the same (Figures 11 and 12). Witch and stepmother appear as two people with matching facial characteristics: the bitter shape of their mouths, the black wart on their right cheek, and the triangular lines around their nose and mouth signal that they are identical. In the illustration in which the witch feels Hansel's chicken bone, her hands are shown to be carefully manicured and her nails are painted with pink polish. Although the stepmother's nails are never shown, the bottle of nail polish that is displayed on her table further supports the parallel.

Moreover, both women are drawn in an ominous black triangle, a symbol that links them in many other images of the book. It is a visual leitmotiv that can be discerned when the mother is standing in the children's bedroom (the stepmother's shadow, the church's tower, the little mouse hole, and the hat on the wardrobe), on the gingerbread house's roof, and around the witch when she looks at the window. Both women have what seems to be a black cone-shaped hat in their house (the stepmother on top of the wardrobe, the witch on top of the oven). No more of these black cones appear after Gretel has pushed the witch in the oven—they seem to have

Figure 11. Hansel and Gretel *by Anthony Browne.*

simultaneously disappeared from the parental home, as has the step-mother.

Browne's illustrations offer the reader an interpretation of "Hansel and Gretel" that may be inspired by Bettelheim or that at least has strong simi-larities to his theory. The parallels between stepmother and witch, on the one hand, and parental home and gingerbread house, on the other, fore-ground identity in difference, and like Bettelheim, the illustrations suggest that the differences can be attributed to a shift in perception rather than the actual change of location that the manifest content of the fairy tale describes. That a loaf of bread is drawn under the window that displays the witch may not be coincidental in this context. Bettelheim stresses the role of the

Figure 12. Hansel and Gretel *by Anthony Browne.*

mother in "Hansel and Gretel" as "the source of all food to the children" (159). The central conflict in the tale stems, according to Bettelheim, from the child's frustration that "Mother no longer serves him unquestioningly but makes demands on him" (163). When she does give the child food, she is mistrusted, like the witch in the story. The loaf under the witch thus signals the cause for the children's ambivalent feelings.

Freudenburg reads Browne's application of Bettelheim's theory as a correction. She observes that Browne adds objects such as makeup and female accessories to the domestic scenes in "Hansel and Gretel" in order to accuse the stepmother of vanity and child neglect (307). This interpretation functions as a critique of Bettelheim: "Using a psychologically informed approach, Browne exonerates the young and dissects the stepmother's emotional makeup in order to expose the real root of the children's troubles—it is not the children who are at fault, but instead, a self-centered, uncaring parent" (308). With this critique, Freudenburg places Browne in a long line of critics (such as Tatar, Zipes, and Tucker) who have pointed out that Bettelheim tends to falsely accuse children rather than parents of all the ordeals that fairy tales describe. Freudenburg thus suggests that Browne undoes the interpretative twist that Bettelheim gave to the story. In the Grimms' version, the adults (stepmother and witch) are blamed for all evil; in Bettelheim's reading, the children are accused, among others, of oral regression and the inability to accept that parents cannot devote themselves completely to them; in Browne, the parents' faults are once again highlighted and the children's innocence restored. That they take only a very modest piece from the gingerbread house in his illustrations supports this view and contradicts the "unrestrained giving into gluttony" that Bettelheim ascribes to the children (161). It could be argued that Browne simply illustrates the allocation of innocence and guilt as it is made explicit in the Grimms' "Hansel and Gretel" and that Bettelheim is an irrelevant intertext. No doubt, for many children and adults this is how the story is read. Yet the fact that Browne incorporates several aspects of Bettelheim's analysis while modifying others means that his visualization of the tale can indeed be read as a correction to *The Uses of Enchantment* (as Freudenburg argues). A psychoanalytic reading can surely find a way out of this critique: in a Bettelheimian interpretation of Browne's picture book, the foregrounding of the mother's vanity can simply be another projection from the children's point of view, who feel neglected when she has interests other than taking care of them.

Possibly inspired by Anthony Browne is the British illustrator Ian Beck.[15] He draws a similar, albeit less striking, parallel between the two houses in his teddy bear version of "Hansel and Gretel" (1999). As in Browne, the two houses in the tale are structured in the same way: both the parents' cottage and the witch's gingerbread house have a central door with a small pointed roof on top of it. In each house, there are windows on both sides of the door and above the pointed roof. Moreover, the windowpanes of both the gingerbread house and the parental home are decorated with small hearts. Each roof has a pointy decorative element on top as well as a chimney to the right of it. Although the gingerbread house is larger than the parental cottage, these eye-catching features do draw the link between the houses as two appearances of the same location. When he illustrated the tale of "Hansel and Gretel" anew for *The Orchard Book of Fairy Tales* (Impey and Beck), Beck drew a parallel between the stepmother and the witch that is similar to Browne's. The positions of the two mirror each other. As the stepmother gives the children a piece of bread, her hands are stretched out, holding a small loaf, and her back is bent, as is her head. Like the stepmother, the witch is drawn in profile. She, too, is handing the children a small piece of food (possibly bread), and her back and head are also bent toward the children. Again, from a psychoanalytic point of view, it is no coincidence that the parallel between the two women is drawn at the moment when they feed the children: the distribution or withdrawal of food is, according to Bettelheim, the core of the conflict between the child and the mother. The faces of mother and witch resemble each other: their eyes are hollow; their mouth has a bitter expression.

As with Browne, the parallel between the two female figures invites and supports a psychoanalytic reading that considers the witch a perverted image that the child projects onto the mother. In contrast to Browne, however, Beck adds no elements that foreground the stepmother's vanity. The fact that the stepmother is only drawn at the moment when she gives food may even nuance the harshness with which she is described in Rose Impey's text. More than Browne or Zelinsky, Beck draws a parallel between Hansel and Gretel through their similar clothing (white shirt, black vest, and green trousers or skirt). Both wear the same red shawl and black shoes with gray stockings. Whereas Browne retains the children's individuality that is suggested by the traditional tale's manifest content, Beck's illustrations draw attention to the identity of siblings that Bettelheim suspects in the latent content.

A fourth illustrator of "Hansel and Gretel" who conflates images of mother and stepmother is Jörg Drühl (1981). Like Zelinsky, Drühl draws a first analogy between the parental home and the gingerbread house in the composition of his images: Hansel and Gretel are pictured on the left of the illustration, standing in front of the house; the stepmother and witch stand on the right. Some analogies arise between the two houses, yet they are not as strong as in the case of Browne and Zelinsky. With Drühl, the windows have the same shape, with a square wooden frame, and are made from the same glass, a semitransparent type of windowpane with a circle motif. The analogy between stepmother and witch is stronger, however. Both women are pictured with a black cat. This may be merely an indication that both women are witches. Yet, even that is an addition to the Grimms' tale, in which the stepmother is portrayed as an evil character but not as a witch. Moreover, there are other similarities in Drühl's illustrations that support the hypothesis that the two adult females in the story may be the children's two perceptions of the same woman. They resemble each other in their facial features as well as in their clothing. Both have a long nose that points down like an arrow. Moreover, stepmother and witch wear a similar cap. In the latter's case, the cap is supplemented with horns, which underline her demonic nature. It is unclear whether the women wear the same clothing, because the witch covers herself with a long cloak. Details from other pictures further support the idea that the witch may be the reincarnation of the stepmother in a further demonized form: one of the beehives that stand next to the gingerbread house could be spotted on top of the stepmother's four-poster bed, as could her walking stick.

Ideas from psychoanalysis do not surface only in illustrated versions of "Hansel and Gretel." The Dutch illustrator Loek Koopmans displays an intertextual link with Bettelheim's theory in his drawings to Perrault's "Cinderella" (1999), effecting a process of condensation. The dresses that the stepmother and stepsisters wear assume a symbolic dimension as the story develops. In the first image of this picture book, Cinderella is drawn facing her three mocking new relatives (Figure 13). In this illustration her stepsisters and stepmother wear identical salmon pink dresses. As they are standing close to each other, they appear as one big person, and it is hard to discern which foot belongs to which woman. In the rest of the book, neither the stepmother nor the two stepsisters are ever standing completely alone. They are always wearing the same salmon pink dresses, and their dresses always touch. The two stepsisters thus function as one inseparable unit, and sometimes even the stepmother is included in this process of visual condensation. As Bettelheim writes about "Cinderella": "Mother and daughters are so closely identified with each other that one gets the feeling that they are one unit split into different figures" (248). Koopmans reverses this process of splitting, combining the three characters again into one and giving a visual indication of the tale's possible latent content.[16] The penultimate illustration in his *Cinderella* depicts the scene in which she tries on the glass slipper and is a visual echo of the first picture. Again, the stepmother

Figure 13. Cinderella, *illustrated by Loek Koopmans.*

and stepsisters form one big cloud of salmon pink dress. With this picture freshly in mind, the reader may wonder why, on the next page, Cinderella is no longer pictured in her shabby dress, nor in the yellow gown that she wore at the ball, but in the same salmon pink dress that her hated relatives wore. In the words that accompany this illustration, there is only a brief mention of the striking metamorphosis. Part of the text still refers to the picture on the previous page (how Cinderella produced the second glass slipper and thus surprised her stepsisters). Then it is said that Cinderella's godmother makes a new magical appearance and transforms the girl's shabby dress into a magnificent dream gown. That this is exactly the gown that her sisters and stepmother were wearing earlier is not mentioned, a clear example of the interpretative potential that an illustration can add to a text.

Several hypotheses can be offered to explain Cinderella's transformation into her stepsisters' look-alike. First of all, it is striking that her physical appearance throughout the book does not differ very much from that of her stepsisters. This becomes particularly clear at the ball, where they look almost identical (except for the color of their dresses). The similarity between the three girls might support Bettelheim's view of brothers and sisters in fairy tales: as stated above, he reads siblings as the symbolic projections of different aspects of the same individual. An alternative interpretation of Koopmans's final illustration, which would contradict Bettelheim's insistence on the importance of flat characterization and a happy ending, is that Cinderella has assumed some of the stepsisters' qualities herself. The pink dress seems to symbolize power and status—power that was abused by Cinderella's stepfamily. Although her facial expression in the final illustration is much more benign than her stepsisters' ever was, the identification with her steprelatives that is established by the dress undermines the unambiguously happy ending that is presented in the text. "Then Cinderella was brought to the prince and their wedding was celebrated a few days later," it is stated (my translation). The illustration contradicts or destabilizes the traditional fairy-tale ending. Whether Cinderella has simply inherited her stepsisters' and stepmother's clothing, or whether she has potentially inherited their evil traits, remains unresolved.

Recondensation of split images also occurs in Bettelheim's interpretation of "Little Red Riding Hood." As briefly mentioned above, Sandra Beckett draws a parallel between Bettelheim and Jean Ache's *Le monde des ronds et des carrés,* an abstract picture book that is loaded with sophisticated color symbolism. Red Riding Hood is represented by a red dot, her grandmother is a brown dot, and the wolf is a black one. Interestingly, the mother's symbol unites two colors—she is half-red and half-brown—suggesting as Beckett argues, "her intermediary position (both mother and daughter) between the other two generations of women." The illustrations also incorporate Bettelheim's interpretation of the evil stepmother: "The representation of the mother as half red and half brown seems to combine the fairy-tale stereotypes of the good mother and the evil stepmother into a single character with a negative and a positive side" (*Recycling* 62). This may seem problematic for several reasons. First, because "Little Red Riding Hood" does not feature a wicked stepmother or any other evil female character in the story. Second, one should consider the fact that the grandmother is also represented by a brown dot. The similarity of brown and black helps explain why Red Riding Hood does not recognize the wolf after he has eaten her grandmother. It is unclear whether the colors indicate only a similarity in appearance or also indicate a likeness in character. Beckett assumes that they do: "Ache's portrayal of the grandmother as a dark brown dot creates a striking similarity between her and the wolf, paving the way for Little Red Riding Hood's confusion in the 'collapse of roles' that Marina Warner considers so crucial" (62). Warner indeed argues that "the wolf is kin to the forest-dwelling witch, or crone" (181). And although Bettelheim does not identify the grandmother with the wolf as strongly as Warner, he does highlight certain ambiguities in her role in the story. "Grandmother, too is not free of blame," he writes, accusing her of placing her own benefit above that of the child by spoiling her. In addition, grandmother puts the child at risk by giving her a "too attractive red cloak," which, Bettelheim argues, is loaded with sexual symbolism and which the girl is still too immature to wear (173). Moreover, like Ache, Bettelheim partly equates mother and grandmother when he discusses "Little Red Riding Hood" in light of the Oedipus complex. In his interpretation, Red Riding Hood deliberately directs the wolf to her (grand)mother's cottage because she wants her "out of the way."[17] By an elaborate detour, Bettelheim again identifies the wolf with the grandmother: "The girl feels she deserves to be punished terribly by the mother, if not the father also, for her desire to take him away from Mother" (175). The mother, whom Bettelheim equates with the grandmother, thus becomes a danger to the little girl—a threat that can indeed be represented by the brown color of Ache's illustrations.

These six examples show that illustrations can add an interpretation to a given text through the content they depict and the styles and perspectives they use and that some of these interpretations can be intertextually linked to psychoanalytic theory. All of the illustrations that were analyzed are combined with a traditional textual version of the fairy tale or a duplicate adaptation. The pictures offer or support an interpretative direction without intruding into the text but instead providing a supplementation or counterpoint. Like the poetic retellings defined by Anna Altmann and discussed in the previous chapter, the fairy-tale picture books and illustrated versions rely on an active reader to make the comparison between word and image. Several meanings and conclusions can be attached to this relationship between the verbal and the visual; yet, in comparison to Bettelheim's fairy-tale interpretations and to other retellings, the illustrations are limited in the number of meanings that they can express with reasonable clarity. I have mainly focused on parallels that suggest an identical latent content behind different manifestations of the same person or location (condensation) and on composition and perspective, which can draw attention to the point of view from which a story is told. More abstract meanings, for instance Bettelheim's idea that Hansel and Gretel's stepmother is the children's projection of negatively experienced aspects from their biological mother, would be much more complex to express visually.

Dream Mechanisms in Retellings for Children

The Dutch children's author Peter Van Gestel combines a psychoanalytic and a feminist critique in his retelling of "Sleeping Beauty." The introduction to "Prinses Roosje" (Little Princess Rose) signals that he shares Bettelheim's view about the tale's central message. " 'Prinses Roosje' is slightly longer and also slightly different from 'Briar Rose' but it tells the same story: little girls grow up, the people around them simply have to live with it," Van Gestel explains (Kuijken 11; my translation). Bettelheim offers a similar interpretation, with a more explicit stress on the adolescent's sexual maturation: "The central theme of all versions of 'The Sleeping Beauty' is that, despite all attempts on the part of the parents to prevent their child's sexual awakening, it will take place nonetheless" (230). Before maturity and sexual awakening can be reached, Bettelheim argues, the adolescent typically goes through a period of lethargy: " 'The Sleeping Beauty' emphasizes the long, quiet concentration on oneself that is also needed. During the months before the first menstruation, and often for some time immediately following it, girls are passive, seem sleepy, and withdraw into themselves. [. . .] The turning inward, which in outer appearance looks like passivity (or sleeping one's life away), happens when internal processes of such importance go on within the person that he has no energy for outwardly directed action" (225).

In the Grimms' "Briar Rose," this period is symbolized by the hundred years of sleep after the young girl pricks herself—an event that, according to Bettelheim, symbolizes the girl's first menstruation (233). There is no reference to an actual passive period in Sleeping Beauty's life in the Grimms' version. It is symbolically represented by her sleep, which appears suddenly (by magic) and before which she is quite active. In "Prinses Roosje," by contrast, Van Gestel adds a period of lethargy even before Roosje has pricked herself:

> At the age of twelve Roosje thought all games were boring. She no longer played with her dolls. [. . .]
> One morning, when the sun was still hiding behind the highest palace towers, she sat on her swing.
> Her legs didn't move, the swing didn't swing.
> Rose counted the blades of grass under her feet. Still far from one hundred she fell asleep. (Van Gestel, "Roosje" 121; my translation)

Both Bettelheim and Van Gestel extend the period of Sleeping Beauty's passivity to the moment right before she pricks herself, and both substitute the long period of magical sleep with a more realistic alternative. Moreover, they insert a phase of puberty that is not described in the manifest content of the traditional story: there Briar Rose moves straight from childhood to adulthood. The description of the tale's protagonist after she has encountered a black stork, which in Van Gestel's story assumes the function of the magic spindle, dramatizes Bettelheim's interpretation of Briar Rose as a solipsistic pubescent girl: "Roosje didn't understand anyone anymore; nobody understood Roosje anymore. The years were long and sad for the king and queen. Their daughter spoke the strangest language they had ever heard. [. . .] Roosje slept nearly all day. When she didn't sleep, she lay on a couch with languid eyes and snacked on cookies, sweets, and cakes, which she consumed with one single bite" (Van Gestel, "Roosje" 125; my translation). Some magic is retained in Van Gestel's tale—the enchantment lies in the fact that Roosje says everything backward—but the relationship that she has with her surroundings is reminiscent of the more realistic pubescent struggles as described by Bettelheim.

A third parallel can be observed in the narcissism that is ascribed to Briar Rose in Bettelheim's interpretation and in Van Gestel's description. Roosje is pictured in a scene that contains clear allusions to the Greek adolescent Narcissus: before she is pricked, she stands naked in a pond and looks at her own reflection in the water. That Roosje sighs with admiration (123) is ambiguous. Does she marvel at the black bird, which she also sees reflected, or at herself? Her unreasonable self-centeredness was apparent in the preceding scenes, in which she started commanding the sun: " 'Mind your own business,' she ordered the sun. 'And shine a little less fiercely' " (122; my translation). "The world becomes alive only to the person who herself awakens to it," writes Bettelheim (234). In Van Gestel's tale, this awakening happens both in a romantic and in a Marxist sense: it is only when Roosje falls in love with a socialist-minded prince and opens up to the needs of other people that she can begin to communicate with her surroundings and break the black stork's curse.

As in most of his analyses, Bettelheim considers several interpretations at once when discussing "Sleeping Beauty." Fairy tales, he argues, can address the unconscious of different people in different ways, and a tale's meaning to a child can develop as it grows older (16). The psychological explanation of Sleeping Beauty's passivity as a natural part of puberty is combined with a psychoanalytic interpretation that places the tale in Freud's model of the "family romance." Bettelheim focuses his attention particularly on the girl's father, who in the Grimms' tale appears most preoccupied with preventing his daughter's sleep by having all the spindles in his kingdom destroyed. Bettelheim refers to Giambattista Basile's "Sun, Moon, and Talia" to argue that the latent content of "Sleeping Beauty" deals with an Oedipus complex:

> In Basile's story Talia is the daughter of a king who loved her so much that he could not remain in his castle after she fell into a deathlike sleep. We hear nothing more about him after he left Talia ensconced

on her throne-like chair "under an embroidered canopy," not even
after she reawakened, married her king, and lived happily with him
and her beautiful children. One king replaces another king in the
same country; one king replaces another in Talia's life—the father
king is replaced by the lover king. Might these two kings not be sub-
stitutes for each other at different periods in the girl's life, in different roles, in different disguises? (228)

In "Prinses Roosje," Van Gestel adds a suggestion of incestuous feelings
to the king's relationship with his daughter Roosje, a suggestion that is not
as explicitly present in the overt content of the Grimms' tale. The latter text
describes how the king is so happy with the birth of his beautiful daughter
that he throws a magnificent feast. When she is cursed, it is stated, "Since
the king wanted to guard his dear child against such a catastrophe, he issued an order that all spindles in his kingdom were to be burned" (Grimm,
"Brier Rose" 696). In Van Gestel's tale, as in Bettelheim's interpretation,
the feelings of the father are described in greater detail:

> "Isn't she beautiful and delicate? I'm afraid we'll never find her a
> suitable prince. A prince who is as strong and brave as I am." Roosje
> started crying.
>   The young king comforted her. "There there," he said, "who
> knows, maybe we'll find such a prince, and if not, we'll keep you our-
> selves."
>   Now Roosje cried even louder. ("Roosje" 118; my translation)

That the father compares himself to his daughter's future husband, that
he comes to the conclusion that no one will equal his own qualities, and
that he is later pictured sitting by her bed are all reminiscent of the incestuous relationship that Bettelheim sees hidden in "Sun, Moon, and Talia."
Yet, it immediately becomes clear that Van Gestel offers a different interpretation than does Bettelheim in one crucial aspect. Bettelheim ascribes
the incestuous desire to the child: "We encounter here again the 'innocence' of the oedipal child, who feels no responsibility for what she arouses
or wishes to arouse in the parent" (228). The child's reaction in Van Gestel's tale is quite different, and her innocence does not need to be put in
quotation marks, as Bettelheim does for Briar Rose. Roosje's incessant

crying indicates her shock and protestation about what her father suggests.

In the prequel to "Briar Rose" that Van Gestel includes in "Prinses Roosje," a number of symbols appear that further invite an intertextual comparison with Bettelheim's interpretation. Van Gestel gives the rose garden, for instance, more prominence than it has in the Grimms' version. Bettelheim associates the hedge of roses with sexuality: its impenetrability and harmful thorns represent the destructive aspects of premature sex, and the flowers symbolize sexual maturity and fulfillment (233). In the Brothers Grimm's version, the roses do not appear until Briar Rose falls asleep. In Van Gestel's version, it is mentioned in the prequel that her mother tends roses, and the associations to a latent sexual content in this symbol are suggested more powerfully. The queen asks her husband for a rose garden, and it is a place where the couple meets daily and to which only they have access, like monogamy in marriage. It is in this garden that the frog makes his prediction to the queen that she will have a daughter born to her within a year, again a reference that not only Bettelheim associates with sexuality. The parents' prohibition becomes more explicit when Roosje is trespassing and receives her near-fatal prick. The king and queen had forbidden her access to the rose garden. Biblical associations with the Fall of Adam and Eve arise when she ignores their interdiction: "Now I can finally discover the rose garden's secret. Shortly after that she walked into the forbidden garden past the bushes with bright red roses" (Van Gestel, "Roosje" 122; my translation). And as the eating of the apple in the story of the Fall has often been associated with the acquisition of carnal knowledge, Roosje's trespassing leads to a first step in her sexual awakening. The pond asks her to undress and immerse herself in the water (another sexual symbol): "Come on, girl, take off your clothes, come with me, I'm delightfully cool" (123; my translation). It is when she is naked in the water, contemplating herself, that she gets pricked by the black stork's beak (Figure 14).

The most important difference between the Grimms' "Briar Rose" and Bettelheim's interpretation of it, on the one hand, and Van Gestel's retelling, on the other, is that Roosje does not feel scared after her symbolic first sexual experience, nor does she fall asleep. On the contrary, she invites the stork back. The roses as sexual symbols support this suggestion of her maturity: when Roosje enters the garden, the roses are already blooming. Van Gestel mixes a psychoanalytic, a feminist, and a Marxist interpretation of

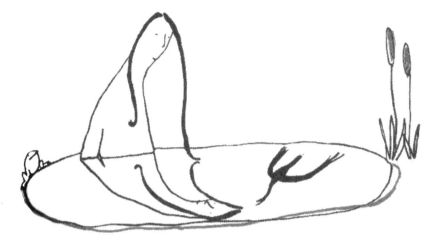

Figure 14. Prinses Roosje illustrated *by Sabien Clement*.

"Sleeping Beauty." He provides the female characters with intelligence and self-consciousness. Roosje's first sexual awakening, which does not yet involve a man but an exploration of her own body, becomes more positive in Van Gestel's retelling than in Bettelheim's reading. The subsequent crisis of communication between Roosje and her parents seems to have less to do with her sexuality than with her lack of interest in the needs of others.

Central to Bettelheim's interpretation of the evil fairy in "Sleeping Beauty" is the process of doubling, which is similar to that of the stepmother in "Hansel and Gretel": "in Perrault, as in the Brothers Grimm's version, at the very beginning of the story we find the (fairy god)-mother(s) split into the good and the evil aspects" (230). Van Gestel, although he zoomorphizes the evil fairy and transforms her into a stork, keeps this dualism. In his tale, there is only one good fairy, a white stork, and an evil counterpart, a black stork. The associations with yin and yang are clear, and a link with Jungian theory can be drawn. In an epilogue to the tale, the dualism is explicitly resolved:

> In the pond's clear water the queen saw the black stork's
> reflection.

> She shivered.
> Now not only was the white stork very close to her but the
> black one also.
> "Who's that?" she asked quietly.
> "That's me too," the white stork said.
>   (Van Gestel, "Roosje" 131; my translation)

The accompanying illustration by Sabien Clement supports this (Figure 14). The black bird is shown as the shadow of the white bird, as its reflection. It is perhaps not a coincidence that it is Roosje's mother who learns that the black stork and the white stork are two aspects of one and the same animal. In the quotation above, the parentheses in Bettelheim's reference to "(fairy god)-mother(s)" indicate that he sees the good and evil fairies or godmothers as aspects or symbols of Sleeping Beauty's mother. In Van Gestel's tale, the stork dissociates her from an evil counterpart in female form.

In the article "Dromen, sprookjes, en verhalen" (Dreams, Fairy Tales, and Stories), Van Gestel explains his views on fairy tales. He disagrees with Bettelheim, whom he does not mention explicitly, in another crucial respect: the importance of a happy ending. Like Bettelheim, Van Gestel pleads for the preservation of cruelty in fairy tales, and he likes the idea that fairy tales tell stories about people who are not subject to a higher force (137). Although Bettelheim sees these higher forces as internal to the human psyche (that is, as symbols of the superego), he also prefers fairy tales to myths for reasons similar to those of Van Gestel: the pessimistic myth disturbs the child and makes it feel helpless, whereas the optimistic fairy tale reassures and empowers it (Bettelheim 37–39). However, unlike Bettelheim, Van Gestel claims that he prefers stories without a happy ending: "Well, with regard to fairy tales and stories, everyone cherishes their own happy endings, all those children's literature pedagogues always want fairy tales and stories for children with a happy ending. One day I'm going to write a story in which a children's literature pedagogue comes to a terrible ending" ("Dromen" 142; my translation).

When it comes to writing his own fairy-tale retelling, however, Van Gestel does stick to Bettelheim's pattern: Roosje is cured from her speech impediment, she is reconciled with her parents, and she marries her prince.

Her husband respects her as an intelligent woman, which contains a promise that their marriage will work even better than her parents' does. This is an unambiguously happy ending, on Van Gestel's terms as well, for it combines aspects of the traditional fairy tale's romantic closure with an optimistic Marxist and feminist twist. That Van Gestel abstains from a direct association of Roosje's (biological) mother with another evil female and retains the fairy tale's optimistic conclusion makes him exemplary for most fairy-tale retellings that are aimed at a young audience. Although occasionally retellings for children can be found that break with these conventions, positive images of parents, especially mothers, and happy endings still prevail.[18]

Retellings for Adults

Given his noninterventionist policy with regard to children, the only addressee of an orthodox application of Bettelheim's theories in literature must be the adult, who is also the intended reader of *The Uses of Enchantment*. Although both the illustrated fairy tales and Van Gestel's retelling contain powerful suggestions for recondensing split projections, it is indeed in retellings for adults that the process of splitting in the fairy tale is most openly discussed and explained. Steven Gould's "The Session" (1995) is a sequel to the Grimms' "Snow White." The psychoanalyst is here introduced to the fairy-tale world, as the story is initially set up as a discussion between Snow White and her therapist. A wife and mother now, Snow White has everything in life to make her happy, but the depressions that plague her and the hostile feelings that she harbors toward her two-year-old daughter prevent her from enjoying her new life to the full. As can be expected, the therapist takes her back to her childhood, where he believes the cause of her present troubles can be found. In this retrospective narrative, the fairy tale is retold from Snow White's angle—the perspective, Bettelheim has argued, that also dominates the traditional version of the tale:

What happened to your mother?
> She died when I was little, but I remember her. She was beautiful and kind and she'd sing me lullabies.

So, your father remarried?

> Yes. But it's like she cast a spell on him. She must have, for him to
> marry her. I don't remember the wedding, but I remember the first time
> she came into the nursery. I'd spilled some paint on my clothes and she
> grabbed me by the back of the neck and screamed at me. "Look what
> you've done! Look what you've done!" She hit me. (Gould 91)

That Snow White does not remember the wedding, nor her biological
mother's funeral, is revealing, as is the fact that she has only retained positive memories of her. The stepmother first appears at a moment when the
little girl is punished for something bad, and this is a significant overlap
with Bettelheim's interpretation. In *The Uses of Enchantment*, he attempts
to uncover what Snow White's perspective represses, and that is also what
her therapist tries to do in Gould's retelling. His conclusions come remarkably close to Bettelheim's, as he confronts Snow White with what she refuses to see:

Your father never remarried. Your mother didn't die when you were little.

> What are you talking about? What is this nonsense?

I don't lie. I've never lied. What I just said is the truth.

> But—but, that doesn't make sense. Of course she died. Or that crea-
> ture wouldn't have come to ruin my childhood.

Mothers love their children.

> Of course.

Your mother would never push you down the stairs.

> No, she wouldn't.

Your mother held you and sang lullabies and was kind.

> Yes!

*I'm sorry. Check the court history. Your mother didn't die until she "overdid
it" at your wedding. Your father never remarried. This is the truth.*

———

*Sometimes it's easier to believe that a parent has died and been replaced by an
evil creature than to believe they would—*(Gould 91–92)

The therapist explains that Snow White could not accept her image of the ideal mother to be compromised, an interpretation of the traditional version that intertextually links Gould's retelling to Bettelheim.[19] However, this revision too is a correction. Snow White's reasons for keeping up her false belief in a stepmother until adulthood are justified by the extreme form in which her biological mother deviated from the ideal. The story says that the young Snow White was indeed badly molested and that she had to flee for her life. This part of her account is confirmed by the therapist, who at the end of the story is revealed to be the magic mirror that has witnessed the events from the very beginning and is known in the fairy-tale world to speak the truth. Maria Tatar's critique of Bettelheim's accusations of children is thus corrected in "The Session," and Snow White's anger toward her mother is presented as fully justified by the facts of reality, not by self-centeredness. Gould's story, which at some points seems to function as an introduction to fairy-tale psychoanalysis for beginners, shows that the first step for Snow White to deal with her anger and its consequences in her adult life is to acknowledge her act of repression and the fact that she has been mistreated. This insight also releases her from the vicious circle through which victims of child abuse become molesters themselves.

A young girl who releases herself from such a pattern in a more confrontational manner is Cindy, the protagonist of Willy Spillebeen's *Doornroosjes Honden* (1983, Briar Rose's Dogs). In contrast to Gould's sequel, the child abuse (in this case a severe form of child neglect) is not described retrospectively but witnessed directly through the eyes of the little girl, who is the focalizer of this novel. She projects the split not on an external figure, as Snow White does in Gould's short story, but on herself: "In her bed she once thought that her day was made up of two parts: the day itself was happiness, the evening and night were sadness. [. . .] And again Cindy thought, surprising herself, that maybe there were two Cindy's and that one was always present and the other not. It was a mystery to her where the other one was then and she wondered who she could ask about that" (Spillebeen 13–14; my translation).

Like Gould's more fantastic tale, Spillebeen's realistic retelling draws attention to the fact that child abuse is not only an imaginary projection but also a fact of life. In spite of Bettelheim's experience with "severely disturbed children" (4), this is something that rarely surfaces in his interpretations. Instead of creating a second, bad mother figure, as Gould's Snow White does when she is mistreated, Cindy splits herself. She seems to make this split, moreover, on a more conscious level. The consequences are disastrous, as Cindy projects her ever-increasing anger and frustration against her other self—a process that eventually leads to self-destruction. The girl swallows several boxes of sleeping pills and the final, uncompromising lines of the novel describe her death. She becomes a Sleeping Beauty for whom no happy ending lies in store. Like Gould's rewriting of "Snow White," Spillebeen adds a Tatarian correction to the psychoanalytic perspective. Similar to, for instance, Henry James's *What Maisie Knew*, the narratological point of view of the innocent child is retained and exploited to produce a vehement clash with the harsh reality that she witnesses and often cannot understand. The ironic distance between the neglected child and the informed adult reader invites compassion and sympathy. The fairy-tale frame is in this respect presented as anything but therapeutic: Cindy focuses on Briar Rose's hundred-year sleep as the happy ending to the tale, rather than the kiss that awakes her. Thus the fairy tale feeds her dream of escape from a world that insufficiently acknowledges the needs and rights of the child. Spillebeen corrects Bettelheim in showing that children's problems do not merely exist in their imagination or unconscious yet supports the psychoanalyst's claim that if fairy tales are not shared in a loving and supportive environment, no healing effect can ever be achieved.

Resexualizing the Fairy Tale

In several of the stories that enact the therapeutic function of the fairy tale or a split of characters, a possible sexual undercurrent in the fairy tale is highlighted. This resexualization of the fairy tale, as I will call it, remains by no means limited to these tales. Of course a resexualization presupposes a desexualization. Folktales and fairy-tale collections that are older than the Grimms' illustrate that sexuality once formed a popular theme in fairy tales—most notably, this is the case for Giovan Francesco Straparola's *Le piacevoli notti* (1550–53, The Delectable Nights), Giambattista Basile's *Lo cunto de le cunti*, also known as the *Pentamerone* (1634–36), and some tales by the seventeenth-century French *conteuses*.[20] The sexual dimensions of the fairy tale were censored substantially in the collections of Perrault and, especially, the Brothers Grimm. Whereas the moral to Perrault's "Chaperon Rouge," for instance, still contains a strong hint that the wolf's appetite may be sexually loaded, this dimension is suppressed in *Die Kinder- und Hausmärchen.* "When it came to passages colored by sexual details or to plots based on Oedipal conflicts," Maria Tatar argues, "Wilhelm Grimm exhibited extraordinary editorial zeal. Over the years he systematically purged the collection of references to sexuality and masked depictions of incestuous desire" (*Hard Facts* 10). The sanitized tales are the versions that have entered the fairy-tale canon for Western children, often in duplicates that were censored even further.[21]

Some critics have argued that sexuality is a dimension that was never absent from the fairy tale. In popular culture, as well as in several fictional works, the sexual aspect of the fairy tale was also maintained or reintroduced long before Bettelheim published *The Uses of Enchantment.*[22] Catherine Orenstein, for instance, notes the use of Little Red Riding Hood as a common sex symbol in cartoons and commercials of the 1930s and 1940s. However, the humor or erotic tension in these parodies can be argued to result from the fact that Red Riding Hood is a sexually innocent character in the overt content of the canonized versions of the tale. Since the 1960s, feminist, philologist, and psychoanalytic critics have increasingly addressed the more explicit sexual references that were present in folktales and older fairy-tale collections. The growing awareness that the best-known fairy tales had once contained more overt sexual themes (as well as different role patterns, descriptions of class, and so forth) led to the production of several anthologies in which these themes received particular prominence. In *The Old Wives' Fairy Tale Book* (1990), for instance, Angela Carter "aim[s] at reasserting precisely those dimensions in a woman's life—including sexuality—that male editors had suppressed" (Haase, "Scholarship" 9). The voices of all these scholars and authors have helped popularize the idea that fairy tales are stories about sexual awakening and erotic desire as well as fear of sex; about menstruation and pregnancy; and about incest, rape, and adultery. It is for this reason that the introduction of sexual references in post-1970 retellings can be called a *re*-sexualization: these works return to an older convention of the fairy tale. Although the resexualization of the fairy tale cannot be credited to Bettelheim alone, he (as well as Freud) can be said to have been an important factor in this process. Bettelheim has been reproached with a lack of knowledge of the fairy-tale tradition, but in many of his analyses he does draw upon older (mainly European) fairy-tale collections and myths, and he highlights themes of incest, oedipal desire, and sexual awakening in these stories. These older fairy tales are treated as narratives in which there was less repression. Bettelheim tries to recover these references as well as to reveal other symbols that have a latent sexual content in the Grimms and Perrault. In this sense, he becomes a relevant intertext for fairy-tale retellings that do the same.

Oedipal Desire in Retellings for Adults and Adolescents

Several critics have drawn parallels between the work of the American poet Anne Sexton and the theories of Sigmund Freud.[23] In explanations of her own poetry, Sexton also invokes psychoanalytical terms and processes: "Sometimes the doctors tell me that I understand something in a poem that I haven't integrated into my life. In fact, I may be concealing it from myself, while I was revealing it to the readers. The poetry is often more advanced in terms of my unconscious, than I am. Poetry, after all, milks the unconscious. The unconscious is there to feed it little images, little symbols, the answers, the insights I know not of" (qtd. in Miller 61). In the last sentence Sexton reformulates and applies to her work one of the basic principles on which Freudian and Bettelheimian interpretations of literature are founded. She still modestly seems to accept that the psychoanalyst can interpret and explain these symbolic meanings to the author, reader, or patient. This is something that more recent authors and critics have rebelled against.

Like many critics, Zipes reads Sexton's fairy-tale retellings as autobiographical: "*Transformations* is unique in that [Sexton] gains distance on her personal problems by transposing them on to fairy-tale figures and situations" ("Sexton" 461). Although in the quotation above Sexton claims that her literary work contains insights that she is not conscious of, Alicia Ostriker ascribes to her the more empowered position of the psychoanalyst: "An important source of Sexton's effectiveness is her striking ability to decode stories we thought we knew, revealing meanings we should have guessed" (85). Two different aspects of her writing surface here, which cause a tension in Sexton's poetry. Ostriker views Sexton as the interpreter of fairy tales (like a psychoanalyst), as someone who decodes fairy-tale symbols. Zipes sees her as an autobiographical writer who tries to interpret her own life by referring to fairy tales, as someone who encrypts her meanings with fairy-tale symbols. As a result and in contrast to a psychoanalyst such as Bettelheim, Sexton's explanations of the fairy tales are not as clearly structured and accessible as possible but rather pose a challenge to interpreters. Whereas some see the code that Sexton uses as a conscious choice (Ostriker), others see it as a more naïve discourse in which the unconscious finds an outlet (Sexton's doctors).

Whether Sexton's poem "Briar Rose" can be read as a reflection of (neo-)Freudian interpretations is a much debated issue, especially among feminist critics. Ostriker asserts that "[Alt]hough Sexton is obviously indebted to psychoanalytic method in the retrieval of latent content, she is not limited by its dogmas" (85). She refers here to Bettelheim's interpretation of Briar Rose's hundred-year sleep as a symbol of feminine pubescence, whereas Sexton reads "Briar Rose" as a story of incest. Bettelheim knew at least some of Sexton's poems that were based on fairy tales. He quotes *Transformations* in his discussion of "Snow White" and "The Frog Prince," but *The Uses of Enchantment* does not mention her "Briar Rose (Sleeping Beauty)." There are several striking similarities between Bettelheim's interpretation of "Sleeping Beauty" and the transformations of the traditional story in Sexton's retelling, however. In his discussion of Basile's "Sun, Moon, and Talia" as a variant of "Briar Rose," Bettelheim notes the absence of the father after Talia is woken by the prince. By interpreting Talia's father and her husband as identical, Bettelheim combines two different phases of a young girl's development: the Freudian Electra complex (childhood) and the young girl's first love (adulthood). For him, this combination of prince and king does not make it a story about incest but a narrative that symbolizes the projected feelings of an oedipal child (228). Bettelheim was not the first to focus on the relationship between the princess and the king in "Sleeping Beauty." Eight years earlier, Sexton had formulated a similar interpretation. When her Briar Rose wakes up, the equation of prince and father becomes explicit:

> In due time
> a hundred years passed
> and a prince got through.
> The briars parted as if for Moses

and the prince found the tableau intact.
He kissed Briar Rose
and she woke up crying:
Daddy! Daddy!
    (Sexton 171)

The association of the kiss with her father suggests that the king may
have usurped the prince's role when the girl was young. The repetitive-
ness of the kiss—both in the multiple references throughout the poem, as
in the described repetition of her behavior as a habit—supports this interpretation:

But if you kissed her on the mouth
her eyes would spring open
and she'd call out: Daddy! Daddy!
    (Sexton 172)

The childish name for the father is an indication that the association goes
back to the girl's childhood. The mechanical fierceness with which she
cries out "Daddy!" stands in stark contrast to the endings of the Grimms'
and Perrault's "Sleeping Beauty" and suggests that the previous kisses may
have caused a trauma. The prologue to the poem, a description of Sleeping
Beauty's childhood, sets up the theme of incest more clearly with the description of the games that father and daughter play:

Little doll child,
come here to Papa.
Sit on my knee.
I have kisses for the back of your neck.
A penny for your thoughts, Princess.
I will hunt them like an emerald.
Come be my snooky
and I will give you a root.
That kind of voyage,
rank as honeysuckle.
    (Sexton 169)

The child is objectified by the father, who calls her a doll—in combination with this reification the comforting line "come here to Papa" acquires an ominous ring. As Dawn Skorczewski notes, by calling his daughter "little doll child," her father "emphasizes his power over her by virtue of size and age" (314). That he announces a hunt for her thoughts suggests that she is his prey, another way of stressing the aggressive assertion of power that is later reinforced when the girl compares him to a shark circling around her bed. As the father offers his "little doll child" kisses on the back of her neck as well as the phallic symbol of the root, in combination with the sexual associations in the components of "honeysuckle," the theme of incest becomes more concrete.

The incest is only thinly veiled at the end of Sexton's poem, which also stresses the little girl's helplessness and disempowerment (in the images of the prison and the abyss), fear (the shark), and disgust (the jellyfish):

> Daddy?
> That's another kind of prison.
> It's not the prince at all,
> but my father
> drunkenly bent over my bed,
> circling the abyss like a shark,
> my father thick upon me
> like some sleeping jellyfish.
> What voyage this, little girl?
> (Sexton 173)

In an achronological intertextual comparison, Sexton's stanza can be read as an ironic comment on Bettelheim's interpretation of "Sleeping Beauty." Bettelheim ascribes a positive value to the protagonist's development ("voyage") in the Grimms' "Sleeping Beauty." He reads the story as the coming of age of an adolescent girl, with all the typical problems that may accompany this phase in life: the difficulty in detaching oneself from overprotective parents, the anxiety about the first menstruation, a period of passivity and lethargy, and fear and insecurity about marriage and sexuality. Yet by the end of the story, these problems are resolved and Sleeping Beauty is sexually mature and ready for marriage. This contrasts with Sexton's Briar Rose, who is traumatized and cannot break free from the prison in which her father has locked her up—the jellyfish is an animal unlikely to transform into a charming prince. Whereas Bettelheim associates the prince and the king on a symbolic level, Sexton takes the equation more literally and shows how the father took over the prince's initiation of Sleeping Beauty. The psychoanalyst can attach positive value to the symbolic equation, but Sexton, and many feminists with her, transport it to a realistic frame of reference and deny its healing effect. "There was a theft," the poem spells out, as if the young girl's virginity, happiness, and subjectivity have been stolen. The eyes that flip open mechanically suggest that as an adult, she has become the selfless doll that her father called her as a child. Sleeping Beauty's premature sexual awakening has led her to become a perpetual insomniac, plagued by awful memories that no prince can chase away.

Although Bettelheim could not have influenced Sexton's rewriting of the tale of "Sleeping Beauty," *The Uses of Enchantment* has affected the reception of this work, as Skorczewski concludes her historical survey of reviews and interpretations. Some critics who have applied Bettelheimian interpretations to Sexton's poem managed to do so by largely ignoring the incestuous theme.[24] Skorczewski mentions Robert Philips and Vernon Young as two examples of critics who have diagnosed Briar Rose as having an Electra complex, thus putting the origin of the erotic fantasy with the child rather than the father. In a similar critique and with explicit reference to a misapplication of Bettelheimian theory on Sexton's poem, she comments on Cynthia Miller's interpretation of "Briar Rose (Sleeping Beauty)": "It is difficult to understand how a critic whose attention is so focused on the language of Briar Rose [as Cynthia Miller] could interpret 'my father thick upon me / like some sleeping jellyfish' as a cry for support and supervision. The interpretation does make sense, however, when coupled with Bruno Bettelheim's explanation of the Sleeping Beauty tale" (Skorczewski 333).

Skorczewski's critique of the reception of Anne Sexton's poem draws on a more general critique targeted against Bettelheim and other psychoanalysts. In his interpretations of fairy tales, Bettelheim claims to have an insight into a child's psyche, even in the child's unconscious experience of stories. In addition to the epistemological doubt that can be raised with regard to this contention, what is even more problematic to feminists and critics of children's literature, such as Tatar, Tucker, and Zipes, is that Bettelheim locates the desire in the female child, from which it is not a big step to infer that the fairy tale presents an incest fantasy. Sexton's "Sleeping

Beauty," like Van Gestel's "Prinses Roosje," retains the perspective of the child, but shifts the incestuous desire to the father, the king.

The American poet Denise Duhamel similarly interprets "Sleeping Beauty" as a tale of incest in her "Sleeping Beauty's Dreams" (1996). Duhamel also sees the parallel that Sexton and Bettelheim draw between father and prince: "She's kissing her dead father when the Prince kisses her awake."[25] The multiple sexual symbols that Duhamel incorporates into her poem are all threatening, sharp, and lifeless objects: from the "popping bobbins and evil spindles, / lethal injections" to "the needle, up and down" that "repeats, like sex, like sex with the Prince / who hasn't woken her yet."[26] The result of the suggested incest is that this Sleeping Beauty too can never truly wake up from her traumatic experiences. At the end of the story, she is still "groggy" and looking "for infinity through his eyes, / dark and small like dustpan's holes" (92). The emptiness of this image suggests the failure of her search; the dustpan trivializes the idea that she will only turn to dust. Like Sexton, Duhamel stresses that incest is not the result of Sleeping Beauty's desire and that it has turned her life into a perennial nightmare. The contrast to Bettelheim's optimistic reading of the tale could not be greater. Van Gestel, although he opens up the possibility of the king's sexual attraction to his daughter, does return to the happy ending: the desire is never acted upon. Sexton and Duhamel are further removed from the traditional tale in form and content: they make the sexual component of the king's desire more explicit and show how the ensuing traumatic experience renders a happy ending impossible. They do so in a form that is coded and complex in its own right—their denial of the protagonist's subjectivity is expressed in a fragmentary and alienating language that reflects her disturbed, restless personality.

Briar Rose is not the only fairy-tale protagonist who Bettelheim diagnoses as having an Electra complex. The tale that deals with a girl's attachment to her father most elaborately is "Beauty and the Beast." Francesca Lia Block bases her retelling, "Beast" (2000), on de Beaumont's version. In accordance with Bettelheim's interpretation of this tale, and like Sexton and Duhamel, Block emphasizes the possible oedipal dimensions in the relationship between Beauty and her father: "Beauty's father loved his youngest daughter, the child of his old age, more than anything in the world. Maybe too much. After all, it was he who had named her" (170). Later in the story, the father asks himself whether his wife died because he had loved his daughter too much: here it is not a king who replaces another king, as in Bettelheim's analysis of "Sun, Moon, and Talia," but a daughter who replaces a wife. In de Beaumont's version from 1756, the scene in which Beauty's father plucks the rose is rendered rather briefly: "As he passed under an arbor of roses, he remembered that Beauty had asked for one, and he plucked a rose from a branch filled with roses" (808). Like Bettelheim, Block's narrator stresses the sensual and sexual symbolic meaning of the rose and adds incestuous connotations to the father's crime:

> That was when Beauty's father noticed the rose. The rose that had proved he loved his daughter too much. There was a little sign in front of it that read, Please Do Not Pick the Flowers.
>
> The rose reminded him of his daughter—open, glowing, pink, and white, fragrant. Did he know it reminded him of her because it was forbidden? He only knew that he had to have it. (177–78)

Picking a flower is a common euphemism for taking a girl's virginity, and Block's tale transforms the prohibition and consequent violation to a more explicitly sexual transgression. The similarities in focus that mark Block and Bettelheim's interpretations of "Beauty and the Beast" do not make Block's retelling a fictional counterpart to Bettelheim's nonfictional analysis, however. Two crucial shifts in her tale would render such a straightforward link problematic. First of all, Bettelheim sees Beauty as the central figure of the entire tale and he interprets it exclusively from her point of view. Block makes use of two alternating focalizers in her third-person narrative: in the second part, the protagonist is indeed Beauty, but in the first part the events are seen through her father's eyes. The oedipal attachment that Bettelheim locates in the daughter is once again shifted to the father, as was the case for Van Gestel, Sexton, and Duhamel. It is he who loves his daughter too much; it is he who plucks the rose because it reminds him of his daughter. Block lifts the responsibility for the oedipal attachment from Beauty, who is pictured as feeling oppressed by it. At first it is stated that "Beauty [. . .] had her father's love and so didn't feel a need for much else" (171), but later the narrator asserts that "secretly, without even knowing it herself, she had been waiting for a Beast to go to" (184). The narrator's comment fits in with the analysis of Bettelheim, who claims that Beauty needs to detach herself from her father and transfer her love to the

Beast. But Block modifies Beauty's feelings when she leaves the house. Whereas de Beaumont writes that "Beauty was the only one who did not cry because she did not want to increase their [her family's] distress" (809), Block pictures her as truly liberated: "She had never felt so free" (185). When her father dies, she is relieved rather than sad. The balance between affection for the father and love for the husband that Bettelheim finds so vital to the resolution of "Beauty and the Beast" (308) is absent from Block's retelling.

Linked to this modification is a second crucial difference between Block and Bettelheim, which concerns their evaluation of the beastly versus the civilized. Bettelheim writes that "the oedipal love of Beauty for her father, when transferred to her future husband, is wonderfully healing" (303). Block's retelling suggests the same: the time that Beauty spends with the Beast is the happiest of her life (190). Yet, for Bettelheim, it is necessary that the Beast shed his animal shape in order for the couple to achieve this happiness: "Mature love and acceptance of sex make what was before repugnant, or seemed stupid, become beautiful and full of spirit" (304). In Block's retelling, the beastly is not repugnant, but desirable—it is essential for Beauty's happiness that the beast keep his animalistic traits and that she can share them with him. Bettelheim opposes the beastly and the beautiful: "Once detached from the parent and directed to a partner of more suitable age, in normal development, sexual longings no longer seem beastly—to the contrary, they are experienced as beautiful" (308). Block portrays the beastly *as* beautiful. She therefore refutes Bettelheim's authoritarian claim that "these artificially isolated aspects of our humanity [the dual existence of man as animal and as mind] must become unified; that alone permits human fulfillment" (308). In Bettelheim's interpretation, it is "Beast's true nature" that surfaces when he becomes human; according to Block it is Beauty's true nature that appears when she is allowed to become beast. Or, to use psychoanalytic terminology—whereas Bettelheim values the "humanization and socialization of the id by the superego" (309), Block revalues the id, or rather a version of the id that is enriching without being threatening.

As a result, Block's retelling denies its characters and readers the perfectly happy ending that is vital to de Beaumont and Bettelheim's views of the story, indicating instead Beauty's sustained ambivalence. That the time Beauty spends with the Beast is the happiest of her life can be taken literally.

His transformation partly disturbs her bliss: "Beauty loved him more than anything, her Beast boy, but, secretly, sometimes, she wished that he would have remained a Beast" (198). As Beast acquires speech, his previously physical communication with Beauty loses its intensity. Bathing, wearing shoes, and walking function as markers of socialization—markers that entail for Beauty a clear and irrefutable loss of their entanglement. In Zipes's critique of Bettelheim it is stated that "the patterns of the fairy tales allegedly [according to Bettelheim] foster ideal normative behavior which children are to internalize; yet some of these literary patterns like the forms of social behavior are repressive constructs which violate the imagination of both children and adults alike" (*Magic Spell* 185). Block's alternative ending to "Beauty and the Beast" reveals such a normative model of behavior in de Beaumont's story and Bettelheim's unquestioning praise of it.

Whereas Block questions the complete happiness in the ending to the traditional version, others have revised that closure so that it can be a blissful ending on their terms. Highly influential in this respect is Angela Carter's "The Tiger's Bride" (1979). At the end of this retelling, the traditional ending of "Beauty and the Beast" is reversed, as it pictures the protagonist while the beast licks her human skin from her body and beautiful fur appears (*Boats* 169). No such harmony is achieved, however, in Anne Provoost's *De Roos en het Zwijn*, a retelling for young adults that draws on both de Beaumont's "Beauty and the Beast" and Straparola's "The Pig Prince." The author herself names Bettelheim as an influence when it comes to the foregrounding of sexuality in *De Roos en het Zwijn*: "The sexual messages that Bettelheim addresses have been made more explicit than in the original version. To me *Belle et la Bete* [sic] has always and foremost been the story of how young women first have to distance themselves from the father figures in their lives in order to be able to become sexually mature" (Provoost, *Anne Provoost*; my translation).

The quotation is indeed an echo of Bettelheim's interpretation of the tale: "Only after Beauty decides to leave her father's house to be reunited with the Beast—that is, after she has resolved her oedipal ties to her father—does sex, which before was repugnant, become beautiful" (308). Provoost denies, however, that she was directly influenced by Bettelheim. To the critique that she had applied Bettelheim's retelling by the book, she replied that she only read it after she had written the first version of *De Roos en het Zwijn*: "What are you going to talk about if you have to avoid all psychology: the relationship with the lover, with the father and the mother, with the child? It's not because you apply Freud, that you're an adherent. You simply cannot know" (Vandevoorde; my translation). Drawing the link with other influential thinkers such as Charles Darwin, Provoost argues that you cannot escape these theories when you live in modern times. Like most authors who incorporate Freudian or Bettelheimian elements in their retellings, Provoost modifies the psychoanalytic interpretation of the fairy tale, making different emphases and opening the possibility for the retelling to be read as a dialogue with, or a critique of, psychoanalysis.

Parallels between Bettelheim's and Provoost's interpretations of "Beauty and the Beast" abound. Provoost reintroduces an explicitly sexual theme and foregrounds the relationship between Rosalena (Beauty) and her father, adding strong oedipal connotations. This becomes clear from the reasons given for the hatred between Beauty and her sisters. The sisters' negativity is never explained in de Beaumont's tale as a rivalry for the father's affection. The narrator suggests different interests, as well as jealousy because of her beauty in general (not the father's acknowledgement of it in particular). As with all sibling rivalry, Bettelheim argues that the negativity between Beauty and her sisters "has only incidentally to do with a child's actual brothers and sisters. The real source of it is the child's feelings about his parents" (238). In Provoost's retelling, Rosalena also links her sisters' jealousy explicitly to her father: "They had reached the age when young girls become jealous, and everything indicated that my father privileged me" (20; my translation). Whereas in de Beaumont's tale, it is Beauty who decides to stay at home with her father, in Provoost's retelling, it is her father's choice: "I couldn't give you away first because you're not the eldest" (50–51; my translation). It is unclear whether the affection of Beauty's father is her interpretation or even, as Bettelheim would argue, her projection of oedipal feelings onto her father. This issue remains unresolved, as the narrative is restricted to Rosalena's point of view. Although it is never claimed that Rosalena has sexual longings for her father, she does have a physically intimate, at times even erotic relationship with Zoran, the little pig that her father gave her. In a psychoanalytic reading, Rosalena transfers her oedipal feelings to this animal. Both Bettelheim (following Freud) and Provoost situate sexuality not only in adults but also in children. Van Gestel can be argued to do the same in his description of a narcissist Prinses

Roosje, but Provoost's protagonist is substantially younger. Already when Rosalena is five years old, her little pig Zoran fulfills her sexual desire, and he does so until she reaches puberty: "Now and then I sneaked out of the house to the little shed, where I heated the oven, undressed and lay down in the hay. Zoran knew my need. He stood over me as he had when I was five, and licked the skin of my throat, my thighs with his rough, massaging tongue" (31; my translation). The scene is reminiscent of the ending to Carter's "The Tiger's Bride." Yet, in comparison to the fairy-tale pre-text and Bettelheim's interpretation, Rosalena's sexual intimacy with Zoran becomes a reversal and subversion of the traditional ending. Rosalena's transfer does not take place in an adult heterosexual relationship but is part of a child's sexual longing. No transformation takes place, yet this does not mean that Rosalena's desire remains unfulfilled.

However, Provoost also acknowledges the fear, repression, and guilt related to a young girl's awakening sexuality, and they bring Rosalena to a severe form of penitence. Bettelheim sees a similar pattern in "Cinderella." The Flemish critic Annemie Leysen considers Rosalena's self-inflicted atonement an indication of a Freudian morality (698): "Rosalena feels guilty about her awakening sensuality. Only by bidding her father farewell for good can she allow a man to enter her life and come to full sexual maturation" (698; my translation). This interpretation indeed fits into a Freudian or Bettelheimian reading of "Beauty and the Beast," but it is odd that Leysen would suggest that Rosalena, like Beauty, resolves her feelings of guilt at the end of the story. Instead I would argue that Provoost modifies or leaves out several aspects that Bettelheim considers vital to the fairy tale's therapeutic function. The main difference between their interpretations of the tale lies exactly in the (im)possibility of resolution. Although Provoost states in the quotation above that she sees the transference of oedipal love from father to beast as central to the tale (a Bettelheimian reading), Rosalena in *De Roos en het Zwijn* never completes this process. Instead, the story ends with her eternal oscillation between father and beast: "I know I will always go back and forth, a whole life long. [. . .] Who shall kill me, release me from this eternal movement? Whom shall I kiss to turn the tide?" (109; my translation). Bettelheim argues that as long as Beauty does not pass on the love for her father to the beast, there can be no transformation of the beast into a prince. In this sense, Provoost's ending fits into Bettelheim's interpretation. But like many of the feminist retellings discussed in the previous chapter, Provoost questions the traditional ending of "Beauty and the Beast," unmasking it as a superficial validation of external rather than internal transformations. Rosalena has "a strong belief that an external change could never be an interesting change" (29; my translation). Bettelheim shares this idea, explaining the external metamorphosis as a symbol of a more significant internal transformation in Beauty's perception of the Beast. However, in contrast to Bettelheim and de Beaumont, Provoost underlines the impossibility and undesirability of such an internal transformation: she unmasks their ideal of a gradual process of maturation and harmonious resolution as an illusion. As Rosalena keeps oscillating between the Beast and her father, Provoost's retelling oscillates between a Bettelheimian and an anti-Bettelheimian reading of "Beauty and the Beast." Provoost's awareness of psychoanalytic theory, as well as her skepticism of it, thus leads to a complex and rich literary dialogue that leaves the reader with more questions than answers.

Resexualized Fairy Tales in Illustrated Children's Books

The foregrounding or uncovering of repressed sexual desire does not remain limited to adult and young adult literature but occasionally also appears in picture books and illustrated fairy tales for young children. The 1978 edition of a collection of the Grimms fairy tales, translated by Brian Alderson, features a remarkable illustration by the British artist Michael Foreman (Figure 15). Sleeping Beauty's prince is shown as he is about to enter a hole in the thorn hedge that surrounds the royal castle. The sexual symbolism in this image is unmistakable: the prince holds up his sword in front of a big bush that looks more like pubic hair than a hedge of roses. The hole itself is black and surrounded by pink dots. Again these dots are more reminiscent of female labia than of the roses that are mentioned in the Grimms' text, especially since they only surround the black hole and appear nowhere else in the hedge. The prince does not seem to have made this hole, but rather he has discovered it: this is suggested by the fact that he carefully holds one of the briars with his hand, to make the entrance bigger.

Foreman's illustration appears as a visual counterpart to Bettelheim's explanation of the hedge of thorns. The psychoanalyst argues that it protects Sleeping Beauty from untimely suitors but that when she is ready for sex and marriage, the "wall of thorns suddenly turns into a wall of big,

Figure 15. Sleeping Beauty and Other Favourite Tales *by Michael Foreman.*

beautiful flowers, which opens to let the prince enter" (233). In Foreman's illustration, as in Bettelheim's interpretation, an association is suggested between the opening of the hedge of thorns and a first sexual encounter. Typical Freudian associations are invoked: the sword as a phallic symbol, and flowers that "indicate women's genitals, or, in particular, virginity" (Freud, *Lectures* 188, 192). Eva Bednářová's illustration to Perrault's "Sleeping Beauty" (1978) adds a similar sexual symbolism. Her bird's-eye view of the castle shows a hole in the bush of roses that also looks like a vagina. Like Foreman, Bednářová couples this reference to female sexuality with a symbol of male sexuality: long daggers and blooming flowers adorn the frame around her illustration of the castle.

A few years after his work on the Grimms' translation by Alderson, Foreman illustrated "Sleeping Beauty" once again, this time for the translation by Angela Carter (1982). The previously discussed image is missing here, but it is replaced by a picture that is equally loaded with sexual suggestion. The prince is shown as an archer riding across a landscape that has the distinct form of a naked woman (Figure 16). In the following picture, in which Sleeping Beauty is represented in profile, one can see that her face has the exact same shape as the landscape.

Again, the archer and the phallic symbol of his arrow, in combination with a naked female body, make visible the strong sexual associations that psychoanalysis ascribes to the fairy tale. By reflecting a Freudian interpretation in his illustrations, however, Foreman can also be said to incorporate the patriarchal view that psychoanalysis has been reproached with: the prince is the conqueror; Sleeping Beauty lies passive and is objectified. On the other hand, the magnification of her body and vagina signal the prince's smallness in front of his conquest, and the illustrations thus draw attention to the mixture of desire and fear that he too is confronted with.

Foreman's and Bednářová's illustrations to "Sleeping Beauty" form an exception in children's literature. The sexual aspects of psychoanalytic theory are usually softened or ignored when it is applied in literature for the very young. Moreover, when sexual aspects are highlighted in fairy-tale retellings for children, they are rarely located in the child itself, as they are in Bettelheim and Freud. Gerard Gielen's collection of retellings serves as a good example here. In the epilogue, in which he explains several opinions on the fairy tale, Gielen makes an interesting reduction when it comes to Bettelheim:

Figure 16. Sleeping Beauty and Other Favourite Tales *by Michael Foreman.*

In his book *The Uses of Enchantment* Bruno Bettelheim says that fairy tales matter so much for the child because they deal with the reality of life itself. Fairy tales address deep truths of life, feelings, questions, fears, and doubts. When we tell a child a fairy tale, we offer images that the child can recognize in its own struggle with illness and death, loss and separation. The fairy tale takes the child's fears and dilemmas seriously and tackles them directly: the need that someone cares for it, the will to live, and the fear of death. At the same time, the fairy tale presents solutions in a way that the child can access both consciously and unconsciously. Fairy tales thus offer relief by giving shape to unconscious fears, without the child being conscious of it. (Gielen 235; my translation)

Illness and death are present in the margins of Bettelheim's theory, as are concerns about a parent's death or the skills that a child needs to replace the older generation, which Gielen mentions later (235). Much more central to the analyses of tales in *The Uses of Enchantment*, however, are unconscious fears and desires caused by Oedipus and Electra complexes ("Snow White," "Sleeping Beauty"), masturbation ("Jack and the Beanstalk"), penis envy and castration anxiety ("Cinderella"), and the dangers of premature sex as well as the child's desire for it ("Little Red Riding Hood," "The Frog Prince"). The sexual aspect of Bettelheim's interpretations is for the most part ignored by Gielen. When he does address it, for instance in his retelling of "Hansel and Gretel," the child is portrayed as the victim of adult sexual desire, which does not take place in the child's unconscious but in real life. As we have seen, Bettelheim, in contrast, situates sexual desire in the child itself (320); yet this is an aspect of his theory that is frequently adapted in popularized criticism as well as in retellings for children and adults.

Critical Responses to Bruno Bettelheim

Few of the literary examples with parallels to Bruno Bettelheim's interpretations integrate his theory in a straightforward manner. All the retellings and illustrations mentioned in this chapter overlap with only some aspects of his analyses and differ in others. Even larger than the corpus of works that match Bettelheim's ideas is the number of texts that use literature as a means to critically engage with psychoanalytic theories. This is not surprising if we keep in mind Bettelheim's criticism of fairy-tale adaptations and retellings: for him the traditional versions were the highest good. The genre of the fairy-tale retelling thus becomes a forum for resistance to Bettelheim's theories on two levels: first, by their mere existence these retellings violate Bettelheim's rule that the Grimms' tales should not be modified; and second, on the level of content, these retellings critically engage either with Bettelheim as a person or with his ideas about fairy tales. It is striking that, with a few exceptions, such as Anne Provoost and Yves Pommaux,[27] hardly any writers are willing to name Bettelheim as a direct and positive influence. Several authors have testified, however, to writing their retellings in debate with Freud's or Bettelheim's theory, including Angela Carter (Haffenden 82–83).

In fairy-tale criticism, Bettelheim has been under fire for several reasons, both professional and personal. With the appearance of his most influential works, Bettelheim was embraced by the general public and his fame rose with lectures, newspaper articles, and television documentaries. After his suicide in March 1990, a controversy about his work ethics was raised by some of his former patients at the Orthogenic School of Chicago, who accused him of psychologically and physically abusing them as children. This put his whole view on childhood into a new perspective (Sutton 1–15).[28] However, even before his death, Bettelheim's research ethics and methodology had come under fire.

The elaborate critical discussion of *The Uses of Enchantment* can be boiled down to a few central ideas. Several critics have expressed the idea that Bettelheim's thinking is universalistic. Feminists have scolded him for his equation of boys and girls, reader response critics for his disregard of age, class, and the child's individual personality. Anthropologists and sociohistorians have dismissed *The Uses of Enchantment* because it supposedly ignores all variants of fairy tales except the Grimms'.[29] Psychoanalytic studies are more generally criticized for "postulat[ing] absolute universality on the basis of a scattering of case histories—all typically from Western cultures" (Dundes, "Folklore" 18). Bettelheim is reproached with ignoring the cultural and historical specificity of *Die Kinder- und Hausmärchen*, and while claiming to uncover universal, transhistorical truths,[30] he turns a small selection of tales from this nineteenth-century European collection into a model for all fairy tales.[31] Bettelheim's universalism has been attributed in part to the faults in his methodology. His alleged lack of knowledge of the fairy-tale scholarship available in the 1970s, for instance, can explain why he gives the Brothers Grimm so much credit—too much credit, Perry Nodelman argues: Bettelheim "wrongly believe[s] that the tale [sic] accurately represent an anonymous oral tradition" (*Pleasures* 257–58). This romantic myth had already been contested before *The Uses of Enchantment* was published, yet Bettelheim "virtually ignored any proper discussion on how fairy tales came to exist and to be written down in the first place" (Tucker, "Dr. Bettelheim" 33). Scholars' opinions differ with regard to Bettelheim's intentions. Whereas Nodelman attributes the gaps in his study to ignorance, others see them as part of a manipulative psychoanalytic methodology. According to critics such as Maria Tatar, Bettelheim's selection of tales is biased and excludes "stories that run counter to Freudian orthodoxy."[32] She also claims that he has manipulated the tales that he discusses so that they fit into a psychoanalytic model (*Heads* xxii, xxiv).[33] Bettelheim's scientific ethos has been shown to be problematic in several other ways. A scandal arose after his death when *The Uses of Enchantment* was argued to contain several plagiarized passages from Julius Heuscher's *A Psychiatric Study of Myths and Fairy Tales* (1963) as well as ideas from other scholars, such as Géza Róheim and Otto Rank.[34] Moreover, Tucker claims that Bettelheim leaves out all evidence, as well as research, that contradicts his views on reader response and the beneficial effect of fairy tales ("Dr. Bettelheim" 34–35). The dubious therapeutic function has indeed come under further discussion. Patricia Guérin Thomas argues that there is no proof for it (Haase, *Reception* 242); Tucker contrasts Bettelheim's theory with Arthur Applebee's and Norman Holland's research ("Dr. Bettelheim" 35);

and Zipes refutes it with reference to Basil Bernstein's work (*Magic Spell* 189–90).

The result of Bettelheim's interpretive acrobatics is what Nodelman calls wish fulfillment of his own fantasies (*Pleasures* 258). Critics such as Maria Tatar and Shuli Barzilai have pointed out that his analyses are generally more informative about himself than about the fairy tales. Their feminist response to Bettelheim's works reveals a patriarchal bias, among others, in the fact that Bettelheim mainly selects tales that feature "a girl's sexual rivalry with her mother for the attention and affection of a father/husband" (Tatar, *Heads* xxvi). It has been mentioned several times that Bettelheim is "oddly accusative" toward women and children and has frequently been criticized for "blaming the victim." Tatar points out that Bettelheim pretends to have the child's interest in mind but represents an adult view of the tales: he always charges the child characters in the fairy tales with what goes wrong, never the parents. Bettelheim interprets "Hansel and Gretel," for instance, as a tale about children's regression and oral greed rather than a story about parents who abandon their children or an evil witch who tries to kill them.[35] He "quickly erases the 'evil deeds' of the impoverished parents to focus on the 'frustrations,' 'destructive desires,' 'uncontrollable craving,' 'ambivalent feelings,' and 'anxieties' of the children in the tale. [. . .] Bettelheim's reading of 'Hansel and Gretel' turns the children, who are viewed as burdens on the parents and strains on the family budget, into the real villains of the story" (Tatar, *Heads* xviii).

Finally, like feminist scholars such as Lieberman, Bettelheim has been criticized for a reduction of the fairy tale's wide range of possible functions and for rationalizing its magic.[36] Tatar (*Heads* xxii) and Darnton (10) note that Bettelheim treats fairy-tale characters as real persons on the psychoanalytic couch. I will now explore in more depth the disregard of the fairy tale's complexity and literariness as a recurrent critique of Bettelheim's approach. The starting point of my analysis will be the response to Bettelheim of three influential scholars: Ruth Bottigheimer, Pierre Péju, and Jacqueline Rose.

A Translation of Sexual Symbols (Ruth Bottigheimer)

In the most basic popularized understanding, the psychoanalytic study of literature is frequently understood to be a mere translation of sexual references into symbols or, as Bottigheimer explains, "the willingness to see a phallus in everything that is longer than wide, whereas everything that is hollow is equated with the vagina" ("Bettelheims Hexe" 299; my translation). In "Bettelheim's Hexe" (Bettelheim's Witch), Bottigheimer notes the propensity in fairy-tale criticism to explain everything that is red, for instance, as a symbolic reference to menstruation (296). To compare Bettelheim's theory with such a simplistic model of interpretation would be a reduction too, but this is nevertheless how *The Uses of Enchantment* is perceived by some critics. As Wilhelm Solms, for instance, writes, Bettelheim "isolates individual images from the fairy tale, does not ask which function they fulfill in the fairy-tale plot, but ascribes to them the meaning found in Freud and invented by Freud" (13; my translation). The examples that Solms mentions are reminiscent of Bottigheimer's critique: Bettelheim reads the shoe in "Cinderella," for instance, predictably as a symbol of the vagina.

It is the psychoanalytic view of literature as a simplistic symbolic translation of sexual references that has most often been satirized in fairy-tale retellings, even before *The Uses of Enchantment* appeared. Most of these have the same format. They reformulate the plot of a well-known fairy tale, adding terms or typical explanations borrowed from psychoanalysis. Willy Pribil (1971) rephrases "Snow White" freely after Sigmund Freud (*Schneewittchen, frei nach Sigmund Freud*): "Once upon a time there was a princess. She loved her father, since she had a repressed Electra complex. Because she was so beautiful her stepmother, loaded with a strong sadistic libidinal component, was seized by sexual envy and she ordered the hunter to take Snow White to the forest and thus to her lethal end. But here the queen committed a faulty act [*Fehlleistung*] because the hunter was a fetishist" (44; my translation).

Such reformulations of the fairy tale in a specific jargon are not exclusive to psychoanalysis. James Finn Garner and David Fisher, for instance, perform similar critiques when they rephrase the tales in politically correct euphemisms or legalese. One of the effects of such an unexpected combination of subject and register is that the inappropriateness of the discourse is highlighted. These retellings do not communicate a critique or an interpretation of the fairy tale; rather they ridicule the method and jargon of the analysis that is applied. Moreover, by summarizing the more elaborate discussions of fairy tales by critics like Grant Duff and later Bettelheim, Pribil relies on the popular impression that for psychoanalysts, the fairy tale is no more than a succession of neuroses. The retelling thus humorously addresses the reduction of the fairy tale in an exaggerated, simplistic psychoanalytic interpretation.

The work of Iring Fetscher was introduced in the first chapter of this book. One of the three critical paradigms that are the subject of his mock fairy-tale interpretations is psychoanalysis. In the preface to *Wer hat Dornröschen wachgeküßt?*, Fetscher addresses Karl Popper's critique of the incontestability of psychoanalysis: "It is irrefutable. Every attempt to refute it, yes even the silently raised doubt, can easily be explained by the analyst as the typical symptom of a *resistance* that comes from the unconscious, which—contrary to the conscious intention of the person in doubt—appears as clear proof that the interpretation was right. [. . .] Thus the analyst cannot be contradicted or criticized" (*Dornröschen* 14; my translation).

Fetscher finds in the literary parody of psychoanalysis a way to escape its premises. His satirical interpretation of "Sleeping Beauty" is based on a reading of the tale as her victory over her fear of defloration. Fetscher here mocks the exact passage that Bottigheimer criticizes, that is, the psychoanalytic interpretation of the magic spindle that "jumps around so merrily" (Grimm, KHM 1: 258; my translation)[37] as a phallic symbol. Fetscher adds, "As is known, in the popular vernacular the male sexual organ is often designated by 'that thing' or 'my thing,' which undoubtedly indicates an alienated relationship to one's sexual characteristic" (*Dornröschen* 170; my translation).

The retellings by both Pribil and Fetscher highlight the apodictic self-evidence with which psychoanalysis equates fairy-tale elements with sexual symbols and complexes. Dundes noted this arrogance in the works of Erich Fromm (1951), writing about "Little Red Riding Hood" that "most of the symbolism in this fairy tale can be understood without difficulty" ("Interpreting Red Riding Hood" 31).[38] Imitating this assertion of obviousness, Pribil argues, "Surely the symbolism of this passage does not need to be further explained" (44; my translation). Fetscher inserts words such as "*bekanntlich*" (as is known) and "*zweifellos*" (undoubtedly). It is no coincidence that the psychoanalyst who features in Fetscher's fake fairy-tale conferences is called Peter Sicherlich or Peter Surely (*Dornröschen* 209). One metacomment in Fetscher's mock analysis of "Sleeping Beauty" is particularly important for the critique of Bettelheim that will be discussed in the following section: "The claire-obscure of the fascinatingly polysemic fairy tale gives way to the clear light of science" (*Dornröschen* 168; my translation). Not only does Fetscher (like Popper, Zipes, Tatar, Tucker, and Solms) doubt psychoanalysis' claim to being science, he also suggests that the understanding that is gained when the fairy tale becomes subject to rigid scientific analysis may entail the loss of a variety of meanings and interpretations, a loss of literariness. This criticism of the enlightened aspects of psychoanalytic fairy-tale criticism lies at the base of Pierre Péju's critique of Bruno Bettelheim.

A Different Kind of Desire (Pierre Péju)

One of the critiques of Lieberman's and others' "images of women" studies was that this approach reduces the fairy tale to a cliché, and likewise Bettelheim has been criticized for limiting his choice of fairy tales and fairy-tale passages to examples that illustrated his theory. Bettelheim (14–15) and Lieberman use the same principle for limiting their corpus: they study only the small number of tales that are still widely known and read.[39] Both have been criticized for ignoring the literary dimensions of the fairy tale, stressing instead its utilitarian dimension, either as an instrument of socialization (feminism) or as a means of therapy (psychoanalysis). In both cases, the aesthetic value of the tales takes second place.[40] Pierre Péju is a French critic and philosopher as well as an author of fairy tales and novels. His elaborate discussion of Bettelheim in *La petite fille dans la forêt des contes* (1981, The Little Girl in the Fairy-Tale Forest) seeks to draw the reader's attention exactly to the literary features of the fairy tale and to open up different perspectives for the interpretation and experience of the tales.

Péju's critique is aimed primarily at the enlightened aspects of Bettelheim's approach. Instead of accepting the magic in the tale as supernatural, Bettelheim is accused of turning magic into mystery. Referring to André Breton, Péju explains that the difference lies in the fact that a mystery can be solved and that a rational explanation underlies the supernatural (72). This is the "clear light of science" in Fetscher's mock analysis, which literally and figuratively elucidates the meaning of the story. The fairy tale is presented as a riddle or detective story that invites the reader to look for the true meaning that lies beneath the supernatural symbols (Péju 73). As Solms has argued, Bettelheim divides the fairy tale into a superficial layer and a deeper meaning (12–13) and consequently treats the literary qualities primarily as belonging to the superficial layer, as aspects of the fairy tale that can be virtually ignored. Bettelheim does stress fairy tales' aesthetic qualities in his introduction: "The delight we experience when we allow ourselves to respond to a fairy tale, the enchantment we feel, comes not from the psychological meaning of a tale (although this contributes to it) but from its literary qualities—the tale itself as a work of art" (12). Yet in the following sentence it becomes clear that this dimension is instrumentalized in light of the tale's therapeutic function: "The fairy tale could not have its psychological impact on the child were it not first and foremost a work of art" (12). This applies also to the approach that characterizes Bettelheim's case studies, in which literary features are rarely taken into account. In her seminal essay "Against Interpretation" (1964), Susan Sontag warns that such Freudian "digging" behind a text can become an aggressive activity that risks excavating and destroying the text (6). Like her, Péju condemns the rationalistic approach, asking respect instead for the beauty of the tale itself. The stories should not be read merely for keys to solve a mystery, he argues, and implicit in his argument is the appeal to treat magic as an intervention of the supernatural, not as mystery.

In addition to this critique, Péju reveals the politics of power that underlies Bettelheim's rationalistic approach, an aspect that was also addressed in Fetscher's parody. If the fairy tale is a mystery, a detective story, then the psychoanalyst is the chief inspector (Péju 73).[41] Bettelheim is reproached with putting himself in the authoritative position of the analyst or teacher who will uncover the true meaning of the tale: "He who interprets reigns supreme" (60; my translation). That this authority can be reversed when the psychoanalyst in turn is analyzed is something that can be observed in the reception of Bettelheim's work (among others, by Paul Pelckmans and Jack Zipes).

Péju sees Bettelheim's reading as an enforced enlightened lesson in which the fairy tale supposedly "helps to gain consciousness; it makes one progress; it makes one 'grow up.'" Péju's choice of words hints at what is lost in this model of progress, and his romantic views on literature as well as on the child become apparent: psychoanalysis "allows us to pass from the innocent magic lantern of memories of 'Cinderella' to the understanding of its symbolist mechanisms and latent contents" (59–60; my translation). Péju cannot reconcile his romantic ideals of magical and innocent experiences with Bettelheim's enlightened ideal of rational understanding, and Péju's plea for the literary qualities of the fairy tale soon takes the form of a more general anti-criticism. He writes that "there is absolutely no need for interpretation" (73; my translation), and in a heroic rhetoric he launches a defense of the fairy tale "against that powerful mincing machine of psychoanalysis" in order to save it from "the ravages of interpretation" (60; my translation).

In opposition to this destructive form of interpretation, Péju places the French epistemologist Gaston Bachelard's concept of "rêverie"—an aspect of the imaginary in the fairy tale that he believes to appeal to both children and adults and that can be described as a "perpetual movement of images that will always escape the categories and levels they are put in" (61; my translation). Whereas Bettelheim grants supreme authority to the (adult) psychoanalyst, when it comes to knowing both the child's psyche and the fairy tale, Péju argues that the child's understanding of the fairy tale as literature is superior to the adult's (62). He takes the alleged power from the adult and, in a romantic move, places it in the hands of the child. That it is then an adult (i.e., Péju himself) who explains the child's superior understanding of the fairy tale to other adults is a paradox that he does not sufficiently address. Like Bettelheim, Péju claims an understanding of the child that can easily be unmasked as an adult construction.

Bettelheim's reduction of the fairy tale is, according to Péju, clearest in his application of the Oedipus complex to every single tale: "The interpretation of symbolism is only exciting if it is flexible and capable of following unforeseen turns and shifts in the images. Yet, there is with Bettelheim a rigidity of interpretation dominated by the Oedipus complex that forbids straying onto tracks where the principle of identity is lost" (Péju 74; my translation).

The rigid frame of reference of the Oedipus complex leads to the omission or misrepresentation of several fairy tales: "All the passages that deviate from the path of oedipalization and that are also valuable in their own right are reinstalled by Bettelheim in a teleological chronology" (Péju 75; my translation). It is here that fairy-tale retellings inspired by psychoanalysis have helped to foreground other interpretations so that passages that are ignored or distorted by Bettelheim can be reinterpreted and reevaluated. Péju mentions "Snow White" as a tale reduced by Bettelheim, most notably the episodes that describe Snow White's life with the seven dwarves. Bettelheim merely glances over this part of the tale, describing it as a "phase of latency" in her maturation process (Péju 75). The implication is that this period in her life is only a temporary stage, which has little meaning and needs to be surpassed as soon as possible. Péju points out that while she is living with the dwarves, Snow White does not have the desire to return anywhere, nor to proceed to another place: "She lives there in the heart of the forest; it's like that and she does not think of 'becoming'" (137; my translation). And although Bettelheim gives little attention to this part of "Snow White," Péju points out that many children are especially fond of the period with the dwarves.

Péju gives back to the dwarves their potential of a truly unsettling perversity, one that Bettelheim has ignored because of his rigid focus on family relationships:

> And was there no form of sexuality in what brought Snow White and the seven dwarves together? Didn't they love each other, all eight of them? Sure, in a way that differs from maternal, filial, or fraternal love, in a way that escapes sociosexual goals and for that reason can be called perverse. But they loved each other. [. . .] And if one tells us next about the prince's desire for Snow White at the moment when he discovers her recumbent posture, why not mention the extraordinary emotion of the dwarves in front of their companion's white corpse, which they cannot bring themselves to bury in the black earth? (Péju 75; my translation)

Péju reverses a more conservative critique that is often raised against psychoanalysis: whereas many opponents of this approach were scandalized by its sexualization of the child and the fairy tale, he claims that Bettelheim does not go far enough in interpreting the perverse nature of some fairy-tale characters. That he then alternates between a sexual dimension in this relationship (*désire*) and the broader concept of love (*aimer*) marks an ambivalence that eventually takes him back to the more romantic view of the child. Perversity is used to cover a broader range of relationships, including nonsexual ones, which escape Bettelheim's model of progress into heterosexual monogamy.

In his reevaluation of Snow White's stay with the seven dwarves, Péju indicates a lacuna that has not escaped several contemporary authors. It is a popular strategy in fairy-tale retellings to change the point of view to highlight passages or characters that are usually deemed of secondary importance. Francesca Lia Block's "Snow" is such a tale. The beginning intensifies the oedipal undercurrents in the Grimms' story of "Snow White" as they have been analyzed by Bettelheim. It is Snow's mother who rejects her, not her stepmother. Her later jealousy of Snow is caused by a rivalry for the attention of the same man, a gardener. Snow is pictured as a maturing young woman experiencing her first sexual longings. However, by her deletion of passages that precede and follow this period in the traditional version, Block draws particular attention to the time that Snow White spends with the seven dwarves. Péju's stress on their love is echoed in Block's "Snow" in a passage that functions as a self-reflection on the intertextual correction that this retelling undertakes: "She loved them. That's what no one tells. She loved them" (13). Bettelheim, Péju has shown, indeed belongs to those who "do not tell." Yet, Block, in contrast to Péju, explicitly denies any perversity in their relationship and returns to a model of "maternal, filial, or fraternal love" that Péju (75) explicitly rejects: "They loved her as their daughter, sister, mother [. . .] they loved her. That maybe has been hinted at before, but not that she loved them" (Block 13).

   In contrast to and as a possible critique of Bettelheim and other neo-Freudian fairy-tale interpretations, Block's Snow White does not value a heterosexual relationship as the ultimate goal. Snow rejects the gardener, who in this tale functions as a substitute for the prince. For Block, as for Péju, Snow White's stay at the seven dwarves' house is more than a necessary but temporary stage in the progress to mature heterosexual adulthood. Both highlight alternative and equally fulfilling states of being. A Bettelheimian reading might suggest that the Snow White figure at the end of Block's "Snow" remains stuck in a phase of latency, that she is a "freak." Yet, the closure is presented as a well-considered choice and, rather, seems to call for respect for other goals in life than the resolution of oedipal desire in marriage:

> She wanted them. More than gardeners or mothers. She wanted them the way she needed the earth and the flowers and the sky and the sea from her tower room and food and sleep and warmth and light and nights by the fire and poetry and the stories of going out into the world and almost being destroyed by it and returning to find comfort and the real meaning of freak. And I am a freak, she thought, happily. I am meant to stay here forever. I am loved. (Block 30)

Péju likewise presents Snow White's stay with the dwarves as a conscious choice to step out of a restrictive oedipal triangle that places her between the mother and the prince: *"The little girl in the fairy-tale forest* is a fictional being who indicates that if 'femininity' apparently means being cornered between the grand figures of the mother, jealously feminizing, and the husband-Prince Charming, at the same time it has at its disposal an *escape route,* whether that is called the forest, the heath, the wilderness, the desert, wandering or madness" (139; my translation). Block's Snow finds her *escape route* at her new home with her friends. As in *Weetzie Bat,* the series that made her famous, Block here offers an alternative form of living to the nuclear family that was still central to the Grimms' tales and to Bettelheim's analysis. Péju recognizes the openness and flexibility of the fairy tale (89), Block exploits it by offering alternative readings.

Like Péju, Block's revision of "Snow White" is inspired by a critique of rigid meanings and fixed identities. And as in Péju, in Block this critique is accompanied by a glorification of nature as another desire of the unconscious, the need for "pure ways of escaping human behaviour, social and family roles" that take the shape of "complex combinations between the human body, plants, and stones. They cause reversible slips between the organic and the inorganic" (Péju 89; my translation). About "Snow White" in particular, Péju writes: "The tale of 'Snow White' tells us about a little girl whose mother has to pursue her into the depths of the forest and recall her to femininity because she has started to establish other types of links with the vegetal, the animal, the wilderness, and with beings that escape anthropomorphism" (139; my translation).

In Block's tale too, the desire for the organic and the inorganic go hand in hand: from Snow White's love for "the earth and the flowers and the sky and the sea" (30) to her associated affection for the seven dwarves. It may be no coincidence that she rejects the incarnation of the prince as gardener, traditionally someone who domesticates and brings order in the untamed nature that Péju idealizes. Block's feminist and ecocritical perspectives on the traditional "Snow White" find a communal target in this character. Whereas she dreams of the gardener "cutting down trees with an ax [so that] blood ran from their trunks" (18), the dwarves have built their cottage "without chopping down one tree" (5). Block also shifts their profession from miners, who exploit nature, to environmentally friendly builders.

The "reversible slips" between the human body and nature are reflected in the large number of organic similes and metaphors that permeate Block's sensory writing: "The mother looked broken like a rose bush" (3); "her eyes like black rose petals" (4); her lashes like "tassels" (8); Snow's "green color of certain white flowers" after she has eaten the poisoned apple (26), with the smell of "a bouquet" (29). The dwarves have animal names and smell "of woodsmoke and sweet earth, where flowers grow" (13). The boundary between organic and inorganic material is also crossed in the imagery applied to the dwarves' cottage, which "looked like part of the canyon itself, as if it had sprung up there. It smelled of woodsmoke and leaves" (5–6). Again inorganic and organic materials mingle, not only in the smell but also in the image of growth, comparable to a plant or a vegetable, which is applied to the cottage.

At the end of Block's story, one may wonder in which direction Snow's earlier described sexual longing will take her, and how her need for a mother will affect her life, a need that has been intensified by the visit of her mother to the dwarves' cottage. These are questions that Block leaves to the imagination of the reader. In this and other ways, her retelling responds to Péju's critique of the tendency in some fairy-tale critics to reduce the fairy tale in order to project their own interpretations onto the tales. Whereas Péju argues in favor of the richness of literature and the beauty of what Bettelheim considers only a surface layer or temporary stage, Block demonstrates this richness through a text that allows multiple meanings and open closures and that is written in a suggestive, sensory style. In her tale, there is no master who reigns supreme, only an invitation to enter into a dialogue with the various layers of the fairy tale, as well as with various critics who have reflected on these tales.

Mimicking Psychoanalysis

Probably one of the earliest fictional reactions to *The Uses of Enchantment* was published in Germany in 1976. It is Dorothea Runow's "rotkäppchen—auch für erwachsene—gedanken zu bruno bettelheim" (little red riding hood—also for adults—thoughts on bruno bettelheim).[42] Runow wrote her retelling in response to an article by Bettelheim that was published in the newspaper *Welt am Sonntag* (World on Sunday) and most notably to his claim that "cruel fairy tales are exactly what children need" (Runow 50; my translation). Runow's text consists of two parts: a free retelling of "Little

Red Riding Hood," plus nine footnotes, which take up as much space as the retelling itself. Her critique of Bettelheim can be found in both parts. In the fictional text, it is present on an explicit and implicit level. Implicit criticism can be read in the parts of "Little Red Riding Hood" that Runow rewrites and that modify elements in the tale to which Bettelheim had given prominence in his analysis. The red cap from which the protagonist derives her name is a good example. According to Bettelheim, "Red is the color symbolizing violent emotions, very much including sexual ones. The red velvet cap given by Grandmother to Little Red Cap thus can be viewed as a symbol of a premature transfer of sexual attractiveness" (173). Runow gives a more pragmatic dimension to this symbol of "sexual attractiveness": when the mother discovers that her little girl has lice, she shaves off her hair. "little eva cried terribly," the story continues, "she didn't want to walk around with her bald head. out of sympathy the mother took her good red silk dress, cut off a piece from the hem and sewed for her daughter a little red cap" (50; my translation). The little girl's name, eva, implies a second critique of Bettelheim. It suggests an allusion to the biblical Eve (of which it is the German equivalent), especially when her friends emphatically sing, "eve is now called red riding hood, eve is now called red riding hood" (50; my translation), and when she is repeatedly referred to as "eve alias red riding hood." Although Bettelheim only mentions Eve in his chapter on "Snow White" when he deals with the poisoned apple, the reference can be read as part of Runow's critique of his approach. In the long subtitle that introduces her tales, Runow calls psychoanalysis *"religionsersatz,"* a substitute for religion.[43] Feminists have reproached Christianity for putting all the blame for the Fall on Eve and claim that she has been used as an excuse for women's suppression for centuries. In Bettelheim's analysis Little Red Riding Hood likewise functions as a scapegoat, and Tatar and Zipes have accused him of blaming the girl for her own rape. Read in this context, Runow's assertion that "eva heibt jetzt rotkäppchen" can be read as a feminist critique of Bettelheim, or "pater bruno von bettelheim" (father bruno from bettelheim), as she calls him with another clear reference to Christianity. If psychoanalysis is a substitute for religion, than Red Riding Hood is the new Eve, the new female scapegoat. However, Runow immediately corrects this and pictures an eva or red riding hood who is by no means restricted to the role that psychoanalysis and Christianity have reserved for her. The girl's critical curiosity and the guidance she receives from her mother arm her with the necessary knowledge and empowerment to guarantee her own happy ending.

A more explicit critique of psychoanalysis occurs when eva's mother replaces her warning of the fairy-tale wolf with a warning of "der pater bruno aus bettelheim." This critique is elaborated on in the paratext. When the mother explains that this friar suffers from "*die wiener krankheit*" or "vienna disease," the footnote explains that this is the "search for people who need treatment." Runow attacks psychoanalysis for the commercialization of its theories and for its lack of originality and profound insights: "psychoanalysis, styled to an accommodating psychology, has degraded with bettelheim, as with horst & richter, to the laws of the bestseller that doesn't live up to any title anymore, merely repeats tiresome thoughts, only blows up what others have already said in dark prehistory" (51; my translation).

Not only does Runow's story anticipate Bettelheim's later status as an international bestseller, but she also draws attention to his problematic use of ideas from other critics. Linked to the reproach of false appearances in the footnote is the critique of eva's mother, who questions Bettelheim's credibility and accuses him of mimicry. The description of the term that she gives differs slightly from the meaning that was attributed to "mimicry" by French feminists such as Luce Irigaray. Eva's mother explains the biological use of the concept to her daughter in the garden, referring to the flowers that grow there: "that is a grasshopper; it looks exactly like an orchid blossom, has the same flesh-tinted color, only it doesn't hold any honey, but instead deceives the flower-visiting insects, so that they come to it voluntarily and it can devour them" (Runow 50; my translation). "Mimicry" here stands for "deceit" in a narrow sense. It can be applied to Bettelheim in two ways. First, in the footnote cited above, Runow describes how Bettelheim's book does not live up to its title, and she argues that readers' attraction to him is based on false promises. Second, mimicry can also be attached to the aforementioned "wiener krankheit." Bettelheim, like a wolf in sheep's clothing, is accused of exploiting his patients under the pretence of curing them. In the retelling, both Freud and Bettelheim are indeed intertextually linked to wolves, the fairy-tale equivalent of the carnivorous flower that pretends to be harmless. Eva's mother warns her that father bruno von bettelheim dwells in the forest, and Freud appears in a short retelling-within-the-retelling of "The Wolf and the Seven Kids," in which he kidnaps six children who are never retrieved. A contradiction arises when this interpretation of mimicry is linked to a statement of the mother earlier in the text, when she warns her daughter that Bettelheim "believes that he is either a giant or a bad wolf, he pretends and applies mimicry!" (50; my translation). Here she seems to claim that Bettelheim falsely presents himself as a bad wolf, something that she then claims he actually is but tries to hide. Another contradiction can be observed when little eva asks for a second time what mimicry is during the mother's short retelling of "The Wolf and the Seven Kids." The mother does not answer that Freud pretends to cure his patients with psychoanalysis when he in fact harms them, as one might expect after the explanation about the grasshopper. Instead she returns to a form of mimicry present in the Grimms' collection, the transvestism of the wolf:

> "And what is mimicry here?" eva alias red riding hood asked.
> "first," the mother said, "that the man dresses in women's clothing, and second, that he has hidden the children under his cassock, as if he were pregnant. also the slender hands do not exactly indicate hard men's work and the high-pitched voice is also part of the deception. all of that is mimicry." (Runow 51; my translation)

Although these are valid examples of mimicry as deceit, they do not relate to the mother's earlier observation that Bettelheim thinks he is a wolf and engages in mimicry. At this point in the story, one may wonder who exactly pretends to be what and why? With her new explanation, eva's mother herself draws upon Bettelheim's interpretation of the tale of "Little Red Riding Hood," in which he too argues that the wolf imitates pregnancy (177). The incorporation of a psychoanalytic interpretation in a retelling that actually criticizes this interpretative approach is an indication that the tale can be read as practicing a different type of "mimicry," with the new connotations that the term acquired in French feminism. As Vivian Liska explains, "When woman herself has playful and creative control over the defining characteristics that restrict and instrumentalize her, she can unmask their alleged predetermination by nature as a cultural construct and transform the formerly fixed role models into a 'mask'" (*Moderne* 86; my translation). Liska borrows the term "mimicry" from the French feminist Luce Irigaray, who describes mimicry or "mimesis" as follows: "To play with mimesis is thus, for a woman, to try to recover the place of her exploitation by discourse, without allowing herself to be simply reduced to it. It means to resubmit herself—inasmuch as she is on the side of the 'perceptible,' of 'matter'—to 'ideas,' in particular to ideas about herself, that are elaborated in/by a masculine logic, but so as to make 'visible,' by an effect of playful repetition, what was supposed to remain invisible: the cover-up of a possible operation of the feminine in language" (Irigaray 124).

If we replace the word "woman" in the first lines of this quotation with "fairy tale," it becomes clear in what sense Runow's retelling can be read as a performance of "mimicry" in response to the fairy tale's treatment by psychoanalysis.[44] Like the woman in Irigaray's theory, the fairy tale can use the form of a retelling to explore the site of its exploitation without being simply reduced to one interpretation. In the case of Runow's retelling, the fairy tale enters into a dialogue with psychoanalysis and appropriates its ideas in a form of repetitive play. Runow imitates and mocks psychoanalytic interpretations, among others, in the following quotation: "each day grandma went to the rich people to do their dirty wishes—what am I saying, washing." This Freudian slip of the tongue so obviously confuses a sexual allusion (dirty wishes) with a harmless word that it can be read as a parody of Freudian analysis, especially when Freud himself appears a few lines down as "der pater siegmund aus freudenhal" (51). The castration anxiety that is so central to Freudian theory seems to have affected "der pater" himself: "he had sung in the boys' choir for a long time and had a really high-pitched voice" (50; my translation). Moreover, when eva asks her mother why some people use mimicry, she immediately resorts to explanations from their childhood background and hidden fears and desires, just as a psychoanalyst would (51). With this exposing imitation or mimicry of psychoanalysis, the retelling accuses Bettelheim of reducing, misrepresenting, and taking commercial advantage of its literary pre-text. As Runow, echoing Otto Gmelin, writes in a footnote: "*the* fairy tale does not exist. That is bettelheim's capital mistake" (52; my translation).

To Be Or Not To Be Tamed? (Jacqueline Rose)

Runow's slippery use of terms and explanations makes further sense if we relate it to Jacqueline Rose's response to Bruno Bettelheim in *The Case of Peter Pan, or the Impossibility of Children's Fiction* (1984). This Lacanian study of the origin and reception of J. M. Barrie's *Peter Pan* has more general implications for children's literature and its criticism. As Rose argues in a now famous quotation: "If children's literature builds an image of the child inside the book, it does so in order to secure the child who is outside the book, the one who does not come so easily within its grasp" (2). She extends this critique to include not only children's literature but also its criticism and Bettelheim's study in particular. In her chapter on "Peter Pan and Freud," Rose stresses the subversive nature of Freud's views on the child and the unconscious. Both Freud's radically unsettling concepts were adapted, however, when they were applied by other critics and authors. Rose accuses Bettelheim of such a modification, which she claims is a safe reduction. Whereas in Freud's theories, both childhood and the unconscious form a permanent challenge to a stable, rational identity, Bettelheim creates the illusion that it is possible to "master" the unconscious and achieve a coherent identity:

> Bettelheim's work is distinguished by its attention to the complexity of unconscious process [sic] for both adult and child; but the concept of mastery—with its associated meaning of coherence in psychic and sexual life—is none the less the central term through which this complexity is conceived and by means of which it is finally resolved. The unconscious does not therefore challenge the human ego, its seeming coherence and identity; the unconscious "enriches" the ego, and much as a quantity of energy or a current, it can be transferred into the ego where it becomes neutralised and safe. (Rose 14)

Bettelheim claims that fairy tales can reassure children, yet Rose reveals how it is rather *The Uses of Enchantment* that reassures adults by modifying Freud's theories and suggesting the possibility of a happy ending in reality. It can be argued that Rose simplifies Bettelheim in the same way that she accuses him of simplifying Freud. Bettelheim does seem to realize the impossibility of permanently taming the unconscious. He notes that "failure to experience recovery and consolation is true enough in reality," and he does stress that fairy tales cannot guarantee happiness in real life but can give children the necessary confidence to deal with their fears and desires (Bettelheim 147). Yet Rose is right that Bettelheim often seems to forget this: his concrete interpretations of the fairy tales do give the impression that a balance is achievable in which the unconscious can be permanently mastered.

Rose denies the possibility of a unified subject and links this impossibility to the lack of fixed meanings in language: "Language is something we do not simply use to communicate, as everything in psychoanalytic practice makes clear" (16). She uses Freud's multifarious references to the child as a case that demonstrates "the often contradictory and inconsistent ways" in which the same term can be used (18). Rose here turns one of the typical critiques of psychoanalysis, its lack of consistency[45] and supposedly random and manipulative interpretations, into something positive. She suggests that Freud not only recognizes the instability of referential meanings in language but that he is also consistent in putting this instability of terms into practice. Bettelheim simplifies Freud's approach to language, Rose claims. She bases this critique of Bettelheim's use of unambiguous referentiality with regard to another semiotic system, that of psychoanalytic symbols: "It remains the form of interpretation—where one thing straightforwardly *equals* another—which seems to predominate in the analysis of children's writing" (19). Again, Rose can be accused of misrepresenting Bettelheim, who explicitly and implicitly acknowledges the multifarious meanings that can be attributed to one and the same psychoanalytic symbol— explicitly when he writes that "fairy stories speak to our conscious and unconscious, and therefore do not need to avoid contradictions" (174); implicitly when he gives several explanations for the same fairy-tale symbol or passage. It is odd that Rose should base her critique of Bettelheim on "Little Red Riding Hood," which is one of his most elaborate fairy-tale analyses and one in which he does give the possibility of various and contradictory interpretations. When Bettelheim tries to explain why Red Riding Hood gives the wolf directions to her grandmother's house, for instance, two competing interpretations emerge. On the one hand, he argues that the grandmother represents the mother so that the passage is an indication of Red Riding Hood's unresolved oedipal conflict, in which she "arrang[es] things so that the wolf can do away with the mother figure" (172). On the other hand, Bettelheim considers the possibility that Red Riding Hood realizes she cannot master the wolf alone and pushes the problem onto someone else, "an older person, a parent or parent substitute" (174). Moreover, if the passage in which Red Riding Hood gives the wolf her grandmother's address illustrates one thing, it is indeed that "language is something we do not simply use to communicate" (Rose 16). This message is implicitly as present in Bettelheim as it is in Freud, and it plays an important role in both Runow's and Gillian Cross's retellings.

If we return to Dorothea Runow's retelling of "Little Red Riding Hood," we see that the unambiguous referentiality of terms is problematized when Runow brings into play so-called shifting signifiers. Runow's polysemantic application of the word "mimicry" would, in this interpretation, be true to Freud's view on and use of language. It is more likely, however, that she uses slippery meanings as a critique of psychoanalysis' inconsistency rather than as a positive appreciation of it. On the basis of the fictional text and the footnotes, I would rephrase Runow's critique as follows: by applying shifting meanings, psychoanalysis manages to force the fairy tale into a limiting frame of reference. Psychoanalysis exploits the instability of referentiality to make possible a reduction of the fairy tale on its own terms. Runow's retelling contains a plea to acknowledge the complexity of the fairy tale and its multiple meanings—its own shifting signifiers.

Several other retellings reintroduce the radically challenging nature of the unconscious and draw attention to the unsteady meanings of (psychoanalytic) terms and symbols. By denying the fairy tale its traditional happy ending, texts by Priscilla Galloway, Gillian Cross, and Paul Biegel contradict Bettelheim's neutralization of the unconscious. In "The Woodcutter's Wife" (1995), Galloway, like Bettelheim, draws a link between Hansel and Gretel's stepmother and the evil witch. However, contrary to Bettelheim, she ascribes truly evil characteristics to this character, which are not only portrayed as projections of the child but also affirmed by the stepmother as a first-person narrator. Galloway's potential resistance to Bettelheim's theory can be derived from the fact that the evil character in this retelling is not killed but merely locked away. On several occasions Bettelheim stresses that the punishment of evil is necessary to realize the fairy tale's consolatory function. And the only suitable punishment seems to be death:

> Prettified or bowdlerized fairy tales are rightly rejected by any child who has heard them in their original form. [. . .] The child knows better what needs to be told. When a seven-year-old was read the story of "Snow White," an adult anxious not to disturb the child's mind, ended the story with Snow White's wedding. The child, who knew the story, promptly demanded: "What about the red-hot shoes

that killed the wicked queen?" The child feels that all's well with the world, and that he can be secure in it, only if the wicked are punished in the end. (Bettelheim 147)

Many duplicates and retellings indeed have alternative endings that strip the traditional tales from cruelty in order to spare children from fear. Such a concern for the child's well-being is unlikely to have motivated Galloway's rewriting, however. "The Woodcutter's Wife" deviates from the traditional ending to "Hansel and Gretel" by leaving open the potential for return that Rose claims is vital to Freud's concept of the unconscious. Galloway's witch, a predator who lives on the blood of humans, is not burned but locked up. When she is plotting her return to Hansel and Gretel's house, she realizes that an adult woman is not the ideal shape: "If I become a small child, I won't be able to get very far. Luckily I don't want to go very far. My work is here, and I'm too old to start over. When I go to their door with big dark eyes and a hungry look, I know they will take me in" (123). The threatening force of the evil witch here takes the form that Rose links to the ever-threatening unconscious: the child. The narrator assumes a guise of innocence and need, believing that this appearance will work best to hide her harmful intentions. That the shape of the child is the only human form that the witch can envisage to escape between the bars of her cage supports Rose's idea of the child as a concept that can never be grasped and confined.

The ending of Gillian Cross's *Wolf*, a novel discussed earlier in this chapter, at least leaves a gap so the unconscious can return. Throughout the book, the protagonist Cassy is disturbed by dreams that refer to "Little Red Riding Hood." Central to these dreams, as to the tale, is the threatening figure of the wolf. As Cassy herself realizes, her image of the wolf is fragmented and escapes conscious control: "What had she ever had to do with wolves? She tried to make some kind of picture in her mind, but the image slid about shapelessly, splitting into disconnected fragments. [. . .] The question irritated her so much that she sat up and reached for her suitcase. She meant to find a pen and a piece of paper, so that she could try to draw the wretched animal" (43).

Like the unconscious, or as part of what she has repressed in her unconscious, the wolf irritates Cassy, who can be argued to represent the ego: it is shapeless, fragmented, she cannot grasp it but nevertheless feels that she has to address it. When she tries to get a grip on the wolf by drawing it, that is by creating a fixed representation of it, she grabs instead the "solid lump inside its newspaper wrapping" that her grandmother has put in her bag. The yellow, malleable material becomes a metaphor for language with which Cassy tries to shape the unconscious: "That would do. Better than paper, in fact, if she could really mould it" (43). But she cannot—the signifying system is used to explore the signified, without yielding a definite result. The signifiers keep shifting: "Her fingers struggled, moulding and re-moulding, trying to find the exact shape that would answer the image in her mind, the shape that would mean *Wolf*" (44). The yellow lump is later revealed to be a piece of the plastic explosive semtex, and it can be read as the ultimate symbol of danger and destruction in the book. The shapeless semtex shares with the unconscious (and the wolf and the child) the impossibility of being pinned down, of being "mastered," and like the wolf it invests the story with a permanent sense of unease and threat. It is no coincidence that in a book so loaded with references to psychoanalysis Cassy falls asleep while trying to shape the lump. She meets the wolf in her dreams, where she further explores the meaning of it without managing to control it for good. That the signifying system in this fragment is represented by a shape-shifting explosive is not the only occasion in *Wolf* in which language is proven to be slippery and treacherous. On other occasions in the book, Cassy's use of language leads her into dangerous situations. Several messages do not arrive with the right person or pass on information to the wrong one; others are not understood or are misunderstood. When Cassy writes her grandmother a postcard with Goldie's new address, for instance, what she tries to communicate is a cry for help: "It was a signal, that meant, *Here I am. Come and get me*" (65). The message does not reach Nan, however, but Mick, who will "come and get" Cassy, not to help but to hurt her.

The figure of the wolf is a shifting signifier that can be related to several characters and concepts both in Cassy's dreams and in real life: her father; her stepfather; Cassy herself; and the wolf as endangered animal, as evil, as victim, as symbol, as figure of speech, and so on. Given the intertextual link to "Little Red Riding Hood" this dynamic process is eventually expected to end and yield one definite counterpart to the wolf. For a long time it is unclear who the incarnation of the evil wolf is in Cross's novel—the speculation on its identity invests the book with a narrative tension.[46] When at the end of *Wolf*, Cassy's father is arrested as an Irish Republican

Army terrorist, this question is answered. Cassy has faced and resolved the mystery of her childhood memories, and it is assumed that her nightmares will cease. This is also how Susan Clancy interprets the end of *Wolf:* "Within this [kaleidoscopic] structure, Cross sets out to achieve balance. [. . .] The final view of the wolf, as achieved in the performance piece, is a balanced depiction. In this way, Cross maintains the order within society that is necessary to achieve harmony" (79).

Clancy reads *Wolf* as Bettelheim reads the fairy tale: balance and harmony are the ultimate goals, goals that are not beyond reach. However, she seems to ignore two important aspects of Cross's novel. First, the performance is by no means the final image of the wolf that the retelling leaves us with. Second, it is odd that this performance should be described as a "balanced depiction" of the wolf. Although it is true that several aspects of the wolf are addressed in the school performance that Lyall, Goldie, Robert, and Cassy set up, these aspects do not balance each other out but rather clash and cause more confusion and anxiety. Cassy panics during the performance, which results in her "primal scream":

> She couldn't speak, couldn't think, couldn't breathe. The wilderness came up round her, savage and animal. The ancient forest closed in on her—a
> Danger—
>
> . . . and the thing leaped out of the shadows—mouth open, vast, black, slavering—its red eyes glaring and its hot, foul breath strong on her face—huge and grey, with the wolf legs kicking free of the human clothing. [. . .]
>   no time and no defence and nothing to do except scream and scream and screamandscreamandSCREAM—(Cross 167–68)

The passage is the equivalent of the moment in which Red Riding Hood recognizes the wolf in her grandmother's clothing and is attacked and eaten. The boundaries between Cassy's mind and her surroundings are dissolved— the darkness inside her head is matched by the equally threatening forest that closes her in from the outside. It is strange that Cassy's fear and primal scream (which mark the end of the performance, as she then runs away) are ignored in Clancy's discussion and that she describes the image of the wolf

in the performance in terms of harmony and balance. Similarly, her assertion that Goldie's boyfriend "Lyall works to construct a harmonious unit"
(79) equally disregards many references to chaos in his squat. The nostalgic longing for a simpler world that marks the introduction of Clancy's text
influences her concept of the kaleidoscope as a means of structure rather
than a device that eternally shifts fragments, and it also determines her
reading of Cross's *Wolf*.[47] Order and harmony are revealed in the book to
be at best temporary illusions, if not treacherous deceptions.

The performance is not the last instance in the book in which wolves appear. Several ambiguities in the last pages of Cross's novel further undermine the possibility of a safe closure. When Cassy and her friend Robert
visit the zoo, the wolves in the enclosure become a metaphor for the wolf
of her past that has plagued her for so long:

> "And what about—him [Mick, Cassy's father]?" [Cassy asked].
> "No need to worry about that. They'll put him away for years
> and years, until you're grown up. You can forget all about him."
> Cassy ran her finger slowly up and down one of the railings. But
> she didn't say anything. She just watched the circling, vigilant
> wolves, padding in their barren cage.
> "They'll soon be gone, too," Robert said, following her eyes.
> "No more big bad wolves to remind you. The keeper told Lyall.
> *They're not enough of a draw, so they're being phased out.*"
> "And all we have to do is live happily ever after?" Cassy said.
> And she laughed. (Cross 185)

The word "enclosure" for the wolves' habitat suggests that the wolf is confined to a manageable space with clear boundaries. A parallel can be drawn
to Bettelheim's view on the unconscious as criticized by Rose: the wolves
are separated from human beings who can observe them from a safe distance. And when people are no longer interested, they can "phase them
out." Bettelheim claims that the fairy tale can suggest the same for the child's
unconscious: "Consolation is the greatest service the fairy tale can offer a
child: the confidence that, despite all tribulations he has to suffer [. . .] not
only will he succeed, but the evil forces will be done away with and never
again threaten his peace of mind" (Bettelheim 147). More specifically about
"Little Red Riding Hood," Bettelheim writes that the tale "projects the girl

into the dangers of her oedipal conflicts during puberty, and then saves her from them, so that she will be able to mature conflict-free" (172). Robert seems to align himself with Bettelheim when he says that now that Cassy has dealt with her father, he will not be able to harm her for a long time. The same parallel can be drawn to her unconscious: she has faced her worst fears, and has learned to "master" them. Yet at the same time, when the association is made between the wolves in the enclosure and Cassy's father in prison, the metaphor (of the wolf) as a figure of speech reintroduces a dynamic of shifting meanings. The wolf has already escaped from its figural enclosure in language while Robert is reassuring Cassy. This in reinforced by the behavior of the wolves in the zoo: they are still "circling" and "vigilant."

Like Galloway in "The Woodcutter's Wife," Cross modifies the ending of the Grimms' "Little Red Riding Hood." By having the wolf imprisoned rather than killed, Cross creates a first opening for the unconscious to reenter. "Years and years" do not last forever, and just as Rose argues that childhood and adulthood cannot be separated in Freudian psychoanalysis, Robert leaves open the possibility of a reappearance of her father when Cassy is grown up. Her childhood past may find her again when she is an adult, as her infant self found her when she was a child. Not that Robert sees this as a threat: the next sentence ("You can forget all about him") suggests that by the time Cassy is an adult, she will be in control enough that she is no longer threatened by her father. At the end of *Wolf,* Robert displays a firm belief in the possibility of a stable, fixed identity. Cassy, however, seems to have internalized a piece of advice that Robert gave her earlier in the book: " 'What's this thing you've got about real life?' Robert said quietly. '*Real* life and *real* people. That doesn't mean anything. It's just a way of making walls, to shut out what's uncomfortable. And it doesn't work, you know' " (107). Rose, like Robert, has stressed that shutting out what is uncomfortable does not work. Cassy, too, realizes that prison walls may keep away her father for a while, but he cannot be wiped away or "phased out" as easily as the wolves in the zoo. She laughs away the possibility of a happy ending when Robert suggests this.

Moreover, it is clear that Cassy does not *want* to shut away her father completely. Added to the ending discussed above is a metareflective coda, which takes up the idea of a happy ending and Cassy's hopes and doubts on this matter:

". . . and they all lived happily ever after." Nan closed the book and leaned over the cot to give Cassy a brisk kiss.

"But what happened to the wolf?" Cassy said.

"Oh, he went far, far away, dear, and they never had to worry about him, ever again."

"But didn't he *mind*?"

"That's enough!" Nan said sharply. "You'll only give yourself bad dreams, thinking about things like that. Close your eyes and go to sleep, like a good girl." She pulled the curtains, turned out the light, and shut the door behind her as she went out.

Cassy lay with her eyes open and gazed into the darkness, making up a letter in her head. *Dear Wolf, Don't vanish into the dark forest again. I still need to know about you. Perhaps I can come and visit you, or . . . or . . .*

Slowly her eyelids drooped. She knew that she wouldn't finish the letter in this dream, but she wasn't worried.

She would write it when she woke up. (185–86)

Again, Cross brings up the wolf to disturb the illusion of an unambiguous happy ending. Nan, in her role as substitute parent/superego, first tries to reassure Cassy that the wolf will disappear and that she should stop worrying about him. The girl's reply is an immediate violation of that advice: she is already worrying about her father. Nan's reaction shows that she is not so sure that the wolf has been dealt with for good either. Her attempts to close off Cassy's room can be interpreted in two ways if we link them to Jacqueline Rose's views on the child: on the one hand, by closing the curtains and the door, Nan (the superego) tries to protect Cassy (the ego) from the threats that come from outside (the wolf or id). On the other hand, this is also a way for Nan to shut Cassy off from Nan herself: the child is troubling the adult, who needs to resort to an aggressive assertion of power to stay in control.

Several temporal layers intermingle in this coda: the cot indicates that the story returns to Cassy's early childhood, before her struggles with her father and before his arrest. The last sentence, in contrast, refers to Cassy's ability to write, which indicates that this ending takes place later in her life, probably after her father's arrest. That she seems to know the wolf's address supports this. A second ambiguity is introduced near the end of the quotation, linked to the blurring of temporal layers: Cassy says that she is dreaming. It is unclear at what point she has fallen asleep. Does the whole passage take place in a dream and did she fall asleep before the quotation started? Does she dream about falling asleep? Or did she fall asleep while making up the letter in her head? The fact that the passage is marked off from the rest of the text, as are the other dreams in the book, supports the first interpretation. The coda is by all means reminiscent of the opening motto of *Wolf* when Nan asserted that *"Cassy never dreams."* Nan now admits that Cassy does dream and warns her about nightmares, and indeed the whole book has proven Nan wrong. Cassy's dreams have been vital to the development of her personality and to the resolution of the plot. The same forcefulness with which Nan now tries to ban Cassy's thoughts of her father can no longer be taken seriously, and it is not surprising that Cassy violates Nan's command as soon as Nan has left the room.

Although the coda shows that Cassy has not finished dealing with her father or the wolf yet, it is indicated that his impact on her will be different. She now knows that she cannot ignore the wolf as a symbol of the unconscious and of her father. Previous attempts to do this have invariably failed, causing anxiety and nearly ending in disaster. In spite of his danger and in contrast to Nan, Cassy realizes that the wolf is an important part of her life and seeks to get in touch with him herself. Although she does not claim complete knowledge of him (*"I still need to know about you"* and not "I still need to know you"), her intention to write the letter does indicate that she invites him back into her life, that she wants to explore what he can mean to her. And in line with Bettelheim's view on the fairy tale, this willingness to explore the unconscious is reassuring: "she wasn't worried" (186). Or in Bettelheim's words, "Once we have mastered those [overwhelming feelings], we need not fear any longer the encounter with the wolf" (181).

But again, the reader can question Cassy's reassurance, especially if this ending is linked to the previous passage at the zoo in which Cassy still laughs at the possibility of a happy ending. It is as if Cross oscillates between Bettelheim's and Rose's views of the unconscious. Her first ending (at the zoo) is in accordance with Rose, the coda with Bettelheim (and with the still-dominant expectation of optimism at the end of children's books). Even the hopeful coda is riddled with gaps that may undermine Cassy's poise. Cassy plans to write her letter when she wakes, but will she remember to do so? The information from her previous dreams did not enter her conscious as easily as she expects these present thoughts will. And what if she does write the letter—will it reach the addressee in the way that Cassy intends, or will it be lost or misunderstood, as her previous writing has? Cassy still longs for the wolf as a parental figure, as a protective and caring father. Will Mick be prepared to be a father to her now that he is imprisoned? The last time Cassy tried to talk to him, he tried to shoot her, and it is partly due to her intervention that he was caught by the police. Moreover, what will be the impact on Cassy if Mick *is* willing to explain his motives for terrorism?

A reflection on the tale of "Little Red Riding Hood" further destabilizes the happy ending. Although Cassy appears at the end of *Wolf* as the reincarnation of the self-confident Red Riding Hood from the coda to the Brothers Grimm's tale, the traditional protagonist takes quite a different attitude toward the wolf. When Red Riding Hood meets the second wolf, she runs away, she warns her grandmother, and together they kill him (Grimm, KHM 1: 160). Cassy, by contrast, seems to be as interested in and hence vulnerable to the wolf as Red Riding Hood was at the beginning of the Grimms' tale. Bettelheim, who praises the Grimms' Red Riding Hood for having learned her lesson and immediately engaging her grandmother in the battle against the wolf (something that Cassy obviously defies), would deplore her voluntary return to the wolf. For Rose, such a return and concomitant vulnerability are inevitable.

A similar comeback of the wolf occurs in Paul Biegel's *Wie je droomt ben je zelf.* As described above, Biegel explicitly rephrases Bettelheimian theory for children in the preface. Sandra Beckett deplores Biegel's didactic turn as well as his assumption that "readers of all ages are expected to make the same journey into their inner selves as the characters" ("Biegel" 88).[48] None of this didacticism can be perceived in the retelling itself, which Beckett does believe to offer elements for readers of all ages. I would argue that the book cannot be read only as a reflection of Bettelheim's theories, but like Cross's retelling, it contains a Rosean modification of his view of the unconscious. Both the overall plot of Biegel's "Little Red Riding Hood" retelling and the various imbedded dreams of the characters are concerned with shifting shapes: nothing is what it appears to be. Humans "are enchanted themselves," the wolf claims, "and they don't even know it" (32; my translation). The performance of roles is a theme that is also present in the traditional versions of "Little Red Riding Hood": the wolf seems kind and helpful when he crosses Riding Hood's path, but he is in fact a man-eater; what the girl believes to be her grandmother is in fact the wolf in disguise. Dressing up is the structuring principle of Biegel's retelling, and this motif can be read as a self-reflective comment on the retelling's practice of transforming the traditional tale, dressing it up as it were, not only to give it a new shape but also to return to what lies behind its surface meaning. The disguise helps the reader to come to a truer shape, as Biegel explains in the preface.

Yet the exact meaning that lies behind the masquerade is hard to distinguish, and the dressing up soon takes the form of a perpetual circle: the wolf dreams that he is a wolf who dies, the grandmother dreams that she is death disguised as a younger woman, the girl dreams that she is first a princess and then an enchanted wolf. In their dreams, these characters dress up once again so that it becomes impossible to tell any true shape behind the concealing outfits. The rather postmodern conclusion of this retelling seems to be that everything appears as a disguise, that no stable subjectivity can ever be discovered, only temporarily constructed. The truest and very Freudian understanding of the self seems to be offered when Red Riding Hood sees her reflection as a split image in two mirrors: both human and wolf (Biegel 51). As in Cross's novel, the wolf appears in Biegel's story as something that cannot be understood, tamed, or eradicated. "I cannot be destroyed," it says to Red Riding Hood in her dream (58; my translation). And indeed, in Biegel's modification of the traditional ending, the wolf does not drown in the brook with his belly filled with stones but pukes them out one by one.

Does Biegel come then to a Rosean modification of the tale's ending? Possibly, but not necessarily: the story does offer a strategy to deal with the wolf. "The wolf, that is your own fear" (62; my translation), grandmother explains to the huntsman. She is aware of this, and so is Red Riding Hood, the two characters who have lived and dreamed inside of the wolf. Their awakening is described as a rebirth: "I dreamed that I was dead, then came the light, and now I can finally start living," is the grandmother's reaction when she is released (54). Red Riding Hood's comment parallels this: "I dreamed I was wolf, then came the light, now I can also be human" (55; my translation). The confrontation with their worst fears in the safe environment of the dream has proven to be healing. In contrast to the huntsman, who is trembling, they have accepted the presence of the wolf and are at peace with it. When in the final lines of the tale, the wolf knocks at the door, the grandmother is by no means surprised and offers him a drink. The gap that the wolf's reaction to this invitation leaves can be filled in reassuringly by the reader who follows Bettelheim's optimism. For the reader who shares Rose's skepticism toward the mastery of the unconscious it can be the start of a new cycle of disturbing conversations and events.

The Dynamics of the Intertextual Dialogue

Authors of fiction who have engaged with Bettelheim's work form important players in the reception of *The Uses of Enchantment*, Donald Haase argues:

> Writers like Margaret Atwood, Angela Carter, and Robert Coover have understood the sociohistorical dynamics of the fairy tale and produced fairy-tale adaptations that complicate, undercut, and frustrate conventional psychoanalytic readings—especially as they relate to the psychology of identity, socialization, gender, and sexuality. Such revisions challenge readers to rethink classical psychoanalytic premises and search for new models to understand the psychological implications of the fairy tale in social, historical, and cultural contexts. ("Psychology" 407–8)

The three authors that Haase mentions have been supplemented in this chapter with several others who have rewritten and illustrated fairy tales for both children and adults. Few have done so in an entirely affirmative mode, as Haase also notes, but enter into a creative dialogue with Bettelheim's theory. There is something artificial about the distinction that was made in this chapter between retellings that support Bettelheim's theory and retellings that criticize or contradict it. Instead, the corpus under discussion can be envisaged as a continuum. On one end stand the works that largely remain true to his theory, most notably the collections of traditional Grimms' tales whose editors rephrase psychoanalytic theories for adult mediators in the introduction. On the other end we find the works in which ideas from psychoanalysis as well as the analysts themselves are ridiculed. As Linda Hutcheon notes about parody in general, such scornful responses at the same time undermine and affirm the importance of psychoanalytic

fairy-tale theory: "The very act of parodying invests the Other [the parodied pre-text] with both authority and an exchange value in relation to literary norms" (*Parody* 77). When authors such as Jean-Marie Poupart include references to Pruneau von Betterave (Beckett, *Recycling* 244) or
Dorothea Runow to "der pater bruno aus bettelheim," they can assume
that at least some readers will understand this as an allusion to the psychoanalyst and thus attest to his importance.

In between these two poles lies a whole range of works that overlap with
some elements from neo-Freudian theory, while at the same time modifying, criticizing, or disregarding other elements: Atwood, Biegel, Browne,
Carter, Cross, and many others who have and have not been dealt with in
this chapter belong here. Children's literature seems to have embraced Bettelheim's claim that fairy tales are therapeutic and ignored his vehement
disapproval of illustrations and fairy-tale retellings. However, both in the
introductions to fairy-tale collections and in retellings that can be intertextually linked to Bettelheim, his theory appears as substantially "softened,"
not to say censored. The latent content that Bettelheim reveals clashes with
the horizon of expectations of even recent children's literature, and Bettelheim himself prohibits adults to explain the symbolic meaning of fairy tales
to children. As a consequence, when his ideas on the latent (sexual) content
of the tales do enter children's books, they rarely do so explicitly, but they
appear, for instance, as allusions in illustrations (Browne, Beck, Koopmans, Ache, and Foreman) or as elaborations of Freudian symbols that exploit children's literature's double address.

Two aspects of Bettelheim's theory have been repeatedly modified in
the retellings for children and adults as well as in the critical discourse on
The Uses of Enchantment. First, most authors and critics resist his tendency
to blame the victim. In critical discourse, this problem has been noted explicitly. Some of the retellings have tried to shift the balance again by
stressing the perpetrator's guilt (for instance in the form of first-person narration in Galloway) or the victims' long-term suffering (for instance Sexton's poetry). Second, Bettelheim's lack of respect for the complexity and
literary qualities of the fairy tale has been addressed—explicitly in criticism, implicitly in literature. Several of the retellings have not yielded a
single, definite interpretation (Cross, Van Gestel, Biegel, Provoost, Sexton, Block, Browne) but oscillate between different readings and thus re-
install the polysemantic potential of literature. Whereas most—though not

all—fairy-tale retellings for young children conform to the happy ending that Bettelheim deems so important, we see that in retellings for older children, adolescents, and adults, the resolution of the fairy tale is substituted with more open endings, whose gaps of meaning invite reader participation and critical distance. Moreover, authors like Block, Provoost, Sexton, and others rewrite the fairy tale in a rich language that draws attention to itself in addition to expressing ideas about life and literature. Although feminists were among Bettelheim's fiercest critics, some have been influenced by *The Uses of Enchantment*. Sandra M. Gilbert and Susan Gubar's palimpsestic reading of "Snow White," which will be the focus of the next chapter, is partly inspired by Bettelheim's view of the fairy tale; yet it reveals the traditional story as well as his interpretation as manifestations of a patriarchal ideology.

4 Sandra M. Gilbert and Susan Gubar's
The Madwoman in the Attic

    The impact of Sandra M. Gilbert and Susan Gubar's *The Mad-woman in the Attic* (1979) on feminist literary criticism is undisputed as is the importance of their discussion of "Snow White" for fairy-tale studies.[1] The analysis of the tale forms the final part of the introductory chapter to *The Madwoman in the Attic*. Whereas the rest of the book focuses on literature written by woman authors, in "The Queen's Looking Glass" Gilbert and Gubar explore the origin of nineteenth-century women's unease with authorship through the analysis of metaphors of male writing, as well as the representation of women in texts written by men. "Is a pen a metaphorical penis?" is the famous opening phrase of their first chapter (*Madwoman* 3). Given the relatively small number of woman authors in history and in the literary canon, the image of women in literature has come to be dominated by male writers, Gilbert and Gubar argue. The "male expectations and designs" of what it means to be a woman prove to be limiting and biased. Gilbert and Gubar identify "two mythic masks male artists have fastened over her human face both to lessen their dread of her 'inconsistency' and [. . .] to possess her more thoroughly" (*Madwoman* 17). On the one hand, they discern the pervasive idealist image of the angel, the woman who is selfless and pure; on the other hand, stands the female monster, the woman who is active, aggressive, and unfeminine. In Charlotte Brontë's *Jane Eyre*, the enraged monster is Bertha Mason, the madwoman in the attic after whom Gilbert and Gubar's book is named. In the Grimms' tale of "Snow White," the two extremes are embodied by the angelic Snow White and her wicked stepmother.

In contrast to Marcia Lieberman, who mainly puts forward character identification as the reading strategy that the fairy tale stimulates, Gilbert and Gubar stress literature's ability to speak simultaneously on different levels: "No human creature can be completely silenced by a text or by an image. Just as stories notoriously have the habit of 'getting away' from their authors, human beings since Eden have had a habit of defying authority, both divine and literary" (*Madwoman* 17). And whereas Lieberman envisages the fairy tale's primary implied reader as a female child, Gilbert and Gubar recognize the relevance of "Snow White" for adult readers as a multi-layered text that provides insight into the construction and possible subversion of the two female archetypes. The reflection on Snow White's and her stepmother's imprisonment in and possible escape from the stereotypes they have come to embody is continued in the various contemporary retellings and illustrated versions of "Snow White" that are discussed in this chapter. I will focus on three aspects of Gilbert and Gubar's analysis: the function of the mirror, the deconstruction of the angel and the monster, and the development of the woman author. Although Gilbert and Gubar's view of "Snow White" proves to be the most pervasive, my analysis will show that the retellings, too, have "the habit of 'getting away,'" not only from their authors but also from the critical intertexts with which they can be linked.

Patriarchy and Female Entrapment: The Voice in the Mirror

Gilbert and Gubar read the Grimms' tale of "Snow White" as the literary reflection of woman's confinement in nineteenth-century bourgeois culture. The tale stages the battle between the two mythic images with which patriarchy has tried to grasp women: the angel and the witch. On the surface level, it is the angel who conquers and the witch who is defeated and punished. The tale thus seems to comply with patriarchal ideology, whose fears and ideals are confirmed and transmitted. Yet, Gilbert and Gubar suggest that every woman in patriarchy is entrapped in *both* these images, which do not oppose but succeed each other. The first queen, the wicked queen, and Snow White are all read as female role models that do not exclude each other but between which every woman has to negotiate. The three female figures in the tale are thus, in a sense, one and the same.

Patriarchy can only master woman if she is restricted and confined, Gilbert and Gubar argue. In "Snow White," the continued imprisonment of woman is symbolized by a succession of glass enclosures that affect all three of the female characters: from the window through which Snow White's biological mother stares at the snow, to the evil queen's magic mirror, to Snow White's glass coffin. Gilbert and Gubar interpret the last two objects moreover as "the tools patriarchy suggests that women use to kill themselves into art" (*Madwoman* 36), to become lifeless objects of the male gaze. Of the three glass prisons, the mirror takes the most prominent place in the traditional versions of "Snow White" and in Gilbert and Gubar's interpretation. Like Lieberman, they see the beauty contest as an instance in which the subordination of women to male judgment, to the male gaze, becomes clearest. In "Snow White," this competition takes place in the dialogues between the queen and her magic mirror that tells her "who is the fairest of them all." According to Gilbert and Gubar, this mirror fills a remarkable gap in the story. The reader may wonder indeed what role Snow White's father plays after he is remarried.[2] The Grimms' version of 1857 does not mention his death, and it is puzzling that he would tolerate the evil deeds his new wife afflicts on his daughter. Gilbert and Gubar argue that the king is by no means absent from "Snow White," as the Brothers Grimm's text suggests. Drawing on Bettelheim's interpretation of the tale as an oedipal drama, they claim that the voice of the patriarch is represented by the magic mirror: "There is one way in which the King *is* present. His, surely, is the voice of the looking glass, the patriarchal voice of judgment that rules the Queen's—and every woman's—self-evaluation. He it is who decides, first, that his consort is 'the fairest of all,' and then, as she becomes maddened, rebellious, witchlike, that she must be replaced by his angelically innocent and dutiful daughter, a girl who is therefore defined as 'more beautiful still' than the Queen" (Gilbert and Gubar, *Madwoman* 38).

Gilbert and Gubar see the death of the first queen as a metaphorical death, a transformation into her more wicked self.[3] In the Grimms' tale of 1857 it is stated, "A year later the king married another woman. She was a beautiful lady, but proud and arrogant and could not bear being second to anyone in beauty" ("Snow White" 83). That the mirror initially calls the queen the fairest in spite of these flaws is an inconsistency that Gilbert and Gubar ignore—in this tale's universe, where only two women matter, a possible explanation would be that Snow White is still too childlike to enter the beauty contest.

If the mirror is a metaphorical prison, as Gilbert and Gubar posit, rather than an instrument of knowledge, as it is presented in the surface layer of the Grimms' tale, it is paradoxical that the queen would voluntarily seek its company time and time again. From the psychoanalytical theory that partly informs their interpretation, Gilbert and Gubar draw an explanation of why it is the queen herself who interrogates the mirror in the Grimms' tale and why it is she herself who initiates the beauty contest: "To the extent, then, that the King, and only the King, constituted the first Queen's prospects, he need no longer appear in the story because, having assimilated the meaning of her own sexuality (and having, thus, become the second Queen) the woman has internalized the King's rules: his voice resides now in her own mirror, her own mind" (*Madwoman* 38). In several realistic retellings the mirror is indeed present only as an instrument for physical as well as mental self-reflection rather than as an exterior voice that judges the queen and drives her to jealousy and madness. Questions and answers in these disenchanted retellings are provided by the people who look in the mirror, while the object itself remains silent. In Róisín Sheerin's "Snow White" (1991), this is stated literally by the queen: "I get the most satisfaction out of my mirror *even though it just reflects my own opinions*. I consulted it about Snow White, told it how I had decided to wash my hands of her, had resolved to have nothing more to do with her. I asked the mirror if it thought I was being too harsh. I was reminded that I too had been awkward and rebellious when I was young" (49; my emphasis). The "I was reminded" is ambiguous: is it the mirror that reminds the queen, or does she remind herself? The fact that the rest of the retelling is devoid of magic suggests that it is the queen. Her internal dialogue with the mirror is reassuring rather than distressing, and the relationship between this stepmother and Snow White is determined by an effort to understand and love each other. The happy ending of this tale does not lie in the heterosexual marriage and punishment of the queen that a patriarchal model would promote, according to Gilbert and Gubar, but in the successful female bonding that they deem impossible in a society where the king's voice resides in the mirror and in the female mind.

Retellings that retain the theme of intense rivalry between (step)mother and -daughter more frequently externalize the voice of the mirror and mark it, like Gilbert and Gubar, as a distinctly patriarchal instrument. By making judgments about women in terms of youth and beauty, the mirror is shown to encourage rivalry and destroy female friendships. In several retellings in which the mirror is omitted or not enchanted, Snow White's father himself assumes its voice, as if the process of literary symbolization that Gilbert and Gubar describe as taking place in the Grimms' tale is reversed and undone. In psychoanalytic terms, these retellings bring to the surface the repressed, unconscious meaning of the tale; in feminist terms, they reveal the patriarchal ideology that is implicit in the traditional versions. Moreover, the retellings not only correspond to Gilbert and Gubar's critique of the Grimms' tale but also return to a convention present in some oral variants of "Snow White," in which male figures fulfill the role of the mirror.[4]

Jane Yolen's "Snow in Summer" (2000) provides a recent literary example in which the mirror is substituted by Snow White's father. This retelling relocates the traditional plot to a twentieth-century setting but retains the strong opposition between Snow White and her stepmother as the central action of the tale. The story is narrated by Snow and presents the stepmother in the unfavorable light of the traditional version. Yolen describes, however, more clearly and elaborately than the Brothers Grimm, the origin of the stepmother's hatred. In the beginning of the tale, it is stressed that Snow White's father chooses his new wife for her beauty: "The day she moved to Cumberland he said she was the queen of love and beauty"—the parataxis suggests that for him, love and beauty go hand in hand. That the father claims his new wife to be "prettier than a summer night" (92) can be read as the first hint of a competition, because in this tale the figure of Snow White is called "Snow in Summer" (abbreviated to Snow). The phrase "summer night" not only contains part of her name but also echoes William Shakespeare's comparison of his lover's beauty to a "summer day" in Sonnet 18. The change from "day" to "night" makes sense because "summer night" bears strong phonetic resemblances to "Snow White," the daughter's counterpart in the traditional tale. It is thus suggested that the stepmother is prettier than the protagonist and first-person narrator of the story, Snow, who later recalls that her father had never called her beautiful before she was thirteen years old. This observation strengthens the intertextual link between the father and the mirror, which does not mention Snow White until she is seven. As in Gilbert and Gubar's interpretation of "Snow White," it is also Snow's father who calls his wife's attention to his daughter's beauty. With his remark, Snow observes how her father now stimulates her stepmother's jealousy:

> Papa said, as if surprised by it, "Why, Rosemarie . . ." which was my Stepmama's Christian name, "Why, Rosemarie, do look at what a beauty that child has become."
> And for the first time my Stepmama looked—really looked—at me.
> I do not think she liked what she saw. ("Snow in Summer" 92)

The father is perceptive of his daughter's beauty, but it is the stepmother herself who interprets his remark as a reason for rivalry. Or, rather, that is how Snow interprets the course of events and presents it to the reader. In contrast to the mirror, the father comments but does not explicitly compare. If "Snow in Summer" is read as the account of a naïve or prejudiced narrator,⁵ another factor appears that stimulates the competition between Snow and her stepmother: in the margins of the tales moves the figure of Miss Nancy, her biological mother's best friend. She tells Snow magic stories, which are later suggested to be fairy tales, stories that end "happy-ever-after" (95). As Lieberman and Gilbert and Gubar have pointed out, such magic stories may influence a girl's expectations of the threats that a stepmother or any other woman brings. That Miss Nancy does not favor her employer's new wife is affirmed in several passages: "She [the stepmother] was a beautiful woman, everyone said. But as Miss Nancy down at the postal store opined, 'Looks ain't nothing without a good heart.' And she was staring right at my Stepmama when she said it" ("Snow in Summer" 91).

For Snow White to tell her own story in a traditional version would be contradictory to Gilbert and Gubar's interpretation of her role in the tale: they envisage her as a voiceless figure, "the heroine of a life that *has no story*" (*Madwoman* 39). Inevitably, when Snow White appears as a narrator, she must adopt some of the aspects that Gilbert and Gubar reserve for the queen, the artist and plotter, as I will discuss more elaborately below. Whereas critics such as Brownmiller fear that fairy tales train girls to be victims, "Snow in Summer" shows that fairy tales can equally promote female bonding and function as cautionary stories that indirectly teach female agency. Thanks to Miss Nancy's stories, Snow has learned to distrust her stepmother and take responsibility for her own happiness. At the moment when her stepmother approaches her in disguise while she is living with the seven dwarves, a reversal of the traditional roles takes place. While her mother is sitting at the table eating apple pie, Snow kills her with a frying pan. Not only is Snow's role reversed from victim to murderer (supported by her transformation from the recipient to the dispenser of apples), her stepmother's character is also modified. She is now the naïve woman who lets herself be tricked—she becomes the victim who eats the apple and is killed. A judgment of whether she deserved this ending depends on whether the reader is willing to take Snow's perspective to be accurate. In this respect, the surprising closure may raise the question of to what extent Snow has acted out a plot that Miss Nancy designed for her—the tale does not end with Snow's wedding, but with the union of Miss Nancy with her father. "Make your own happiness," was her advice to Snow ("Snow in Summer" 95), and this may indeed be what Miss Nancy has done for herself.

In Yolen's tale, the stepmother is perceived exclusively from the narrative perspective of Snow, who does not change her opinion of her throughout the tale. In contrast, the first-person narrator of Emma Donoghue's "The Tale of the Apple" (1997) does adapt her view of her stepmother and reflect on the construction of her initial prejudices. In this process, Donoghue links the figure of the king and the magic mirror even more clearly than Yolen does: not only does she put the words of the mirror more literally into the king's mouth, but she also includes the oedipal tension and the competitive aspect more explicitly. In the traditional version of "Snow White," as well as in Yolen's retelling, there is no mention of any sort of bonding between Snow and her stepmother. Donoghue shows that a hesitant friendship *is* developing between the two young women, who do not differ much in age in her retelling. Their fragile bond is, however, soon disrupted by a deceptively casual remark of Snow White's father:

> Once when he came to [my stepmother's] room at night he found us both there, cross-legged on her bed under a sea of velvets and laces, trying how each earring looked against the other's ear. He put his head back and laughed to see us. Two such fair ladies, he remarked, have never been seen in one bed. *But which of you is the fairest of them all?* We looked at each other, she and I, and chimed in the chorus of his laughter. Am I imagining in retrospect that our voices rang a little out of tune? [...]
>
> He let out another guffaw. Tell me, he asked, how am I to judge between two such beauties? I looked at my stepmother, and she stared back at me, and our eyes were like mirrors set opposite each other, making a corridor of reflections, infinitely hollow. (Donoghue 47–48; my emphasis)

In contrast to the mirror in the Grimms' tale and similar to "Snow in Summer," the father compares his wife and daughter spontaneously, without being asked or provoked. Although Donoghue, like Yolen, mentions fairy tales as a negative influence on Snow White's image of her stepmother, the father's words are suggested to be the strongest stimulant for their rivalry. The mirrors in the women's eyes function as an intertextual marker, drawing attention to the object that speaks the father's words in the traditional tale. In addition, these mirrors show that Snow White and her stepmother have internalized the king's voice in the same way that Gilbert and Gubar argue is the case for the Grimms' wicked queen. Before the king's ominous words, the two women tried to enhance each other's beauty as friends ("trying how each earring looked against the other's ear"). Once the competition has been instigated, they can no longer take each other for what they are, it is suggested, but only see the other in comparison to themselves: these are the "mirrors set opposite each other."

An important difference from the traditional tale is that, both in Yolen and in Donoghue, Snow White too is implicated in this process, that she too is affected by the king's words, whereas she is absent from the scenes in which the mirror makes his judgment in Grimm. In retrospect, Donoghue's narrator realizes that her father's comparison was based on standards that are "infinitely hollow," dictated by a patriarch who is pictured in the rest of the story as treating women mainly as sex objects and breeding machines. That the two young women have internalized the king's words explains why their rivalry continues after his death. Like Yolen, Donoghue thus extends the internalization of the king's voice from the wicked queen to include Snow White as well.

Many other retellings do not equate the mirror with Snow White's father but with another male character. They also appear as relevant intertexts for Gilbert and Gubar's analysis of "Snow White," although they are not as close to the intertextual core as Yolen and Donoghue are. The aforementioned "Snow Night" by Barbara Walker provides the clearest example. In this feminist revision, it is the hunter who tries to stimulate the competition between Snow Night and the queen. For Gilbert and Gubar, "the huntsman is really a surrogate for the King, a parental—or, more specifically, patriarchal—figure" (*Madwoman* 39). This is another aspect in which they are inspired by Bettelheim. In the postpatriarchal society that Walker depicts, the hunter tries to regain control after Snow Night has rejected his proposal for marriage: "One evening he found the queen alone in her anteroom, consulting her magic mirror, which always told the truth. He sat quietly while she asked the mirror several questions. Then, as she was turning away, he said, 'I wonder if Your Majesty has ever asked the mirror who is the fairest lady in the land?'" (22). In this story, the traditional roles of king and mirror are not united as in Donoghue's and Yolen's retellings and Gilbert and Gubar's analysis, and the mirror is restored as an instrument of truth. However, the need for male judgment that the queen has internalized, according to Gilbert and Gubar, is externalized once again and projected onto a patriarchal figure. As in Donoghue and Yolen, the queen does not solicit a male opinion, instead the hunter tries to stimulate female jealousy spontaneously. In "Snow Night," however, the differences in age and beauty between stepmother and stepdaughter do not raise the slightest doubt or competition. Female rivalry is immediately discarded as "one of the ridiculous traditions about women invented by men." The queen knows that Snow White is the fairest but does not consider this observation a reason to cause "unnecessary strife" (Walker 23). The third-person narrator supports this feminist correction of the traditional story, stressing from the beginning that the queen was "also famous for her beauty, of a more mature type than that of the young princess" (21). "Snow Night" differs from the traditional versions as well as from most retellings of the tale, in which the queen immediately and uncritically lets herself be infected with jealousy by her mirror's or her husband's words. In Walker's feminist fairy tale, it is not the stepmother who is a threat to Snow White but the hunter, who does not realize that his patriarchal ideas are no longer valid and that his own role in the other (female) characters' lives is marginal. "Snow Night" thus builds on a stark contrast with the traditional "Snow White," to which it self-reflexively refers as the better-known version of the tale written by Lord Hunter.

In Fiona French's classic *Snow White in New York* (1986), the mirror's role is taken over by a different medium, the newspaper. The *New York Mirror* fulfills the function of the judge in the beauty contest—it proclaims Snow White's stepmother to be the "the classiest dame in New York" and Snow White "the Belle of New York City." Later in the book, a newspaper article reveals to the evil stepmother where Snow White is hiding, as the mirror does in the traditional tale. That this medium, too, represents a man's voice is suggested by the fact that at least the second article is written by a male journalist: "The very first night Snow White sang there was a newspaper reporter in the club. He knew at once that she would be a star. Next day Snow White was on the front page of the New York Mirror." Again a male character is presented as the judge in a competition for celebrity: he decides "who's hot and who's not." The journalist's opinions are even more powerful because they are more public than the queen's private mirror. At the end of *Snow White in New York* it becomes clear that the voice of the mirror does not coincide so much with that of the father as with that of the prince: Snow White marries the reporter. In the modern setting where "high society" and appearing on the newspaper's front page are the highest goals that can be achieved, his power is comparable to that of the monarch in the traditional tale.

Adèle Geras's *Pictures of the Night* (1992) draws the link with reality more strongly than the previous retellings. In contrast to French's book, in which Snow White's deathlike sleep after she swallows a poisoned cherry is an undisputed instance of magic, for all the supernatural events in *Pictures of the Night* there is a rational explanation. In this realistic, novelized retelling set in the early 1960s, it is a hairdresser, Monsieur Armand, who fulfills the role of the mirror. As in Yolen's and Donoghue's retellings, the Snow White figure, Bella, narrates the incident in retrospect, with a claim to psychological insight into the stepmother's feelings toward her: "Marjorie's attitude towards me changed when I was seven. I can pinpoint the very day: it was the day of my first visit to Monsieur Armand's hairdressing salon, Chez Armand. Up until then, Marjorie loved me in the way that someone loves a pretty doll" (32). Like the stepmother in Donoghue's tale, Marjorie likes to share clothes and makeup with Bella at first and although her attitude is patronizing, it does not seem as unloving as Bella describes it. This initial bond ends abruptly the moment the two female characters are compared by a male:

> "*Voilà!*" He turned to Marjorie with a flourish, to show her the re-sult of his labours on me. "Do you not think this is *merveilleux?*"
>
> "Oh, that's very nice," said Marjorie. "Thank you so much, Armand."
>
> "Thank you," I said, "I think it's lovely."
>
> "You are going to become . . . how do you say? . . . the competi-tion for Madame Lavanne, *n'est-çe pas* [sic]?"
>
> Marjorie was almost silent on the way home. My father was very pleased with the new hair-style.
>
> "You look simply lovely, Bellissima!" he said and kissed me. "More like your mother than ever. It quite takes me back!"
>
> Maybe his words were less than diplomatic. Marjorie became even quieter. (Geras 35)

Geras redistributes the mirror's function between two male characters: the hairdresser and the father. As is typical of hairdressers, Monsieur Armand talks to his clients while looking at them in the mirror. Geras thus retains the intertextual reference to the talking mirror but resituates its words and function in a realistic frame. Not only does Monsieur Armand compare the two women in terms of beauty, but it is also he who tells Marjorie later in the story where Bella is hiding. He explicitly and spontaneously calls the relationship between the two women a "competition." Although the judg-ment of Monsieur Armand makes a big impression on Marjorie, it is not the opinion of this man that matters most to her. Bella's father reinforces the rivalry initiated by Monsieur Armand by using the superlative "*Bellissima*," the fairest, and by bringing in the association with his first wife (as does the father in Yolen's retelling). It was also Bella's father who first placed his daughter in front of a mirror and pointed at her beauty (Geras 26), an ele-ment that overlaps quite literally with Gilbert and Gubar's reading of the mirror as a "patriarchal" or "fatherly" instrument in "Snow White."

As Gilbert and Gubar argue about the queen in the traditional versions, Marjorie can be said to internalize the voice of the mirror. After the first incident at the hairdresser's, she keeps asking Monsieur Armand who he sees as the winner of the beauty contest:

> Visits to the hairdresser continued, of course, and each time we went, Marjorie would ask Monsieur Armand, sometimes in a round-about way and sometimes straight out, which one of us was the more beautiful. Monsieur Armand twisted and turned his replies into complicated knots of words that always worked out as the message that Marjorie wanted to hear: there's nothing to choose between you. Then, one day when I was ten, she caught him off guard.
>
> "Tell me truly, Armand," she said after a particularly successful session with scissors and rollers, "how does the competition look now?" (Geras 40)

Although some of Geras's alterations to the traditional tale reflect similarities with Gilbert and Gubar's interpretation, her retelling diverges from their vision on the tale in several aspects. First, the narrator stresses the unease with which Monsieur Armand has to make his judgment after he has perceived the effect that his first statement has had, and he denies afterward that any such competition should take place or continue ("there's no choosing between you"). Second, in Geras's retelling, it is not only the step-mother who visits Monsieur Armand but also Bella herself. In the Grimms' tale, Snow White is always the object of the mirror's gaze and never the gazing subject. Bella, in contrast, is present from the very beginning when her father and Monsieur Armand make their judgments: she is thus conscious of her own beauty and of her progress in the competition. Her beauty is revealed not to be as "natural" as that of the Grimms' Snow White, but contrived with "scissors and rollers." Moreover, Bella also has a mirror in the house that she shares with seven friends, the equivalent of the dwarves' cottage (Geras 22). That Snow White assumes some of the queen's characteristics is one of Gilbert and Gubar's most central points, as will be discussed in detail below. However, their timing is different from Geras's. "Innocent, passive, and self-lessly free of the mirror madness that consumes the Queen" (*Madwoman* 38), they describe Snow White, and note that she only displays some "hint of self-interest" at the point when she disobeys the dwarves. By turning Bella into the narrator of her own story, Geras, like Yolen and Donoghue, breaks with Gilbert and Gubar's view of Snow White as an innocent, helpless victim, a heroine without a story. Bella presents herself as a sharp observer from a very young age and an active participant in the story of her life.

That Bella has a story to tell does not mean, however, that the reader has to take her word for it. In a confessional passage at the beginning of the novel, which paradoxically underlines and undermines the authenticity of her voice, Bella discredits herself as an unreliable narrator. She writes that her friends are "forever telling me off for exaggerating, making an exhibition of myself, being what you call melodramatic" (Geras 9). Further on, she states, "Long live melodrama, say I, and passion and bright scarlet dresses and loud music and everything that isn't flat and dull and grey and little and ordinary" (11). Not only does she distinguish herself in these sentences from the rather dull protagonist that Gilbert and Gubar have revealed Snow White to be in comparison to her inventive and passionate stepmother, but Bella's introduction of herself also warns the reader that her personality may color her account. It is through her voice that we hear about Monsieur Armand's and her father's beauty contest, in which indeed Bella presents herself as the center of the action, the fairest of them all. By adapting the traditional fairy tale's narrator, Geras makes explicit what Shuli Barzilai had argued about the Grimms' "Snow White" all along: "'Snow White' is the daughter's story. Her perspective orients the narrative form from beginning to end. [. . .] The text is full of indications of Snow White's perspectival dominance" (523). In *Pictures of the Night,* this perspectival dominance finds continuation and reinforcement in Bella's first-person narrative. As in Yolen's "Snow in Summer," from Bella's account too, the reader can distill alternative explanations for Marjorie's hatred. The main reason may not be Bella's beauty but rather her resemblance to her biological mother, the first and idealized wife of Marjorie's husband. This would still be a form of female competition, but one in which Bella's role is only secondary.

From a comparison of the revisions of "Snow White" by Yolen, Donoghue, French, Walker, and Geras, it becomes clear that the scene with the mirror functions as a poetological, self-reflexive moment, which not only marks an intertextual connection with the traditional tale but also comments on the elements of that pre-text that are reflected or distorted in the intertextual transformation. In French and Walker, Snow White is absent from the scene in which the equivalents of the mirror (the newspaper and hunter, respectively) comment on her beauty. In the rest of these retellings, the Snow White figures remain subject to the plots and help of others. In Yolen, Donoghue, and Geras, the Snow White equivalents are present when the conversation with the mirror is reflected in the text: they witness the mirror's judgment not only as characters but also as narrators. If the opposition of females that Gilbert and Gubar see at work in the traditional "Snow White" is retained, the subsequent loss of innocence in Yolen, Donoghue, and Geras is the condition that needs to be fulfilled to make Snow White an author. Moreover, in these three retellings the equivalent of the mirror is dissociated from the truth—its judgment is shown to be biased and constructed. Similarly, as the mirror loses its status of omniscience and objectivity, so does Snow White as the narrator or mirror of the events: her perspective can equally be called biased and reductive.

The Voice of the Therapist

Gilbert and Gubar's analysis of "Snow White" is influenced by Bettelheim in several ways, most notably by the fact that he considers the king to be the central point of reference in the conflict between the queen and Snow White. Gilbert and Gubar consequently interpret the voice in the mirror as being the voice of the king but strip him of the positive connotations that Bettelheim attaches to him and ignore Bettelheim's emphasis that the fairy tale represents the child's projection. In chapter three it was mentioned that according to Pierre Péju, the psychoanalyst assigns himself the role of the king: "He who interprets reigns supreme" (60; my translation). In the short story "The Session," Steven Gould makes the circle complete: this sequel to "Snow White" locates the voice of the therapist in the mirror. When she returns to her father's castle after her wedding and after her father's death, Gould describes Snow White as finding a listening ear in her mother's mirror. She has plenty to discuss with it, including her marital problems and the hostile feelings that she harbors toward her own daughter. Throughout their conversation, the mirror stresses that it does not wish to guide Snow White but merely have her reflect her own feelings and ideas: "*I don't 'see' people. I help them to see themselves,*" it claims, and "*If I reflect things back at you or ask questions, it's to steer you to where you can find insight*" (87–88).

Just as Péju argues that Bettelheim grants supreme authority to the psycho-analyst, several times the mirror in Gould's tale underlines its omniscience, or at least its superiority in knowledge to Snow White: "*I know a great many things and I suspect others, but for me to tell you what I know or suspect is not going to do any good unless you're ready to see it for yourself*," it states, and, "*I know details, but it's your perspective that we need here*" (88–89). With its insistence that it can only tell the truth (91–93), the mirror stresses the authority of its judgments and opposes itself to Snow White's more limited, subjective point of view. Like Geras's tale and Barzilai's analysis, Gould draws attention to Snow White's perspectival dominance in the traditional story, because the mirror each time invites her to give her viewpoint (88, 89) and her answer invariably corresponds to the traditional version of the tale.

Keeping Péju's critique of Bettelheim's self-proclaimed authority in mind, one may ask what the mirror's viewpoint is and whether it is as neutral and truthful as it claims. After all, excluded from any other perspective, the reader has to take its word for it: the tale is only polyphonic at the beginning of the story. Toward the end Snow White accepts that the mirror's perspective is more reliable and complete than her own: she is the patient brought to insight by the psychoanalyst. One may wonder, however, what role the mirror played when Snow White's mother was still alive. It briefly hints at this period by stating, "*I don't lie. That's what started this whole mess in the first place*" (Gould 92), presenting itself as a victim rather than an accomplice in or instigator of the conflict. Gould's sequel takes the liberty of fiction to step into a story at a certain point, without the obligation to encompass or explain as many aspects of the pre-text as possible. When the comparison between "The Session" and the traditional tale is drawn, a number of questions still linger: why could the mirror not dissuade the first queen from abusing her daughter? Did she remain immune to its therapeutic advice? And even if it could not lie, why did it not refuse to be her accomplice, as it now refrains from providing Snow White with easy answers? Although the mirror dissuades Snow White from asking the same questions as her mother, its therapeutic sessions give it considerable power over her, as becomes clear in the final lines:

> When should I see you again?
> *Same time next week?*
> All right. [. . .]

> *Thank you, your Highness.*
> No, no—thank you, Mirror.
>   (Gould 93)

Although this mirror promises to function differently from the one in the traditional tale, it is clear that Snow White is as much under its influence as her mother was. And if the therapist is as much an authoritative, patriarchal voice as Bettelheim has been argued to be, she may not be better off.

"Snow White" Illustrations

It is not only textual fairy-tale retellings that can be intertextually linked to the debates Gilbert and Gubar have initiated on the patriarchal ideology in "Snow White." In a large number of illustrated versions of the tale, the mirror has distinct masculine traits or is associated with the face of a man. Like the textual revisions analyzed above, these illustrated fairy tales practice what Bacchilega has identified as an ideology-critical strategy in postmodern fairy-tale retellings: "Assuming that a frame always selects, shapes, (dis)places, limits, and (de)centers the image in the mirror, postmodern retellings focus precisely on this frame to unmake the mimetic fiction. These retellings make the implicit link between narrative and gender (re)production in 'Snow White' apparent, and narrative and psychological claims to truth can be questioned" (Bacchilega, *Postmodern Fairy Tales* 35–36).

In some fairy-tale illustrations, this postmodern process of denaturalizing a mimetic narrative by focusing on the ideological nature of its (narratological) frame can be taken quite literally. The illustrations invest the mirror's frame with additional meanings and thus problematize its neutrality. By rooting the mirror in a more specific context, these pictures create the potential for a commentary on the accompanying text, which usually retains the traditional illusion of a neutral third-person narrator. Trina Schart Hyman's, Charles Santore's (Grimm, *Snow White*), and Wim Hofman's illustrations, for instance, add Christian symbols to the mirror and thus draw attention to the Christian dimensions and perspectives in the story. The examples discussed below all contextualize the tale of "Snow White" in the same ideology as Gilbert and Gubar do: patriarchal society. They do so moreover, like Gilbert and Gubar, by identifying the mirror not with a natural truth but with a gendered, masculine voice.[6]

Figure 17. Snow White and the Seven Dwarfs *by Bernard Canavan.*

Although it is debatable whether the mirror in Gregory Maguire's retelling *Mirror Mirror* ever speaks, the illustrations by Douglas Smith that are included before the chapters in which it appears show that its top is decorated with the face of a beastlike man. Moreover, the mirror displays an aestheticized and passive Snow White as Gilbert and Gubar see her constructed through the male gaze.

In Bernard Canavan's illustrations to Leslie Gower's adaptation of "Snow White" (1986), the mirror is part of the body of a masculine figure, and it is the head that speaks (Figure 17). In several of Canavan's drawings (5, 11), the mirror's face expresses actual pleasure when he shows the queen that Snow White is her superior in beauty. Wim Hofman concludes his elaborate retelling of "Snow White" with the words and an image of the mirror (Figure 18). The illustration is particularly impressive because although the mirror has played an important role throughout the story, it has never actually been shown before. Given the game of seduction it has played with the stepmother and the glee with which it has directed her to her tragic fate, in a reading in the vein of Gilbert and Gubar it is not surprising that this mirror too has a distinctly masculine face. Its frame combines, moreover, visual allusions to God as well as to the devil, indicating that it combines omniscience with evil.

Female Voices

Retellings and illustrated versions that represent the mirror with a male, human voice incorporate a feminist critique of the traditional versions and may stimulate a reflection on the distribution of gendered roles in these tales. It is rare in variants of "Snow White" that the role of the mirror is associated with a woman. Steven Swann Jones mentions only one oral variant, a Mexican version from Robe in which a crone tells the queen that Blanca is fairer than she (103). The same is true for the retellings, in which it is rare that the mirror's function is taken over by a female figure. This may be due to the masculine genus of the German word *"Spiegel."* Yet, English translations and adaptations usually do not render the derived masculine pronoun "er" as "he" but as "it," showing that the mirror is considered gender neutral. In many retellings, it is clear that the mirror's masculinity can be read as an added feminist critique that displays an intertextual overlap with Gilbert and Gubar.

Figure 18. Zwart als inkt *by Wim Hofman.*

Mira Mirror by Mette Ivie Harrison (2004) is one of only two examples in my corpus in which the mirror is inhabited by a woman. This fantasy retelling may in fact be the exception that confirms Gilbert and Gubar's rule that the mirror is a patriarchal instrument, because the function and character of this mirror highly differs from the more traditional versions and from the retellings that expose a patriarchal attitude. Mira is the adopted sister of a young woman who bears strong resemblances to Snow White's stepmother. In an attempt to attain physical perfection, she literally kills her sister into art, capturing her soul. The magic mirror is not only a metaphorical but also a physical entrapment for Mira:

> I tried to open my mouth, but it seemed I had no lips to open, no tongue to form words, no throat to make sound, no lungs to give me breath. The only sound that came from me was that of breaking glass. And then the sound again, in reverse. The glass, once shattered, had reformed itself.
>
> What had happened? I looked to my sister for help, but my neck was so stiff that my view of her was limited to a small circle—no more than that. I began to realize I had changed. I had become something that could not move. (Harrison 9)

A stark contrast arises between Mira's narrated experience and Canavan's visual representation of the masculine mirror (Figure 17). Whereas Mira feels claustrophobic and her sight is restricted by the wooden frame, the masculine figure in Canavan's picture surrounds the mirror and still has the ability to see and move around. Moreover, Mira uses her powers very differently from the mirror in the traditional tale. Once her sister has haunted Snow White and apparently failed, as in the traditional tale, the mirror is abandoned and hangs alone in a cottage in the forest for many years, expecting to die. When Mira finally gets a new owner, she initially tries to manipulate this girl so that she can collect enough power to retransform herself into a human being. However, a friendship develops between Mira, her new owner, and another girl who they meet along the way, and when Mira finally does get the chance to regain her human shape, she is not prepared to do so at the expense of another woman's happiness. She is even able to forgive her sister and finds that her sister's love for her is greater than her craving for youth and beauty. Harrison's fairy tale thus ends with a romantic plea for sisterhood, a plea that is also implicit in Gilbert and Gubar's discussion of "Snow White."

Gail Carlson Levine's *Fairest* (2006) is a second example in which the mirror is inhabited not only by a male ghost, Skulni, but also by a woman. Skulni is its permanent resident: "He had a man's face, a sharp face—

small features and small ears and a nose that came to a point. He was smiling [. . .] , his eyes splits of merry spite" (205). As in most retellings that
invest the mirror with a personality, Skulni plays a far greater role in the
story than the mirror in the traditional tales: not only does he show beauty,
but he also distributes it and thrives on the competition that is the result of
it. Skulni does experience the mirror as a form of entrapment, but it also
gives him pleasure. Occasionally he likes to leave for a holiday to the human world, and in order to have that chance, he needs to have a person
killed to take his place. When Ivi, the wicked queen, kills Aza, the Snow
White figure, with a poisoned apple, the latter's spirit is transported into
the mirror. Her attitude to this event marks a great contrast with the male
ghost. Aza immediately feels trapped and confined and is not willing to
take Skulni's place, even though she knows that his position would make
her extremely powerful: "I watched him, paralyzed with horror. I should
have taken his seat, but I didn't think of it" (272). Like Mira in Harrison's
retelling, Aza would rather die herself than be responsible for someone
else's death: "I threw myself—shoulder, elbows, knees, all my singing
weight—into the mirror. I sang, 'I won't remain in a mirror, a beauty in
a—' A roar drowned me out. The mirror crumbled in a bedlam of jan-
gling notes" (291–92). Aza's attempt to kill herself and the mirror by
breaking its glass corresponds to the moment when her corpse is revived
and her spirit is transported back into her body: a coincidence that secures
the happy ending but that she is unaware of. Thanks to this stroke of luck
and in contrast to the less fortunate Mira, Aza does not have to complete
her self-sacrifice.

Both Aza and Mira build a strong contrast to the majority of personified
mirrors. Harrison and Levine imagine what would have happened if the
voice in the mirror were a woman, and their answer is clear: "Snow White"
would have been a completely different story. Instead of abusing their
power and stimulating rivalry, Aza and Mira try to bond with the female
subjects who look into the mirror. When the female protagonists are forced
to choose between power and death, they both refuse to betray their strong
moral principles. Moreover, by inhabiting the mirror, these female characters come to realize the subsidiary value of physical beauty and learn to
value kindness, loyalty, and freedom. For the women in the majority of
fairy-tale retellings, the mirror remains a symbol of imprisonment, whether
they inhabit it or see themselves reflected in it.

The Male Gaze

For Gilbert and Gubar, the central action of "Snow White" is the conflict between Snow White as the stereotypical angel woman and her stepmother, who is portrayed as a monster woman. The bulk of their critique consists of a revaluation of the monster woman, who in their interpretation is an artist and a plotter, and a devaluation of the angel woman, who is considered to be voiceless and selfless. Retellings that are thematically related to this critique have used different strategies to address the underlying patriarchal ideology of this imagery. As discussed in the previous section, authors have drawn attention to, and thus denaturalized and criticized, the male gaze from which these archetypes allegedly stem. In several retellings, this foregrounding of the gaze does not remain limited to the mirror but also includes the prince, whose view of Snow White is problematized as it is by Gilbert and Gubar. A second strategy is to stress and exaggerate the negative aspects of the female angel so that the desirability of this archetype becomes questionable.

According to Gilbert and Gubar, Snow White's innocence, beauty, and passivity are the main reasons she is the patriarch's preferred woman—an interpretation that is supported by several retellings that foreground a causality between Snow White's powerlessness and the prince's affection. Alice Friman's "Snow White: The Prince" (1984) is a sequel to the traditional tale narrated by the prince. He testifies explicitly why he chose Snow White as his bride:

> She was my perfection once—
> An ivory heart
> A white bud stopped in stone.
> And because she'd never change
> I could have filled cathedrals with my love.
> My cold virgin. My wafer. My cup.
>
> I did not count on the accident.
>   (218)

In this poem, it is stressed that the prince fell in love with his wife when she was still "the eternally beautiful, inanimate *objet d'art*" that Gilbert and

Gubar consider her to be (*Madwoman* 40). He compares her to a list of in-animate materials—materials like ivory and stone, which are used to create art. Later in the text, the prince shows that he is an amateur of art objects. The Egyptian ankh, for instance, he appreciates as a "symbol of life / Frozen in its own silence" (218)—the ideal of still perfection that he also held for "Snow White." With the mention of the virgin, the cathedral, the wafer, and the cup, the prince draws the link with the Christian imagery of which the angel and the Virgin Mary are also a part—the Virgin Mary is, according to Gilbert and Gubar, another appearance of the virtuous female archetype that Snow White represents. The association with the Holy Communion and the body of Jesus Christ through the wafer and the cup (of wine) makes the prince central: he believes that he is the one for whom Snow White has been sacrificed.

That Friman's prince describes Snow White's "resurrection" as an "accident" affirms what Andrea Dworkin has argued about the Grimms' tales in a broader feminist context: "For a woman to be good, she must be dead, or as close to it as possible" (42). The crucial difference between Dworkin's and Gilbert and Gubar's analyses on the one hand and Friman's poem on the other lies in the potential of the fictional text to dissociate the speaking voice from that of the author. Friman's poem stages as a narrator the former prince, who is now king and patriarch. Whereas in the traditional fairy tales this patriarchal view of woman is communicated as implicit, "hidden," and naturalized ideology, here the prince rephrases it explicitly, even blatantly, and apparently unaware of the feminist critique that his testimony may raise. Such an unawareness of the reader is typical of the poetic form of the "apostrophe," in which the lyrical I speaks with his back turned to the reader, who thus gets access to the speaking subject's most intimate feelings (Van Alphen, Duyvendak, Meijer, and Peperkamp 9–10). Under the fictional pretence of providing the reader with the prince's uncensored thoughts, Friman's poem presents a "female mimicry of a male perspective" (Felski 75), an imitation of the male gaze that invites critical distance.

The Grimms' "Snow White" follows the typical narratological pattern of the traditional tale with an omniscient, third-person narrator. Cristina Bacchilega, relying on Mieke Bal's theory of narratology, observes that this narrator bears strong similarities to the voice of the mirror in the traditional tale. As Gilbert and Gubar have shown in another context, Bacchilega points out that this voice should not be accepted as objective and authoritative:

"Like the mirror, the narrator knows all, telling—or even better, showing—things as they are. But there is no pure mimesis in narration, only its illusion; language necessarily mediates 'showing' through a 'telling,' which cannot be innocent, because whether through a voice, or on the page, a narrator exists only in the first-person" (*Postmodern Fairy Tales* 34).

Retellings like Friman's shift the generic, narratological, and stylistic features of the fairy tale so that the ideological perspective from which the traditional content is supposedly presented gains visibility. In Friman's poem, the prince as first-person narrator is used as a mouthpiece for the patriarchal ideology that Gilbert and Gubar argue pervades the traditional tale's third-person narrative. The male gaze, or rather what feminists argue is the male gaze, in turn becomes the object of the reader's gaze. The explicitness with which the prince's ideals are described is an invitation for readers to distance themselves from this ideology. In a second step, which relies on the intertextual connection with a fairy-tale pre-text, readers are challenged to reconsider the prince's motives in the traditional tale and the narratological perspective that presented these as natural.

Perhaps more than any other fairy tale in the Grimms' collection, "Snow White" is a story about seeing and being seen—from the window in the opening scene through which the first queen stares at the snow to the glass coffin in the final paragraphs in which Snow White is displayed for the dwarves and other passersby to see. As Bacchilega has pointed out, it is hence particularly interesting to look at retellings that foreground this process of seeing and to question who sees what and how. In the already mentioned short story "Snow," Francesca Lia Block describes the gardener's reaction to the dead Snow White in a way that is similar to the retrospective testimony of Friman's prince. Here the man is not the narrator but the focalizer:

> The gardener went to her and held her hand. It felt like it would slip away, it was so thin and light; it felt boneless. The gardener said he was going to take her away with him, help her get better. Why was he hesitating? He wanted to look at her like this, for a while. He wanted this stillness. She was completely his, now, in a way she would never be again. His silent, perfect bride. [...] He leaned close to her, breathing her like one would inhale a bouquet. He looked at her lips, half parted as if waiting for him. He wanted to possess. (28–29)

Snow is literally the object of the male gaze here, as the prince or gardener is described looking at her. The reader is given access both to what the man sees and his inner thoughts and associations. The use of focalization as a narratological strategy allows a complex mix of the gardener's direct, internal thoughts with the narrator's external comments. From his inner monologue, the reader can deduce that for Block's prince, perfection is once again associated with frailty, silence, and stillness. These are also the reasons that Gilbert and Gubar ascribed to the prince in the traditional tale, and his subjection of Snow White is confirmed by the narrator's comment: "He wanted to possess."

The reaction of Block's gardener is similar to Snow's mother, who has internalized the patriarchal gaze, as Gilbert and Gubar argue:

> Through the window she saw them, the girl and the gardener. The girl was nightmare. Young young young. Silver white. Perfect. Untorn. Perfect.
>
> The gardener was haloed by her light. Dripping her light. [. . .] After all, she was young, perfect, untouched. [. . .]
>
> Poison, the mother thought, poison. [. . .] She had thought of using it on herself in the past. Wouldn't this almost be the same thing? (Block 20–21)

The scene that the woman witnesses is framed by a window, as if she observes her daughter through the patriarchal lens that Gilbert and Gubar have identified with the glass frames in "Snow White." What the stepmother sees is not a girl but a patriarchal archetype: the perfect, unsoiled virgin. The radiant halo makes visible her saintlike status, as the gardener becomes her dubious worshipper. The poison that the mother immediately thinks refers to the poison she wants to kill her daughter with, but she also seems to feel that her daughter is poison to herself. The scene supports Gilbert and Gubar's argument that it is not just her rival that the mother wants to kill, it is rather the type of angelic woman that she feels threatened by.

The final line of the citation from Block indeed shows that Snow and the queen have more in common than the Grimms' tale suggests. Block returns to the older variants of the story in which Snow White was still persecuted by her own mother. Their similarity and affinity is stressed at several moments in the short story, implicitly and explicitly. "This was not a stranger,"

Snow thinks when she meets her mother, whom she has not seen since she was an infant, "this was someone she sensed deep in her bones. Like marrow" (22). Both are also shown in a similar constellation with regard to the gardener. When the mother is the focalizer at the beginning of the story, it is said that "the gardener stood before the colored winter sun, blocking the light with his broad shoulders" (3). When Snow White sees him for the first time, "she liked the way he towered over her and the way his shoulders blocked the moonlight" (16). The women's subordination is symbolized by their small size and frailty; the fact that the gardener blocks the light with his shoulders marks his position for both women as the ultimate point of reference that he will become in their lives (permanently for the mother, temporarily for Snow). They stand literally and figuratively in a man's shadow—a contrast to Snow White's glorious and generous halo that the mother saw shining onto the man in the passage cited above.

Yet, unlike Gilbert and Gubar, Block does not see the conflict between mother and daughter as the central theme of the tale. Instead she attributes new value to Snow White's relationship with the seven dwarves. The gardener's possessive and the mother's inimical views on Snow stand in stark contrast to the seven dwarves' "benevolent gazes" (7) through which the reader has come to know her in the bulk of the tale. Although this Snow White does not have a female role model to live up to, nor does she have any other woman or "sister" to bond with, she finds alliance with the dwarves, who are, like her, cast away—not from their parents but from society. In the company of these "freaks," Snow is pictured as a happy young woman who has learned how to "hammer and build, cook, sew and garden" (11), who enjoys stories, who knows about sexual longing, and who enjoys the respect of the dwarves (17).

Through the perspective of the dwarves, Snow is shown to be much more than the white, virginal archetype to which her mother and the gardener reduce her. The prince's unresolved reaction to her death is juxtaposed with the seven dwarves', who do not hesitate or stare at her for a moment. Instead, their immediate response is to try and wake her up (Block 26): "My darling," they think, "we never deserved you. Wake up and we will let you go into the world where you belong" (27). While the prince lingers and observes the dead Snow as the art object that Gilbert and Gubar argue he would like to possess, the dwarves are busy making gifts in the hope that she will awaken, imagining her needs as a person who is truly alive—from dresses and necklaces to champagne glasses and quilts (28), almost like a traditional dowry. In contrast to the gardener, they place themselves modestly at her service, wishing a life of luxury for her, and not realizing that all she wants is to share their simple existence in the forest. When the gardener eventually does kiss her, Snow seems to have been aware of his gaze: "In her sleep she had seen love. It was poisoning. It was possessing. Devouring. Or it was seven pairs of boots climbing up the stairs to find her" (31). Renouncing the fairy-tale and arguably patriarchal ideal of a heterosexual union, Block's Snow White prefers to stay with the dwarves and live.

A Lovely Number

That Snow White can only be patriarchy's ideal woman at the price of her own identity and free will is an aspect of Gilbert and Gubar's analysis of the Grimms' tale that overlaps with Lieberman's critique and that is incorporated into several retellings for adults. Anne Sexton stresses Snow White's selflessness by calling her a "number"—the association with the adjective "numb" also underlines her lifelessness and voicelessness. Moreover, the virgin as numb-er, someone who makes others numb, corresponds to the patriarchal role model of silent femininity that Gilbert and Gubar see represented by such figures as the Virgin Mary and Snow White. Like Friman's prince, Sexton's narrator compares Snow White's features to a long list of inanimate, mainly fragile objects and thus creates the impression that she is barely alive, even when she is not lying in the glass coffin:

> No matter what life you lead
> the virgin is a lovely number:
> cheeks as fragile as cigarette paper,
> arms and legs made of Limoges,
> lips like Vin Du Rhone,
> rolling her china-blue doll eyes
> open and shut.
>   (Sexton 149)

The image that Sexton creates of Snow White as a delicate doll or a "dumb bunny" has proven to be pervasive in other feminist fairy-tale poems.[7]

Snow White's doll-like state is evoked in the conclusion of Nikolaus Berg-wanger's poem "schneewittchen öffne deine augen" (1980, snow white open your eyes), which reproachfully asks,

> snow white
> when will you finally open
> your eyes
>   (11; my translation)

after having stressed Snow White's coma several times. The phrase "we are living / in the age of the dwarves" (10–11; my translation), which is equally foregrounded through repetition, seems to indicate the "dwarfed powers" (*Madwoman* 40) to which she has been limited, temporarily in the Grimms' tale and permanently in Bergwanger's and Sexton's versions. Several other authors and poets explicitly stress the passivity of Snow White and her bio-logical mother, as Sexton and Gilbert and Gubar do. "She has nothing to do but to die" (46) writes Patricia Carlin in "The Stepmother Arrives" (2002), after the first queen has given birth. This formulation is repeated with reference to Snow White, whose role in the fairy-tale script is interpreted as being as vapid as her mother's: "She has nothing to do but lie there" (47).

Gilbert and Gubar's view of the queen as a woman who wants to kill not so much Snow White as a person but rather the ideal of innocence and res-ignation that she represents is taken up and elaborated in a "Cinderella" retelling by Sara Maitland, "The Wicked Stepmother's Lament" (1996). Here, Cinderella's stepmother problematizes the usual positive connota-tions attached to the concept of innocence: "I have grown out of innocence now and even of wanting to be thought innocent" (*Angel Maker* 222). This woman, like the queen in "Snow White" in whom she recognizes herself, clearly prefers to live what Gilbert and Gubar call "a life of significant ac-tion" (*Madwoman* 39). Maitland gives the same reason for her hatred of Cinderella as they do for the queen's attempts to kill Snow White: "Snow White represents the ideal of renunciation that the Queen has already re-nounced at the beginning of the story" (*Madwoman* 38). Maitland adds to her resentment of Cinderella's passivity an aversion to the biological moth-er's resignation: "What she was not was powerful. She wouldn't look out for herself. She was so sweet and so hopeful; so full of faith and forgiveness and love" (*Angel Maker* 223). This woman's tragic fate serves as a warning for all women, the stepmother argues: "She was too good. Too giving. She gave herself away, indiscriminately. She didn't even give herself as a precious gift. [. . .] She equated love with suffering, I thought at one time, but that wasn't right, it was worse, she equated loving with being; as though she didn't exist unless she was loved" (223).

The self-sacrifice of Cinderella's mother is pictured not as generous or praiseworthy but as pitiful and pathological. Possibly referring to Bettelheim's split mother figure, which is reflected in Gilbert and Gubar's analysis, Maitland shows how the ideal of the "good mother" must inevitably die—either physically or through a transformation into the "bad mother," the mother who claims her own needs. Cinderella's biological mother has followed the first path: "The mother who denied her little one nothing, the good mother, the one we all longed for, pouring herself out into the child. [. . .] Well she could not, of course she could not [stand up for her rights], so she did not survive" (*Angel Maker* 224). The stepmother in Maitland's tale has witnessed both options: death in the person of her friend, Cinderella's mother, and the transformation into the bad or powerful mother in herself after she had her daughters.

Gilbert and Gubar indicate the cyclical pattern that lies behind the figures of the angel and the witch. The narrator of Maitland's story anticipates this cycle and wants to make sure that Cinderella will make the right choice when she becomes a mother herself. The trials through which she puts Cinderella are then provocatively explained as an attempt to save her stepdaughter's life: "I only meant to tease her a little, to rile her, to make her fight back. I couldn't bear it, that she was so like her mother and would go the same way" (*Angel Maker* 224). Yet the stepmother's alleged well-meant campaign to force Cinderella into some form of agency is to no avail: "So yes, in the end I was cruel. I don't know how to explain it and I do not attempt to justify it. Her *wetness* infuriated me. I could not shake her good will, her hopefulness, her capacity to love and love and love such a pointless and even dangerous object. I could not make her hate me. Not even for a moment. I could not make her hate me" (225).

The rhetorical second sentence of the fragment is immediately undermined by the explanations that precede and follow it: the stepmother does explain her actions and tries to justify her behavior toward Cinderella. The "inconsistencies that result from multiperspectival accounts of the same event" can be a clue to position a narrator as unreliable, argues Ansgar

Nünning with reference to Shlomith Rimmon-Kenan ("Unreliable Narration" 97). Such a multiperspectival dimension is added by the intertextual dialogue between Maitland's story and the traditional versions of "Cinderella." Maitland stages a Cinderella who is even more passive and self-sacrificing than her traditional equivalent. If readers accept this account as truthful, they may even wonder if this is not her way of getting back at her stepmother: it would certainly be a strategy that has succeeded in irritating and infuriating the narrator. Is this Cinderella the "proficient victim" that Belinda Stott (15) believes her traditional counterpart to be?

In contrast to Gilbert and Gubar, who take into account the complete tale of "Snow White," Maitland ends the "Cinderella" retelling before the ball. Like Gould, this author uses the artistic freedom of fiction to suspend the retelling's interpretation and corrections at a crucial point in the story. The final command that the stepmother gives to Cinderella refers to a turning point in the traditional story, the moment when the stepdaughter is finally empowered:

> "Wake up, hurry up, stop daydreaming, no you can't, yes you must, get a move on, don't be so stupid." And "You're not going to the ball, or party, or disco, or over your Nan's, dressed like *that*."
> She calls it nagging.
> She calls me Mummy. (*Angel Maker* 227)

Is the final word of the story, "Mummy," a sign of weakness or a clever provocation? And how does the story continue? As the narrative breaks off at this point, the reader is not informed of whether Cinderella will rebel in secret, whether she will go to the ball or not. The beginning of the Grimms' traditional tale was included at the beginning of Maitland's story and commented on as "You know the rest I expect. Almost everyone does" (*Angel Maker* 222). This makes the lack of an explicit comment on the traditional ending all the more surprising. On the one hand, the ellipsis could imply that the traditional ending has not changed. The reader already knows that part of the tale—the stepmother does not need to elaborate on it but rather wants to explain the motives for the part of the story in which she does play an important role, that is, in Cinderella's persecution. On the other hand, the open ending leaves the possibility that this part of the story never takes place. The Cinderella that she has pictured may not be willing to enter into a plot that tricks her stepmother, whom, if we believe the narrator, she loves like her own mother. Even if the reader assumes that Cinderella does go to the ball and meet with the traditional ending that Perrault and the Grimms' have imagined for her, her happiness is not without blemish as it was in the traditional tale. Will she be the good mother that her dead mother tried to be, a role that eventually killed her, or will Cinderella evolve to become more like her stepmother, as Gilbert and Gubar imagine Snow White to become? And are these indeed the only two options that she will have, since these are presented to the reader by a stepmother who is arguably an unreliable narrator?

The Queen Snow White

Briefly imagining a similar sequel to "Snow White," Gilbert and Gubar come to the conclusion that Snow White will not be able to escape her stepmother's fate once she becomes a mature woman (and a mother) herself. "What does the future hold for Snow White?" they ask themselves. "When her Prince becomes King and she becomes a Queen, what will her life be like?" (*Madwoman* 42). As patriarchy only favors young and innocent women (those who are powerless and easier to control), it is most likely that the Queen Snow White will be vilified too. Several sequels to the traditional tale suggest a similar cyclicality. In Polly Peterson's "The Prince to Snow White" (2000), the prince announces what the future holds for his wife:

> You shall have
> your mother's love.
> Indeed, you have it now,
> even as you
> usurp her place.
> Did you think that I found you
> by chance, Maiden?
> You are beautiful, sublime,
> yet not so lovely
> as our daughter will be:
> your mother's daughter's child—
> her immortality.

Here is another author who stages the prince as a mouthpiece of patriarchy, as described by Gilbert and Gubar, inviting a feminist critique similar to Alice Friman's poem. The prince in Peterson's and Friman's sequels has replaced the king to become a patriarch himself. The line "Did you think that I found you / by chance, Maiden?" contradicts the overt content of the Grimms' tale, in which the prince's finding of Snow White is indeed described as a coincidence. The prince ascribes to his wife a naïvety that he transcends. The answer to the implicit question of how he found her if not by chance may be double. That the prince calls her "Maiden" is an indication of the qualities that marked her attraction for him. She was the ideal, white virgin, the damsel in distress. Alternatively, it is suggested in Peterson's poem that Snow White's mother gave the prince directions. Gilbert and Gubar argue that the queen made a mistake when she killed Snow White because she involuntarily amplified her stepdaughter's attraction: "After the Queen's artfulness has killed Snow White into art, the girl becomes if anything even more dangerous to her 'step' mother's autonomy than she was before, because even more opposed to it in both mind and body. For, dead and self-less in her coffin, she is an object, to be displayed and desired, patriarchy's 'marble opus,' the decorative and decorous Galatea with whom every ruler would like to grace his parlor" (*Madwoman* 41).

Snow White's increased appeal as a selfless being explains why the queen would send the prince to kiss her awake in Peterson's poem: only when Snow White lives and develops can the cycle of archetypal images be resumed. That the prince claims that Snow White has her mother's love now can be read in this context, especially in reference to Delia Sherman's "Snow White to the Prince," to which Peterson wrote her poem in response. Sherman pictures a Snow White who has become conscious of her function as the artistic object of the patriarchal gaze and voices her objections to this role. Snow White realizes that her beauty is cursed because it has turned her into the frozen object of a male gaze and alienated her from the mother that she holds dearer than the prince. If Gilbert and Gubar argue that the queen hates Snow White for her innocence and selflessness (*Madwoman* 39), Peterson suggests that she may appreciate her more now that (at least in Sherman's poem) she has gained a voice and a critical distance from her former self as an innocent maiden.

Although Peterson's prince claims that Snow White's new status may alter her mother's appreciation of her, it will also change his. He announces to his wife that there will be a time when her features will be weighed against her own daughter's beauty and that such a comparison will always turn out to be unfavorable for the older woman. Implicitly he puts himself forward as the judge, as he has also chosen her for her beauty. "Her immortality" refers, then, not to a specific person but rather to the repetition of a female pattern. What will be reborn with the new child is the role that every (step)mother plays in patriarchy, that of the older woman who feels threatened when she is about to be replaced. The "immortality" equally signals the reincarnation of the model that every daughter fulfills in contrast: the innocent maiden. It is this cycle, this eternal exchange of the female archetypes, that becomes immortal in Gilbert and Gubar's analysis of the fairy tale. That Peterson's prince presents the female cycle as natural and inevitable marks his advantage in this pattern. Yet, returning to Sherman's poem, the prince may be revealed as naïve in his own right. In "Snow White to the Prince," Snow White corrects the image of the perfect virgin that the prince had of her: she explains that she had accepted the poisoned apple consciously, that it was a regression to her childhood, when the relationship with her mother was still harmonious. Such a conscious and controversial act as suicide blemishes the prince's image of the selfless Snow White, and hence she is already considered a usurper before she has become a mother herself, even before she has become patriarchy's "marble opus."

As shown above, Gilbert and Gubar attribute to the mirror an important role in stimulating the rivalry between mother and daughter. Several retellings include this element to suggest a cyclical pattern after the traditional "Snow White" has finished. According to Max Lüthi, it is typical of European fairy tales that magical objects are only referred to as long as they have relevance for the plot, and then disappear from the story (*Europäische Volksmärchen* 31). This rule also applies to the Grimms' "Snow White." What happens to the magic mirror after the stepmother dies is not revealed: it speaks one last time before the queen goes to Snow White's wedding and is not mentioned again. Several duplicates and retellings make an addition in this respect: they mention that the mirror is broken, either because it falls from the wall (for instance, in Leslie Gower's *Snow White and the Seven Dwarfs*) or because somebody destroys it (for instance, in Levine's *Fairest*). Bettelheim stresses that evil needs to be punished and eradicated in order for the fairy tale to have a reassuring effect on children, and the fact that these additions are made may indicate that the mirror is indeed considered to have a threatening dimension.

Gilbert and Gubar view the mirror as a symbol of patriarchy, and as such it cannot simply be destroyed. It still has a role to play after the queen has died, as the traditional ending to "Snow White" promises a continuation of the status quo with regard to gender roles. Gilbert and Gubar predict that the looking glass will eventually turn against Snow White when she is a mature woman: "Snow White has exchanged one glass coffin for another, delivered from the prison where the Queen put her only to be imprisoned in the looking glass from which the King's voice speaks daily" (*Madwoman* 42). The fact that the magic mirror with all its terrible consequences for a young queen will be passed on to the next generation has also been suggested in various "Snow White" retellings as well as in some illustrated versions of the tale. Like Gilbert and Gubar, several retellings fill in the gap in the Grimms' tale of what happens to the mirror and end with an image of Snow White looking into the mirror for the first time. In Anne Sexton's *Transformations* from 1971, the poem "Snow White and the Seven Dwarfs" ends with an ominous reference to the looking glass:

> Meanwhile Snow White held court,
> rolling her china-blue doll eyes open and shut
> and sometimes referring to her mirror
> as women do.
>   (*Transformations* 153)

Snow White is still pictured as a "dumb bunny," and it is left to the imagination of the reader what the effect of the mirror will be. Such an open ending can be also found in some illustrations in which the mirror reappears at the end of the tale without any further comment. The final image in Charles Santore's *Snow White* (1996, Grimm) contains a visual allusion to Jan van Eyck's famous masterpiece *The Arnolfini Betrothal* (1434), in which the couple's backs are reflected in a convex mirror, as well as the painter himself (Figure 19). This convex mirror appears in Santore's illustration as a visual addition between Snow White and her prince as it does in the Arnolfini painting and shows a similar reflection (Figure 20).[8]

In the left-hand corner of van Eyck's work, a pair of slippers is portrayed, which Santore includes in the frame that surrounds the text describing the end

Figure 19. The Arnolfini Betrothal *by Jan van Eyck.*

of the evil queen (as a reference to the red-hot shoes with which she dances herself to death). The distinctive shape of the convex mirror in Santore's illustrations makes it all the more obvious that the very same mirror once belonged to the queen (Figure 21). The text does not explain how the mirror came to be owned by the young couple and what its effect will be on them.

The visual intertext that *The Arnolfini Betrothal* provides may suggest a metacomment that is similar to Bacchilega's interpretation of the fairy-tale narrator in light of Mieke Bal's theory. *The Arnolfini Betrothal* clearly marks the painter's presence, by including the Latin statement "Johannes de eyck

Figure 20. Snow White *by Charles Santore.*

Figure 21. Snow White *by Charles Santore.*

fuit hic" (Jan van Eyck was here) above the mirror and by showing himself in it (Hall xix). As the artist's presence is foregrounded within the painting, he becomes, to use Genette's narratological terms, homodiegetic (part of the story) rather than heterodiegetic (external to the story). That this is done in and above a mirror, the symbol of mimesis, cannot be a coincidence. The extended view of the convex mirror captures more than a traditional mirror could (in the case of *The Arnolfini Betrothal*, both the ceiling and the floor and both the bed and the window); yet at the same time it distorts to a greater extent what is reflected. Both convex mirrors, moreover, have a frame that contains smaller medallions—images that draw attention to the frame itself, which contextualize the image in the mirror and nuance the idea of an objective, unmediated gaze. In van Eyck's painting, the medallions in the mirror's frame depict scenes from the Passion of Christ, signaling the marriage's holy status. In Santore's *Snow White*, they contain references to the devil, pagan symbols, and two images of the goddess of justice. The devils signal the queen's as well as the mirror's evil nature, and the Lady Justice may be included to remind the queen that she will be judged and punished for her evil deeds. When the mirror appears again at the end of the story, the medallions are not as clearly visible as before (the image is also smaller); yet one image of the devil can still be discerned. If the Christian symbols in *The Arnolfini Betrothal* are a promise of bliss, the mirror at Snow White and the prince's wedding announces a future that is burdened with a heavy past that may, or as Gilbert and Gubar argue *must*, repeat itself. The text states that "Snow White and the prince lived in the palace and reigned happily over the land for many, many years." The deviation from the more permanent "happily ever after" can be read as a further indication that the mirror will eventually have the impact on Snow White that Gilbert and Gubar consider inevitable.

Like Santore's book, Trina Schart Hyman's illustrations to *Snow White* (1974), published a few years before *The Madwoman in the Attic*, closes with an image of the mirror. A contrast between this image and the earlier occurrences of the magic object can be noted, however, that may (but must not) contradict Gilbert and Gubar's interpretation. The visual symbolism throughout Hyman's pictures relies strongly on the juxtaposition of different Christian symbols: Snow White's mother does not have a mirror on her wall, but a triptych of the Virgin Mary with child (Figure 22).

ONCE in the middle of winter, when were falling like feathers from the sky, sewing by a window, and its frame w ebony. As she sewed, she glanced up at the snow her finger with the needle and three drops of blo the snow. Since the red seemed so beautiful white, she thought to herself, "If only I had a ch as snow, as red as blood, and as dark as ebony."

Soon afterward, she gave birth to a little girl white as snow and as red as blood, and whose black as ebony. She was named Snow White. A moment the child was born, the Queen died.

Figure 22. Snow White *by Paul Heins.*

A parallel between the mother and the Madonna is visually suggested by the fact that they wear clothes of the same colors (blue, red, and white) and by the similarity in their position: both sit at a window. The Blessed Virgin already has a child; the good queen wishes for one. A similar triptych can later be discerned when Snow White is living in the seven dwarves' house, only here the Virgin Mary (or another female saint who bears strong similarities to Snow White) is represented with flowers, not with a child. This underlines not only the similarity between Snow White and her mother, which Gilbert and Gubar have also stressed, but also the two women's saintly piety.

On the second double spread of the picture book, the room where Snow White's mother sat is repeated, but now with a new queen, Snow White's stepmother. The parallel composition draws attention to the fact that the triptych has been removed, and the wall is now dominated by a huge mirror.

Figure 23. Snow White *by Paul Heins.*

The frame consists of several heads and bodies, mainly of trolls, skulls, and devils (Figure 23). The new queen's own head can be distinguished in the frame as well, on the right-hand side. At the bottom hangs the figure of a smiling she-devil with both horns and breasts, in a position that seems a parody of a crucified Jesus. Its mixture of male and female characteristics is what Gilbert and Gubar argue the queen to be reproached with in patriarchy, that which turns her into a monster woman.

On the penultimate page of Hyman's *Snow White*, a remarkable transformation takes place in the mirror. Whereas the queen stands in exactly the same position with regard to the mirror as on the second page of the book, she is no longer reflected in it. Rather, the mirror reflects the sky and the moon that can be seen through the window outside. The mirror has either become a window, or the queen has already ceased to exist for the mirror. Support for this interpretation can be found in the text, which describes Snow White's preparations for her wedding and announces the queen's ultimate defeat. A second transformation of the mirror is located in its frame: whereas the right-hand side of the frame still pictures the same skulls, trolls, and female heads as before, the left-hand side has started to fade. The panic on the faces of the figures on the right may signal that they have witnessed their companions' annihilation and can now expect the same fate. When on the final page the image of the mirror is resumed as a frame around the text, it still pictures the moon and now a setting sun as well (Figure 24). The evil faces are replaced with more benign and dominantly female ones, as well as some children's heads and male faces. The skull on top has now become the head of a beautiful woman, and as she slightly bends over the glass surface, the mirror acquires the shape of a heart, underlining the romantic outcome of the story and the mirror's approval. The devil at the bottom of the frame is cut off from the page, and it is suggested that it has disappeared as well. Whereas before it clutched the branch of a tree, its arms and hands are now feminized and pictured as open and welcoming.

That the mirror is not destroyed but left at the palace may indicate that Snow White will one day inherit it. The dominant message of the final illustration is that the mirror has changed and will fulfill a more positive function for its new owner. Yet, not all disturbing elements have disappeared from its frame: at the bottom a few dark figures still lurk in the shadow, and from the way the page is cut it is unclear whether the devil has vanished or is simply waiting for the next queen, Snow White. Moreover, one may wonder if the mirror has not become more dangerous because it has adapted itself to the needs of its new owner and most of the threatening faces have been replaced by more attractive ones. Whether the nature of the mirror has changed or it has retained its manipulative function under a different guise remains unclear.

Wim Hofman's *Zwart als inkt* goes one step further along the lines that Gilbert and Gubar have traced. At the end of his retelling, Hofman pictures

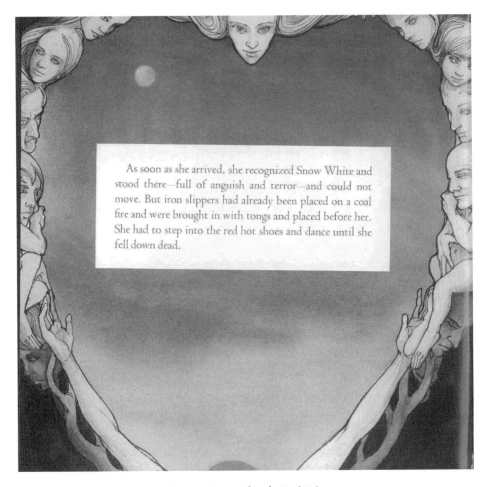

As soon as she arrived, she recognized Snow White and stood there—full of anguish and terror—and could not move. But iron slippers had already been placed on a coal fire and were brought in with tongs and placed before her. She had to step into the red hot shoes and dance until she fell down dead.

Figure 24. Snow White *by Paul Heins.*

Snow White and her prince in a moment of bliss as they travel back to the prince's palace. A metafictional comment disrupts this evocation of spotless happiness:

> *We are now on page x*
> *and this will do. They appear to be like hand and glove*
> *and so we could let everything end nicely here*
>   (178; my translation)

Could but *will not* is the implication of this irrealis. The addendum indeed introduces an unsettling element when the mother's mirror is offered as a wedding present to Snow White:

> On the last day (bride and groom
> were just about to leave) a woman came to visit.
> She had come from far, she said, and knew the bride well.
> As a gift, she brought a pack, an embroidered
> cloth with birds and flowers and fish
> and wrapped in it was a wonderful mirror,
> big as a gate, a frame with golden curls. [. . .]
>
> After the party, Snow White had the mirror
> hung up on her bedroom wall.
> She wanted to have a look at herself.
> And when she had, the mirror said:
> "Well done, beautiful."
>   (179–80; my translation)

Gilbert and Gubar link the window and the mirror as two frames that limit a woman's horizon of possibilities. The mirror may resemble a gate in Hofman's retelling, but only in size: the golden curls that frame it are reminiscent of the golden cage that the queen has inhabited and that her daughter now faces. The mirror has the final word in *Zwart als inkt* and expresses his satisfaction that Snow White hangs it up and wants to look at herself. The accompanying image shows him as a godlike, male figure, whose gleeful smile suggests that he knows that he will soon be in control once again. The embroidered cloth in which the mirror was wrapped may be the same one that Snow White's mother was sewing when she pricked herself and made her wish (12) and thus establishes an intratextual connection with the scene by the window, which Hofman has extended. It is associated with the "good mother," a role that Snow White is expected to fulfill in the near future. That this object wraps or hides the most cherished possession of the "bad mother," the mirror, suggests the duplicity of the gift of motherhood that the queen passes on to Snow White.

Patricia Carlin's imagination takes this situation a few years ahead in "The Stepmother Arrives," and she makes an even stronger suggestion to relate Snow White's end to her stepmother's:

> The stepmother dies
> in the burning shoes. Her dancing
> days are over. The girl acquires
>
> a castle, a kingdom, a mirror,
> and a new daughter.
> She dances away her days in the castle.
>
> "Mother, my glass eyes
> are open," she sings
> at night in her silent dream mouth.
>
> The face in the mirror changes.
> It's time for an ending.
> Upstairs they are heating the iron shoes.
>   (47)

In Carlin's poem, Snow White receives the mirror after her stepmother has died. Once she is married, her life doubles the evil queen's: when she becomes a mother in turn, the mirror starts to oppose her. "The face in the mirror changes" is an ambiguous line in this respect: on the one hand, it may indicate that Snow White's daughter has replaced her as the fairest in the land; on the other hand, it may imply that she herself is changing, that she is growing old or dismayed. For Gilbert and Gubar, the two changes go hand in hand, one leads to the other. I read Snow White's nighttime song, "Mother, my glass eyes / are open" as an intertextual reference to Sexton's poem, in which Snow White's eyes were compared to that of a china doll, rolling open and shut. Here the image is linked to a feminist awakening, a moment of insight, that paradoxically takes place in a dream. Carlin's poem provides a sequel then not only to the traditional tale but also to Sexton's retelling, which ended with Snow White looking in the mirror. The glass, moreover, builds an association with the looking glass, the mirror to which

Snow White has also opened up. Carlin shows the effect that time has had on Snow White: she has lost her innocence and finally understands her mother. The last line of Carlin's poem, in which Snow White's ending is announced, is the most obvious link with her stepmother's painful death, one that Gilbert and Gubar explicitly draw on in their critical analysis as well: "In fiery shoes [Snow White] will do a terrible death-dance out of the story, the looking glass, the transparent coffin of her own image" (*Madwoman* 42). Both the critics and the author pessimistically stress the cyclical pattern that is displayed in "Snow White." Carlin's penultimate line may indicate not only the end of her poem as well as of Snow White but also the wish for this cycle to come to a standstill.[9]

The Snow White Queen

Whereas sequels or retellings that make additions to the fairy-tale ending frequently suggest that Snow White assumes the features of the evil queen, there are a few prequels or retellings that expand the beginning of the story, in which the queen is said to have characteristics that formerly belonged to Snow White. Priscilla Galloway's "A Taste for Beauty" was mentioned in chapter two as a retelling that can initially mislead the reader with regard to the identity of the first-person narrator. The occurrence of a stepparent, the expulsion from home, and the refuge to an all-male environment would support the hypothesis that the narrator is the intertextual equivalent of Snow White. As the narrative proceeds, it becomes clear that this supposition is wrong and that the first part of the story is a prequel to the traditional tale, told by Snow White's stepmother. By providing insight into the history and psychology of this character, the retelling shows that the two women have more in common than the Grimms' traditional version would suggest, a hypothesis that also lies at the basis of Gilbert and Gubar's analysis of the tale.

The characteristics of Snow White and the queen merge more extensively in Michael Blumlein's science fiction story "Snow in Dirt" (1997). In the figure of the narrator, Martin, the roles of the king, the prince, and the dwarves are conflated. One day he digs up the body of a woman from the soil wrapped in a bodysuit made of skin or leaves. The words that Martin uses for her, "still as a statue, beautiful" are reminiscent of the prince's and the dwarves' to describe Snow White (21). When after some time, the young woman starts breathing and wakes up, she and Martin begin a relationship. Vexing—she is named after the initially "vexing situation" of her coma (31)—resembles the traditional Snow White in several other aspects in addition to this miraculous revival: she has dark hair and pale skin (22) and claims that she loves miners (33). Moreover, "the role of mother and housewife certainly seemed familiar to her" (42), Martin claims, which confirms the Snow White image created by traditional versions such as the Grimms' and Disney's. As Vexing grows more accustomed to her new life and becomes more empowered, she begins to resemble the evil queen. Her fame as a top model grows, and so does her desire to become the fairest of them all: "She loved it when people stared, for like all models she craved attention" (37). Given the shift in characteristics from Snow White to the queen, it is not surprising that at this point the mirror also enters the story: "She liked to adorn herself with mirrors and other reflective objects [. . .] appliquéd to her dresses or woven in the fabric itself" (37). Vexing not only looks in the mirror, the mirror becomes a part of her. Nevertheless, these decorative objects seem to function more as markers of an intertextual link than taking on the role of the mirror as the judge in the beauty contest. As in *Snow White in New York*, it is the newspapers that decide who is the fairest of them all: "The tabloids dubbed her 'the Queen,' and if not omnipotent, she was certainly ubiquitous" (39). Other shifts in the story support Vexing's transformation from Snow White into the stepmother. Whereas she had first admitted to loving miners, she later says that she hates short men for being bossy and domineering and acting like children (38). This seems contradictory if the retelling is linked to the traditional tale of "Snow White," in which the seven dwarves *are* miners. However, the change in attitude underlines the fact that she has evolved from the dwarves' ally, Snow White, to their enemy, the evil stepmother. Moreover, Martin himself is described as short and as being a miner (for digging up Vexing), and her scorn of dwarves seems to mark a shift in her feelings toward him.

The wheel turns when Martin wants a child and Vexing cannot conceive. At the same time, all the mirrors in the story, including the press, start to oppose her: "Mirrors, which had always been allies, became enemies" (Blumlein 44). Gilbert and Gubar's idea that Snow White and the queen are in fact two aspects of the same woman, that is that the queen tries to kill the Snow White in herself, is taken up literally in Blumlein's retelling. Vexing may not have a daughter to compete with, but she is haunted by her former self. Martin has decorated his cottage in the backyard with her pictures: "Every surface, including the ceiling, was covered with her picture. Vexing the ingenue, the vixen, Vexing the girl next door, the starlet, the fresh-scrubbed housewife. Vexing the princess, radiant and happy, athletic, sultry and gay. She looked upon me wherever I turned. Vexing the pinup. The dreamboat. Vexing my lover, my queen, my wife" (44). Given the intertextual link with the traditional Snow White, it is logical that Martin uses a cottage to build this homage to his wife's former beauty; the cottage is also where Snow White fled and was safe from the enraged queen. The images that Martin uses all date back to Vexing's time of glory, often showing her in roles that reflect a patriarchal ideal of femininity or female subordination. The possessive pronouns with which Martin ends his enumeration show that the images give him power, put him in control. Yet they also suggest that he loves her in all her forms, including the mature woman that she has become at this point in the story ("my queen").

In Gilbert and Gubar's analysis, as well as in all the sequels discussed above, the transformation from Snow White into the queen is unidirectional: once Snow White has aged and gained consciousness, there is no way back. The angel may transform into the monster woman, but the monster will never change back to the angel. In Blumlein's science fiction retelling, however, the cycle is reversed toward the end of the story. When Vexing discovers the cottage with the images of her former self, she decides to volunteer for a medical experiment that will undo her physical deterioration. It takes her three months to grow back to the age at which Martin dug her up, and then her regression goes one step further: she falls asleep again. Not being able to wake her up with a kiss, Martin decides to bury her, "white as snow," and hopes that someday "a new and better prince would come along" (Blumlein 55). The end of the tale links up with the beginning, not only in content but also in the echo of words: "I found the girl of my dreams in the garden. She was covered by dirt" (21) and "She was the woman of my dreams. [. . .] The night sang as I covered her with dirt" (55). The price of Vexing's return to youth is selflessness—again she becomes the catatonic object that she was at the beginning of the story. Whether or not she will be her subservient self when she wakes up again (or for that matter, whether she will ever be dug up again at all) is a question that the story does not answer, as it also leaves to the reader's imagination what had happened to Vexing before Martin discovered her body and whether she had lived through similar cycles before.

Several other retellings portray the queen as a victim or address mitigating circumstances to defend her case. Gilbert and Gubar see the mirror as an important stimulant in the queen's rage and rebellion. Yet, in their interpretation it is not the instigating factor, nor was it in the Brothers Grimm's tale, as we have seen above. Some retellings correct this and ascribe even more power to the mirror than the Grimms do. In *P. W. Catanese's The Mirror's Tale* (2006), a fantasy sequel to the traditional "Snow White," the mirror is retrospectively put forward as the initial agitator of the queen's jealousy. Before she comes under its power, the queen is pictured as "someone you'd want for a friend, as long as you weren't daunted by her beauty" (63). Although she cared about the way she looked, her main occupations were helping the poor and the sick: "It was only in her final years that she became the hateful Witch-Queen, jealous of anyone whose beauty approached her own" (65). In this sequel, the queen's change in nature is attributed entirely to the impact of the mirror, which houses a horrific spirit that preys on the souls of its victims. Her innocence is thus restored in a rehabilitating move that goes even further than Gilbert and Gubar's but that strips the queen of the artistic rebellion that they value so positively. Whereas Gilbert and Gubar plead for a revaluation of the monster woman, Catanese's *The Mirror's Tale* transforms the queen into another angelic victim, another Snow White.

The Queen as Plotter

In *The Madwoman in the Attic* Gilbert and Gubar couple the devaluation of the voiceless angel woman with a revaluation of the witch: "The Queen, as we come to see more clearly in the course of the story, is a plotter, a plot-maker, a schemer, a witch, an artist, an impersonator, a woman of almost infinite creative energy, witty, wily, and self-absorbed as all artists traditionally are" (*Madwoman* 38). In the antiauthoritarian move with which they approach patriarchal literature, the former manifestations of evil are redeemed as rebels against the status quo. Gilbert and Gubar link the queen to the female artists who are the subject of the rest of their book, and thus introduce the suppressed woman author to the fairy-tale universe. Several recent retellings have cast the queen in a more positive light by similarly portraying her as an intelligent and resolved plotter, though not so much as a writer. In Tanith Lee's "Red as Blood," (1983), she is a cunning slayer who manages to trick and heal the vampire Snow White; in Pat Murphy's "The True Story," (1997), she deceives the king to protect Snow White from his pedophilic assaults; in Jacey Bedford's "Mirror, Mirror" (2004), she is a political mastermind who has to sacrifice her step-daughter in order to make long-lasting peace in the country. Susan Thomas's "Snow White in Exile" (2000) describes Snow White's wish to become the schemer that her stepmother was. According to Maria Tatar, Gilbert and Gubar were probably inspired by Anne Sexton's poetic retelling of "Snow White," especially by the passage in which she watches herself in the mirror after the queen's death as well as by the image of the mobile queen (*Classic* 77). None of these retellings come as close to Gilbert and Gubar's interpretation, however, as that of the American author Robert Coover.[10]

Written six years before *The Madwoman in the Attic* appeared, Coover had thematized remarkably similar speculations on the queen's motives for killing Snow White in "The Dead Queen" (1973). For the type of intertextual comparison between fiction and criticism that I undertake in this book, the prior publication date does not make it an irrelevant intertext. In Coover's retelling, the polysemantic potential of fiction is exploited to the full, and what Pfister calls the degree of "dialogicity" is particularly high. In *Cycles of Influence*, Stephen Benson argues that Coover "uses narrative [. . .] as a means of revealing the fictional nature of particularly pervasive narratives that have taken on the mantle of truth—'static facts' " (153), and this throughout his fictional work. The myths of the angel and the witch are two such pervasive images that Coover deconstructs as he uncovers "the transformational energies" (Benson, *Cycles* 155) contained in the tales. The first-person narrator of Coover's short story is Prince Charming. The plot begins where the Grimms' version of "Snow White" ends, after the happy couple's wedding and the death of the queen: "The old Queen had a grin on her face when we buried her in the mountain, and I knew then that it was she who had composed this scene, as all before, she who had led us, revelers and initiates, to this cold and windy grave site, hers the design, ours the enactment, and I felt like the first man, destined to rise and fall, rise and fall, to the end of time" (Coover, "Dead Queen" 304).

The narrator of this tale is the one who, according to Gilbert and Gubar, will be the new king, the new patriarch. He is, however, far less self-confident than the traditional prince and feels himself to be involved in the cycle of "rise and fall" that Gilbert and Gubar described for women in patriarchy. That the prince compares himself to the biblical first man marks his vulnerability—Adam, after all, was cast out of paradise—and associates him with the forbidden fruit. The queen in "Snow White," like the snake, has offered a poisonous apple to Snow White, and she, like Eve, has accepted it, disobeying the dwarves' counsel to be on her guard. This is an indication that Snow White may not be so innocent, as the Grimms had portrayed her, but that she has acquired carnal knowledge and will ultimately cause her husband's fall. In contrast to Eve, however, Coover's Snow White does not seem to regret her act but has grown into the plotter that her stepmother was. "The Dead Queen" thus combines, like Gilbert and Gubar, a revaluation of the queen with the supposition that after her stepmother's death Snow White will be her successor not only in title but also in spirit.

In their analysis of eighteenth-century literature written by male authors, Gilbert and Gubar stressed that the patriarch's confidence is a false poise, a reassurance against the threat of a constitutive other that is beyond his grasp; "woman's inconstancy" explains why male artists have felt the need to pin women down with the two images or "masks" of the angel and the monster (*Madwoman* 17). This process of literary fixation is described explicitly in Coover's sequel to "Snow White." Prince Charming sees a facial expression on the dead queen that he cannot understand and begins to suspect that this woman may be more empowered than he had guessed. He needs his father's reassurance that woman can be grasped and contained. "My father saw this, perhaps I was trembling, and as though to comfort me, said: no, it was a mere grimace, the contortions of pain, she had suffered greatly after all, torture often exposes the diabolic in the face of man, she was an ordinary woman, beautiful it is true, and shrewd, but she had risen above her merits, and falling, had lost her reason to rancor" (Coover, "Dead Queen" 304).

By explaining the queen's transgressions as madness and meaningless aggression, the king tries to rationalize them in the way that patriarchy tried to control women, according to Gilbert and Gubar: "Female speech and female 'presumption'—that is, angry revolt against male domination—are inextricably linked and inevitably daemonic" (*Madwoman* 35). The prince's father tries to fit a new mask on the queen's face, stressing her suffering rather than her superiority, suggesting that she has failed rather than triumphed. This is affirmed when the image of the mask appears literally later in the tale: "I held my breath and stared at the dead Queen, masked to hide her eyes, which to what my father called a morbid imagination might seem to be winking, one open, the other squeezed shut" (Coover, "Dead Queen" 306). The passage can function as a symbol for the kind of literary reading that Gilbert and Gubar, as well as Coover's prince and Coover himself, practice: underneath the mask imposed on women by patriarchy, that is underneath the fixed images and stereotypes, they look for palimpsestic indications of subversion in "works whose surface designs conceal or obscure deeper, less accessible (and less socially acceptable) levels of meaning" (*Madwoman* 73). Like Gilbert and Gubar's analysis, Coover's tale is the exploration of the possible deeper significance of the figures of Snow White ("the true meaning of her name," 307–8) and the queen. However, Coover stages the rather dubious figure of Prince Charming to undertake such a palimpsestic interpretation. The queen's wink may be addressed not only to the prince but also to the reader; it is indicative of the irony with which Coover's tale itself is invested.

In contrast to the feminist critics Gilbert and Gubar, the male fictional character Prince Charming is alienated by what he finds under the patriarchal surface. Believing that he sees through his father's excuse, he is not the least reassured by the mask imposed on the queen's face: "But I did not believe him, I could see for myself, did not even entirely trust him, this man who thought power a localized convention, magic a popular word for concealment, for though it made him a successful King, decisive and respected, the old Queen's grin mocked such simple faith and I was not consoled" (Coover, "Dead Queen" 304).

Contrary to other retellings and to Gilbert and Gubar's analysis, Coover's prince does not automatically succeed his father as the new patriarch but distances himself from the king. Or does he recapitulate an earlier stage in the way patriarchy deals with women, the phase in which they still produce anxiety and are not yet controlled by stereotypical fixations? As Gilbert and Gubar argue, once man has realized that it lies in a woman's power to be and remain unknown to him, every woman becomes threatening. Because literature provides several examples of monster women who have successfully deceived men by pretending to be ladylike and angelic, it could be suspected that "all women were inexorably and inescapably monstrous, in the flesh as well as in the spirit" (*Madwoman* 31). Indeed, when Coover's prince observes his new wife, he sees certain disturbing aspects of the dead queen displayed in her: "My young bride, her cheeks made rosy by the mountain air, smiled benignly through the last rites, just as she had laughed with open glee at her stepmother's terrible entertainment at our wedding feast the night before, her cheeks flushed then with wine. I tried to read her outrageous cheerfulness, tried to understand the merriment that such an awesome execution had provoked. At times, she seemed utterly heartless, this child, become the very evil she'd been saved from" (Coover, "Dead Queen" 304).

Coover's sequel here fills in a gap in the Grimms' tale and in most other traditional versions in which the queen is punished: how does Snow White react when her stepmother appears at her wedding, and how does she behave when the woman is put to death? The fact that Snow White does not forgive her stepmother, as for instance Perrault's Cinderella does with regard to her stepsisters, allows a second smudge on the perfect image of the angelic woman that she had come to represent for the prince, after the "birdshit on the glass coffin when I found her" (Coover, "Dead Queen" 308). Coover exploits this gap to the full and further tarnishes the image of perfection. Snow White's glee is perceived as "outrageous," unladylike, and thus evil. The patriarchal images of angel and monster have started to break down and merge in the prince's perception, just as Gilbert and Gubar argue that Snow White and her stepmother are in a sense one and that in patriarchy every angelic woman is feared to hide a monster woman.

The prince tries to give various explanations for his wife's delight at her stepmother's suffering, but unlike his father, he cannot rationalize his fear away and has to admit that his wife is and will remain a stranger to him: "Has all our watchfulness been in vain, had that good and simple soul been envenomed after all, was it she who'd invited her old tormenter to the ball, commissioned the iron slippers, drawn her vindictively into that ghastly dance? Or did she simply laugh as the righteous must to see the wicked fall? Perhaps her own release from death had quickened her heart, such that mere continuance now made her a little giddy. Or had she, absent, learned something of hell? How could I know?" (Coover, "Dead Queen" 304). In contrast to his father, the prince acknowledges that he does not understand his wife. Gilbert and Gubar argue that Snow White's condition is the inevitable fate of all women in patriarchy: "There is, after all, no female model for her in this tale except the 'good' (dead) mother and her living avatar the 'bad' mother" (*Madwoman* 42). In relation to this stand the prince's observations about his own mother, whom he now realizes he does not really know (Coover, "Dead Queen" 307). In the prince's speculation about his wife's gloating delight, Snow White's image of angelic perfection once again becomes compromised by the association with the monster and hell. More importantly and more positively from Gilbert and Gubar's point of view, the prince imagines Snow White not only as a monster but also as the artist, the plotter that Gilbert and Gubar claim that her stepmother was: she may have secretly invited her stepmother, she may have arranged the iron slippers, she may have tricked not only her stepmother but also all those who still believe in her innocence.

Related to this new view of his wife is the reason that the prince gives for the queen's subversive actions. These do not differ very much from Gilbert and Gubar's analysis: "An angel in the house of myth, Snow White is not only a child but (as female angels always are) childlike, docile, submissive, the heroine of a life that *has no story*. But the Queen, adult and demonic, plainly wants a life of 'significant action,' by definition an 'unfeminine' life of stories and story-telling" (*Madwoman* 39). As Coover's Prince Charming explains about his mother-in-law: "What she had lusted for was a part in the story, immortality, her place in guarded time" ("Dead Queen" 305). But her ambition reaches further than this: not only does she want to have a part in the story, she wants to *write* the story, to be the "composer" as the prince calls her in the opening passages of Coover's retelling ("Dead Queen" 304). If we follow Gilbert and Gubar's analysis, Coover's prince has also understood exactly why the queen had tried to kill Snow White. It is her selflessness and renunciation that drive the queen mad. As the prince explains, "She suffered no losses, I thought, in fact that's just the trouble, that hymen can never be broken, not even by me, not in a thousand nights, this is her gift and essence, and because of it, she can see neither fore nor aft, doesn't even know that there is a mirror on the wall. Perhaps it was this that had made the old Queen hate her so" (Coover, "Dead Queen" 305). Coover's prince, however, believes that the queen may have been wrong in assuming her stepdaughter to be innocent, that Snow White had possibly become a conniving trickster in her own right. The prince, moreover, seems to realize his part in the cycle that Gilbert and Gubar have described and wishes to preserve the image of purity that his wife was valued for, if only for his self-assurance. Is that why he finds that her hymen cannot be broken? On their wedding night, when Snow White proves to be a more practiced lover than the prince had imagined his virginal wife would be, the images of Snow White and the Queen mingle, not surprisingly, in the mirror: "I'd gazed into the mirrors to see, for the first time, Snow White's paradigmatic beauty, but instead it had been the old Queen I'd seen there, flailing about madly in her redhot shoes" (Coover, "Dead Queen" 310). The mirror is the place where the images of the two women were confronted in the traditional tale, and this is the place where they now merge. Moreover, by associating Snow White's reflection with the red-hot shoes, the prince may catch a glimpse of her future as Patricia Carlin and Gilbert and Gubar also later imagine it.

I have listed several retellings in which Snow White becomes more like the queen, but in Coover's tale, as in Blumlein's, the queen also becomes more like Snow White, in a provocative conflation of symbolic objects. The dead queen is buried in the very glass coffin that Snow White had been exposed in before, and the prince expects that she may even wake up. In his reconstruction of the queen's secret plot, the prince comes to the surprising conclusion that "maybe the old Queen had loved me, had died for *me*! [. . .] It was as if she'd lived this exemplary life, died this tragic death, to lead me away from the merely visible to vision, from the image to the imaged, from reflections to the projecting miracle itself, the heart, the pure snow white . . . !" (Coover, "Dead Queen" 313). At this point the prince paradoxically relapses into the traditional "imaging" of patriarchy, and the queen's plotting is interpreted as being at the service not of herself, but of him, a man. The passage functions as a metacomment and a warning with regard to the palimpsestic reading that the prince has been practicing: underneath the visible, the image and the reflection, the prince ultimately finds not the queen, but himself. His analytic strategy has not opened a window but reflects back on him like a narcissistic mirror. Similar critiques have been addressed to the palimpsestic reading of Gilbert and Gubar. Rita Felski, for instance, has noted that their "description of Victorian women struggling against a repressive society to find their true selves often made these women sound remarkably like American feminists of the 1970s" (67). The unexpected meaning that Coover's prince "discovers" shows that analysis sometimes reveals more about the critic than about the text that is its object. Read in an intertextual comparison with Gilbert and Gubar's analysis, it may remind us of the bias not only in patriarchal fairy tales but also in feminist criticism.

As the narrator of Coover's tale, the prince is of course presented as a plotter himself, exemplifying "the human propensity to use story structures to organize experience and construct meaning" that is such an important preoccupation in Coover's work (Benson, *Cycles* 151). His "quasi-existential and reflective mode" does not only lend itself, as Bacchilega has argued, "to comic effects" (*Postmodern Fairy Tales* 39), it also invites ironic, critical distance. What Charming does not realize is that the meaning that he has so desperately tried to attribute to the queen is a construction, a solipsistic interpretation. Toward the end of the story, he believes that through his palimpsestic reading he has finally grasped the true nature of the queen. In the following fragment, it is not so much the queen who "has" him but he who thinks he "has" the queen: "The old Queen had me now, everything had fallen into place, I knew now the force that had driven her, that had freed me, freed us all, that we might live happily ever after, though we didn't deserve it, weren't even aware of how it had happened, yes, I knew her cause, knew her name—I wrenched open the coffin, threw myself upon her and kissed her lips" (Coover, "Dead Queen" 313).

His claim of knowledge contrasts with his earlier admission that he did not understand the queen, or his wife. What the prince does not seem to notice at this point in the story is that he has put another mask on the woman's face, perhaps a mask that is different from the traditional patriarch's— who would not deem possible the relapse of the monster woman into the angelic woman, let alone her transformation into a new messiah—but a mask nevertheless. The queen's cold, rubbery lips immediately remind Charming, however, that he has not understood her in the least: "I'd been wrong about her, wrong about everything." When the corpse tumbles from the coffin down the hill, "the mask fell away from her open eye, now milky white." The repulsive image of the dead eye and the sight of her burnt feet cast the prince back to the more traditional interpretation of the tale: "If this is the price of beauty, it's too high. I was glad she was dead" (Coover, "Dead Queen" 313). The prince is cured from his idea that the queen died for him and resorts to the explanations that the traditional fairy tale gives for her actions and death: she had wanted to be the fairest in the world and paid the price for it. No longer does he consider her the conniving plotter who had tricked them all.

Although the prince is revealed as an unreliable narrator and his plan to wake up the queen is absurd, not all of his observations can be as easily discredited and even his final conclusions (that he was all wrong) can still be undermined. First, the images of Snow White and the dwarves cannot easily be restored to their former innocence after the orgy in which they have all participated. Second, although the prince's meaning-making narrative is unmasked as an illusion, the story has laid bare undercurrents in the fairy tale that may possibly deconstruct its traditional evaluation of the queen. Benson explains about Coover's literary work that the "emphasis [lies] on the fictional nature of narrative against the historical fixing of narrative as seeming 'truth'—myth or metanarrative" (*Cycles* 151). This is also what seems to be at stake in "The Dead Queen." If we go along with the prince's and Gilbert and Gubar's interpretation that the queen was a plotter and a "master of disguises" (Coover, "Dead Queen" 309), has she not, after all, reached the ultimate goal, the ultimate subversion of patriarchy? She has struck the monarchy in the heart and affected its hope for the future. By the end of the sequel, the prince has lost all his dignity and can no longer be deemed a worthy successor to the throne, Snow White has fainted, and the king has lost his previous composure and has tears of anger and shame in his eyes. Patriarchy has been undermined, and the happy ending to "Snow White" has proved to be very short. If the queen had wanted to subvert patriarchy, as Gilbert and Gubar argue, she is the only winner in Coover's tale.

One can thus question Bacchilega's conclusion that the stepmother in "The Dead Queen" "has no real transformative power" (*Postmodern Fairy Tales* 41). Although Bacchilega is highly aware of the postmodern strategies that Coover uses to expose "truth-making" rather than truth itself, she does follow the prince's point of view to come to her conclusion about the queen's (dis)empowerment. When she writes that "the prince fails to see that the Queen's actions and plots do not break away from the mimetic conventions and imagination of the 'innocent persecuted heroine' fairy tale" (41), it should be added that it is only through the limited perspective of the prince that the reader is presented with the content of the queen's actions and plots. One can speculate about the extent of his insight into her schemes and how far his projection goes. The same holds true when Bacchilega writes that the queen "compulsively returns to it [the mirror] in order to establish the 'truth.' [. . .] In her fight to free herself, she has 'used the mirror as a door, tried to'" (*Postmodern Fairy Tales* 41). Again Bacchilega echoes the prince's point of view to draw conclusions about the queen's success, quoting his words almost literally. The reading that I have presented above leaves open the possibility that the prince did not have the knowledge of the queen's motivations that he claimed, and acknowledges that her plotting ultimately did have a radically subversive, transformative effect.

Black as Ink: The Author Snow White

The bulk of *The Madwoman in the Attic* does not concern the representation of women in male-authored texts, which are discussed in the introduction, but the literary strategies through which nineteenth-century women writers expressed their discomfort with authorship, their repressed anger, and their subtle rebellion. In a few retellings in which Snow White assumes her (step)mother's characteristics, she becomes a plotter and artist in a more literal sense, that is, as a writer. Wim Hofman's *Zwart als inkt* (Black as Ink) and Sine van Mol's *Een vlekje wolf* (A Patch of Wolf) show that authorship is as difficult for a female fairy-tale character as it was for nineteenth-century women according to Gilbert and Gubar. The introduction of writing to the analphabetic world of the fairy tale fits into the psychologization of fairy-tale characters, who gain a roundness through their literary work, the use of self-reflexive passages in the retellings, and a broader feminist critique.

From the title of Hofman's *Zwart als inkt*, it is clear that writing occupies a central place in this retelling. It is explicitly mentioned that Snow White learns to write (an addition to the Grimms' tale) when she is still living at the palace, and she writes letters to her mother to which she never receives a reply. Her mother—here never replaced with a stepmother—is alienated from her daughter shortly after she is born; the king dies in the war and in her ensuing postpartum depression, the mother holds her daughter responsible for his death. If she had been a boy, the king would have come home and survived. Snow White's expulsion from the palace brings no profound relief for the girl. Hofman's seven dwarves exercise an extreme form of suppression on her, their endless list of chores leaving no personal freedom. The warnings and commands to stay in the house soon dominate every conversation with her housemates. The first time that Snow White asks for pen and paper it is to write down all their instructions:

> "Don't you have paper?" Snow White asked them.
> "And a pen?"
> "What do you want paper and pen for?"
> they asked her. "You can talk, can't you?
> Can you write then?
> And what do you want to write?"
> "I want to write down everything you say,"
> she replied. "Then I'll remember it."
> They liked that of course.
>   (67; my translation)

The repressive dwarves are initially suspicious of Snow White's writing: they had apparently assumed that she, like the traditional Snow White, could not write at all; they do not see the need for it and want to control its content. When she tells them that it is merely their words that she wants to reproduce and that they will determine the content, they are reassured— although they warn her to use their paper and ink economically, another discouraging note.

Hofman extends the minor "acts of disobedience" (*Madwoman* 40) that Snow White risks in the traditional tale. Her writing is presented as a rebellious "quest for self-definition" under the kind of "acceptable facade" that Gilbert and Gubar find in the work of nineteenth-century woman authors (*Madwoman* 74, 76). At first, Snow White follows the dwarves' discouraging guidelines. She limits her writing to small pieces of paper cut from the large sheets on which the dwarves draw maps and schemes (Hofman 67); her writing is literally and figuratively constrained and marginal. Her handwriting consists of narrow letters, and the content is a literal rendition of what the dwarves tell her. In contrast to the woman writer that Gilbert and Gubar describe, Snow White does not get to see much male writing, only the bible. Later in the book, it is said that the dwarves do not want to share their drawings with her, telling her to go and write and draw by herself. By that point, her writing has become something that they consider harmless, something that keeps her quiet.

Once Snow White has been granted this liberty, writing soon becomes compulsive, a way for her to express herself and make her mark. The lists of tasks that she writes down gradually become more subversive. It is unclear whether Snow White's initial request for pen and paper contains a critical comment in itself, pointing out that the dwarves' instructions are so numerous, trivial, and illogical that no one could possibly remember them all. Later, her written organization of commands becomes more clearly, though still tacitly, rebellious. She ranks them in such a way that contradictions become apparent:

> *Every night, before you go to sleep*
> *look under your bed. There, in that darkness,*
> *may be something, you never know.*
>
> *Put boxes and crates with potatoes or cobblestones*
> *under your bed, so that no monster*
> *can hide there.*
>
> *You must put no junk, no boxes or crates*
> *under your bed. All sorts of creepy things*
> *can easily come and sit between or in them.*
>   (Hofman 72; my translation)

This marks the first step in Snow White's evolution into a more creative kind of writing. Her list becomes a parody, a repetition with a critical distance, to recall Hutcheon's definition. Just as "creepy things" can hide between crates, a subtle subversion has crept between the lines of Snow White's text. One can assume at least that the dwarves did not utter the two contradictory statements one after the other. By the way Snow White selects and recombines what are supposedly literal quotations from the dwarves, she undermines their meaning and releases herself from them. It is not surprising that in the passage that follows this list she violates one of its most elaborate commands for the first time and starts playing with her toes.

Soon after her parodic list, Snow White also detaches herself from her promise to use pen and paper economically, that is, for writing down the dwarves' instructions only. She composes various letters and experiences writing as a joyful and liberating activity:

> Did she not write on paper,
> then on the table
> with some soup that was spilled there.
> With her nail she wrote
> in the white sand on the floor,
> with a stick in the soil
> in front of the door, imaginary letters
> on the door. On the windowsill
> she wrote invisible things and on the window.
> She wrote with a finger in the sky,
> the sky was blue, the whole sky
> she wrote full of blue letters, full of white clouds,
> full of birds, full of thoughts. She did not empty.
> On the path to the brook
> she wrote a long line
> and in the brook she wrote:
> brook,
> water,
> fish, fish, fish, fish.
>   (78; my translation)

Much of this writing is imaginary and volatile, a romantic ode to and affirmative adornment of her natural environment. It is both imaginary (the letters in the sky) and descriptive (brook, water, and fish), and the style is reminiscent of the Flemish poet Paul Van Ostaijen. Drawing and writing overlap as Snow White decorates the sky with letters and birds. The notes that she later writes mark a movement from this exterior focus to a preoccupation with her inner longings and frustrations, as her life also becomes more limited to the domestic space.

Even when Snow White is living with the dwarves, the most frequent addressee of her letters is her mother, who has rejected her. Other recipients of her letters are animals, vegetables, and domestic objects. She never addresses any of her writing to the seven dwarves, who are the only ones who might respond to her, but who are also the ones who confine her and who have clearly told her to keep her writing to herself. As a result, Snow White is an author who is not read, something that becomes painfully clear from the fact that she never gets any replies, in spite of her vehement pleas (76, 83, 100). This lack of an audience soon leads to doubts about her own writing: "*Why do I still write to you? / You never write back anyway*" (79; my translation). Her letter to "nobody" most explicitly voices her concerns about her writing and herself:

> *dear nobody,*
>
> *you cannot read*
> *what I write*
> *that is too bad*
> *if you had eyes*
> *you could see what is written here*
> *nobody is nice*
> *now I can quietlie*
> *rite missteikes*
> *and cawl u neimes*
> *you are an idijot*
> *no one who sees*
> *and you never write*
> *back no one gets*
> *a letter from me ever*
> *I might as well not*
> *Write*
>
> (133; my translation)

In the middle of the letter, Snow White seems to realize the freedom of an author who is not read; these are liberties that nineteenth-century woman authors who confined themselves to marginal genres or private writing (diaries) could also take according to Gilbert and Gubar. Not being read releases her not only from the conventions of writing (spelling mistakes) but also from insincere decorum (calling names). However, toward the end of the letter, it is the lack of a communicative context and not the liberation from writing conventions that marks her experience.

It does not take a sophisticated reader to see that Snow White uses her letters as a barely covered way of addressing her personal dilemmas. The first angry letter that she writes is the fourth one: *"Why don't you run away?"* (79; my translation), she reproaches a chair, and herself. It places her in a long line of nineteenth-century woman writers described by Gilbert and Gubar, including Charlotte Brontë, who "wrote obsessively, often in what could be (metaphorically) called a state of 'trance,' about their feelings of enclosure in 'feminine' roles and patriarchal houses, and wrote, too, about their passionate desire to flee such roles or houses" (*Madwoman* 313). The dwarves' house is not only literally but also metaphorically too small for Hofman's Snow White, and her feelings of suffocation grow ever more intense. Once she has admitted her anger in her letters, her writing soon takes a dark turn and the topic of death starts to surface as her most prominent subject. The fly that she warns for the clash with a windowpane still comes off unharmed, with only a "dent in his bowler hat" (Hofman 81), but the beans, carrots, fire, chickens, and candle do not escape the deaths that she has planned for them. The chickens in particular are reminiscent of her former self, as the dwarves tell her to cut out the hearts and liver, and Snow White knows that this is what her mother had ordered the huntsman to do to her. She now subjects the chickens to the plan that he could not execute, identifying with her mother and not with her former self. The massive slaughter—it is stressed that Snow White kills all the chickens, and that there was no need to do so—functions as a rehearsal for her own annihilation.

References to suicide become more and more explicit: "If only I could get away too" (Hofman 171), Snow White writes, and, in a letter to God: "What do you think, shall I come to you?" (172; my translation). When eventually her mother comes to offer her the poisoned apple, Snow White becomes not only her victim but also her ally:

"I am not scared," Snow White said.
She recognized the woman's voice
all too well.
Was this what she had been waiting for all along?
"I think I know
who you are," she said, "and what kind of apple this is,
both sweet and bitter . . ."

The rain rustled, the brook rustled,
the wind rustled more than ever.

She took the apple.
She saw where the woman had put her teeth.
She saw how the dark red
of the apple shone like a mirror
and bit there. The world turned
like the page of a book.
"O, Mother," she said and slid
away in a sea of blood and ink.
    (Hofman 124; my translation)

Snow White's death is a suicide, presented as the result of many pleas not heard and many letters not read. Hofman thus dissociates her from the image of the "dumb bunny," the naïve victim, as she is presented in so many traditional versions and retellings. Her death is a conscious choice, a refusal to live under conditions from which she sees no other means of escape. That the apple is compared to a mirror shows patriarchy's complicity in the creation of these conditions. The metaphorical association with objects that relate to reading and writing—the turning page of the book and the sea of ink—further relate her death to literature. The turning page and world can be read as a self-reflection on the text's use of revisionist intertextuality; indeed *Zwart als inkt* turns the traditional tale upside down. The sea of ink also shows Snow White's writing to be so overwhelming and frustrating that it becomes life threatening.

Hofman invests the tale of "Snow White" with alternative and often controversial meanings but retains the possibility of a happy ending. Not only is Snow White's prince a writer himself, but he is also a reader. When he arrives at the seven dwarves' house, he gets to know Snow White through her writing, going through her letters. Now that she is dead, Snow White finally finds an audience—she is loved not only by the prince but also by the seven dwarves, who have finally become interested in her letters. The prince's affection and respect continue after she has been revived:

> "You do not have to be afraid anymore,"
> the prince said. "And you can
> write as many letters
> as you want."
> "Will you write back?"
> Snow White said. "Never
> has anyone written back to me."
> "Of course I will write back," he said.
>   (178; my translation)

This traditional happy ending, which takes the form not just of marriage but also of a writer who finds a reader, is affirmed by God as well as by the natural elements. God's approval is suggested by the star that has guided the prince to Snow White, reminiscent of the three magi's journey to Bethlehem. The relationship between Snow White and the prince is romantically lauded by nature in the scene that follows his promise to write back: "The wind was favourable. Clouds / blew along" and played games in an attempt to distract the lovers (178; my translation). Nevertheless, the reintroduction of the mirror at the end unsettles the idea of a problem-free "happily ever after," as I have argued above. It is unclear whether Snow White will be able to rebel against the mirror as she has against the dwarves or whether the cycle of female resentment will repeat itself.

Possibly inspired by the acclaimed *Zwart als inkt* is Sine van Mol's poetry collection *Een vlekje wolf* (2003). The tale of "Snow White" is evoked in a section called "Haar brieven" (Her Letters). These are all highly reminiscent of Hofman: Snow White addresses the letters to, among others, the forest and the mirror, but also to the dwarves and her father. Like Hofman's Snow White, she never receives a reply and stresses her frustration over this:

Papa,

where are you?
Shall I put my letter
in a bottle?
Give it to the wind
or the dove?
   (van Mol 34; my translation)

Unlike in Hofman's story, Snow White's father is not reported dead, and she still tries to communicate with him. Van Mol thus underlines an inconsistency in the traditional tale that has also been indicated by Bettelheim and Gilbert and Gubar, a gap that Hofman has filled. Like Hofman's Snow White, van Mol's protagonist would gladly grant her mother the victory in the beauty contest. She recognizes her each time she attempts to murder her and she too chooses death over loneliness:

Dear dwarves,

you no longer need to stand guard
because
I will sleep
in
a glass coffin.
   (37; my translation)

And again, like Hofman's Snow White, this young woman's suicide seems motivated by the fact that her pleas are not heard, her letters not read. Writing in a patriarchal society, whether one is surrounded by oppressive dwarves or desperately seeks the attention of a king, is portrayed as an isolated activity that leads to frustration rather than creative communication or artistic fulfillment. It is unclear what the outcome will be in van Mol's short book, in which Snow White's letters are not embedded in a frame tale. Does her ending follow the traditional tale, in which Snow White finds a prince to replace the former object of her affection, the father? Or does the absence of any letters after she has announced her suicide signal the end of her writing activities, if not of her life altogether?

Critical Responses to Sandra M. Gilbert and Susan Gubar

Gilbert and Gubar's influence has been undisputed, not just in feminist criticism but also in fairy-tale studies. Nicholas Tucker's impression that the most influential voices in children's literature studies often come from outside the field certainly proves valid for Gilbert and Gubar. However, as can also be argued for Bettelheim, such critics sometimes lack the broader historical context in which fairy tales have been placed. Within feminist fairy-tale studies, Gilbert and Gubar's approach to the fairy tale has generally been less radically contested than Lieberman's or Bettelheim's, although several critical voices have emerged concerning their analysis.[11] Donald Haase sees the isolation of Gilbert and Gubar's work from previous fairy-tale studies as its main flaw ("Scholarship" 13). Of course their analysis of "Snow White" is part of a larger argument within their feminist project, but it is striking that they do not treat this fairy tale in a manner that is notably distinct from the nineteenth-century poems and novels that they discuss. Yet, as Steven Swann Jones has argued about "Snow White" (though not with reference to Gilbert and Gubar specifically), "Even though it is easier to work with and find logical continuities within one coherent text, this method does not provide us with the most accurate and comprehensive picture of what a given folktale is really about. In order to understand the significance and themes underlying a specific fairy tale, we must analyze its composite existence in oral tradition" (Jones 37). Although Gilbert and Gubar's analysis does not display a particular knowledge of or interest in the oral and written variants of "Snow White," some of the conclusions that Jones draws from his comparative analysis of a large corpus of historically and geographically varied tales come remarkably close to those presented in *The Madwoman in the Attic*. The following example illustrates this: "From this range of representative motifs, we can see that the Jealousy episode is primarily concerned with dramatizing the conflict between the mother figure and the developing child. We can also see from these motifs that this conflict is apparently a product of the heroine's oedipal rivalries with the mother. [. . .] Even when they are not competing for the attentions of the father, however, the heroine and the persecutor are competing sexually for the attention of other men" (Jones 43).

The lack of a sociohistorical context leads to a large number of missed opportunities in Gilbert and Gubar's discussion of "Snow White"—

opportunities that have partly been addressed by some of the scholars following in their footsteps, including Bottigheimer, Barzilai, Jones, and Rowe. Influential in the philological gender analysis of *Die Kinder- und Hausmärchen* was Ruth Bottigheimer's *Grimms' Bad Girls and Bold Boys* (1987), in which she argues that "identifying the real narrative voice in the spinning tales is crucial [. . .] because mixed and often contradictory messages emerge from different narrative levels within these tales, and because narrators seem to favor heroic figures of their own sex" (10).

Whether such a "real narrative voice" in a polyphonic genre as the fairy tale can ever be discerned is questionable, and in practice Bottigheimer indeed focuses on revealing the various threads from which the Grimms' tales are spun. Concrete paths that Gilbert and Gubar miss include the fact that in some oral variants of "Snow White," a male character fulfills the role of the mirror (Bacchilega, *Postmodern Fairy Tales* 34) or that the wicked queen is Snow White's biological mother in the manuscripts and published versions of *Die Kinder- und Hausmärchen* prior to 1819. Various fairy-tale retellings exist that draw back on earlier printed or manuscript versions of the Grimms' tales, or that reimagine the interaction between the Grimms and woman storytellers (see Joosen, "Novelizing the Fairy Tale" and "Back to Ölenberg"). In most of these, the way the Brothers Grimm treated the female oral material is envisaged as a true battle of the sexes. Written in the 1980s, when the genesis of *Die Kinder- und Hausmärchen* was high on the agenda of fairy-tale studies, Linda Kavanagh's "The Princesses' Forum" explicitly and elaborately refers to the Grimms' revisions. When Sleeping Beauty complains that in many stories women are depicted as enemies, Cinderella reformulates Bottigheimer's conclusions in an extreme fashion: "That's because men wrote the stories. [. . .] It makes them feel good to have women fighting among themselves for male attention" ("Princesses' Forum" 8). More recently, Barbara Walker likewise reminds her readers that the ideological message of a tale is determined by the teller who narrates it. In "Snow Night," the author is Snow White's rejected admirer: "As for Lord Hunter, his reason quite gone, he lived confined for the rest of his life as the dwarves' prisoner. In later years he sometimes passed the weary hours by writing stories. It is said that he wrote an entirely different version of the story you have just heard" (Walker 25). Although Lord Hunter is a fictional character and his tale exists only in Walker's fictional realm, the ending of "Snow Night" suggests a similar male bias in the traditional "Snow White" that the reader may know.

Other retellings form the link between Gilbert and Gubar's reflection of woman authorship and the sociohistorical research on woman fairy-tale collectors and authors. Cathleen O'Neill's "Revenge of the Sisters Grimm" (1989) invents for the Brothers Grimm what Virginia Woolf had imagined for Shakespeare in *A Room of One's Own:* a fictional sister with the ambition to write constrained by a male-dominated society. There are three Sisters Grimm who live in Patri-Ark, "the land of he and him":

> The laws of former Patri-Ark
> Kept sisters past hid in the dark,
> where rules were made by he for she
> and written out of his story.
> No trace was found of woman-kind
> save what the bravest one could find
> by delving through the olden lore
> of memory, songs and tales of yore.
>   (O'Neill 11)

O'Neill's story reminds the reader that the information available about the Brothers Grimm greatly surpasses what is known about their oral sources or their sister: "The arkives contained only his story. The annals were full of He and Him. Sisters, wives, mothers and daughters were not worthy of record." The voice of the women can only be accessed through stories written down by men (the so-called Patri-Arkives), in which, as O'Neill's characters suggest, "We must look for the secret sign" (12). These observations find their nonfictional parallel in the works of feminist researchers such as Gilbert and Gubar's and, more specifically for fairy tales, Jeannine Blackwell and Valerie Paradiž.

The critique that Gilbert and Gubar do not sufficiently take into account the geographical and historical context can be supplemented by the reproach that they attribute too much value to the author of the text. One of the most prominent and recurrent critical comments on *The Madwoman in the Attic* is Gilbert and Gubar's "unstated complicity with the autobiographical 'fallacy'" (Jacobus 520). Not only has their "author-centered focus [. . .] been criticized as naïve and over-simplistic" (Gamble 244; see also Cain xxxii), for the fairy tale in particular this approach is problematic. The Grimms' tales, after all, draw back on an oral tradition, and male and female voices unmistakably intertwine in the genesis of "Snow White." Again I believe that some aspects of Gilbert and Gubar's critique would provide interesting views on this interaction, but it is a fact that they themselves do not consider the fairy tale in light of the interaction between the Grimms and their female sources. Nor do they discuss how the tale of "Snow White" evolved during the Grimms' lifetimes and beyond. In "To Spin a Yarn" (1986), Karen Rowe argues that telling fairy tales is "semiotically a female art" (308). She refers to Ovid's Philomela, who told the story of her rape by weaving it into a tapestry after she had her tongue torn out by her rapist and her speech was thus literally stolen from her. Rowe turns Philomela into a metonymic figure who is representative of all woman storytellers: "Ironically, Philomela, the innocent woman who spins, becomes the avenging woman who breaks her enforced silence by simply speaking in another mode—through a craft presumed to be harmlessly domestic, as fairy tales would also be regarded in later centuries" ("Spin" 301). Typical of the history and development of fairy tales, as is the case for Philomela's story, is that the female tales survive in the writings of men. In his *Metamorphoses*, Ovid "lays claim to or attempts to imitate the semiotic activity of woman par excellence" ("Spin" 302). As Rowe argues, "Based on this paradigm, we can begin to explore the lineage of women as tale-tellers" (297), from Scheherazade to the sources of the Brothers Grimm. Fairy-tale retellings can take the artistic liberty to reimagine such lineages of woman storytellers and place themselves at the end of it, as Nicole Cooley's "Snow White" and Emma Donoghue's *Kissing the Witch* illustrate.

Several of the aspects of criticism that were discussed with regard to Lieberman can be and have been addressed to Gilbert and Gubar. The duality that was present in Lieberman's discussion of female stereotypes in male-authored fairy tales is perpetuated by Gilbert and Gubar and has been labeled by Charles Altieri "male resentment ad nauseam" (qtd. in Cain xix). As Susan S. Lanser has noted (1989), Gilbert and Gubar oppose, even more elaborately and explicitly than Lieberman, "an essentially false and problematic 'male' system beneath which essentially true and unproblematic 'female' essences can be recovered" ("Feminist Criticism" 422). In *Literature after Feminism*, Rita Felski (2003) stresses that the kind of reading that Gilbert and Gubar practiced may still be how feminism is conceived in the popular understanding; "among feminist scholars, however, the once irresistible metaphor of the madwoman has lost its luster" (69), and this for both aesthetic and political reasons. Linked to the dichotomy of male and female essences is the critique that Gilbert and Gubar naturalize a universalizing tendency with regard to women on the one hand and to literature on the other hand. As discussed with regard to Lieberman, Felski notes that Gilbert and Gubar take the madwoman in the attic as representative for every woman, disregarding differences in race and class.[12] Felski also finds fault with Gilbert and Gubar for painting an image of the Victorian woman that lacks nuance; she stresses that not all Victorian women were helpless in every domain of their lives (70) and shows that, again, the impact of class should not be underestimated.

Not only are Gilbert and Gubar said to have done insufficient justice to differences between women, but they have also been argued to have neglected the differences between woman authors. Felski describes how other metaphors for women writing have succeeded the burdened madwoman in the attic, most notably the "sexy masquerade" of the woman writer as trickster and parodist (75), the "celebration of the female performer" (77). Thus Gilbert and Gubar have been reproached with a reduction of the historical context, as well as of the literary text. Whereas they were once praised for providing an entirely new and convincing perspective on classics such as *Jane Eyre* and "Snow White," Felski refers to feminist critics such as Mary Jacobus and Susan Lanser, who were "troubled by what they saw as a flattening out of literary ambiguity, a zealous desire to impose a single framework and a false coherence onto a many-voiced and many-sided history of women's writing" (70). As Coover's Prince imposed a mask on the Queen's face and ignored or misinterpreted the wink beneath it, Gilbert and Gubar have been argued to project their own, modern views on the historical texts. Jacobus relates this alleged reduction of literature to Gilbert and Gubar's exclusive preoccupation with plot. Their reading strategies thus "become a form of tight lacing which immobilizes the play of meaning in the texts whose hidden plots they uncover" (518) and as a result of their specific, ideology-driven focus eventually produce the same interpretations over and over again. Thus *The Madwoman in the Attic* "reenacts endlessly the revisionary struggle, unlocking the secrets of the female text again and again with the same key" (519). As we have seen, fairy-tale retellings of "Snow White" approach the traditional tale with different keys, adding fictional layers of interpretation to the palimpsestic text. Several of these, most clearly Coover's and Hofman's, refuse to be tightly laced into one meaning and spark reflection on meaning-making itself. Moreover, Hofman, as I have argued in "Back to Ölenberg," goes back into the fairy tale's history and includes elements from "Snow White" versions prior to the final Grimms' version from 1857. He reveals the Grimms' tales to be not just palimpsests that cover one meaning but rather the result of complex interweavings in which various voices and meanings compete. Many of these cannot be retrieved, only reimagined.

Backlash Retellings

The most popular ideas and elements in Gilbert and Gubar's interpretation, often shared with other feminist critics and authors, have been corrected and parodied on several occasions. In the retellings discussed above, it was evident how fictional tales that implement these ideas often leave room for critical distance or alternative interpretations. Yet, some texts seem more clearly written with an intent to parody the feminist treatment of fairy tales in the vein of Gilbert and Gubar, aligning themselves more with their critics than their supporters. Garrison Keillor's "My Stepmother, Myself" (1983) may be considered part of what Susan Faludi called the "backlash decade" of the 1980s, referring to a discourse in the media and in academic criticism through which the credibility of feminism was questioned, "in an attempt to push women back into their 'acceptable' roles" (Faludi qtd. in Gamble 227). Keillor's parody is part of a group of retellings that exaggerate feminist critiques and parody them by putting them in the mouths of fairy-tale characters. Aspects from Gilbert and Gubar's interpretation of "Snow White" are almost literally rephrased by the protagonist of the tale: "In trying to come to terms with myself, I've had to come to terms with my stepmother and her envy of my beauty, which made our relationship so destructive. She was a victim of the male attitude that prizes youth over maturity when it comes to women. Men can't dominate the mature woman, so they equate youth with beauty. In fact she was beautiful, but the mirror (which of course, reflected that male attitude) presented her with a poor self-image and turned her against me" (Keillor 182). Both in Keillor's and in Gilbert and Gubar's texts, the mirror is identified explicitly with the voice of a patriarch. This is interpreted twice as a way for men to encourage rivalry between women, and this rivalry is a strategy to control or marginalize mature women. The explicitness, predictability, and self-evidence ("of course") with which Snow White generalizes the issue invite an alternative interpretation of Keillor's tale: rather than as a feminist critique of "Snow White," it may also function as a parody of Gilbert and Gubar's analysis.

Keillor's Snow White further testifies on her marriage to the prince, who turned out to be not so charming. Gilbert and Gubar could have predicted this outcome, since the traditional prince loves, in their interpretation, not a woman of flesh and blood but the "inanimate *objet d'art* patriarchal aesthetics want a girl to be": "dead and self-less in her glass coffin, she is an object, to be displayed and desired" (*Madwoman* 40–41). Several retellings, as well as some radical feminists, take this interpretation a step further. They read the passage as describing not a symbolic but a realistic, sexual desire and picture the prince as a necrophiliac.[13] Such extreme subversions of the traditional tale and its heroes are highly popular in fairy-tale retellings, which are restrained less than fairy-tale criticism by criteria of plausibility or faithfulness to the pre-text. Hints of necrophilia are present in several of the retellings discussed above, such as Blumlein's and Coover's.[14] In Keillor's sequel, Snow White describes the necrophilic lusts of her husband at length: "Now I can see how sick our marriage was. He was always begging me to lie still and close my eyes and hold my breath. He could only relate to me as a dead person. He couldn't accept me as a living woman with needs and desires of my own. It is terribly hard for a woman to come to terms with the fact that her husband is a necrophiliac, because, of course, when it all starts, you aren't aware of what's going on— you're dead" (182).

Keillor does not tell the story of "Snow White" from the traditional third-person point of view, but instead gives Snow White a voice as the narrator of the tale. By means of this strategy, as well as by taking the analysis of critics such as Lieberman, Dworkin, and Gilbert and Gubar to the extreme and combining it with a confessional talk-group style, Keillor conflates and ridicules the feminist discourses on fairy tales and on family relationships.[15] Taking Gilbert and Gubar's words literally, this author implicitly advocates the inappropriateness of feminist fairy-tale analysis.

A less humorous but equally conservative message can be found in Regina Doman's Christian retelling of "Snow White." In their interpretation of the tale, Gilbert and Gubar draw links with Christian imagery, in which the female archetypes of angel and witch are rooted. Snow White is considered a manifestation of the archetype of which the Virgin Mary was the medieval form (20). In the adolescent novel *Black as Night*, Regina Doman reclaims this ideal, adapting aspects of it to a modern standard of what a young Catholic girl can be. As the author explains, "I was snared by the challenge of making this the story of modern temptation of a girl contemplating her vocation in the modern world" (432). The image of the Virgin Mary is one with which the Snow White figure, Blanche, consciously struggles, as becomes explicit when she dresses up like Mary for a play at the church. She is chosen for the part not only because she is the only female living among a group of seven friars—the equivalents of the seven dwarves—but also because the part corresponds to the virtues of kindness, sympathy for the poor and sick, and self-sacrifice that she displays throughout the book.

Like Gilbert and Gubar, Doman sets up the queen and Snow White as two contrasting types of women. Blanche is depicted as a symbol of goodness and modesty, Elaine as an egocentric career woman and superficial capitalist. The reader is invited to share the girl's perspective as she looks at Elaine:

A flawless blonde lady stood at a podium, making a speech and basking in the applause, smiling. [. . .] The girl wondered what it must be like to be divinely beautiful, and apparently wealthy and powerful as well. *That's who I should want to be like*, she thought, *if I were a really modern girl. Up there in front of the crowd, fit and fashionably dressed, at the pinnacle of some career, not showing a sign of weakness.*

> The girl smiled ironically. *With my small plans for the future, I*
> *never would be anyone's poster girl. Some might even say I'm a traitor,*
> *betraying the cause of women's empowerment.* (Doman 93)

In the final lines, a distance is created between Blanche and the feminist movement, of which Elaine is staged as a representative. *Black as Night* is a novelization of "Snow White" that replaces the flat characterization of the traditional story with ample psychological analysis. Blanche is not as naïve as Gilbert and Gubar argue Snow White to be. She knows what role models are available and consciously chooses to be different from the career woman Elaine. The phrase "some might even say" leaves room for differing opinions, and emancipated womanhood is presented as one option but not necessarily the most desirable one—rather the contrary.

The backlash ideology of Doman's novel is affirmed later in the book when Blanche defends her doubts about going to college: "I just can't help thinking that it's not my path" (303). Father Francis encourages her to think long and hard about her choices, whether they concern marriage or college, but Brother Leon more or less closes the discussion when he says, "Don't feel that you have to go to college just because all your friends are. [. . .] When I graduated from high school, I went because it was 'the thing to do.' I wasted my first two years trying to decide what I wanted to study. I probably would have spent my time better if I'd just gone to work instead of spending all that money taking courses I didn't need. Plus it caused trouble when I wanted to enter a religious order and had student loans to pay off first" (Doman 303–4). By stressing the high cost of college education and describing his time there as wasted, Brother Leon's words are rather discouraging for a girl who is, like his former self, in doubt. In her reply, Blanche casts herself in the passive waiting role that feminists such as Lieberman and Gilbert and Gubar have criticized elaborately in "Snow White": "It's all theoretical. I might want to get married, but I can't very well do that until the man I want to marry proposes. And unless he figures out what he's doing with his life, I'm sort of in limbo" (304). The uncritical way in which this conclusion is received signals that this postfeminist[16] retelling brings the Snow White figure back to the heavily criticized ideal of "Some Day My Prince Will Come."

The Virgin Mary is reclaimed in this novel as a positive force and one that is morally superior to and more powerful than the figure of the witch.

On several occasions in this retelling, Blanche and Elaine discuss what a woman can and should be. Elaine rationalizes the attraction of the Virgin Mary:

> These monks, they have their Mary, right? [. . .] Pale and cold and above and beyond them. That's what they like. That's how you are, right? So transparent and clear, like a pane of crystal glass, no fingerprints on it. Untouchable. [. . .] You've taught me, about being beautiful. You don't have to be scarlet. You're a white maiden, white as snow, aren't you? Pure as the driven snow. That's what they want. Someone who's untouchable. Beauty above them like a star. [. . .] No you, you have it right. You stay above and beyond the men. You can still get what you want. You be a snow maiden, and they'll serve you like a queen so long as they believe you're above it all. (253)

The dichotomy between the two women is enforced in this book by various contrasts: the association with colors (white for Blanche, red for Elaine); the fact that Blanche is described as glass without fingerprints, whereas Elaine has a fondness for stained glass (344); the association of Blanche with the Virgin Mary and Elaine with a snake (335); and the fact that Blanche seeks refuge in a church versus Elaine's aversion of churches (344). As Gilbert and Gubar have tried to reveal the downsides to Snow White, Elaine describes the Virgin Mary's purity as paleness and coldness, her reservation as haughtiness. These are all features that the preceding 250 pages of the novel contradict, as they are mostly written from Blanche's perspective or from the point of view of people who care about her. Elaine tries to discredit Blanche's good nature by interpreting her innocence as a pose—she later calls her "a conniving little tramp" (291). Moreover, in her view, Blanche does not remain "untouchable" in order to preserve something for herself but to give her power over others. She is "playing hard to get," making herself more desirable by presenting herself as unavailable. Readers are invited to contrast the implicit, naturalized view of Blanche with the explicit judgment that Elaine expresses and to distance themselves from Elaine. Her critical description of the Virgin Mary is further corrected by the friars, who characterize her as mild faced and picture her as a warm "Blessed Mother" with "rays of the sun coming out all around her"

(275). Elaine performs not only the role of the witch, but also that of the snake, trying to tempt Blanche with knowledge, freedom, and independence (335). She presents herself as an informed feminist by using such terms as patriarchy[17] and by addressing the opposition of "her story" versus "his story" (335). These issues are discredited through the association with a greedy murderess, who abuses concepts like "her story" not as an interest in female experiences but as a way of biding time, luring Blanche into her trap. As such, Regina Doman's novel can be seen as part of the backlash movement against feminism that has discredited its representatives and merits.

In Blanche's dream during her coma—the realist equivalent in this tale of Snow White's deathlike state—Elaine rephrases the command in the title of Zipes's *Don't Bet On the Prince:* "You can wait forever, and the prince will never show up. He's not coming, Blanche. He never does. Your trust was in vain. You were better off alone" (392). The fact that this is not Elaine speaking but rather Blanche's unconscious representation of Elaine illustrates that the reincarnated figure of the wicked queen has managed to shake her confidence (403). In this evocation, Elaine's plea and Blanche's consecutive doubts tie in to wider feminist fairy-tale debates, recalling Anne Sexton's imagery of Snow White as a china doll and Gilbert and Gubar's description of the nineteenth-century "aesthetic cult of ladylike fragility and delicate beauty" (25): "Princes never come. What's the point in being a china doll? Why not be a power goddess, feeding on strength, remaking yourself in the image of every threat to your supremacy that came along? As Elaine had done. She was being like a silly fainting heroine in some Victorian semi-classic, whimpering and dying of consumption, too fragile to keep herself together, barely suspending disbelief. The weaker vessel. But she couldn't shed her biology like a cracked eggshell and rise to do battle with nature. She was weak. And she was dying" (Doman 403). Blanche's self-critical feminist phase takes the female archetypes to an extreme in the opposition of the china doll to the merciless power goddess. What may be called a brief feminist "awakening" paradoxically—yet, most revealingly—takes place in a dream and is presented as only temporary. Moreover, her feminist self-reflection only occurs when Blanche has given up hope that her prince will save her, as a second choice. At this moment in the multifocalized novel, the reader knows that Bear, her boyfriend, has done everything in his power to find her. And of course Blanche's prince does show up in time. Before he kisses her awake, he commits to her in a union that he knows will have God's approval (427).

Black as Night displays an awareness of feminist discussions yet presents the traditional heterosexual union as the option that is still most desirable. In comparison to the evil stepmother in "Snow White," Elaine in *Black as Night* is even more of an independent plotter and schemer. Yet, Doman draws the reader's attention back to those passages that Gilbert and Gubar downplay or ignore in their analysis. She strongly dissociates Elaine from Snow White—the two are here unrelated—and underlines that Elaine's primary goal is banal personal enrichment, not a higher cause. Through its association with greed and evil, feminism is represented as a temporary aberration, a diversion from the right path that Blanche refinds soon enough.

The Dynamics of the Intertextual Dialogue

In their palimpsestic analysis of "Snow White," Gilbert and Gubar practice in theory what many fairy-tale retellings perform in fiction with regard to their traditional pre-texts. First, they place the story in a broader literary context. Second, they add depth to the character psychology so that black-and-white distinctions are reversed or disappear (Snow White versus the queen). Third, they fill in gaps, such as the silent disappearance of Snow White's father from the scene. Fourth, they problematize happy endings (the female cycle) and finally, they rationalize elements of the supernatural (the magic mirror). Most of these changes are common practice in fairy-tale retellings; so it is not surprising that elements of Gilbert and Gubar's discussion of "Snow White" are mirrored in a large corpus of fictional revisions. Particularly widespread is the rehabilitation of the evil stepmother. The examples discussed above provide only a selection of a much broader group that includes not only retellings of "Snow White" but also revaluations of wicked female characters in "Cinderella," "Hansel and Gretel," and "Sleeping Beauty" as creative plotters and determined survivors. The justification or alternative interpretation of the queen's character and deeds fits into the larger trend in fairy-tale retellings in general to novelize the traditional plot and to step away from flat characterization in favor of round characters with psychological depth (see Joosen, "Novelizing").

As I showed in chapter two, the reversal of gender characteristics is a popular strategy in feminist retellings, in which former negative and positive features are redistributed among male and female characters. Indeed, the rehabilitation of the queen often happens at the expense of the male characters in the story (king, hunter, dwarves, and prince). They tend to be described in largely negative stereotypical terms, whereas the female characters are redeemed, acquire agency, and gain profundity. This seesaw effect can be noted not only in Gilbert and Gubar's article, as Altieri and Lanser have noted, but also in the fictional revisions of "Snow White." Most retellings that promote female bonding, something that Gilbert and Gubar deem highly difficult in patriarchy, do so at the expense of the male characters; this is particularly the case in Sheerin's "Snow White," Donoghue's "The Tale of the Apple," and Walker's "Snow Night," as well as in a few tales that have not been discussed in depth, such as Joni Crane's "No White and the Seven Big Brothers" (1985) and Grainne Healy's "Snow-Fight Defeats Patri Arky" (1989).

When a male character narrates the "Snow White" retelling and produces elements from Gilbert and Gubar's analysis in the form of explicit comments, retellings like Coover's or Peterson's suggest an ironic distance from the narrative perspective. This practice is noticeable in children's literature as well. In Günter Seuren's "Die Fragen der sieben Zwerge" (1964, The Seven Dwarves' Questions), for example, the dwarves reduce Snow White to a useful housemaid:

> Who will now cook heaven and earth for us
> serve it on our favorite plate
> and serve gelatin in all possible colors
> for dessert?
> (96; my translation)

Similarly, in *Das Neueste von den Sieben Zwergen* (2000, The Latest News from the Seven Dwarves), Hubert Schirneck presents the sexist perspective of the seven dwarves in such a blatant manner that it invites a critical distance: "All of a sudden they noticed how much they missed Snow White, not just because she was so beautiful, but especially because she had kept their house so clean. The dwarves had become rather used to it, because it was quite comfortable to have such a cleaning fairy in the house. But now the dirty dishes were piling up, the laundry remained unwashed, the floor filthy, and nobody made the beds" (9; my translation).

Schirneck's example comes from an adventure story for young children, which presents a sequel to "Snow White" from the perspective of the dwarves. The seven spoiled dwarves suggest an analogy between ungrateful children and a Snow White who plays the role of an unappreciated mother and housewife. The retelling thus invites young readers to link the feminist critique to their situation at home and offers a more self-critical model of identification than the victimized and idealized character Snow White.

In the previous analyses, no distinction was made on the basis of the target audience of the fictional texts. Gilbert and Gubar's ideas surface in retellings for children as well as for adults, though it is clear from the range of examples that more intertextual links can be drawn with adult texts. In children's books, the alternative feminist interpretations are left to a great extent to the imagination and inference of the reader: hints are given in the text and the illustrations, and the multilayered texts seem to exploit to the full the possibilities that the double address of children's literature offers. A picture book such as Trina Schart Hyman's *Snow White*, for instance, combines a traditional tale in the text with more complex undercurrents in the illustrations, which require an intertextual competence and cultural knowledge that extends far beyond the fairy tale. Retellings for slightly older readers, such as Hofman's or van Mol's, introduce disturbing elements to the text without making a definite statement on what their impact may be. Again, this leaves room for readers to imagine different endings according to their emotional and intellectual capacities as well as their view of the fairy tale.

One of the most important and challenging insights that Gilbert and Gubar have provided for the study of "Snow White" is their approach to it as a story in which the acts of looking and seeing play a central role. As we have seen, several retellings of "Snow White" invest the narratological flexibility (first-person narrator, focalization, multiple points of view) and author detachment that are typical of fiction in foregrounding the perspectives that are naturalized in the traditional tale. Through these narratological adaptations, as well as through additions about framed watching, the retellings hold a mirror to the male viewer and make him more explicit as a spectator with a patriarchal, possessive gaze.

In this context, it should be noted that there are two remarkable absentees in the long list of first-person narrators or focalizers of "Snow White" retellings: the king and the hunter, the two representatives of patriarchy in Gilbert and Gubar's interpretation. All the other characters in the story have had ample opportunity to give their point of view of the events. Most retellings with a first-person narrator are told, as can be expected, from the perspective of the protagonist, Snow White (Donoghue, Geras, Gould, Keillor, Levine, Maguire, Sherman, Sheldon, Thomas, van Mol, and Yolen), and the antagonist, the queen (Bedford, Gaiman, Galloway, Murphy, and Sheerin as well as Lee and Tom Naegels). Occasional examples can be found for the dwarves (Delessert and Kumpe as well as Maguire and Martin Mooney)[18] and the prince (Coover, Friman, and Peterson). Some retellings even give voice to the main objects in the tale, the mirror (Harrison, Friman, and Thylias Moss) and the apple (Sue Owen). The scarcity of retellings narrated by the king and hunter can be explained not only by their relatively minor roles in the traditional tales. In the interpretations of critics such as Gilbert and Gubar and Bettelheim, the king is granted a central role in the story. That his part as a character is often extended illustrates that several authors of fairy-tale retellings (Geras, Donoghue, and Yolen) equally perceive him as an important character.[19] This makes it all the more puzzling that as a narrator the king is notably absent from fairy-tale retellings. His place as the representative of patriarchy seems to be usurped in part by his successor, the prince who marries Snow White. In most texts, this prince turns out to share the ideology and values that were ascribed to his father-in-law by Gilbert and Gubar. The retellings can thus be argued to supplement the female cycle with a male one in which only one type of masculinity is put forward. Because many retellings narrated by the prince are sequels, he functions as the patriarch in his own right. The large number of woman narrators and the lack of a king narrator illustrate, moreover, the compensatory function that many feminist fairy-tale retellings attempt to fulfill, also with regard to the patterns that Gilbert and Gubar criticize. As the fairy-tale retelling is a genre that to date stands under the important influence of feminist criticism, it is to be expected that woman narrators and protagonists dominate. The seesaw effect thus seems to have an influence not only on the level of content representation within one tale but also on the level of narratological organization within a large corpus of retellings.

Revisiting "Snow White"

In the discussion above, I put *The Madwoman in the Attic* at the center of an intertextual network in which several retellings and illustrations can be placed and consequently interpreted. More than fifteen years after the appearance of *The Madwoman in the Attic*, Gilbert and Gubar revisited "Snow White" in the concluding chapter of *No Man's Land* (1994), in which they in turn included several retellings of the tale. They observe that "the old fairy tales about relationships between men and women have mutated in increasingly complicated ways, so that many of us—feminist critics, cultural historians—seem to be lost in a forest of stories about the future of sexuality and sex roles" (*Land* 359). "Snow White" may have worked to dramatize the situation for nineteenth-century women, but as they approached the twenty-first century, Gilbert and Gubar realized that a new set of tales was required to explain the multiple roles that women have been able to play since, both as authors and as characters. As I briefly addressed in the first chapter, Gilbert and Gubar recast "Snow White" into a hypertext with multiple versions that further split up into multiple endings. They claim to be inspired for these rewritings by both feminist criticism and feminist literature. Readers are invited to pick their favorite tale and, at the end of the chapter, imagine their own stories—or, at least, the female readers are. A final short retelling is added, which once again highlights the gender bias that Gilbert and Gubar take: "Sometimes when this Queen looked into the mirror of her mind, she passed in her thoughts through the looking glass into a forest of stories so new that only she and her daughter could tell them" (*Land* 403).

All of Gilbert and Gubar's retellings of "Snow White" are built upon the same principle, and the following discussion will serve as an example to illustrate a technique of rewriting that also applies to the others. This specific example is meant, in Gilbert and Gubar's own words, "to crystallize controversies about the erotic that have persisted from the turn of the century to the present" (*Land* 363). The scene in which Snow White is led into the forest by the hunter is rewritten as follows: "The handsome huntsman seduced Snow White in the middle of the forest. By the time she arrived at the sybaritic mansion of the dwarves, she was quite adept in the arts of love. Indeed, she was ready to teach the dwarves a thing or two. 'I give myself when I please, where I please,' she told them. And when the Queen arrived on a visit, bringing in tow a charming and fabulously handsome Prince, it seemed Snow White was going to live happily ever after" (*Land* 363).

At this point, the tale is split into three possible endings that are inspired by other stories about female desire, such as Margaret Atwood's *The Edible Woman* and Kate Chopin's *The Awakening*. In the first ending, the prince is unnerved by Snow White's "jouissance." She refuses to marry him and happily disappears into the forest. In the second, the prince cannot satisfy Snow White's lust but they settle down and start an apple strudel factory. In the last variant, the S&M prince chains up a naked Snow White in the glass coffin and the couple is observed by the voyeuristic dwarves, queen, and king.

Rather than considering these retellings literary texts, I read them as humorous fictional passages that bring a light touch to the literary analyses in *No Man's Land*. As Gilbert and Gubar explain after the last variant: "Our variations on the theme of 'Snow White' are meant to be monitory and ironic, for they reflect just a few of the countless plots proposed not only by the writers whose works we have studied in *No Man's Land* but also by a range of contemporary theorists, critics, and poets" (367). A further interpretation of their meanings and implications is left to the readers. Not only can they choose their favorite version, but they also need to make sense of them. In this aspect, Gilbert and Gubar's rewritings remind me of the retellings by Willy Pribil, James Finn Garner, and Iring Fetscher discussed in the previous chapter, tales that were rewritten according to certain formulas. The implied critique, I argued there, affects the formula or applied paradigm probably more than the traditional fairy tale. Indeed, Gilbert and Gubar's retellings seem to cast an ironic light over all the feminist approaches to which they subject "Snow White," turning several into a caricature—whether the titular heroine worships the Queen Mother as a goddess (*Land* 362) or interprets the world as "merely signifiers, signifying nothing" (366). Likewise, their evaluation of the various feminist approaches in and to literature is ambivalent: they are both celebrated as a source of inspiration and visualized as a forest in which one can easily get lost. Finally, although it is clear that Gilbert and

Gubar take into account several of the avenues that *feminist* criticism has followed in the course of the twentieth century, it is striking that they still keep *fairy-tale* criticism out of consideration in this revisiting of "Snow White." Although the views of femininity may have changed and become more diverse, the fairy tale is still used here as an instrument to "crystal-lize controversies" and illustrate certain views in a wider discussion with a sociopolitical goal but with a manifest disregard of its own tradition and literary potential.

Conclusion

In the introduction to this book, I referred to Jack Zipes's description of the evolution of the fairy tale in terms of Darwinist and epidemiologic analogies. Indeed, on the basis of the primary texts that have been presented and analyzed, the flexibility and wide dissemination of the stories cannot be denied. Some retellings retain the structural and stylistic features of the fairy tale but produce variations on the content through reversals, deletions, small additions, or alternative endings. Others revitalize the traditional tales through formal adaptations, merging the plots with generic features borrowed from the picture book, poetry, the psychological novel, the historical novel, the short story, and other forms and genres. Together, all these retellings, even those that take such a critical position that they seem far removed from the traditional fairy tale, do sustain and reinforce the interest in this genre. They rely on its popularity to be understood as revisions and reinforce it by repeatedly using it as a pre-text.

The three case studies illustrate that fairy-tale retellings display a wide variety of intertextual overlaps with critical discussion about the traditional fairy tale. In some retellings, metacritical ideas are explicitly phrased by either the narrator or the fictional characters; in many others, they can be derived from deletions, additions, exaggerations, and corrections. Some retellings evoke arguments from critical fairy-tale debates to explain their raison d'être in autoreflective passages or fictional claims for truth. In most analyses of the retellings in fairy-tale studies, criticism is referred to in order to explain the attitude of these texts with regard to the traditional pretexts. Conversely, fairy-tale retellings and illustrated fairy tales can also actively contribute to the reception of fairy-tale criticism; and theories of intertextuality, when used in a sense that allows for achronological and nonintentional parallels, can be invoked to make aspects of this reception clearer.

In the variety of genres and age groups that they address, fairy-tale retellings have certainly succeeded in implicating readers other than academics in the fairy-tale debates. These audiences have their own specific characteristics and needs, and the difference in the implied readership affects which ideas are expressed in literature and how certain effects are achieved. The fact that the retellings are usually written by nonacademics and address a nonspecialized audience may explain why some fairy-tale critiques find a belated equivalent in the retellings. In this sense, the fairy-tale retelling does not serve the survival of the traditional fairy tale alone. From the parallels that I have drawn between critical texts from the 1970s and some very recent retellings, it can be argued that the fairy-tale retelling is also a site where outmoded critical views of the traditional fairy tale live on. Some of these fictional texts recapitulate the development of certain lines of thought with regard to the fairy tale, expressing views of the fairy tale that have long been problematized in academic circles. These views of the fairy tale are detached from the historical context in which they were topical in fairy-tale criticism, and their presence in recent retellings demonstrates the relativity of categories such as conservative and progressive. Especially in retellings for young children, early feminist and Marxist views still find equivalents today, as if new readers are expected to run through the evolution of these critical paradigms beginning with the most basic views and gradually evolving to more complex ones. This is not to say that all retellings for children rely on simplistic corrections: many of them pose high demands on the intellectual capacities of the readers as well as on their intertextual competence. This is particularly true for retellings that overlap with psychoanalytic interpretations. The latent content of fairy tales as critics such as Bettelheim analyzed it also finds its way into children's books in softened versions or through literary techniques that demand active reading strategies and thus leave room for several interpretations. Illustrations, and the wide array of interactions they can have with a text, often play a vital role in this process. Moreover, recent retellings for children occasionally return to the older versions of Western culture's most popular fairy tales before they were adapted for children (see Joosen, "Back to Ölenberg"). This evolution supports a further shift in the image of the young reader, who is offered literature that enhances not only identification but also alienation and that makes strong demands on the intellectual and emotional competence of the child. Although feminist and Marxist retellings for children also defamiliarize the traditional versions that their young readers are deemed to know, critics who work within these paradigms attach a critical evaluative component to the interpretative function and a need for correction and revision. This does not necessarily imply a shift in the implied young reader, who is still considered to be the more or less passive recipient of ideology. However, early feminist and Marxist ideology critiques have merged with other approaches, both in criticism and in literature, and many of the most demanding retellings for children and adults also imply a correction of traditional models of gender and class. Indeed, in all three case studies, as well as in most of the fairy tales under discussion, the impact of feminist fairy-tale criticism has proven to be particularly pervasive, whether feminist ideas are applied, denied, or parodied.

In literary theory and criticism, the question has been raised how effective literature can ever be in communicating metacritical interpretations and evaluations. In addition to differences between retellings and criticism that can be explained by the disparity of the implied readership, the status and impact of an idea is affected by the discourse and medium in which it is expressed. In fiction, the promotion of explicit ideology or the foregrounding of interpretations can easily have the opposite effect. The clarity of criticism quickly lapses into parody when it is applied to fiction, and indeed the boundary between serious, emphatic assertion and parody becomes particularly blurred in several of the stories discussed in this book. Although some have welcomed the mixture of fiction and criticism, retellings have also been claimed to fail both as literary and as critical texts. Their literariness is believed to get in the way of their clarity, whereas their overt didacticism is argued to obstruct their aesthetic qualities. Although simplistic parodies and role reversals have been rejected as being one-dimensional and too moralistic, these retellings may still qualify as literary texts if literariness is based on polysemantics (Iser, *Appellstruktur*) rather than beauty of language and form. Several of the ideology-driven retellings can be deconstructed to reveal contradictory messages, which open up to the reader a number of gaps, an escape route from an overly didactic stance. The implicit lesson that they teach through their contradictions is one that refuses unity and authority and is thus more in line with post-modern poetics.

None of the retellings that have been discussed can be read as a straight-forward translation of literary theory or political views into fiction. When literature and criticism express similar ideas, the possibilities and the limits of the two genres come into play. Fiction invites a different attitude from the reader than the referential meaning that is communicated through a nonfictional text. Even texts that do not foreground the unreliability of their narrator by their mere fictionality suggest a distance between author and narrator. This again provides the reader with the liberty to read even—or perhaps, especially—the most didactic retellings against the grain. Such antiauthoritarian retellings can still be perceived as interesting literary texts in their own right when they generate the same skeptical attitude in the reader toward themselves.

Fairy-tale retellings have not provoked negative responses alone—on the contrary. Critics have recognized quite a few of these texts for their aesthetic qualities and for a literary complexity that transcends the critical distance that they take with regard to the fairy-tale pre-text as well as their relationship with a critical intertext. Unreliable narrators, exposed gazes, open endings, embedded tales, mismatched collages, ironic metacomments, and shifting signifiers are but a few techniques that have been analyzed in this book as complicating clear-cut messages and opening up gaps that invite the reader to rethink and reexperience the traditional tales. These retellings account for an active exploration of the fairy tale's form and con-tent, providing a literary counterpoint to the reproach that criticism instrumentalizes the fairy tale and that it does not do justice to its aesthetic richness and polysemantic potential. Many of these retellings stretch the generic boundaries of the fairy-tale genre, creating hybrids in combination not only with the critical discussion of the pre-texts but also with other literary genres. In this sense, one may wonder to what extent "the traditional fairy tale" really survives in the fairy-tale retelling. Whereas some of the traditional features are retained, the function of these stories radically changes: conservative morals are transformed into antiauthoritarian messages; the utopian function of magic is traded for rational ideological criticism; the simple and linear fairy-tale structure is disrupted in collages that foreground their own constructedness; flat characterization is replaced with elaborate psychological explorations; and so forth. On the one hand, the concept of "the fairy tale" seems to have become so stretched that it threatens to lose all meaning. On the other hand, this elasticity has made it possible for the fairy tale to remain relevant to date, to provide readers in and far beyond academia not only with nice stories but also with reflections on literature and on life. In this sense, the retellings can be argued to return to a flexibility and adaptability that the fairy tale is believed to have had in the oral tradition, merging past with present, not only in content but also in form.

The critical paradigms in fairy-tale studies do not exist in isolation from each other: feminist, psychoanalytic, and sociohistorical criticism often supplement each other. Gilbert and Gubar share Lieberman's anxiety with regard to the negative impact of repeated stereotypical images of women, although they acknowledge the potential of literature to speak at several levels at the same time. Gilbert and Gubar overlap with Bettelheim in the sense that they also read the fairy tale looking for hidden meanings— although they consider them palimpsestic (with the associated possibility of conscious, creative intentionality) rather than unconscious. Lieberman shares with Marxist critics such as Gmelin a concern about the datedness of the traditional fairy tale, about its use in popular culture, and about the conservative attitudes it promotes. Sociohistorian and philological analyses of the genesis of the Grimms' collection supplement the critiques of Lieberman and Gilbert and Gubar with a historical framework on how patriarchal ideology gradually increased in the Grimms' tales. This hybridity and complementarity of critical views becomes even clearer in the fairy-tale retellings. A number of primary texts (including Fetscher, Block, Donoghue, Sexton, and Carter) have made appearances in various chapters, as they can be intertextually linked to several critical paradigms within fairy-tale studies, the ideas of which they sometimes combine and sometimes contrast. Consistency within a critical paradigm is irrelevant to the non-academic reader and to the creative process of transformation.

In the body of primary and secondary texts analyzed in this book, two further tendencies can be discerned. First, both fairy-tale criticism and a large number of retellings display the tendency to disenchant the fairy tale. This attitude to the fairy tale becomes clearest in the sociohistorical approach (see Joosen, "Back to Ölenberg), which investigates the roots of the fairy tale in reality, but also underlies the three key texts that have been discussed. Lieberman criticizes the popular tales for not providing realistic role models for girls, Bettelheim equates the magical objects and occurrences with figures or psychological processes in the child's unconscious, and Gilbert and Gubar rationalize magical occurrences in "Snow White" as symbolic of patriarchy's ideals and strategies of control. Magic is also one of the typical fairy-tale features that frequently disappear or take on new guises in late twentieth-century retellings: inconsistencies are resolved, magic is rationalized, historical contextualization increases, and fairy-tale plots are transferred to updated, realistic settings. Second, the traditional fairy tale is an action-driven genre. The psychological explanations given in criticism, whether they concern the characters or the tellers and readers, are supported in the fairy-tale retellings that create an alliance with genres that are traditionally known for their interest in the human psyche, most notably the novel and lyrical poetry. This hybridity has been touched upon in this book, not only with criticism but also with other literary genres, and certainly opens perspectives for future research.

I stated in the introduction that this book does not provide an exhaustive study of fairy-tale retellings. However, in the large corpus of stories that I have analyzed, I have found a few noteworthy differences between the Dutch, English, and German contexts. The dominance of English fairy-tale retellings and critical analysis in this book cannot be denied. As such, it is a reflection of literary and academic production: since the 1970s, fairy-tale retellings have been produced in English literature in a variety of genres (e.g., novels, poetry, short stories, and picture books) and for a broad range of age groups (children, adolescents, and adults). This interest of authors and illustrators has been matched with an ever-expanding corpus of studies on a wide array of aspects related to fairy tales and fairy-tale retellings in English. In German literature and criticism, the 1970s and

1980s were a period in which the fairy tale was the topic of various pedagogical and scholarly debates and in which it inspired the largest number of
retellings, both for children and for adults, although mostly in short texts
(poems, short stories) rather than in novels. In more recent years, and in
remarkable contrast to English, the genre of the fairy-tale retelling in German literature seems to be relegated more or less exclusively to children's
literature. Although fairy tales are alluded to in adult literature, the wave of
English fairy-tale novels for adults and adolescents does not seem to have a
counterpart in German literature.[1] Given the ambiguous symbolic status
that the Grimms' tales have had in German history and the importance that
has been attributed to literature as a means of emancipation and coming to
terms with the past, it is not surprising that antiauthoritarian and socio-
critical retellings have dominated the German intertextual dialogue with the
fairy tale. In Dutch literature, the fairy-tale retelling has developed fairly
recently as a popular genre in picture books and in stories and books for
children and young adults. In contrast with the German context, in which
recent retellings are mostly characterized by a parodic treatment of the
fairy tale, in Dutch literature the tales are the pre-text of both humorous
and more psychological stories. Several of the Dutch stories are crossover
texts or texts that exploit the potential of children's literature to address informed readers as well as readers with a less literary background. Many of
these retellings break with the traditional horizon of expectation, not only
of the fairy tale but also of children's literature: they can be juxtaposed with
English retellings for adults that refute the happy ending, that address sexual undercurrents in the fairy tale, and that make high demands on the
reader's intellectual and emotional competence. My specific treatment of
Dutch, English, and German retellings has been made more on the basis of
language than on geographic distinctions, and only occasionally have more
specific differences been addressed (e.g., in the American Cinderellas who
represent the spirit of the entrepreneur). Although the mobility of authors
and the presence of publishing houses in various countries complicate the
matter, a further geographical specification may shed light on the diverse
tendencies in the United Kingdom, the United States, Germany, Austria,
Flanders, the Netherlands, and so forth.

Various other questions and conclusions that were raised in this book
provide paths for future research. My selection of key texts, though based on
the marked canonical status that was attributed to them in the metacritical

discourse, could be further supplemented with others, most notably Jung-ian views, Christian interpretations, and criticism that explores the rela-tionship of Western fairy tales with those of other cultures. Finally, the patterns and thematic overlaps that have been distinguished in this book can be further examined in other, nonliterary media, most notably film and theater, whose different technical possibilities would provide an interesting point of comparison to the generic distinctions between literature and criti-cism that have been addressed in this book.

In conclusion, I go back to a quotation by T. S. Eliot that was mentioned at the beginning of this book. Eliot claims about criticism that "for every success in this type of writing there are thousands of impostures. Instead of insight, you get a fiction." That criticism and fiction may share some inter-ests and characteristics but that their modes of expression and communica-tive models have a substantial impact on the way information and views are transmitted has been illustrated amply in this work. Moreover, the retell-ings analyzed in the three case studies have shown that fiction and insight are by no means opposed and that fiction has its own means of producing insight. I would therefore rather conclude with another quotation of Eliot, one that was used as the motto of Hofman's *Zwart als inkt* and illustrates for me the dynamics between fairy-tale retellings and their intertexts in gen-eral: "What we call the beginning is often the end / And to make an end is to make a beginning." This observation has certainly proved valid for the various critical key texts and retellings under discussion in this work, which have sparked further debates and inspired new fictional texts. This inter-textual dialogue is carried on and fuelled with new material, as the most recent developments in fairy-tale criticism and retellings show, with influ-ences from, among others, queer theory, ecocriticism, and postcolonialism. Moreover, the interest in the fairy tale since the 1970s has brought into be-ing several institutions and serial publications that will help keep the inter-est in this genre vibrant.[2] To date, critics and authors continue to take fresh perspectives on the fairy tale, trying new keys and finding new voices that are waiting to be heard or imagined, ready to make a new beginning.

Notes

INTRODUCTION

1. See also Jack Zipes's "The Changing Function of the Fairy Tale" (1988).

2. As Stanley Fish claims, "Interpretation is not the art of construing but the art of constructing. Interpreters do not decode poems; they make them" (327).

3. See, among others, Mieder (*Grimms Märchen* 7), Solms (90), Haase ("Scholarship" 31; "American Germanists" 294), and Zipes ("Introduction" xxx). Haase and Zipes refer not only to Germany but also to an international context (among others, the United States, the United Kingdom, Ireland, France, and Italy).

4. See Born (54), Haase ("American Germanists" 295–96; "Scholarship" 1–2), Solms (1), and McGlathery (*Romance* ix–x).

5. See, among others, Filz's "Märchen nach 1968" (177) and Zipes's *Fairy Tales and the Art of Subversion*.

CHAPTER 1

1. Stephens and McCallum use "fairy-tale reversion," Zipes uses "modern-day revision" and "fairy-tale parody" ("Fairy Tales" 53), Fernández Rodríguez uses "contemporary revision," Warner uses "reworkings" (193), Sipe and Bacchilega use "fairy-tale transformation," many critics, including Bacchilega, use "postmodern fairy tale," Pizer uses "anti–fairy tale," Nikolajeva uses "fractured fairy tale," and Beckett uses "recycled fairy tale."

2. Genette calls this the "hypotext." Stephens and McCallum define "pre-text" as follows: "The pre-texts for a retelling, then, are known, or already given, 'stories,' however precisely or indeterminately evoked" (5). The analyses in this book are limited to retellings that highlight intertextual links with a specific traditional

fairy tale rather than with the more general coded discourse of the fairy tale. I will take into account, however, that a traditional fairy tale as pre-text occurs in an array of variants, textual and nontextual, that all share and expand upon a minimal thematic core. Several of these variants may participate in the intertextual process.

3. In contrast to Elizabeth Wanning Harries, who writes that "most retellings of traditional or classic fairy tales are duplicates" (15), I consider retellings a synonym of revisions, and thus distinguish them from duplicates.

4. It can and has been argued that the fairy tales by the French *conteuses* originally functioned as retellings rather than traditional tales. Indeed my concept of "fairy-tale retellings" corresponds largely to Harries's definition of "complex fairy tales." Yet, for the purposes of this study, I will use the concept "traditional tale" in a broader sense than that of those that Harries calls "compact tales" and that she contrasts with "complex tales." Harries considers the tales by the French *conteuses* complex fairy tales. Although I am aware that de Beaumont's "Beauty and the Beast" may at some point have functioned as a retelling, for the purpose of this study, I will consider it a traditional tale. The retellings that are the subject of this book are "more visibly, massively, and explicitly" hypertextual and more openly "grafted" on the traditional tales (Genette, *Palimpsests* 5, 9) than her "Beauty and the Beast." Moreover, I will contrast de Beaumont's tale not with its contemporaries or literary and oral predecessors but with its more recent revisions.

5. See also Smith (10), who distinguishes between explicit and implicit reference to fairy tales in the title.

6. Genette's term for this type of intertextuality is "hypertextuality" (*Palimpsests* 5); Nikolajeva calls such works "anagrams," which she defines as "texts in which we can easily identify the intertext by rearranging the constituent elements or merely by connecting each element to a similar element in another text" (*Aesthetic Approaches* 37).

7. See also Bacchilega (*Postmodern Fairy Tales*) and Harries (101). Marie-Laure Ryan classifies the fairy tale under "simple narrativity": "The semantic content of the text is a plot and little else." This plot "revolves around a single problem" and "ends when the problem is resolved" (371–72).

8. Exceptions are Pieter Gaudesaboos's *Roodlapje* (Little Red Rag) and Sine van Mol's "Snow White" poems in *Een vlekje wolf* (A Patch of Wolf). Several retellings include disturbing elements in the happy ending, such as Hofman's *Zwart als inkt* (Black as Ink) and Provoost's *De Roos en het Zwijn*. All are marketed for children or young adults and were recently published in Dutch. Fewer examples

of retellings that break with the convention of the happy ending for young readers can be found in the English and German titles of my corpus.

9. A complete chapter of Beckett's *Recycling Red Riding Hood* is devoted to sequels based on the tale. She underlines that there is a historical tradition of the fairy-tale sequel that dates back to the nineteenth century and refers, among others, to a book by Léo Lespès, *Les Contes de Perrault continués* (Perrault's Fairy Tales Continued) from 1865.

10. Tracy Lynn's *Snow* and Gail Carson Levine's *Fairest* are two rare exceptions to this rule: in the former, the number of dwarves is reduced to five; in the latter their number is not specified. In both cases, Snow White's companions are still dwarves so that some form of intertextual marking is retained.

11. For an elaborate discussion of how intertextuality can be understood in relation to fairy tales, see also Kevin Paul Smith's *The Postmodern Fairy Tale*.

12. Clayton and Rothstein make a similar comment about Barthes: "Valuable as Barthes' account of intertextuality is for understanding the literary, it does not provide the critic with a particularly effective tool for analyzing literary texts. The infinite circularity of codes makes every text, potentially, the intertext for every other text. [. . .] If the codes never stop, then where does one draw the line between relevant and irrelevant references?" (23). See also Pfister (15) and Kümmerling-Meibauer (45).

13. Newspapers and magazines still contribute to the popularization of these ideas. Recent articles in Flemish newspapers on Bettelheim, for instance, include Debusschere's "Het aloude succes van Sneeuwwitje en co. verklaard" (2004, The Ancient Success of Snow White and Co. Explained) and "Variaties op het thema" (2004, Variations on the Theme), Messeman's "De mythe van de moederliefde doorgeprikt" (2004, Shattering the Myth of the Mother's Love), and van Nieuwenborgh's "Van pedagoog tot oplichter" (2003, From Pedagogue to Imposter).

14. Runow, for instance, indicates that her parody of Bettelheim is not so much based on *The Uses of Enchantment* as on an article that appeared in *Springers Welt am Sonntag*.

15. For several examples, see chapter four.

16. See also Glinz (124). Drawing on Goodman's nominalistic view on "the world," Wildekamp, Van Montfoort, and Van Ruiswijk (1980) have pointed out that, since reality is "a relative notion" that is "dependent on prevailing norms and ideas of a certain group or individual at a certain time," not all readers will understand a given text in the same way in terms of its fictionality (548).

17. For example, literary criticism often includes citations or paraphrases from fictional texts, and it is not uncommon in fairy-tale studies to make use of the fairy-tale format itself, usually for a short (auto)biography. See, for example, Jeannine Blackwell's "Fractured Fairy Tales" (1987), Günter Lange (2004), Zipes's chapter on Walter Benjamin in *Happily Ever After*, and Maitland's "A Feminist Writer's Progress" (1983).

18. Note that Fetscher wrote a nonfiction, critical article and a mock analysis of the same tale, "The Brave Little Tailor," in 1980 and 1972, respectively.

19. Mary Beth Stein describes Fetscher's "confusion methods" as follows: "He employs what he terms *Verwirr-Methoden* (methods of confusion), borrowing playfully from serious scholarly approaches, such as philological, psychoanalytic, and historical materialist textual criticism, to produce a unique blend of imaginative storytelling and light-hearted criticism" (160). They have received ample praise for this from German ideology critics such as Werner Psaar and Manfred Klein (1976), who claim that "from a literary pedagogical angle, Fetscher's book of fairy-tale confusions cannot be given enough credit" (87; my translation).

20. Traxler's parody can be read as a critical comment on so-called fairy-tale archaeology. *Die Wahrheit über Hänsel und Gretel* reveals the problems that arise when critics interpret all the elements of a fictional text as reflections of a past reality. About Ossegg, Traxler writes that he "read the fairy tale as if it were an account of facts" (21; my translation). This is a practice that was popular with some researchers of the 1960s. Otto Kahn, for instance, used fairy tales to verify historical hypotheses about the period of the Indo-Germanic conquests. By imitating and mocking the style, rhetoric, and method of this type of criticism, Traxler reveals how easy it is to have readers believe illusions that present fiction as fact. This critique of fairy-tale criticism is recurrent not only in mock interpretations but also in several fairy-tale retellings, as the case studies will illustrate.

21. See also Anders Pettersson ("Introduction" 6), who sees "appreciation" as part of "interpretation." Torsten Pettersson remarks that the addressee has a substantial effect on the way interpretations are construed and communicated. "Spearhead interpretations" for other specialists will perform different functions from "initiatory interpretations" for nonexperts (43).

22. Anders Pettersson notes that this distinguishes professional, academic interpretations from nonprofessional ones, which are characterized by "other acceptability conditions" ("Five Kinds" 53).

23. Hans Glinz's distinction between fiction and nonfiction, for instance, is problematic in that he equates such inevitable subjectivity in criticism with

nonfactuality. He states that nonfiction texts may also contain so-called *Erfindungs-Anteile*: components that were "invented" by the author and/or whose factuality cannot be checked. Among his examples to illustrate this point, Glinz also lists "the interpretation of facts (for instance in expressions like 'that all leads to the conclusion that . . .')" (124; my translation). Glinz leaves exactly how he distinguishes between facts, conclusions, and interpretations unspecified. Are the selection, organization, and presentation of facts not always based on an interpretation (which may remain implicit in the text itself)?

24. See also Nodelman ("What Are We After?" 5).

25. Aschenputtel and Aschenbrödel are the two German names of Cinderella.

26. Fetscher here echoes *S/Z*, in which Roland Barthes pleads for a new kind of interpretation of the "*texte scriptible*," which does not attribute a fixed meaning to literature but respects the plurality of meanings that it contains (11).

27. See, among others, Sontag's *Against Interpretation* and, more specifically for fairy-tale studies, Péju's critique of Bettelheim in chapter three.

28. See also Lamontagne (1998) and Krauss (1980).

29. One of the functions of "fictocriticism" comes close to the mock criticism by Iring Fetscher that was described above: "A critique of the traditional interpretative acts in the academy, acts which rely on the essay as a neutral frame to validate the authority of their rhetoric and to objectify the subject of their criticism" (Flavell 203). The difference seems to lie in the fact that Fetscher detaches the critical text from its author, whereas many of the examples that Flavell describes intensify the attachment of the text to the personality of the author, who invests it with subjective, personal meanings and associations.

30. One may wonder if such manifestations of overlap and fictocritical or paracritical texts ultimately destabilize criticism as a genre. Ihab Hassan argues that criticism has always been a relative term and that "even without the de-creations of certain kinds of writing, like my own paracriticism, the configurations we call literature, literary theory, criticism, have now become (quite like postmodernism itself) 'essentially contested concepts,' horizons of eristic discourse" (510). Yet Flavell argues with reference to Deleuze and Guattari's concepts of "territorialization" and "deterritorialization" that genres like "fictocriticism" can only emerge when "the boundaries between theory and fictional writing remain intact. [. . .] Fictocriticism, nor the other contemporary criticisms emerging that blur the distinction between theory and fiction, do not mark THE END to traditional academic criticism, as they rely on its existence to envision a line of flight" (199). Indeed, although the boundaries between fairy-tale retellings and criticism may be argued

to be breaking down, clear distinctions still exist that allow readers to classify most texts unambiguously.

31. "Run, Run, / As fast you can, / You can't catch me, / I'm the gingerbread man."

32. In the interview attached to *The True Story of Hansel and Gretel*, for instance, Louise Murphy explains her interest in "Hansel and Gretel" as follows: "In college I took a folklore course that fascinated me as we traced and studied the folk motifs that are found in every culture" (4). Neil Philip, author of *The Illustrated Book of Fairy Tales*, holds a PhD in myth and folklore. Gillian Cross, author of *Wolf*, obtained a PhD in English literature from Sussex University when Jacqueline Rose was teaching there. In Kate Bernheimer's *Brothers and Beasts* (2007), a book in which male authors testify to their relationship with fairy tales, several mention fairy-tale criticism as a source of inspiration: Bettelheim is named in Steve Almond's text (13), and Neil Gaiman remembers "academic books on folktales and fairy stories that explain why nobody wrote them and go on to point out that looking for authorship of folktales is in itself a fallacy" (67).

33. Lee's *White as Snow*, for instance, contains a long introduction by Terri Windling on the variants and critical perspectives on "Snow White." Several other examples will be mentioned in the following case studies.

34. In the *Arbeitsvorschläge* (suggestions for assignments) attached to Mieder's *Grimms Märchen—Modern* (1979, Grimms' Fairy Tales—Modern), it reads, "In a recently translated American book by the psychologist Bruno Bettelheim [. . .] it is stressed over and over again that modern children need fairy tales too. But what does Josef Reding [. . .] appear to say about this thesis in his short story?" (132; my translation). One of the "questions for discussion" at the end of *The True Story of Hansel and Gretel* also seems inspired by the discussion on the validity of Bettelheim's theory: "Do you think that Murphy is suggesting that too much belief in fantasy can be an obstacle to maturity or to finding resolution? Or do you think that she shows how belief—in fairy tales, magic, and beauty—can help us overcome trials?" (L. Murphy 11).

CHAPTER 2

1. Barzilai's Lacanian reading of "Snow White" provides an interesting contrast to Lieberman's approach, as do the articles assembled in Haase's *Fairy Tales and Feminism* (2004).

2. In 2001, Coppola still wrote, for instance, "In fairy tales human identity is reduced to fixed roles. These legitimate and strengthen images of 'man' and of

'woman' that are stereotypical and restrictive, particularly for women, given the patriarchal and phallologocentric context in which the stories have been created and transmitted" (131). Duncker argued in 1992, "The fairy-tales are dangerous. Identity is defined by role. We are offered patterns of behavior to follow, menaces if we transgress. The divisions between mothers and daughters, between sisters, between all women, are the cornerstones of patriarchy, and the fairy-tales endorse these divisions with sinister predictability. [. . .] So the messages are clear. The boys must go out into the world, fight giants, gain wealth and power, possess women and become kings. For girls the critical metamorphosis into adulthood is sexual. Sleeping Beauty's bleeding finger is the sign of menstruation and sexual maturity. From menstruation she proceeds into marriage: all her life between is one long sleep. As I say, all we have to do is lie still and wait" (153). Although both critics continue to point out that the stories also contain messages that contradict this image of the fairy tale as a patriarchal instrument, the influence from early feminist critics such as Lieberman and Dworkin is obvious. In 2006, the Flemish therapist and critic Gerard Gielen wrote, "In the classic fairy tales the villains are [. . .] always ugly and the heroes stunningly beautiful. Evil characters are nearly always accentuated by unattractive physical features and the 'stunningly beautiful' princess or the prince in shining armour are always attractive as well as morally good. [. . .] In this way, don't we give children the wrong message that only external beauty is good and don't we enhance from a young age the stigmatisation and discrimination of less attractive people?" (9; my translation).

3. Hulsens's critique of the fairy tale was part of a larger reflection on childhood culture.

4. See also Sarland (72), who briefly describes the "dialectal relationship between determination and agency" in the reading process and finds support for this thesis in research by M. R. Cherland and L. K. Christian Smith.

5. Mieder lists the retellings linked with female emancipation and adds questions for discussion, for example, "What emancipatory advice does Josef Reding give to his Sleeping Beauty character, and to what extent does he activate the otherwise passive fairy-tale heroine?" (*Grimms Märchen* 135; my translation).

6. Note that my translation is a literal one and that the original poem rhymes. "Vielleicht aber muß grade deshalb / im Märchen das Alte bestehen, / damit *alle* heutigen Enkel die Umwelt besser verstehen, / um nachher, im Streit mit dem Alten, / das Weltbild neu zu gestalten?"

7. This part of the text is also cited in the introduction to *Märchen für tapfere Mädchen* (1).

8. The title is slightly misleading, as it suggests that the Grimms, not Andersen, wrote "The Little Red Shoes."

9. A good example of the type of conversation that Hollindale wishes teachers to encourage can be found in Davies ("Beyond Dualism"1993). The article contains the transcript of conversations that her research assistant had with a group of primary school children about a traditional version of "Snow White" as well as about Cole's *Princess Smartypants*. They discuss several of Lieberman's central critiques of the traditional fairy tale, such as the beauty contest, the association of interior and exterior qualities, and the importance of wealth. Note also that the paratext of Vande Velde's *Tales from the Brothers Grimm and the Sisters Weird* (1995) invites readers to perform a similar ideology critique. She invites the readers to "fracture" fairy tales for themselves: "1. Make the villain a hero. 2. Make the hero a villain. 3. Tell what really happened. 4. All of the above."

10. See Joosen ("Disenchanting").

11. For a further discussion of the revised endings to "Beauty and the Beast" in light of Bettelheim's theory, see chapter three.

12. Another exception is Doman's *Black as Night*, discussed in chapter four.

13. For an overview of evolutions in this paradigm, see Liska ("Criticism").

14. For other examples of retellings in which female rescuers as well as male victims occur, see Fernández Rodríguez ("Deconstruction").

15. See also Pizer's discussion of Barthelme. Unlike Pizer I do not distinguish between parodies and anti–fairy tales (his term for the "dialectical antithesis" to the traditional fairy tale). I believe that aspects of a fairy-tale parody, for instance the reversal of gender roles, can be equally intended to achieve a dialectic effect.

16. See also Altmann's critique and reader response research by Bronwyn Davies.

17. See Davies ("Beyond Dualism" 150).

18. Note that Pischke (1977) makes a similar distinction. Pischke's equivalent term for "poesis" is *"Märchenverbesserung"* or "improved fairy tale" (104).

19. As Harries argues about Christa Wolf, Olga Broumas, Lisel Mueller, and Carolyn Steedman, "They do not discard the tales that the early feminist critics found so threatening, but rather show us how to use them" (153).

20. A second critique is aimed at the nonfictional parts in Walker's texts: her "introductions mash references to ancient world mythologies, classic fairy-tale collections and studies, and New Age spiritual movements together with nary a footnote or sufficient explanation" (Langlois 188–89).

21. As Zipes writes about German retellings of the early 1970s, including Gmelin's, "There is very little humor in these tales, and whatever innovation there is, is often compromised by a didactic message and contrived closures" (*Brothers Grimm* 250).

22. Fish writes about William Blake's "The Tyger" that "its simple plurality is simply a testimony to the capacity of a great work of art to generate multiple readings" (342).

23. Walker's collection was criticized in Langlois's review, and Kavanagh's story is one of the feminist publications of Attic Press, which Coppola compares unfavorably with Donoghue's retellings. For a critique of Yolen, see Hanlon (147) as well as Jacqueline Lew's "Sleeping Beauty on Exhibition" (2000/2001), in which the retelling is compared to Sexton's "Briar Rose" ("Sleeping Beauty").

24. There is more ambiguity in the prince's choice. When Plain Jane awakes, she wishes for the prince to fall in love with her. It is therefore unclear whether the prince chooses her of his own free will or magic guides him in his choice. The fact that he first kisses the witch and Jane "to practice" before the enchantment suggests the second.

25. For instance, "These stories were plain lies, but they gave hope and pleasure to his children and so he thought them kinder than the truths he could not bring himself to tell" (Brooke 67).

26. See Jay and Glasgow (2–3) and Heilbrun ("Foreword" xiii).

27. See, for example, Silver on Oscar Wilde (551) and Wullschlager's biography of Andersen.

28. See Roderick McGillis's "'A Fairytale Is Just a Fairytale': George Mac-Donald and the Queering of Fairy" (2003).

29. Solis's discussion of this particular book ends with the conclusion that it is informed by a "theological doctrine," in which disability is seen as a punishment (121).

30. Some examples exist of gay fairy tales for children, most notably *Koning & Koning* (*King & King*) by De Haan and Nijland (2000).

31. See also Martine Hennard Dutheil de la Rochère's "Queering the Fairy Tale Canon: Emma Donoghue's *Kissing the Witch*" (2009).

32. For instance, her retelling of "Sleeping Beauty" and "Charm" in *The Rose and the Beast*.

33. The quotation is taken from a paper presented by Jennifer Orme at the University of East Anglia in April 2009, which appeared in slightly modified form in *Marvels and Tales* in 2010.

34. See also Sipe's conclusion on an earlier research experiment: "In the matter of intertextual connections [. . .], not only are children using these connections in a great number of analytical ways to interpret the story, they are also using them in creative, aesthetic ways—to enter the story and talk back to it, to play and perform, and to creatively stitch stories together to form more complicated, overarching narratives" ("Gingerbread" 86).

35. See also Coppola (130).

36. Examples include Yolen and Stanley's *Sleeping Ugly*, Schroeder's *Smoky Mountain Rose*, Hughes's *Ella's Big Chance*, Maguire's *Confessions of an Ugly Stepsister*, and Jackson's *Cinder Edna*.

37. These include Fetscher's "Ur-Schneewittchen" (*Dornröschen*), Kavanagh's "The Ugly Sisters Strike Back," Maher's "Hi Ho, It's Off to Strike We Go," and the Merseyside Fairy Story Collective's "Snow White."

CHAPTER 3

1. I refer to, among others, Dundes ("Folklore" 23; "Interpreting Little Red Riding Hood" 36), Zipes (*Brothers Grimm* 157; *Magic Spell* 179; "Fairy Tales" 51), Warner (203, 213), McGlathery (*Brothers Grimm* ix), Orenstein (71), Bacchilega (*Postmodern Fairy Tales* 2), Heisig (94–95), Pollak (351), Stone ("*Märchen*" 244), Rose (134), and Bosmajian (131). McGlathery sees Bettelheim as reinforcing a new interest in fairy tales and spreading it to an audience beyond academic circles (*Romance* ix–x). Indeed Bettelheim has thus contributed to what Zipes calls "pop psychology" ("Critical Observations" 26). In the United States, Bettelheim's ideas were discussed in all the major newspapers, and in Germany and Switzerland, the book was the subject of several reviews and public debates (Künneman 147).

2. Van Coillie stresses Bettelheim's popularity and importance in Dutch-speaking countries as well (226). In France, a documentary on his theories was broadcasted in 1974, which made a long-lasting impression. For the German context, in which the traditional tales received heavy criticism from pedagogues in the 1970s, Uther claims that Bettelheim helped bridge the gap between critics and supporters of the fairy tale (8).

3. See, for instance, Heisig (1977): "Bettelheim's name has become synonymous with intelligent and devoted respect for the mysterious world of the child" (94).

4. "Neo-Freudian" is used for psychoanalysts who apply concepts of Freud's theories in a slightly altered form. There is, for example, a difference between Freud's and Bettelheim's understanding of the id.

5. Some critics (e.g., Beckett) use the word "subconscious" instead of "unconscious" to address the id. Freud used the equivalent German term, *"unterbewußt,"* in some of his earliest writing but later used *"unbewußt"* or "unconscious" consistently (*Psychologie* 129). As Bettelheim only uses "unconscious," I will do the same when discussing his ideas about the id. Bettelheim makes no distinction between Oedipus and Electra complexes: he also uses the term "Oedipus complex" to describe the desire of girls for their fathers or jealousy of their mothers. Therefore, when referring to Bettelheim's interpretation of fairy tales in which this distinction is relevant, I will also use the term "Oedipus complex."

6. In this respect Bettelheim seems to be influenced by Jungian psychoanalysis as well as conventional views of children's literature. Bosmajian notes that Freud stresses "the ego's inevitable discontent" (130) and argues that "what makes the Jungian approach so attractive to interpreters of children's literature is that the theory assumes an original wholeness that can be regained after alienation is overcome. This coincides with the comic resolution of so many narratives for children and young adults" (132). See also Rose's critique of Bettelheim below.

7. Some authors of fairy-tale retellings who adhere to Bettelheim's theory are aware of this paradox. Gielen, for instance, addresses Bettelheim's negative evaluation of contemporary children's literature and fairy-tale retellings in the epilogue to his collection of fairy-tale retellings. He explains that he endorses several other premises in Bettelheim's theory: that fairy tales are therapeutic for children (253); that they should end happily and reassure the child (248); and that fairy tales are most effective if they are published without illustrations (250). However, Gielen explains that he disagrees with Bettelheim's thesis that fantasy stories should not be mixed with contemporary realistic elements (237), and he does recommend that adults interrupt the fairy tale when they read it with children to ask questions (249). One can argue that Gielen's explicit comments on his selective application of Bettelheimian theory are representative for several authors in this chapter who have not addressed their relationship to Bettelheim as openly.

8. Prefaces to traditional fairy-tale collections often popularize Freud's and Bettelheim's premise that the fairy tale provides insight into the unconscious. For examples, see Luke's introduction to the Grimms' *Selected Tales* (1982), Ghesquière's preface to Van Cleemput's fairy-tale collection (1994), Shah (1979) and Doherty (2000). As these prefaces are usually intended for parents and ignored by children, and as most of them are rather vague, they respect Bettelheim's rule that unconscious fairy-tale material should not be spelled out for young readers. The

absence of any references to sexual conflict in these examples is significant, as we will see below.

9. Cassy's grandmother, Nan, can be said to represent the voice of the super-ego. It can thus be expected that she argues against the importance of dreams, the realm in which the suppression of the id is weakened.

10. Freud describes the unconscious as being "divided between a repressed unconscious and the preconscious, the place of our 'latent memories'" (East-hope 36).

11. Note that Struck echoes this thought of Freud's almost literally in "Erin-nerungen an Hänsel und Gretel" (1974, Memories of Hansel and Gretel): "When I think back on Hansel and Gretel, I think back on myself" (82; my translation).

12. A parallel can be noted with Goldilocks, who is also the temporary occu-pant of somebody else's house.

13. Condensation is defined by Freud as "the fact that the dream has a smaller content than the latent one, and is thus an abbreviated translation of it. [. . .] Condensation is brought about (1) by the total omission of certain latent elements, (2) by only a fragment of some complexes in the latent dream passing over into the manifest one, and (3) by latent elements which have something in common being combined and fused into a single unity in the manifest dream" (*Lectures* 205). It is this third meaning that Bettelheim reverses in his discussion of split images.

14. The parallel between witch and stepmother in Browne's illustrations has also been noted by, among others, Lewis (66–67) and Freudenburg (307).

15. Beck, like Browne, decorates the witch's house with references to her pointy black hat: it is featured on her curtains, bowls, and paintings.

16. Koopmans is by no means the only illustrator to stress the stepsisters' similarity in his pictures. See also Eva Bednářová's illustrations to Perrault's "Cinderella" (Perrault and Aulnoy 67).

17. This explanation for the very precise directions with which Red Riding Hood leads the wolf to her grandmother's house has been offered by other retell-ings as well, for example, *Rood Rood Roodkapje* (Red Red Red Riding Hood) by Edward van de Vendel.

18. Note in this context that the Grimms changed several mothers into step-mothers in the 1819 edition of their collection. For retellings for children that omit the happy ending, see chapter four.

19. A similar process of splitting is described as it takes place in eight-year-old Coira, the protagonist of Lee's *White as Snow*. This girl's mother, Arpazia, rejects her because she was conceived when Arpazia was raped. Unable to accept this

rejection, Coira composes what Freud calls a "family romance" (*Kinderneurosen* 109).

20. See Seifert (2004) for an overview of his publications on this topic since the 1980s. He argues that "some of these tales exceed literary and ideological conventions with (thinly) veiled eroticism" (*Contes de fées* 57).

21. As Hanks (1978) argues, "American versions of ["Red Riding Hood"] have been sanitized to the point where the erotic element disappears" (qtd. in Stone, "*Märchen*" 239).

22. In this chapter, Anne Sexton's poetry will serve as an example of such fictional work.

23. See, for instance, Young, who argues that "Anne Sexton is out to *get* the brothers Grimm, armed with illuminations supplied by Freud" (qtd. in McClatchy 148). The title of Diana George's book on Sexton's Poetry, *Oedipus Anne*, is also telling.

24. The fact that Bettelheim does not mention Sexton in his discussion of "Sleeping Beauty" may indicate his unwillingness to read the tale as a story about incest. This absence supports Skorczewski's claim that "Briar Rose's prison remains intact because her words are interpreted as revealing her desire for her father rather than his for her" (310).

25. There are other similarities between Duhamel and Sexton's poems, most notably the multiple references to twentieth-century culture and the pessimistic conclusion.

26. This is a possible reference to Basile's "Sun, Moon, and Talia," in which the prince (here "another king") indeed impregnates Talia while she is still asleep.

27. See Beckett's *Recycling Red Riding Hood*, in which Pommaux clarifies his indebtness to Bettelheim: "Referring to Bettelheim's interpretation of the hunter as a protective father figure, Pommaux admits that John Chatterton fulfills that role to some extent" (201). It is unclear whether the word "admits" indicates any reluctance on Pommaux's part to name Bettelheim as an influence.

28. Even before this scandal, child psychologists such as Tucker ("Dr. Bettelheim"1984) and pedagogues such as Gmelin had raised concerns about the negative impact of horror in fairy tales on children.

29. For feminist responses, see Bottigheimer (*Bad Girls* 168) and Heisig (104). For reader response criticism, see Tucker ("Dr. Bettelheim" 34), Zipes (*Magic Spell* 190), and Heisig (97). For reactions from sociohistorians, see Crago (9) and Uther (8). Uther's claim that "Bettelheim's attempts at interpretation are always based on only *one* printed version of a fairy tale" (8; my translation) is manifestly

wrong as seen in, for instance, his interpretations of "Little Red Riding Hood," "Sleeping Beauty," and "Snow White."

30. Dundes mentions "Cinderella" as an example: whereas Bettelheim claims that variants of this tale are "distributed worldwide," Dundes shows that the tale is in fact only widely reported in the Indo-European and Asian languages ("Folklore" 24).

31. See Zipes (*Magic Spell* 191), Darnton (8), Künnemann (149), and Tatar (*Heads* xxiii, xxiv).

32. Bettelheim anticipates this reproach and argues, like Lieberman, that he has discussed only a small number of fairy tales because those are the ones that are still widely known (14).

33. See also Tucker ("Dr. Bettelheim" 36) and Brackert ("Märchendeutung" 232–35). Tucker ("Dr. Bettelheim" 40) argues convincingly that Bettelheim's idealization and deification of the fairy tale lead to the exclusion of tales and passages that portray human weaknesses, such as sexism, opportunism, brutal humor, violence, and discrimination against the poor and the plain.

34. See Dundes ("Bettelheim" 79–80), Sutton (13, 573–74), and Pollak (343–47).

35. This is in contrast to Zipes, who in *Happily Ever After* (1997) reads the same tale as a "rationalization of child abandonment," stressing the parents' blame.

36. See, among others, Grolnick (210).

37. The original text is "der so lustig herumspringt." Zipes's translation does not capture the meaning of "*lustig*" or "merrily," which is relevant in Bettelheim's interpretation: "the thing that's bobbing about in such a funny way" (Grimm, "Brier Rose" 697).

38. Further examples, especially from the 1980s, can be found in Horn ("Lebenshilfe").

39. In his introduction, Bettelheim (15) briefly excuses himself for not being able to explore all the facets of the tales under discussion, explaining that he chose to analyze several tales rather than devote his book to just one or two stories. Yet this does not account for certain gaps in his analysis. He completely ignores, for instance, the fact that Hansel and Gretel's stepmother is reported to have died at the end of the story. This gap, whether deliberate or not, allows him to state that nothing has changed "but inner attitudes" (165), which is manifestly in contradiction with the tale's overt content.

40. See also Horn ("Lebenshilfe" 159, 163).

41. The comparison with a detective story is also present in the choice of words in some of the retellings that parody psychoanalysis. Fetscher, for instance, uses terms such as "the keys to dream interpretation" (*Dornröschen* 168), "secrets" (168), and "*Dechiffrierung*" or "deciphering" (170). Block refers to "clues" (170).

42. Like some of Gmelin's texts, Runow's tale does not use capital letters. I will do the same in the quotations.

43. See also Gerhard Haas (13).

44. Liska (*Moderne* 86 n26) rightfully links this form of "mimicry" to Hutcheon's parody.

45. As Zipes writes about Bettelheim, "Perhaps the greatest weakness of Bettelheim's book is his neglect of socio linguistic [sic] studies and his own careless use of terminology which reflects just how faulty his theory of communication is" (*Magic Spell* 189).

46. This strategy is not unusual in fairy-tale retellings. Donald Barthelme mocks the practice of matching characters in fairy-tale retellings with their counterparts in the traditional version. In the middle of his *Snow White*, readers are required to fill out a survey to make sure that they have recognized the intertextual connections. One of the questions is "Have you understood, in reading to this point, that Paul is the prince-figure?" (82).

47. "No longer can we only give children 'the safe, warm, conservative story, the Pollyanna syndrome' that for many of us was part of our own childhoods" (Clancy 75).

48. See also Beckett (*All Ages* 135–47) for an elaborate analysis of Biegel's tale.

CHAPTER 4

1. See, among others, Gamble (240, 244), Haase ("Scholarship" 12), Heilbrun ("Foreword" xi), Nünning (*Metzler* 169), Sordi (278), Jones (*Magic Mirror* 136), Osinski (47–48), Felski (65), Harries (167), and Zipes (*Stick* 134). Its status as a canonical text of fairy-tale criticism is affirmed by its inclusion in anthologies such as Zipes's *Don't Bet On the Prince* and Maria Tatar's *The Classic Fairy Tales*.

2. Earlier versions of the Grimms' text fill this gap, explaining that the king has died in the war. Several retellings do the same. In Hofman's the king also dies in the war; in Delessert's the heartbroken king searches for his daughter everywhere (28).

3. It is unclear to which pre-text Gilbert and Gubar refer when they describe the Grimms' tale. The citations they include stem from a 1972 Random House edition, which contains the final, canonized edition from 1857 (*Madwoman* 655 n79).

4. Bacchilega (*Postmodern Fairy Tales* 34) mentions, for instance, the Italian "Bella Venezia" and "Snow Bella" from Louisiana, Steven Swann Jones (*New Comparative Method* 100–03) a Hispanic version from Llano and a Puerto Rican

one from Mason. In the majority of versions that Jones describes, however, it is a mirror that makes the judgment.

5. Whether or not Yolen intended Snow to be perceived as an unreliable narrator is debatable and only of secondary importance to this argument. Following Nünning's concept of the unreliable narrator, in this study unreliability is perceived not so much as "a character trait of a narrator as it is an interpretive strategy of the reader," a hermeneutic device by means of which "the reader or critic accounts for whatever incongruity he or she may have detected by reading the text as an instance of dramatic irony and projecting an unreliable narrator" ("Unreliable Narration" 95).

6. Examples can be found of older illustrations in which the mirror is visualized with a male face. These include Fr. Müller-Münster's pictures in *Schneewittchen* (Grimm), in which the face strongly resembles that of Wilhelm Grimm, and Charles Robinson's in Walter Jerrold's *The Big Book of Fairy Tales* (1911). The mirror in Disney's animated version also displays a masculine face.

7. This tendency is not exclusive to retellings of "Snow White." Fernández Rodríguez ("Deconstruction," 2002) discusses several similar examples in retellings of "Sleeping Beauty," in which the objectification of the female protagonist is thematized (54).

8. Since the figures in Santore's book (Grimm, *Snow White*) are wearing red clothes, the reflection is adapted to match this color. Note that Santore only depicts the surroundings in the mirror, not in the rest of the illustration where Snow White and her prince stand in a blank space. It is unclear how the depicted room matches the text, in which it is described that the queen is ordered to dance in red-hot shoes. Does she dance in the room? Or does the illustration refer to a scene after the wedding ceremony, in another location?

9. See also Sheldon's "Snow White Turns 39" (1996/97). The happy ending to the Grimms' tale is confronted here with the everyday banalities in the life of a twentieth-century housewife who is growing older—once again the influence of Anne Sexton is evident. This contemporary Snow White seems to have neither the idealization that her former self was bestowed with nor the creative plotting and scheming that feminists have praised her stepmother for.

10. Sexton is mentioned explicitly in *The Madwoman in the Attic* (Gilbert and Gubar) but not with reference to her retelling of "Snow White." Coover is not mentioned.

11. For an overview of the critique of Gilbert and Gubar, see Sordi (1994).

12. Huang Mei questions the claim to universalism of the "Snow White" pattern (Haase, "Scholarship" 35).

13. Dworkin writes, "Snow-white was already dead when the heroic prince fell in love with her" (42) and "One can point out that in fact [the prince] is not very bright. [. . .] His recurring love of corpses does not indicate a dynamic intelligence either" (43–44).

14. In 1961, Pribil suggested the prince had a necrophilic interest in Snow White. In Gaiman (1994), the prince first meets Snow White's stepmother, who seduces him. Their lovemaking is very similar to the necrophilic kind that Snow White describes in Keillor's retelling. See also Garner's *Politically Correct Bedtime Stories,* in which the prince tries to convince the dwarves to leave him alone with Snow White's corpse (54).

15. Snow White's thoughts on her stepmother are a parody of Nancy Friday's *My Mother/My Self* (1977), to which Keillor's title ("My Stepmother, Myself") refers.

16. Gamble notes that two radically different currents are labeled with the term "postfeminism." I use it here not for the postfeminism that "participates in the discourse of postmodernism" and poststructuralism but rather for the more "conservative 'backlash' against feminism" which sees "feminism in its present form as inadequate to address the concerns and experiences of women today" (298–99).

17. Elaine reformulates most notably a critique of the patriarchal God.

18. Maguire has retold "Snow White" on several occasions. Meant here is "The Seven Stage a Comeback."

19. Other examples include Lee's *White as Snow,* in which the king is a murderous rapist, and Pat Murphy's "The True Story," in which he is a pedophile who lusts after his daughter.

CONCLUSION

1. See also Zipes's overview of German retellings (*Brothers Grimm* 231–69). Although Zipes does not draw the same conclusion, the texts that he mentions do support my impression.

2. The European Fairy-Tale Society started a series of fairy-tale studies in 1980, in which new publications still appear. The journal *Marvels and Tales* was established in 1987. Wayne State University Press has recently established a series of academic publications on fairy tales. In 2005, the literary journal *The Fairy Tale Review* was launched.

Works Cited

PRIMARY TEXTS

Abbestee, Adri, et al. 1974. *En ƺe leefden nog lang en gelukkig . . .* 5th ed. Amsterdam: De Bonte Was, 1978.

Ache, Jean. *Le Monde des ronds et des carrés*. Tokyo: Libraire çà et là, 1975.

Andersen, Hans Christian. *Fairy Tales of Hans Christian Andersen*. London: Reader's Digest, 2004.

Anholt, Laurence. *Billy Beast*. Illus. Arthur Robins. London: Orchard, 1996.

———. *Little Red Riding Wolf*. Illus. Arthur Robins. London: Orchard, 1998.

———. *Snow White and the Seven Aliens*. 1998. Illus. Arthur Robins. London: Orchard, 1996.

Atwood, Margaret. *The Edible Woman*. New York: Anchor, 1998.

———. *Good Bones and Simple Murders*. New York: Talese, 1994.

Barrie, James M. *Peter Pan*. London: Hodder, 1928.

Barthelme, Donald. *Snow White*. 1965/67. New York: Atheneum, 1978.

Basile, Giambattista. *Lo cunto de le cunti overo lo tattenemiento de peccerille*. 5 vols. Naples: Beltrano, 1634–36.

———. "Sun, Moon, and Talia." Zipes, *The Great Fairy Tale Tradition* 685–88.

Beaumont, Jeanne Marie, and Claudia Carlson, eds. *The Poets' Grimm: 20th Century Poems from Grimm Fairy Tales*. Ashland: Story Line, 2003.

Beck, Ian. 1999. *Teddy Tales: Hansel and Gretel*. London: Picture Corgi, 2000.

Bedford, Jacey. "Mirror, Mirror." *Rotten Relations*. Ed. Denise Little. New York: Daw, 2004. 120–43.

Bergwanger, Nikolaus. *Schneewittchen öffne deine augen*. Temeswar: Facla, 1980.

Biegel, Paul. 1977. *Wie je droomt ben je ƺelf*. 2nd ed. Haarlem: Holland, 1990.

Block, Francesca Lia. *The Rose and the Beast: Fairy Tales Retold*. New York: Cotler, 2000.

Blumlein, Michael. "Snow in Dirt." *Black Swan, White Raven*. Ed. Ellen Datlow and Terri Windling. New York: Avon, 1997. 21–55.

Borowsky, Lothar. Foreword. *Grimmige Märchen: Cartoons*. By Heinz Langer. München: Deutscher Taschenbuch, 1984. 7–9.

Briggs, Raymond. *Jim and the Beanstalk*. 1973. London: Puffin, 2003.

Brontë, Charlotte. *Jane Eyre*. London: Dent, 1980.

Brooke, William. *Untold Tales*. New York: Harper, 1992.

Broumas, Olga. *Beginning with O*. New Haven: Yale UP, 1977.

Browne, Anthony. *Into the Forest*. Cambridge: Candlewick, 2004.

———. *The Tunnel*. London: MacRae, 1989.

Carlin, Patricia. "The Stepmother Arrives." 2002. Beaumont and Carlson 46–47.

Carter, Angela. *Burning Your Boats: Collected Short Stories*. London: Vintage, 1996.

———. *The Old Wives' Fairy Tale Book*. New York: Pantheon, 1990.

———, ed. *Sleeping Beauty and Other Favourite Fairy Tales*. Illus. Michael Foreman. London: Gollancz, 1982.

Cashorali, Peter. *Fairy Tales: Traditional Stories Retold for Gay Men*. San Francisco: Harper, 1995.

———. *Gay Fairy and Folk Tales*. New York: Farrar, Straus and Giroux, 1997.

Catanese, P. W. *The Mirror's Tale*. New York: Aladdin Paperbacks, 2006.

Chopin, Kate. *The Awakening*. Oxford: Oxford UP, 2000.

Claffey, Anne, et al., eds. *Rapunzel's Revenge: Fairy Tales for Feminists*. Dublin: Attic, 1985.

Claus, Uta. *Total tote Hose: 12 bockstarke Märchen*. Frankfurt am Main: Eichborn, 1984.

Cole, Babette. *Long Live Princess Smartypants*. London: Puffin, 2004.

———. *Prince Cinders*. 1987. London: Puffin, 1997.

———. *Princess Smartypants*. London: Hamilton, 1986.

Conlon, Evelyn. "That'll Teach Her." *Ms. Muffet and Others*. Dublin: Attic, 1986. 32–36.

Coover, Robert. "The Dead Queen." *Quarterly Review of Literature* 8 (1973): 304–13.

———. *Pricksongs and Descants*. New York: Dutton, 1969.

Craddock, Sonia. *Sleeping Boy*. Illus. Leonid Gore. New York: Atheneum, 1999.

Crane, Joni. "No White and the Seven Big Brothers." Claffey et al. 50–56.

Cross, Gillian. *Wolf*. London: Puffin, 1990.

Dahl, Roald. *Revolting Rhymes*. 1982. London: Smart, 1998.

———. *Rhyme Stew*. London: Penguin, 1989.

Datlow, Ellen, and Terri Windling, eds. *Black Heart, Ivory Bones*. New York: Avon, 2000.

De Haan, Linda. *Koning & Koning*. Illus. Stern Nijland. Haarlem: Gottmer, 2000.

Delessert, Etienne. *The Seven Dwarfs*. Mankato: Creative Editions, 2001.

Desy, Jeanne. "The Princess Who Stood on Her Own Two Feet." 1982. Zipes, *Don't Bet On the Prince* 39–47.

Doherty, Berlie. *Fairy Tales*. Illus. Jane Ray. Introd. Doherty. London: Walker, 2000.

Doman, Regina. *Black as Night: A Fairy Tale Retold*. Bathgate: Bethlehem, 2004.

Donoghue, Emma. *Kissing the Witch: Old Tales in New Skins*. New York: Harper, 1997.

Duhamel, Denise. "Sleeping Beauty's Dreams." 1996. Beaumont and Carlson 92.

Ensor, Barbara. *Cinderella (as if You Didn't Already Know the Story)*. New York: Schwarz, 2006.

Fetscher, Iring. *Wer hat Dornröschen wachgeküßt? Das Märchen-Verwirrbuch*. 1972. Frechen: Komet, 2000.

Ford, Michael. *Happily Ever After: Erotic Fairy Tales for Queer Men*. New York: Kasak, 1996.

French, Fiona. *Snow White in New York*. Oxford: Oxford UP, 1986.

Friman, Alice. "Snow White: The Prince." 1984. Beaumont and Carlson 218.

Gaiman, Neil. 1994. *Snow, Glass, Apples*.12 July 2010. www.holycow.com/dream ing/stories/snow-glass-apples.

Galloway, Priscilla. *Truly Grim Tales*. Toronto: Lester, 1995.

Garner, James Finn. *Once upon a More Enlightened Time: More Politically Correct Bedtime Stories*. 1995. Thorndike: Hall, 1996.

———. *Politically Correct Bedtime Stories*. London: Souvenir, 1994.

Gaudesaboos, Pieter. *Roodlapje*. Tielt: Lannoo, 2003.

Gelberg, Hans-Joachim, ed. *Neues vom Rumpelstilzchen und andere Hausmärchen*. Weinheim: Beltz, 1981.

Geras, Adèle. 1992. *Pictures of the Night*. London: Red Fox, 2002.

Ghesquière, Rita. Preface. *De bijenkoningin en 30 andere sprookjes*. By Gerda Van Cleemput. Illus. Rita van Bilsen. Averbode: Altiora, 1994. 8–9.

Gielen, Gerard. *Mooie heksen en lelijke feeën*. Antwerpen: Garant, 2006.

Gmelin, Otto F. *Gmelin—Märchen Venus—Schwänke [Fibel 2]*. Frankfurt: Ifez, 1977.

———. *Märchen für tapfere Mädchen*. Illus. Doris Lerche. Gießen: Edition Schlot, 1978.

Gould, Steven. "The Session." *The Armless Maiden, and Other Tales for Childhood's Survivors*. Ed. Terri Windling. New York: Dohery, 1995. 87–93.

Gower, Lesie. *Snow White and the Seven Dwarfs*. Illus. Bernard Canavan. London: Acorn, 1986.

Grimm, Brothers. "Brier Rose." 1857. Zipes, *The Great Fairy Tale Tradition* 696–98.

———. *The Brothers Grimm*. Trans. Brian Alderson. Illus. Michael Foreman. London: Gollancz, 1978.

———. "Cinderella." 1857. Zipes, *The Great Fairy Tale Tradition* 468–73.

———. *Die Kinder- und Hausmärchen*. Ed. Heinz Rölleke. 3 vols. Stuttgart: Reclam, 2001.

———. "Hansel and Gretel." 1857. Zipes, *The Great Fairy Tale Tradition* 711–16.

———. *Hansel and Gretel*. Illus. Anthony Browne. London: Walker, 1981.

———. *Hänsel und Gretel*. Illus. Jörg Drühl. München: Lentz, 1981.

———. *Schneewittchen*. Illus. Fr. Müller-Münster. Reutlingen: Ensslin, 1946.

———. *Selected Tales*. Introd. and Trans. David Luke. London: Penguin, 1982.

———. "Snow White." 1857. Trans. Maria Tatar. Tatar, *Classic Fairy Tales* 83–89.

———. *Snow White*. Trans. Paul Heins. Illus. Trina Schart Hyman. Boston: Little, 1974.

———. *Snow White*. Illus. Charles Santore. New York: Random, 1996.

———. *Snow White and the Seven Dwarves*. Illus. Elisabeth Wagner-Koch. London: Temple Lodge, 1994.

Harrison, Mette Ivie. *Mira, Mirror*. New York: Speak, 2004.

Healy, Grainne. "Snow-Fight Defeats Patri Arky." *Sweeping Beauties: Fairytales for Feminists*. Ed. Elaine Crowley, Rita Kelly, and Maeve Kelly. Dublin: Attic, 1989. 39–45.

Hofman, Wim. *Zwart als inkt*. Amsterdam: Querido, 1998.

Hughes, Shirley. *Ella's Big Chance: A Jazz-Age Cinderella*. New York: Simon, 2003.

Huiberts, Marjet. *Roodkapje was een toffee meid: Stoere sprookjes om te rappen*. Illus. Wendy Panders. Haarlem: Gottmer, 2010.

Impey, Rose. *The Orchard Book of Fairy Tales*. Illus. Ian Beck. London: Orchard, 2005.

Jackson, Ellen. *Cinder Edna*. Illus. Kevin O'Malley. New York: Lothrop, 1994.

James, Henry. *What Maisie Knew*. Oxford: Oxford UP, 1996.

Janosch. 1972. *Janosch erzählt Grimm's Märchen*. Weinheim: Beltz, 1991.

Jerrold, Walter, ed. *The Big Book of Fairy Tales*. Illus. Charles Robinson. London: Blackie, 1911.

Jones, Diane Wynne. 1986. *Howl's Moving Castle*. New York: Harper, 2001.

Jungman, Ann. *Cinderella and the Hot Air Balloon*. Illus. Russell Ayto. London: Lincoln, 1992.

Kantor, Melissa. *If I Have a Wicked Stepmother, Where's My Prince?* New York: Hyperion, 2005.

Kavanagh, Linda. "The Princesses' Forum." Claffey et al. 5–11.

———. "The Ugly Sisters Strike Back." *Cinderella on the Ball: Fairytales for Feminists*. Ed. Zoe Fairbairns et al. Dublin: Attic, 1991. 20–25.

Keillor, Garrison. "My Stepmother, Myself." *Happy to Be Here*. London: Faber, 1991. 180–85.

Korn, Ilse. *Königin im Leinenkleid*. Berlin: Kinderbuchverlag, 1977.

Kuijken, Belle, ed. *Héél lang geleden: bekende schrijvers vertellen hun lievelingssprookjes*. Tielt: Lannoo, 2002.

Kumpe, Michael. "Schneewittchen." 1975. Mieder, *Mädchen, Pfeif auf den Prinzen!* 99–100.

Langer, Heinz. *Grimmige Märchen: Cartoons*. Foreword by Lothar Borowsky. München: Deutscher Taschenbuch, 1984.

Lavater, Warja. *Le petit chaperon rouge*. Paris: Maeght, 1965.

Lee, Tanith. *Red as Blood, or Tales from the Sisters Grimmer*. 1979. New York: Daw, 1983.

———. *White as Snow*. 1979. New York: Doherty, 2000.

Leprince de Beaumont, Jeanne-Marie. "Beauty and the Beast." 1756. Zipes, *The Great Fairy Tale Tradition* 805–15.

Lesser, Rika. *Hansel and Gretel*. Illus. Paul O. Zelinsky. New York: Dodd, 1984.

Levine, Gail Carson. *Fairest*. New York: Harper, 2006.

Luke, David. Introduction. *Selected Tales*. By the Brothers Grimm. Trans. Luke. London: Penguin, 1982.

Lynn, Tracy. *Snow*. New York: Pulse, 2003.

Maguire, Gregory. *Confessions of an Ugly Stepsister*. New York: Regan, 1999.

———. *Leaping Beauty and Other Animal Fairy Tales*. New York: Harper, 2004.

———. *Mirror Mirror*. Illus. Douglas Smith. New York: Regan, 2003.

———. "The Seven Stage a Comeback." *A Wolf at the Door and Other Retold Fairy Tales*. Ed. Ellen Datlow and Terri Windling. New York: Aladdin Paperbacks, 2000. 137–48.

Maher, Mary. "Hi Ho, It's Off to Strike We Go!" Claffey et al. 31–35.

Maitland, Sara. *Angel Maker: The Short Stories of Sara Maitland*. New York: Holt, 1996.

McCorkle, Jill. *Crash Diet: Stories*. New York: Fawcett Columbine, 1992.

Merseyside Fairy Story Collective. "Red Riding Hood." 1972. Zipes, *The Trials and Tribulations of Little Red Riding Hood* 251–55.

————. "Snow White." 1972. Zipes, *Don't Bet On the Prince* 74–80.

Mieder, Wolfgang, ed. *Grimms Märchen—modern: Prosa, Gedichte, Karikaturen*. Stuttgart: Reclam, 1979.

————. *Mädchen, pfeif auf den Prinzen*. Köln: Diederichs, 1983.

Minters, Frances. *Cinder-Elly*. Illus. Brian Karas. New York: Viking, 1994.

Mooney, Martin. "Dwarves." 2000. Beaumont and Carlson 82–83.

Moss, Thylias. "Lessons from a Mirror." 1989. Beaumont and Carlson 169.

Munsch, Robert. *The Paper Bag Princess*. 1980. New York: Scholastic, 1999.

Murphy, Louise. *The True Story of Hansel and Gretel*. New York: Puffin, 2003.

Murphy, Pat. "The True Story." *Black Swan, White Raven*. Ed. Ellen Datlow and Terri Windling. New York: Avon, 1997. 278–87.

Naegels, Tom. "Spiegelliegeltje." Kuijken 93–99.

Namjoshi, Suniti. *Feminist Fables*. London: Sheba Feminist, 1981.

Napoli, Donna Jo. *The Magic Circle*. New York: Dutton Children's Books, 1993.

O'Neill, Cathleen. "Revenge of the Sisters Grimm." *Sweeping Beauties: Fairytales for Feminists*. Ed. Elaine Crowley, Rita Kelly, and Maeve Kelly. Dublin: Attic, 1989. 11–14.

Osborne, Will, and Mary Pope Osbourne. *Sleeping Bobby*. Illus. Giselle Potter. New York: Atheneum, 2005.

Owen, Sue. "The Poisoned Apple." Beaumont and Carlson 110.

Perrault, Charles. *Cendrillon*. 1983. Illus. Roberto Innocenti. Paris: Grasset, 2000.

————. "Cinderella; or, The Glass Slipper." Zipes, *The Great Fairy Tale Tradition* 449–54.

————. "Sleeping Beauty." Zipes, *The Great Fairy Tale Tradition* 688–95.

Perrault, Charles, and Marie d'Aulnoy. *Sprookjes van Charles Perrault en Marie d'Aulnoy*. Illus. Eva Bednářová. Haarlem: Uitgeversmaatschappij Holland, 1979.

Perrault, Charles, and Guido Stocker. *Cinderella: das Aschenputtel*. Illus. Loek Koopmans. Gossau: Nord-Süd, 1999.

Pescetti, Luis María. *Caperucita Roja (tal como se lo contaron a Jorge)*. Buenos Aires: Alfaguara, 1996.

Peterson, Polly. 2000. *The Prince to Snow White*. 12 July 2010. www.endicott-studio.com/cofhs/cofp2sw.html.

Philip, Neil. *The Illustrated Book of Fairy Tales*. New York: DK, 1997.

Povel, Wim. "De koetsier van Assepoester." *Sprooksels: Verhalen voor wie nog in sprookjes gelooft.* 1980. Bussum: Novella, 1990. 87–94.

Pribil, Willy. "Schneewittchen—frei nach Sigmund Freud." 1961. *Grimms Märchen— modern: Prosa, Gedichte, Karikaturen.* Ed. Wolfgang Mieder. Stuttgart: Reclam, 1979. 44–45.

Provoost, Anne. *De Roos en het Zwijn.* Amsterdam: Querido, 1997.

Pullman, Philip. *I Was a Rat!* New York: Dell Yearling, 1999.

Roberts, Lynn. *Cinderella: An Art Deco Love Story.* Illus. David Roberts. London: Pavilion, 2001.

Röhrich, Lutz. *Gebärden—Metapher-Parodie.* Düsseldorf: Schwann, 1967.

Runow, Dorothea. "rotkäppchen—auch für erwachsene—gedanken zu bruno bettelheim." *Märchen für tapfere Mädchen.* Ed. Othilie [Otto] F. Gmelin. Frankfurt am Main: Ifez, 1976. 50–52.

Schirneck, Hubert. *Das Neueste von den Sieben Zwergen.* Wien: Jungbrunnen, 2000.

Schroeder, Alan. *Smoky Mountain Rose: An Appalachian Cinderella.* Illus. Brad Sneed. New York: Dial, 1997.

Scieszka, Jon. 1991. *The Frog Prince Continued.* Illus. Steve Johnson. London: Puffin, 1994.

———. *The Stinky Cheese Man and Other Fairly Stupid Tales.* 1989. Illus. Lane Smith. London: Penguin, 1992.

Seuren, Günter. "Die Fragen der sieben Zwerge." 1964. Mieder, *Mädchen, pfeif auf den Prinzen* 96.

Sexton, Anne. *The Selected Poems of Anne Sexton.* Ed. Diane Wood Middlebrook and Diana Hume George. London: Virago, 1988.

Shah, Idries, ed. *World Tales.* Introd. Shah. Harmondsworth: Lane, 1979.

Sharpe, Anne. "Not So Little Red Riding Hood." 1985. Zipes, *The Trials and Tribulations of Little Red Riding Hood* 324–27.

Sheerin, Róisín. "Snow White." *Cinderella on the Ball: Fairytales for Feminists.* Ed. Zoe Fairbairns. Dublin: Attic, 1991. 48–51.

Sheldon, Anne. "Snow White Turns 39." 1996/97. Beaumont and Carlson 109.

Sherman, Delia. "Snow White to the Prince." *The Armless Maiden, and Other Tales for Childhood's Survivors.* Ed. Terri Windling. New York: Dohery, 1995. 40–41.

Snydal, Laurence. "Grandmother." Beaumont and Carlson 56.

Spillebeen, Willy. *Doornroosjes honden.* Antwerpen: Manteau, 1983.

Straparola, Giovan Francesco. *Le piacevoli notti.* 2 vols. Venice: Comin da Trino, 1550–53.

————. "The Pig Prince." Zipes, *The Great Fairy Tale Tradition* 51–56.

Struck, Karin. "Erinnerungen an Hänsel und Gretel." *Märchen und Abenteuergeschichten auf alten Bilderbogen*. Ed. Jochen Jung. München: Moos, 1974. 82–84.

Tellegen, Toon. *Brieven aan Doornroosje*. Amsterdam: Querido, 2002.

Thomas, Susan. "Snow White in Exile." 2000. Beaumont and Carlson 81.

Traxler, Hans. *Die Wahrheit über Hänsel und Gretel: Die Dokumentation des Märchens der Brüder Grimm*. Frankfurt am Main: Bärmeier, 1963.

Van Cleemput, Gerda. *De bijenkoningin en 30 andere sprookjes*. Illus. Rita van Bilsen. Averbode: Altiora, 1994.

Van Gestel, Peter. "Prinses Roosje." 1994. Kuijken 115–31.

Van Mol, Sine. *Een vlekje wolf*. Wielsbeke: De Eenhoorn, 2003.

Vande Velde, Vivian. *Tales from the Brothers Grimm and the Sisters Weird*. San Diego: Harcourt, 1995.

Van de Vendel, Edward. *Een Griezelmeisje*. Illus. Isabelle Vandenabeele. Wielsbeke: De Eenhoorn, 2006.

————. *Rood Rood Roodkapje*. Wielsbeke: De Eenhoorn, 2003.

Vander Laenen, Jan. *De Schone Slaper en andere verhalen*. Westerlo: Kramat, 1998.

Wacker, Nelly. 1975. "Veraltete Märchengestalten." Mieder, *Mädchen, pfeif auf den Prinzen!* 16.

Waddell, Martin. *The Tough Princess*. Illus. Patrick Benson. London: Walker, 2002.

Walker, Barbara G. *Feminist Fairy Tales*. San Francisco: Harper, 1996.

Wittmann, Josef. "Dornröschen." 1975. *Neues vom Rumpelstilzchen und andere Hausmärchen*. Ed. Hans-Joachim Gelberg. Weinheim: Beltz, 1981. 31.

Woolf, Virginia. *A Room of One's Own*. London: Grafton, 1987.

Yolen, Jane. *Briar Rose*. New York: Doherty, 1992.

Yolen, Jane. "Fat Is Not a Fairy Tale." Beaumont and Carlson 158.

————. *Sleeping Ugly*. 1981. Illus. Diane Stanley. New York: PaperStar, 1997.

————. "Snow in Summer." Datlow and Windling 90–96.

Zipes, Jack, ed. *The Great Fairy Tale Tradition: From Straparola and Basile to the Brothers Grimm*. New York: Norton, 2001.

CRITICAL TEXTS

Altmann, Anna E. "Parody and Poesis in Feminist Fairy Tales." *Canadian Children's Literature* 73 (1994): 22–31.

Anne Sexton's Feminist Re-reading of the Grimms' Briar Rose. 6 Nov. 2007. www .gwu.edu/~folktale/GERM232/sleepingb/Sexton.html.

Bacchilega, Cristina. "Extrapolating from Nalo Hopkinson's *Skin Folk:* Reflections on Transformation and Recent English-Language Fairy-Tale Fiction by Women." *Contemporary Fiction and the Fairy Tale.* Ed. Stephen Benson. Detroit: Wayne State UP, 2008. 178–203.

————. *Postmodern Fairy Tales: Gender and Narrative Strategies.* Philadelphia: U of Pennsylvania P, 1997.

Bal, Mieke. *Narratology: Introduction to the Theory of Narrative.* Toronto: U of Toronto P, 2002.

Barthes, Roland. *S/Z.* Paris: Editions du Seuil, 1970.

Barzilai, Shuli. "Reading 'Snow White': The Mother's Story." *Signs* 15.3 (1990): 515–34.

Beck, Kathleen. Rev. of *Snow.* 3 July 2010. http://clcd.odyssi.com/cgi-in/mem ber/search/f?./temp/~2VWFer:1.

Beckett, Sandra L. *Recycling Red Riding Hood.* New York: Routledge, 2002.

————. *Red Riding Hood for All Ages: A Fairy-Tale Icon in Cross-Cultural Contexts.* Detroit: Wayne State UP, 2008.

————. "Paul Biegel as a Crossover Author." *Literatuur zonder leeftijd* 73 (2007): 86–91.

Benson, Stephen, ed. *Contemporary Fiction and the Fairy Tale.* Detroit: Wayne State UP, 2008.

————. *Cycles of Influence.* Detroit: Wayne State UP, 2003.

Bernheimer, Kate, ed. *Brothers and Beasts: An Anthology of Men on Fairy Tales.* Detroit: Wayne State UP, 2007.

————. *Mirror, Mirror on the Wall: Women Writers Explore Their Favorite Fairy Tales.* New York: Anchor, 1998.

Bettelheim, Bruno. *The Uses of Enchantment: The Meaning and Importance of Fairy Tales.* London: Thames, 1976.

Blackwell, Jeannine. "Fractured Fairy Tales: German Women Authors and the Grimm Tradition." *Germanic Review* 62 (1987): 162–74.

Bobby, Susan Redington, ed. *Fairy Tales Reimagined: Essays on New Retellings.* Jefferson: McFarland, 2009.

Böhm-Korff, Regina. *Deutung und Bedeutung von Hänsel und Gretel: Eine Fallstudie.* Frankfurt am Main: Lang, 1991.

Booth, Wayne C. *The Craft of Research.* Chicago: U of Chicago P, 2003.

Born, Monika. "Kommt Böses aus Märchen—auch heute noch? Ideologiekritik der 70er Jahre und ihre Auswirkungen auf die westdeutsche Märchendidaktik." *Märchen in der Geschichte und Gegenwart des Deutschunterrichts: Didaktische*

Annäherungen an eine Gattung. Ed. Tatjana Jesch. Frankfurt am Main: Lang, 2003. 53–87.

Bosmajian, Hamida. "Psychoanalytical Criticism." Peter Hunt 129–39.

Bottigheimer, Ruth. "Bettelheims Hexe: Die fragwürdige Beziehung zwischen Märchen und Psychoanalyse." *Psychotherapie—Psychosomatik—Medizinische Psychologie* 39 (1989): 294–99.

———, ed. *Fairy Tales and Society: Illusion, Allusion and Paradigm.* Philadelphia: U of Philadelphia P, 1986.

———. *Grimms' Bad Girls and Bold Boys: The Moral & Social Vision of the Tales.* New Haven: Yale UP, 1987.

Brackert, Helmut. "Hänsel und Gretel oder Möglichkeiten und Grenzen der Märchendeutung." *Und wenn sie nicht gestorben sind . . . : Perspektiven auf das Märchen.* Ed. Helmut Brackert. Frankfurt am Main: Suhrkamp, 1980. 223–39.

———. "Hänsel und Gretel oder Möglichkeiten und Grenzen literaturwissenschaftlicher Märchen-Interpretation." *Und wenn sie nicht gestorben sind . . . : Perspektiven auf das Märchen.* Ed. Helmut Brackert. Frankfurt am Main: Suhrkamp, 1980. 9–38.

Broich, Ulrich. "Formen der Markierung von Intertextualität." *Intertextualität: Formen, Funktionen, anglistische Fallstudien.* Ed. Ulrich Broich and Manfred Pfister. Tübingen: Niemeyer, 1985. 31–47.

Brownmiller, Susan. *Against Our Will: Men, Women, and Rape.* New York: Simon, 1975.

Brunt, Emma. "De vrouw in het sprookje." *Bzzlletin* 92 (1982): 85–90.

Cain, William E. Introduction. *Making Feminist History: The Literary Scholarship of Sandra M. Gilbert and Susan Gubar.* Ed. William E. Cain. New York: Garland, 1994. xvii–li.

Clancy, Susan. "Gillian Cross's *Wolf:* An Exploration of Patterns and Polarities." *Reflections of Change: Children's Literature Since 1945.* Ed. Sandra Beckett. Westport: Greenwood, 1997. 75–81.

Clayton, Jay, and Eric Rothstein. "Figures in the Corpus: Theories of Influence and Intertextuality." *Influence and Intertextuality in Literary History.* Ed. Jay Clayton and Eric Rothstein. Madison: U of Wisconsin P, 1991. 3–36.

Cooley, Nicole. "Literary Legacies and Critical Transformations: Teaching Creative Writing in the Public Urban University." *Pedagogy: Critical Approaches to Teaching Literature, Language, Composition, and Culture* 3.1 (2003): 99–114.

Coppola, Maria Micaela. "The Gender of Fairies: Emma Donoghue and Angela Carter as Fairy Tale Performers." *Textus* 24 (2001): 127–42.

Crago, Hugh. "What Is a Fairy Tale?" *Signal* 100 (2003): 8–26.

Crew, Hilary S. "Spinning New Tales from Traditional Texts: Donna Jo Napoli and the Rewriting of Fairy Tale." *Children's Literature in Education* 33.2 (2002): 77–95.

Daly, Mary. *Gyn/Ecology: The Methaethics of Radical Feminism*. Boston: Beacon, 1978.

Darnton, Robert. *De betekenis van Moeder de Gans: Geschiedenis met een etnografische inslag*. Amsterdam: Athenaeum, 1984.

Davies, Bronwyn. "Beyond Dualism and towards Multiple Subjectivities." *Texts of Desire: Essays on Fiction, Femininity and Schooling*. Ed. Linda K. Christian-Smith. London: Falmer, 1993. 145–73.

———. *Frogs and Snails and Feminist Tales: Preschool Children and Gender*. Sydney: Allen, 1989.

Debusschere, Barbara. "Het aloude succes van Sneeuwwitje en co. verklaard." *De Morgen* 7 Dec. 2004: 30.

———. "Variaties op het thema." *De Morgen* 19 Aug. 2004: 24.

Dion, Robert. "La Narrativité Critique." *Études Littéraires* 30.3 (1998): 77–90.

Dowling, Colette. *The Cinderella Complex: Women's Hidden Fear of Independence*. New York: Summit, 1981.

Duff, J. F. Grant. "Schneewittchen: Versuch einer psychoanalytischen Deutung." *Imago* 20 (1934): 95–103.

Duncker, Patricia. *Sisters and Strangers: An Introduction to Contemporary Feminist Fiction*. Oxford: Blackwell, 1992.

Dundes, Alan. "Bruno Bettelheim's Uses of Enchantment and Abuses of Scholarship." *Journal of American Folklore* 104 (1991): 74–83.

———. "Interpreting Little Red Riding Hood Psychoanalytically." 1988. McGlathery, *The Brothers Grimm and Folktale* 16–51.

———. "The Psychoanalytic Study of Folklore." *Annals of Scholarship* 3 (1985): 1–42.

Dworkin, Andrea. *Woman Hating*. New York: Dutton, 1974.

Easthope, Anthony. *The Unconscious*. London: Routledge, 1999.

Eco, Umberto. *The Limits of Interpretation*. Bloomington: Indiana UP, 1990.

Felski, Rita. *Literature after Feminism*. Chicago: U of Chicago P, 2003.

Fernández Rodríguez, Carolina. "Cuentos de ayer y de hoy: De la 'heterosexualidad obligatoria' tradicional a la inscripción del amor lésbico." *BELLS* 13 (2004). n. pag. 10 Oct. 2009. www.publicacions.ub.es/revistes/bells13/PDF/articles_01.pdf.

————. "The Deconstruction of the Male-Rescuer Archetype in Contemporary Revisions of 'The Sleeping Beauty.'" *Marvels and Tales: Journal of Fairy-Tale Studies* 16.1 (2002): 51–70.

Fetscher, Iring. "Von einem tapferen Schneider: Versuch einer soziologisch-sozialhistorischen Deutung." *Und wenn sie nicht gestorben sind . . . : Perspektiven auf das Märchen.* Ed. Helmut Brackert. Frankfurt am Main: Suhrkamp, 1980. 120–36.

Fetterley, Judith. *The Resisting Reader: A Feminist Approach to American Fiction.* Bloomington: Indiana UP, 1978.

Feyerabend, Paul. *Against Method: Outline of an Anarchistic Theory of Knowledge.* London: NLB, 1975.

Filz, Walter. *Es war einmal? Elemente des Märchens in der deutschen Literatur der siebziger Jahre.* Frankfurt am Main: Lang, 1989.

————. "Märchen nach 1968." *Märchen und Moderne: Fallbeispiele einer intertextuellen Relation.* Ed. Thomas Eicher. Münster: Lit, 1996. 177–97.

Fish, Stanley. *Is There a Text in This Class? The Authority of Interpretive Communities.* Cambridge: Harvard UP, 1980.

Flavell, Helen. "Fictocriticism: The End of Criticism as We Write It?" *Paradoxa* 4.10 (1998): 197–204.

Fokkema, Douwe. "Literariteit." *Sleutelwoorden: Kernbegrippen uit de hedendaagse literatuurwetenschap.* Ed. Will Van Peer and Katinka Dijkstra. Leuven: Garant, 1991. 99–104.

Freud, Sigmund. *Die Traumdeutung.* Vol. 2 of *Studienausgabe.* Frankfurt am Main: Fischer, 2000.

————. *Introductory Lectures.* Trans. James Strachey. Ed. James Strachey and Angela Richards. London: Penguin, 1973.

————. *Kinderneurosen.* Vol. 8 of *Studienausgabe.* Frankfurt am Main: Fischer, 2000.

————. 1913. "Märchenstoffe in Träumen." *Märchenforschung und Tiefenpsychologie.* Ed. Wilhelm Laiblin. 5th ed. Darmstadt: Wissenschaftliche Buchgesellschaft, 1995. 49–55.

————. *Psychologie des Unbewußten.* Vol. 3 of *Studienausgabe.* Frankfurt am Main: Fischer, 2000.

Freudenburg, Rachel. "Illustrating Childhood—'Hansel and Gretel.'" *Marvels and Tales: Journal of Fairy-Tale Studies* 12.2 (1998): 263–318.

Friday, Nancy. 1977. *My Mother/My Self: The Daughter's Search for Identity.* London: Fontana, 1979.

Frye, Northrop. *The Educated Imagination and Other Writings on Critical Theory 1933–1963*. Vol. 21 of *Collected Works*. Toronto: U of Toronto P, 2006.

Gamble, Sarah, ed. *The Routledge Companion to Feminism and Postfeminism*. London: Routledge, 2004.

Genette, Gérard. *Palimpsests: Literature in the Second Degree*. 1982. Trans. Channa Newman and Claude Doubinsky. Lincoln: U of Nebraska P, 1997.

George, Diana Hume. *Oedipus Anne: The Poetry of Anne Sexton*. Urbana: U of Illinois P, 1987.

Gilbert, Sandra M., and Susan Gubar. *Letters from the Front*. Vol. 3 of *No Man's Land: The Place of the Woman Writer in the Twentieth Century*. New Haven: Yale UP, 1994.

———. *The Madwoman in the Attic: The Woman Writer and the Nineteenth-Century Literary Imagination*. New Haven: Yale UP, 1979.

Glinz, Hans. "Fiktionale und nichtfiktionale Texte." *Textsorten und literarische Gattungen*. Ed. Vorstand der Vereinigung der deutschen Hochschulgermanisten. Berlin: Schmidt, 1983. 118–30.

Gmelin, Otto F. "Böses kommt aus Märchen." *Die Grundschule* 3.3 (1975): 124–31.

———. " 'Das' Märchen gibt es nicht! O. F. Gmelin zum Beitrag von G. König." *Die Grundschule* 3.3 (1975): 143.

Godard, Barbara. "F(r)ictions: Feminists Re/Writing Narrative." *Gender and Narrativity*. Ed. Barry Rutland. Ottawa: Carleton UP, 1997. 115–45.

Grant, Judith. "Andrea Dworkin and the Social Construction of Gender." *Signs* 31.4 (2006): 967–93.

Griswold, Jerry. *The Meanings of "Beauty and the Beast": A Handbook*. Ontario: Broadview, 2004.

Grolnick, Simon A. "Fairy Tales and Psychotherapy." 1983. Bottigheimer, *Fairy Tales and Society* 203–15.

Haas, Gerhard. "Märchen heute." *Praxis Deutsch: Zeitschrift für den Deutschunterricht* 103 (1990): 11–17.

Haase, Donald. "American Germanists and Research on Folklore and Fairy Tales from 1970 to the Present." 1993. *German Studies in the United States: A Historical Handbook*. Ed. Peter Uwe Hohendahl. New York: MLA, 2003. 294–98.

———, ed. *Fairy Tales and Feminism: New Approaches*. Detroit: Wayne State UP, 2004.

———. "Feminist Fairy-Tale Scholarship." Haase, *Fairy Tales and Feminism* 1–36.

———. "Hypertextual Gutenberg: The Textual and Hypertextual Life of Folktales and Fairy Tales in English-Language Popular Print Editions." *Fabula* 47.3/4 (2006): 222–30.

————. "Psychology and Fairy Tales." Zipes, *The Oxford Companion to Fairy Tales* 404–8.

————, ed. *The Reception of Grimms' Fairy Tales: Response, Reactions, Revisions.* Detroit: Wayne State UP, 1993.

————. "Yours, Mine, or Ours? Perrault, the Brothers Grimm, and the Ownership of Fairy Tales." Tatar, *Classic Fairy Tales* 353–64.

Haffenden, John. *Novelists in Interview.* New York: Methuen, 1985.

Hall, Edwin. *The Arnolfini Betrothal: Medieval Marriage and the Enigma of Van Eyck's Double Portrait.* Berkeley: U of California P, 1994.

Hanlon, Tina L. "'To Sleep, Perchance to Dream': Sleeping Beauties and Wide-Awake Plain Janes in the Stories of Jane Yolen." *Children's Literature* 26 (1998): 140–67.

Harries, Elizabeth Wanning. *Twice upon a Time: Women Writers and the History of the Fairy Tale.* Princeton: Princeton UP, 2001.

Hassan, Ihab. "Pluralism in Postmodern Perspective." *Critical Inquiry* 12.3 (1986): 503–20.

Heilbrun, Carolyn G. Foreword. *Making Feminist History: The Literary Scholarship of Sandra M. Gilbert and Susan Gubar.* Ed. William E. Cain. New York: Garland, 1994. xi–xv.

Heisig, James W. "Bruno Bettelheim and the Fairy Tales." *Children's Literature* 6 (1977): 93–114.

Hennard Dutheil de la Rochère, Martine. "Queering the Fairy Tale Canon: Emma Donoghue's *Kissing the Witch.*" *Fairy Tales Reimagined: Essays on New Retellings.* Ed. Susan Bobby. Jefferson: McFarland, 2009. 13–30.

Heuscher, Julius E. *A Psychiatric Study of Myths and Fairy Tales: Their Origin, Meaning and Usefulness.* 2nd ed. Springfield: Thomas, 1974.

Hollindale, Peter. *Ideology and the Children's Book.* Stroud: Thimble, 1988.

Horn, Katalin. "Lebenshilfe aus 'uralter Weisheit'? Psychologische und populär-psychologische Märchenrezeption unter ihrem therapeutischen Aspekt." *Märchen in unserer Zeit: Zu Erscheinungsformen eines populären Erzählgenres.* Ed. Hans-Jörg Uther. München: Diederichs, 1990. 159–69.

————. "Über das Weiterleben der Märchen in unserer Zeit." *Die Volksmärchen in unserer Kultur: Berichte über Bedeutung und Weiterleben der Märchen.* Ed. Märchen-Stiftung Walter Kahn. Frankfurt am Main: Haag, 1993. 25–71.

Hulsens, Eric. 1979. "Kabouters tegen decadente massamedia." *Een kinderhoofd is gauw gevuld: kritieken en essays over jeugdliteratuur.* Leuven: Kritak, 1980. 231–35.

Hunt, Peter, ed. *International Companion to Children's Literature*. 2nd ed. 2 vols. London: Routledge, 2004.

Hutcheon, Linda. *A Poetics of Postmodernism: History, Theory, Fiction*. New York: Routledge, 1988.

———. *A Theory of Parody: The Teachings of Twentieth-Century Art Forms*. New York: Methuen, 1985.

Irigaray, Luce. *The Irigaray Reader*. Ed. Margaret Whitford. Oxford: Blackwell, 1991.

Iser, Wolfgang. "Akte des Fingierens. Oder: Was ist das Fiktive im fiktionalen Text?" *Funktionen des Fiktiven*. Ed. Dieter Henrich and Wolfgang Iser. München: Fink, 1983. 121–51.

———. 1970. *Die Appellstruktur der Texte: Unbestimmtheit als Wirkungsbedingung literarischer Proza*. Konstanz: Universitätsverlag, 1972.

Jacobus, Mary. Rev. of *The Madwoman in the Attic*, by Sandra M. Gilbert and Susan Gubar. *Signs* 6.3 (1981): 517–23.

Jarvis, Shawn. "Feminism and Fairy Tales." Zipes, *The Oxford Companion to Fairy Tales* 155–59.

Jauss, Hans Robert. *Literaturgeschichte als Provokation der Literaturwissenschaft*. 2nd ed. Konstanz: Universitätsverlag, 1969.

Jay, Karla, and Joanne Glasgow, eds. *Lesbian Texts and Contexts: Radical Revisions*. New York: New York UP, 1990.

Jones, Steven Swann. *The Fairy Tale: The Magic Mirror of the Imagination*. London: Routledge, 2002.

———. *The New Comparative Method: Structural and Symbolic Analysis of the Allomotifs of "Snow White."* Helsinki: Academia Scientiarum Fennica, 1990.

Joosen, Vanessa. "Back to Ölenberg: An Intertextual Dialogue between Fairy-Tale Retellings and the Socio-Historical Study of the Grimm Tales." *Marvels and Tales: Journal of Fairy-Tale Studies* 24.1 (2010): 99–115.

———. "Disenchanting the Fairy Tale: Retellings of 'Snow White' between Magic and Realism." *Marvels and Tales: Journal of Fairy-Tale Studies* 21.2 (2007): 228-39.

———. "Novelizing the Fairy Tale: The Case of Gregory Maguire." *Expectations and Experiences: Children, Childhood & Children's Literature*. Ed. Clare Bradford, Valerie Coghlan, et al. Lichfield: Pied Piper, 2007. 191–201.

———. "Philip Pullman's *I Was a Rat!* and the Fairy-Tale Retelling as Instrument of Social Criticism." Bobby, *Fairy Tales Reimagined* 196-209.

Kahn, Otto. "Rumpelstilz hat wirklich gelebt." *Rheinisches Jahrbuch für Volkskunde* 17/18 (1966/67): 143–84.

Kamenetsky, Christa. *The Brothers Grimm and Their Critics*. Athens: Ohio UP, 1992.

Kolbenschlag, Madonna. 1979. *Goodbye Sleeping Beauty*. Dublin: Arlen, 1983.

König, Guido. "Kommt Böses aus dem Märchen? G. König zum Beitrag von O. F. Gmelin." *Die Grundschule* 3.3 (1975): 132.

———. "Märchen heute: Unzeitgemäße Gedanken zu einem problematischen Lerninhalt." *Die Grundschule* 3.3 (1975): 136–42.

Krauss, Rosalind. "Poststructuralism and the 'Paraliterary.'" *October* 13 (1980): 36–40.

Kristeva, Julia. 1979. *Desire in Language: A Semiotic Approach to Literature and Art*. Oxford: Blackwell, 1980.

Kümmerling-Meibauer, Bettina. "Im Dschungel des Texts: Kiplings *Dschungelbücher* und das Prinzip der asymmetrischen Intertextualität." *Kinder- und Jugendliteraturforschung 2000/2001*. Ed. Hans Heino-Ewers et al. Stuttgart: Metzler, 2001. 42–61.

Kunneman, Harry, ed. *Wetenschap en ideologiekritiek*. Meppel: Boom, 1978.

Künnemann, Horst, ed. *Märchen—wozu?* Hamburg: Lesen, 1978.

Lamontagne, André. "Metatextualité postmoderne: de la fiction à la critique." *Études Littéraires* 30.3 (1998): 61–76.

Lange, Günter. "Einführung in die Märchenforschung und Märchendidaktik." *Märchen—Märchenforschung—Märchendidaktik*. Ed. Günter Lange. Baltmannsweiler: Schneider Hogengehren, 2004. 3–29.

Langlois, Janet L. Rev. of *Feminist Fairy Tales*, by Barbara G. Walker. *Marvel and Tales: Journal of Fairy-Tale Studies* 11.1–2 (1997): 187–89.

Lanser, Susan S. "Feminist Criticism, 'The Yellow Wallpaper,' and the Politics of Color in America." *Feminist Studies* 15.3 (1989): 415–41.

———. "The 'I' of the Beholder: Equivocal Attachments and the Limits of Structuralist Narratology." *A Companion to Narrative Theory*. Ed. James Phelan and Peter J. Rabinowitz. Malden: Blackwell, 2005. 206–19.

Lernout, Geert. *Schrijven over literatuur*. Leuven: Acco, 1999.

Lew, Jacqueline. "Sleeping Beauty on Exhibition. 2000/2001." 16 July 2010. http://bootheprize.stanford.edu/0001/booth0001.pdf.

Lewis, David. *Reading Contemporary Picturebooks: Picturing Text*. London: Routledge, 2001.

Leysen, Annemie. "Meisje van glas." *Ons Erfdeel* (1999): 698. In: *Ons Erfdeel*, October 1999. 16 July 2010. www.anneprovoost.com/dutch/RoosZwijn/RoosZwijnRecensieOnsErfdeel.htm.

Lieberman, Marcia K. "'Some Day My Prince Will Come': Female Acculturation through the Fairy Tale." 1972. Zipes, *Don't Bet On the Prince* 185–200.

Liska, Vivian. *Die Moderne—ein Weib: Am Beispiel von Romanen Ricarda Huchs und Annette Kolbs*. Tübingen: Francke, 2000.

———. "From Feminist Literary Criticism to Gendered Cultural Studies: A Critical Touchstone." *Literature and Society: The Function of Literary Sociology in Comparative Literature*. Ed. Bart Keunen and Bart Eeckhout. Brussels: Lang, 2001. 93–111.

Lodge, David. "Literary Criticism and Literary Creation." *The Arts and Sciences of Criticism*. Ed. David Fuller and Patricia Waugh. Oxford: Oxford UP, 1999. 137–52.

Lurie, Alison. "Fairy Tale Liberation." *New York Review of Books* 17 Dec. 1970: 42–44.

Lüthi, Max. *Das europäische Volksmärchen: Form und Wesen*. 8th ed. Tübingen: Francke, 1985.

———. 1961. *Volksmärchen und Volkssage: Zwei Grundformen erzählender Dichtung*. 3rd ed. Bern: Francke, 1975.

Maitland, Sara. "A Feminist Writer's Progress." *On Gender and Writing*. Ed. Micheline Wandor. London: Pandora, 1983. 17–23.

May, Jill P. *Children's Literature and Literary Theory*. New York: Oxford UP, 1995.

McClatchy, J. D., ed. *Anne Sexton: The Artist and Her Critics*. Bloomington: Indiana UP, 1978.

McGillis, Roderick. "'Ages: All': Readers, Texts, and Intertexts in *The Stinky Cheese Man and Other Fairly Stupid Tales*." *Transcending Boundaries: Writing for a Dual Audience of Children and Adults*. Ed. Sandra L. Beckett. New York: Garland, 1999. 111–26.

———. "'A Fairytale Is Just a Fairytale': George MacDonald and the Queering of Fairy." *Marvels and Tales: Journal of Fairy-Tale Studies* 17.1 (2003): 86–99.

McGlathery, James M., ed. *The Brothers Grimm and Folktale*. 1988. Urbana: U of Illinois P, 1991.

———. *Fairy Tale Romance: The Grimms, Basile, and Perrault*. Urbana: U of Illinois P, 1991.

Meijer, Maaike. "Vrouw-en-literatuur." *Sleutelwoorden: Kernbegrippen uit de hedendaagse literatuurwetenschap.* Ed. Will Van Peer and Katinka Dijkstra. Leuven: Garant, 1991. 176–87.

Messeman, Sofie. "De mythe van de moederliefde doorgeprikt." *De Tijd* 17 Apr. 2004: 21.

Miller, Cynthia A. "The Poet in the Poem: A Phenomenological Analysis of Anne Sexton's 'Briar Rose (Sleeping Beauty).'" *The Existential Coordinates of the Human Condition: Poetic—Epic—Tragic.* Ed. Anna-Teresa Tymieniecka. Dordrecht: Reidel, 1984. 61–73.

Moi, Toril. *Sexual/Textual Politics: Feminist Literary Theory.* London: Methuen, 1985.

Nikolajeva, Maria. *Aesthetic Approaches to Children's Literature.* Lanham: Scarecrow, 2005.

———. *Children's Literature Comes of Age.* New York: Garland, 1996.

Nikolajeva, Maria, and Carole Scott. *How Picturebooks Work.* New York: Garland, 2001.

Nodelman, Perry. *The Pleasures of Children's Literature.* 2nd ed. New York: Longman, 1996.

———. "What Are We After? Children's Literature Studies and Literary Theory Now." *Canadian Children's Literature* 31.2 (2005): 1–19.

Nünning, Ansgar F., ed. *Metzler Lexikon Literatur- und Kulturtheorie.* 2nd ed. Stuttgart: Metzler, 2001.

———. "Reconceptualizing Unreliable Narration: Synthesizing Cognitive and Rhetorical Approaches." *A Companion to Narrative Theory.* Ed. James Phelan and Peter J. Rabinowitz. Malden: Blackwell, 2005. 89–107.

Odber de Baubeta, Patricia Anne. "The Fairy-Tale Intertext in Iberian and Latin American Women's Writing." Haase, *Fairy Tales and Feminism* 129–47.

Orenstein, Catherine. *Little Red Riding Hood Uncloaked: Sex, Morality and the Evolution of a Fairy Tale.* New York: Basic, 2002.

Orme, Jennifer. "Mouth to Mouth: Queer Desires in Emma Donoghue's *Kissing the Witch.*" *Marvels and Tales: Journal of Fairy-Tale Studies* 24.1 (2010): 116–30.

Osinski, Jutta. *Einführung in die feministische Literaturwissenschaft.* Berlin: Schmidt, 1998.

Ostriker, Alicia. "The Thieves of Language: Women Poets and Revisionist Mythmaking." *Signs* 8 (1982): 68–90.

Paradiž, Valerie. 2004. *Clever Maids: The Secret History of the Grimm Fairy Tales.* New York: Basic, 2005.

Péju, Pierre. *La Petite Fille dans la forêt des contes*. Paris: Éditions Robert Laffont, 1981.

Pelckmans, Paul. "Bruno Bettelheim: een psychotherapeut over kindersprookjes." *Streven* 31 (1978): 876–86.

Pettersson, Anders. "Five Kinds of Literary and Artistic Interpretation." *Types of Interpretation in the Aesthetic Disciplines*. Ed. Staffan Carlshamre and Anders Pettersson. Montreal: McGill-Queen's UP, 2003. 52–81.

———. "Introduction: The Multiplicity of Interpretations and the Present Collection of Essays." *Types of Interpretation in the Aesthetic Disciplines*. Ed. Staffan Carlshamre and Anders Pettersson. Montreal: McGill-Queen's UP, 2003. 3–29.

Pettersson, Torsten. "What Is an Interpretation?" *Types of Interpretation in the Aesthetic Disciplines*. Ed. Staffan Carlshamre and Anders Pettersson. Montreal: McGill-Queen's UP, 2003. 30–51.

Pfister, Manfred. "Konzepte der Intertextualität." *Intertextualität: Formen, Funktionen, anglistische Fallstudien*. Ed. Ulrich Broich and Manfred Pfister. Tübingen: Niemeyer, 1985. 1–30.

Pischke, Hildegard. "Das veränderte Märchen: Untersuchungen zu einer neuen Gattung der Kinderliteratur." *Literatur für Kinder: Studien über ihr Verhältnis zur Gesamtliteratur*. Göttingen: Vandenhoeck, 1977. 94–113.

Pizer, John. "The Disenchantment of Snow White: Robert Walser, Donald Barthelme and the Modern/Postmodern Anti–Fairy Tale." *Canadian Review of Comparative Literature* 17.3/4 (1990): 330–47.

Pollak, Richard. *The Creation of Dr. B.: A Biography of Bruno Bettelheim*. New York: Simon, 1997.

Propp, Vladimir. *Morphology of the Folktale*. Trans. Svatava Pirkova-Jakobson. Austin: U of Texas P, 1975.

Provoost, Anne. *Anne Provoost, auteur*. 16 July 2010. www.anneprovoost.be/nl/pmwiki.php/DeRoosEnHetZwijn/Fragment.

Psaar, Werner, and Manfred Klein. *Wer hat Angst vor der bösen Geiß? Zur Märchendidaktik und Märchenrezeption*. Braunschweig: Westermann, 1976.

Rev. of *Kissing the Witch*. *The Horn Book Guide* (1997). n. pag. 6 July 2010. http://clcd.odyssi.com/cgi-bin/member/search/f?./temp/~G6d4cB:1.

Richter, Dieter, and Johannes Merkel. *Märchen, Phantasie und soziales Lernen*. Berlin: Basis, 1974.

Richter, Dieter, and Jochen Vogt, eds. *Die heimlichen Erzieher: Kinderbücher und politisches Lernen*. Reinbek bei Hamburg: Rowohlt, 1974.

Rochman, Hazel. Rev. of *Watching the Roses*. *Booklist* 89.3 (1992). n. pag. 1 July 2010. www.booklistonline.com/ProductInfo.aspx?pid=935243.

Röhrich, Lutz. *Märchen und Wirklichkeit*. Wiesbaden: Steiner, 1956.

———. "The Quest of Meaning in Folk Narrative Research." McGlathery, *The Brothers Grimm and Folktale* 1–15.

Rölleke, Heinz, ed. *Die älteste Märchensammlung der Brüder Grimm: Synopse der handschriftlichen Urfassung von 1810 und der Erstdrucke von 1812.* Cologny-Genève: Fondation Martin Bodmer, 1975.

Rose, Jacqueline. *The Case of Peter Pan, or the Impossibility of Children's Fiction.* 1984. Philadelphia: U of Pennsylvania P, 1992.

Rowe, Karen E. "Feminism and Fairy Tales." 1979. Zipes, *Don't Bet On the Prince* 209–26.

———. "To Spin a Yarn: The Female Voice in Folklore and Fairy Tale." 1986. Tatar 297–308.

Rudd, David. "Theorising and Theories: The Conditions of Possibility of Children's Literature." Peter Hunt 29–43.

Ryan, Marie-Laure. "The Modes of Narrativity and Their Visual Metaphors." *Style* 26.3 (1992): 368–87.

Sarland, Charles. "Critical Tradition and Ideological Positioning." Peter Hunt 56–75.

Seifert, Lewis C. "Feminist Approaches to Seventeenth-Century *contes de fées*." Haase, *Fairy Tales and Feminism* 53–71.

———. "Gay and Lesbian Tales." *The Greenwood Encyclopedia of Folktales and Fairy Tales*. Ed. Donald Haase. 3 vols. Westport: Greenwood, 2008. 400–02.

Showalter, Elaine. "Feminist Criticism in the Wilderness." *Critical Inquiry* 8.2 (1981): 179–205.

Silver, Carol. "Wilde, Oscar." Zipes, *The Oxford Companion to Fairy Tales* 549–51.

Sipe, Lawrence R. *Storytime: Young Children's Literary Understanding in the Classroom.* New York: Teachers College, 2008.

———. "'Those Two Gingerbread Boys Could Be Brothers': How Children Use Intertextual Connections during Storybook Readalouds." *Children's Literature in Education* 31.2 (2000): 73–90.

———. "Using Transformations of Traditional Stories: Making the Reading-Writing Connection." *The Reading Teacher* 47.1 (1993): 18–26.

Skorczewski, Dawn. "What Prison Is This? Literary Critics Cover Incest in Anne Sexton's 'Briar Rose.'" *Signs* 21.2 (1996): 309–42.

Smith, Kevin Paul. *The Postmodern Fairy Tale: Folkloric Intertexts in Contemporary Fiction.* New York: Palgrave, 2007.

Solis, Santiago. "Snow White and the Seven 'Dwarfs'— Queercripped." *Hypatia* 22.1 (2007): 114–31.

Solms, Wilhelm. *Die Moral von Grimms Märchen.* Darmstadt: Primus, 1999.

Sontag, Susan. *Against Interpretation, and Other Essays.* London: Eyre, 1967.

Sordi, Michele. "Caught in the Crossfire." *Making Feminist History: The Literary Scholarship of Sandra M. Gilbert and Susan Gubar.* Ed. William E. Cain. New York: Garland, 1994. 271–93.

Stein, Mary Beth. "Fetscher, Iring." Zipes, *The Oxford Companion to Fairy Tales* 160.

Steinchen, Renate. "Märchen—Eine Bestandsaufnahme." *Kinder- und Jugendliteratur.* Ed. Margareta Gorschenek and Annamaria Rucktäschel. München: Fink, 1979. 129–64.

Stephens, John. *Language and Ideology in Children's Fiction.* London: Longman, 1992.

Stephens, John, and Robyn McCallum. *Retelling Stories, Framing Culture: Traditional Stories and Metanarratives in Children's Literature.* New York: Garland, 1998.

Stone, Kay. "Feminist Approaches to the Interpretation of Fairy Tales." Bottigheimer, *Fairy Tales and Society* 229–36.

———. "*Märchen* to Fairy Tale: An Unmagical Transformation." *Western Folklore* 40.3 (1981): 232–44.

———. "Things Walt Disney Never Told Us." *Journal of American Folklore* 88 (1975): 42–55.

Stott, Belinda. "Cinderella the Strong and Reader Empowerment." *New Review of Children's Literature and Librarianship* 10.1 (2004): 15–26.

Sutton, Nina. *Bettelheim: A Life and Legacy.* Boulder: Westview, 1996.

Tatar, Maria. *The Classic Fairy Tales.* New York: Norton, 1999.

———. *The Hard Facts of the Grimms' Fairy Tales.* 2nd ed. Princeton: Princeton UP, 2003.

———. *Off With Their Heads! Fairy Tales and the Culture of Childhood.* Princeton: Princeton UP, 1992.

———. *Secrets behind the Door.* Princeton: Princeton UP, 2004.

———. "Wilhelm Grimm / Maurice Sendak: *Dear Mili* and the Literary Culture of Childhood." 1992. *The Reception of Grimms' Fairy Tales: Response, Reactions, Revisions.* Ed. Donald Haase. Detroit: Wayne State UP, 1993. 207–29.

Tucker, Nicholas. "Dr. Bettelheim and Enchantment." *Signal* 43 (1984): 33–41.

―――. "The Grimms' Wicked Stepmothers." *Where Texts and Children Meet.* Ed. Eve Bearne and Victor Watson. London: Routledge, 2000. 41–50.

Uther, Hans-Jörg. Vorwort. *Märchen in unserer Zeit: Zu Erscheinungsformen eines populären Erzählgenres.* Ed. Hans-Jörg Uther. München: Diederichs, 1990. 7–10.

Van Alphen, Ernst, Lizet Duyvendak, Maaike Meijer, and Ben Peperkamp. *Op poëtische wijze: Handleiding voor het lezen van poëzie.* Bussum: Coutinho, 1996.

Van Coillie, Jan. 1999. *Leesbeesten en boekenfeesten: Hoe werken (met) kinder- en jeugdboeken?* Rev. ed. Leuven: Davidsfonds, 2007.

Vandergrift, Kay. *Snow White Criticism: Introduction.* 16 July 2010. www.scils .rutgers.edu/~kvander/swcriticism.html.

Vandevoorde, Hans. 1998. *Schuld en boete bij Anne Provoost.* 16 July 2010. www .anneprovoost.be/nl/index.php/Auteur/.

Van Gestel, Peter. "Dromen, sprookjes en verhalen." *Literatuur zonder leeftijd* 18.65 (2004): 130–45.

Van Nieuwenborghe, Marcel. "Van pedagoog tot oplichter." *De Standaard* 28 May 2003: 16.

Vloeberghs, Katrien. "Kindbeelden in de westerse moderniteit." *Literatuur zonder leeftijd* 70 (2006): 10–23.

Warner, Marina. 1994. *From the Beast to the Blonde.* London: Vintage, 1995.

Weinrebe, Helge M. A. *Märchen—Bilder—Wirkungen: Zur Wirkung und Rezeptionsgeschichte von illustrierten Märchen der Brüder Grimm nach 1945.* Frankfurt am Main: Lang, 1987.

Weinreich, Torben. *Children's Literature: Art or Pedagogy?* Trans. Don Bartlett. Frederiksberg: Roskilde UP, 2000.

Wildekamp, Ada, Ineke Van Montfoort, and Willem Van Ruiswijk. "Fictionality and Convention." *Poetics* 9 (1980): 547–67.

Wilkie, Christine. "Relating Texts: Intertextuality." *Understanding Children's Literature.* Ed. Peter Hunt. New York: Routledge, 1999. 130–37.

Wilkie-Stibbs, Christine. *The Feminine Subject in Children's Literature.* New York: Routledge, 2002.

―――. "Intertextuality and the Child Reader." Peter Hunt 179–90.

Wullschlager, Jackie. 2000. *Hans Christian Andersen: The Life of a Storyteller.* London: Penguin, 2001.

Würzbach, Natascha. "Feministische Forschung in Literaturwissenschaft und Volkskunde: Neue Fragestellungen und Probleme der Theoriebildung." *Die*

Frau im Märchen. Ed. Sigrid Früh and Rainer Wehse. Kassel: Röth, 1985. 192–214.

Yolen, Jane. "America's Cinderella." *Children's Literature in Education* 8.1 (1977): 21–29.

Zipes, Jack. "Anne Sexton." Zipes, *The Oxford Companion to Fairy Tales* 460–61.

————. 1979. *Breaking the Magic Spell: Radical Theories of Folk & Fairy Tales.* Rev. ed. Kentucky: U of Kentucky P, 2002.

————. *The Brothers Grimm.* 2nd ed. New York: Palgrave, 2002.

————. "The Changing Function of the Fairy Tale." *Lion and the Unicorn* 12.2 (1988): 7–31.

————. "Critical Observations on Recent Psychoanalytical Approaches to the Tales of the Brothers Grimm." *Marvels and Tales: Journal of Fairy-Tale Studies* 1.1 (1987): 19–30.

————, ed. *Don't Bet On the Prince: Contemporary Feminist Fairy Tales in North America and England.* 1986. New York: Routledge, 1989.

————. *Fairy Tales and the Art of Subversion: The Classical Genre for Children and the Process of Civilization.* New York: Methuen, 1983.

————. "Fairy Tales and Folk Tales." *The Oxford Encyclopedia of Children's Literature.* Oxford: Oxford UP, 2006. 45–54.

————. *Fairy Tales as Myth—Myth as Fairy Tale.* Lexington: UP of Kentucky, 1994.

————. *Happily Ever After: Fairy Tales, Children, and the Culture Industry.* New York: Routledge, 1997.

————. "Introduction: Towards a Definition of the Literary Fairy Tale." Zipes, *The Oxford Companion to Fairy Tales* xv–xxxii.

————, ed. *The Oxford Companion to Fairy Tales.* Oxford: Oxford UP, 2000.

————. *Relentless Progress: The Reconfiguration of Children's Literature, Fairy Tales, and Storytelling.* New York: Routledge, 2009.

————, ed. 1983. *The Trials and Tribulations of Little Red Riding Hood.* 2nd ed. New York: Routledge, 1993.

————. *Why Fairy Tales Stick: The Evolution and Relevance of a Genre.* London: Routledge, 2006.

Index

Illustration Credits

Figures 15 and 16 from *Sleeping Beauty and Other Favourite Tales* by Michael Foreman reproduced by permission of Michael Foreman.

Figure 17 from *Snow White and the Seven Dwarfs* by Bernard Canavan reproduced by permission of Bernard Canavan.

Figure 18 from *Zwart als inkt* by Wim Hofman reproduced by permission of Querido, Amsterdam, The Netherlands.

Figure 19 *The Arnolfini Betrothal* by Jan van Eyck.

Figures 20 and 21 from *Snow White* by Charles Santore reproduced by permission of Charles Santore.

Figures 22, 23, and 24 from *Snow White* by Paul Heins reproduced by permission of Little Brown and Company. Text by Trina Schart Hyman. Translation copyright 1974 by Paul Heins; illustrations copyright 1974 by Trina Schart Hyman.

DATE DUE

MAY 17 2012	3:40	Pm
MAY 22 2012	2:11	pm
JUN 02 2012	2:54	Pm
JUN 04 2012	1:23	PM